How to Become a More Effective CBT Therapist

How to Become a More Effective CBT Therapist

CBT Therapist

Mastering Metacompetence in Clinical Practice

Edited by

Adrian Whittington and Nick Grey

WILEY Blackwell

This edition first published 2014
© 2014 John Wiley & Sons, Ltd.

Registered Office
John Wiley & Sons, Ltd, The Atrium, Southern Gate, Chichester, West Sussex, PO19 8SQ, UK

Editorial Offices
350 Main Street, Malden, MA 02148-5020, USA
9600 Garsington Road, Oxford, OX4 2DQ, UK
The Atrium, Southern Gate, Chichester, West Sussex, PO19 8SQ, UK

For details of our global editorial offices, for customer services, and for information about how
to apply for permission to reuse the copyright material in this book please see our website at
www.wiley.com/wiley-blackwell.

The right of Adrian Whittington and Nick Grey to be identified as the authors of the editorial material in
this work has been asserted in accordance with the UK Copyright, Designs and Patents Act 1988.

Library of Congress Cataloging-in-Publication Data

How to become a more effective CBT therapist : mastering metacompetence in clinical practice / edited by
Adrian Whittington and Nick Grey.
    pages   cm
  Includes bibliographical references and index.
  ISBN 978-1-118-46834-0 (hardback) – ISBN 978-1-118-46835-7 (paper)   1. Cognitive therapy.
2. Clinical competence.   3. Therapist and patient.   I. Whittington, Adrian, editor of compilation.
II. Grey, Nick, 1970– editor of compilation.
  RC489.C63H69 2014
  616.89′1425–dc23

                                          2013050604

A catalogue record for this book is available from the British Library.

Cover image: © Fenykepez/iStockphoto

Set in 10/12pt Galliard by SPi Publisher Services, Pondicherry, India
Printed in Malaysia by Ho Printing (M) Sdn Bhd

1   2014

For David Westbrook

Contents

About the Editors

Adrian Whittington is Director of Education and Training and Consultant Clinical Psychologist at Sussex Partnership NHS Foundation Trust, where he leads on training programmes in CBT and other evidence-based psychological therapies. He works clinically with people with anxiety disorders and depression and teaches on the postgraduate CBT training programme at the University of Sussex.

Nick Grey is a Consultant Clinical Psychologist and Joint Clinical Director of the Centre for Anxiety Disorders and Trauma (CADAT), South London and Maudsley NHS Foundation Trust, King's Health Partners. His clinical work is providing out-patient cognitive therapy to people with a variety of anxiety disorders both within randomized controlled trials and in a more general NHS service. He is actively involved in disseminating cognitive behavioural therapies, trying to ensure that the most effective treatments are applied in routine care. He is accredited as a practitioner, supervisor and trainer with the British Association of Behavioural and Cognitive Psychotherapies.

About the Contributors

James Bennett-Levy is Associate Professor at the University of Sydney's University Centre for Rural Health (North Coast). He is one of the leading researchers on the training of CBT therapists. He has co-written *Experiencing CBT from the Inside Out: A Self-Practice/Self-Reflection Workbook for Therapists* (2014) and the *Oxford Guide to Imagery in Cognitive Therapy* (2011), and co-edited the *Oxford Guide to Behavioural Experiments in Cognitive Therapy* (2004), and the *Oxford Guide to Low Intensity CBT Interventions* (2010).

Steve Boddington is a Consultant Clinical Psychologist, and Head of Psychology and Psychological Therapies, Mental Health of Older Adults and Dementia, South London and Maudsley NHS Foundation Trust. Steve is a registered Practitioner Psychologist and Chartered Psychologist with 20 years of specialist experience in working with older people. He is an associate fellow of the British Psychological Society and a past chair of the Division of Clinical Psychology's Faculty of Psychology for Older People. He has an interest in the development of accessible psychological services that meet the needs of older people, sitting on various national working groups, and has been involved in the development and delivery of training on the application of CBT for older people.

Gillian Butler is a Consultant Clinical Psychologist working with Oxford Cognitive Therapy Centre and Oxford Health NHS Foundation Trust. She now works in the forensic service and has special interests in the use of CBT during recovery from traumatic experiences in childhood, and in developing a sense of self. She is co-author of Manage Your Mind: The Mental Fitness Guide and of Psychology: A Very Short Introduction, and author of Overcoming Social Anxiety and Shyness.

Suzanne Byrne is the Deputy Course Director for CBT (IAPT Adult Programmes) at the Institute of Psychiatry, Kings College London. She is an honorary Cognitive Behavioural Psychotherapist at the Centre for Anxiety Disorders and Trauma South London and Maudsley NHS Foundation Trust.

Anna Chaddock is a Clinical Psychologist and Cognitive Behaviour Therapist. She is employed by Newcastle upon Tyne Hospitals NHS Foundation Trust in their Specialist Palliative Care and Primary Care Mental Health services. Her special interests include reflection in CBT and interpersonal processes, particularly empathy.

Simon Darnley is the Head of the Anxiety Disorders Residential Unit based at the Bethlem Royal Hospital. He was a psychiatric nurse before training as a Cognitive Behavioural Psychotherapist. Simon has been involved in CBT treatment, training and supervision for over 20 years. He is also now Head of Mood, Anxiety and Personality Disorder Clinical Pathways for Lambeth, within the South London and Maudsley NHS Foundation Trust, managing a wide range of clinical services. He is an award-winning part-time magician, a member of the Magic Circle and President of the Kent Magicians Guild.

Kate M. Davidson is a Fellow of the British Psychological Society and Director of the Glasgow Institute of Psychosocial Interventions, NHS Greater Glasgow and Clyde and University of Glasgow. She completed her clinical training and PhD at University of Edinburgh. She is an Editor of Personality and Mental Health. She developed and evaluated the efficacy of CBT for personality disorders in both community and now in forensic settings.

Melanie Davis is a Clinical Psychologist delivering CBT in both individual and group settings as part of the Durham Pain Management Service. She supports the rest of the multidisciplinary team through consultation and training in psychological approaches to pain management. Her research interests include the interpersonal process in CBT and the use of reflection to enhance therapeutic knowledge and skill.

Nicole de Zoysa is a Senior Clinical Psychologist working in the diabetes and cardiac rehabilitation services at King's College Hospital. She has taught on IAPT training courses for the past three years focussing on adapting step two and step three interventions for people living with long-term conditions. Nicole de Zoysa has also published in the areas of mindfulness-based cognitive therapy and motivational interviewing for primary care nurses and diabetes educators.

Alicia Deale is a Cognitive Behavioural Psychotherapist at the Centre for Anxiety Disorders and Trauma, South London and Maudsley NHS Foundation Trust. She is a part-time clinical tutor and course supervisor on the Postgraduate Diploma in CBT at the Institute of Psychiatry.

Sharif El-Leithy is a Principal Clinical Psychologist and BABCP accredited Cognitive Therapist, specializing in post-traumatic stress disorder (PTSD). For the last 12 years he has worked in the Traumatic Stress Service in Tooting, South London, offering psychological treatment to diverse populations including ex-military and survivors of war and torture. He was part of the screen-and-treat program that followed the 2005 London bombings, and set up similar programs for assault victims within local hospital settings.

Myra S. Hunter is Professor of Clinical Health Psychology with King's College London. She has worked in both clinical and academic roles with people with physical health problems for over 30 years, with a particular interest in oncology, cardiology and women's health. She has developed cognitive behaviourally-based interventions for women with premenstrual and menopausal symptoms and is currently evaluating interventions for people with non-cardiac chest pain and for men with prostate cancer treatment related symptoms.

Jane Hutton was awarded her Doctorate in Clinical Psychology from the Institute of Psychiatry, where she holds an honorary contract. She is employed by South London and Maudsley NHS Foundation Trust and is Consultant Clinical Psychologist in the Department of Psychological Medicine at King's College Hospital. Her research and clinical interests are in mindfulness-based approaches and CBT for people living with physical health problems.

Stephanie Jarrett is a Consultant Clinical Psychologist with a long-standing interest in psychological approaches to physical health problems. Her doctorate was in psychosocial oncology and she now works in the chronic pain service at University Hospital Lewisham where she has set up individual and group services for patients. She has taught a wide range of medical and psychological professionals on the biopsychosocial model of chronic pain and has recently published evidence of the clinical and cost-effectiveness of using this approach.

Louise Johns is a chartered Consultant Clinical Psychologist and coordinator of a specialist outpatient psychological therapies service for psychosis (PICuP: Psychological Interventions Clinic for outpatients with Psychosis), South London and Maudsley (SLaM) NHS Foundation Trust, London. She is also an Honorary Senior Lecturer at the Institute of Psychiatry (IOP), King's College London. She has worked in a clinical and research capacity in the field of psychosis for 15 years, and has published over 50 articles on psychosis, covering development and psychopathology of symptoms, and cognitive behavioural treatments.

Suzanne Jolley is a Research Clinical Psychologist at King's College, London, Institute of Psychiatry and an Honorary Consultant Clinical Psychologist in the South London and Maudsley NHS Foundation Trust, Psychosis Recovery services. She co-developed the King's/IOP PGDip in CBT for Psychosis. Her clinical practice, teaching and research have been primarily in psychosis over the past 20 years, with interests in training, dissemination, workforce development, cognitive models of delusions, and psychosis in children.

Nadine Keen is a Principal Clinical Psychologist at a specialist outpatient psychological therapies service for psychosis (PICuP) based at SLaM, and holds an honorary contract with the IOP where she is involved with teaching and research. She has specialized in psychosis for the past 10 years and was a trial therapist on the multicentre RCT for cognitive therapy for command hallucinations (COMMAND). Nadine was also a therapist on the London Bombings Screen and Treat Programme where she specialized in the treatment of PTSD. She has a longstanding clinical and research interest in the confluence of PTSD and psychosis as well as working with imagery in psychosis.

Helen Kennerley is a Consultant Clinical Psychologist in Oxford Health NHS Foundation Trust and a Senior Associate Tutor with the University of Oxford. She has practiced CBT for over 25 years and is a founder member of the Oxford Cognitive Therapy Centre (OCTC). She has written several popular cognitive therapy self-help books and co-authored and co-edited a number of CBT text books including a very popular introduction to CBT.

Rob Kidney attained his Doctorate in Clinical Psychology in Plymouth in 2003 and completed his Masters in Psychological Therapies (CBT) in Exeter in 2007. He has been the service lead for an adult IAPT service, academic lead for High Intensity CBT at the University of Exeter and trial therapist on the NIHR-HTA funded CoBalT trial (Cognitive Behavioural Therapy as an adjunct to pharmacotherapy for treatment resistant depression in primary care: a randomized controlled trial). He has published in the *British Journal of Clinical Psychology*, and provided workshops at local, national and international conferences. Currently Rob is working for Virgin on behalf of the NHS as Lead Clinical Psychologist in Southern Devon CAMHS with an emphasis upon training, supervising and delivering CBT provision.

Willem Kuyken works as a researcher, trainer and clinician at the Mood Disorders Centre in Exeter. His research and clinical work specialize in CBT and mindfulness-based approaches to recurrent depression. A particular theme of his work is exploring how therapists co-create conceptualizations with their clients that enhance the effectiveness of therapy. He has published several publications on case conceptualization, including the book, co-authored with Christine Padesky and Rob Dudley, *Collaborative Case Conceptualization*.

Sheena Liness is Course Director of the postgraduate adult CBT training programmes at the Institute of Psychiatry, King's College London. Sheena organizes, teaches and supervises on a range of programmes including the High Intensity (IAPT) Programme. She is an accredited BABCP trainer, supervisor and CBT therapist and has worked in CBT clinical practice for 20 years.

Freda McManus is the (acting) Director of the Oxford Cognitive Therapy Centre and has been Director of the University of Oxford's PG Dip in CBT for the past nine years. She has worked in both the University of Oxford's Department of Psychiatry and at the Centre for Anxiety Disorders and Trauma (Kings College London) helping to devise and evaluate cognitive behavioural treatments for anxiety disorders. Freda McManus has published widely in the area of cognitive-behaviour therapy for anxiety disorders, and on training clinicians in CBT interventions.

Stirling Moorey is Consultant Psychiatrist in CBT and former professional Head of Psychotherapy at South London and Maudsley NHS Foundation Trust. He is a trained Cognitive Therapist and Cognitive Analytic Therapist who has been teaching and supervising CBT for many years and has an interest in how the therapy relationship can be understood within the cognitive model. His other area of interest is the application of CBT to people with cancer.

Emmanuelle Peters is Reader in Clinical Psychology at the Institute of Psychiatry (IOP), King's College London, and the director of a specialist outpatients psychological therapies service for psychosis (PICuP), based at South London and Maudsley NHS Foundation Trust. She has specialized in psychosis for the past 25 years as a clinician, researcher and trainer. Her research interests include the continuum view of psychosis, cognitive models of psychotic symptoms, and CBT for psychosis.

Roz Shafran is Professor of Clinical Psychology at the University of Reading and founder of the Charlie Waller Institute of Evidence Based Psychological Treatment. Her clinical and research interests include the development and dissemination of cognitive behavioural theories and treatments. She is an associate editor of "Behaviour Research and Therapy". She recently received an award for Distinguished Contributions to Professional Psychology from the British Psychological Society and the Marsh Award for Mental Health work.

Biza Stenfert Kroese is a Senior Lecturer in Clinical Psychology at the University of Birmingham and a Consultant Clinical Psychologist who until recently managed an NHS psychology service for people with intellectual disabilities (ID). She has co-edited books and published papers on challenging behaviour and the application of CBT for people with ID as well as papers on mental health and ID, parents with ID and staff attitudes on working with people with ID. She is involved in a national research trial of CBT intervention for anger.

Richard Thwaites is a Consultant Clinical Psychologist and CBT therapist, employed as Clinical Lead for a large NHS IAPT service covering Cumbria, UK. In addition to delivering therapy he provides clinical leadership, supervision and training within the service and wider organization. His research interests include the role of the therapeutic relationship in CBT and the use of reflective practice in the process of skill development. He is co-author of the book *Experiencing CBT from the Inside Out: A Self-Practice/ Self-Reflection Workbook for Therapists* (2014).

David Westbrook was a Consultant Clinical Psychologist, and was Director of Oxford Cognitive Therapy Centre (OCTC) until June 2012. He practiced CBT for over 25 years and after stepping down from the role of director he continued to work part-time in OCTC, doing training, supervision and research, and part-time as an NHS clinician, providing a service for patients with severe and complex problems. David edited a number of influential and critically acclaimed books on CBT. Tragically, David died in 2013 during the production of this book. He was known as a brilliant, humble, kind, humorous man.

Michael Worrell is Consultant Clinical Psychologist and director of postgraduate CBT training programmes at Central and North West London Foundation NHS Trust and Royal Holloway University of London. Michael directs a range of programmes including the Post Graduate Diploma and MSc in CBT, The High Intensity Training (IAPT) Programme, Post Qualification Training in CBT Supervision and the Behavioural Couples Therapy Training. His interests include "resistance", managing endings, the therapy relationship and couple therapy.

Foreword

David M. Clark

Professor of Experimental Psychology, University of Oxford

Cognitive behaviour therapies have established their efficacy with a wide range of mental health problems, both in randomized trials and in audits of routine clinical practice. However, there has been a persistent difficulty in providing CBT treatments to everyone who could benefit, due to insufficient numbers of suitably trained therapists.

In 2008 England embarked on an exciting programme to disseminate psychological therapy on a wider scale than has been ever been attempted before, with CBT forming the core treatment to be delivered by the new services for people with depression and anxiety disorders. By 2014 the Improving Access to Psychological Therapies (IAPT) programme will have trained 6,000 new therapists in evidence-based treatments recommended by the National Institute for Health and Clinical Excellence (NICE). The training courses established follow defined curricula, which ensure that the competencies needed to provide many of the leading empirically supported CBT treatments for depression and anxiety disorders are covered, as laid out in Roth and Pilling's (2007) competency framework.

Analysis of the outcomes delivered by the IAPT programme is confirming that CBT and the other treatments can be effective in routine services, but also that, as already observed in clinical trials, not everyone improves, or improvement may be partial (Clark, 2011). To overcome this problem we need to do two things. First, we need continue to improve our treatments. Second, we need ensure that the treatments that we currently have are delivered as competently as possible. This book focuses on the second of these imperatives, providing tools for clinicians to help them remain faithful to the treatments that are effective, while considering how and when treatments need to be tailored or adapted to specific individual circumstances and needs. Of course adaptation and flexing of CBT is not an "add-on" for some cases only, but a method of providing effective therapy in every case. However, the adaptations become more diverse and stretching in the most complex cases or when working with specific client groups that may have particular needs beyond those of the populations with which treatments were developed.

In this book Adrian Whittington, Nick Grey and colleagues explore how to tailor CBT methods while remaining true to the core principles, basing interventions on an individualized CBT formulation, guided by the best evidence and theory. The book is compiled from the distilled knowledge of some of the most skilled and experienced clinicians, who ground their insights in the foundations of CBT while suggesting ways to handle complexity and adaptations for specific adult client groups. Later chapters provide guidance to develop further as a therapist and to ensure that the learning is implemented systematically and successfully. This is a practical book to be read, but above all, to be used regularly to guide one's work.

References

Clark, D. M. (2011). Implementing NICE guidelines for the psychological treatment of depression and anxiety disorders: The IAPT experience. *International Review of Psychiatry, 23*(4), 318–327.

Roth, A. D., & Pilling, S. (2007). *The competences required to deliver effective cognitive and behavioural therapy for people with depression and with anxiety disorders.* London: Department of Health.

Foreword

Tony Roth

Professor of Clinical Psychology, University College London

It is a pleasure to have been invited to contribute to this book, not least because it has given me the chance to preview the contributions of a number of eminent and talented clinicians, and to use this opportunity to reflect on what metacompetences are, and how they are used.

The CBT competence framework (Roth & Pilling, 2007) was the first of what has become a suite of frameworks, now covering a range of therapeutic modalities and clinical populations. As a prototype for what followed, it acted as a test-bed for our ideas about how best to set out the knowledge and skills that underpinned the effective delivery of psychological therapies. One aim was that the framework was oriented towards competence rather than adherence, congruent with the sentiment that clinicians should not only do the right thing, but also do the right thing in the right way. Although the way we phrased competence descriptions reflected this stance, it became clear that some competences seemed to operate at a different level to others, because they focused on the way in which sets of competences were deployed, and in this sense could be seen as "meta" to others. It is fair to say that initially we lacked a well thought through conceptualization or definition that separated the "ordinary" from these "meta" competences, and even as work proceeded and we gathered examples of what they might look like, we still struggled to arrive at robust conceptualization. Without one it was all too easy for this term to become synonymous with complexity, resulting in almost everything beyond the "straightforward" application of therapy technique being flagged as a metacompetence – not a very useful development. The prefix "meta" implies that these competences are in a sense superordinate to some other set of actions, and although they are more likely to be evident when managing therapeutic challenge or complexity, it is this overarching or overseeing quality that is their appropriate focus.

One way of thinking about metacompetences is the idea of "procedural" rules that guide the assembly and sequencing of an action. These often involve balancing one decision about how to proceed in therapy against another, scoping and filtering a range of potential ways forward in order to arrive at a rational choice of action. Initially this decision making is likely to be fairly conscious, but increasingly in most, but not all cases, will become "more automatic" with experience and training, and so can be seen as a formal representation of what is often referred to as clinical acumen. Some examples from the CBT framework may help to illustrate this:

- "Juggling" competing demands: An ability to maintain adherence to an agreed agenda and to "pace" the session in a manner which ensures that all agreed items can be given appropriate attention (i.e., ensuring that significant issues are not rushed)
- Monitoring and responding to the way a session unfolds: An ability to be aware of, and respond to, emotional shifts occurring in each session, with the aim of maintaining an optimal level of emotional arousal (i.e., ensuring that the client is neither remote from, or overwhelmed by, their feelings).
- Constructing the intervention in a way that holds in mind a holistic sense of the client's needs: An ability to implement the CBT model in a manner that is consonant with a comprehensive formulation that takes into account all relevant aspects of the client's presentation

Hopefully these examples make it clear that metacompetences are not abstruse; their challenge lies in the fact that they require clinicians to make particular types of judgment. The common thread is that these judgments usually involve titration: weighing the consequences of one action against the other and arriving at a decision about how best to implement the therapeutic process.

In their introduction Adrian Whittington and Nick Grey adopt an analogy for metacompetence that I also find myself using. Great cooks are distinguished not by their ability to adhere to a recipe but by their ability to use the recipe as a guide, bringing to bear knowledge of the general principles that underpin cookery and a capacity to implement specific techniques, and where necessary developing bespoke recipes that take account of missing ingredients and the utensils that they have at their disposal. This is a critical, even if obvious, observation: it means that recipes – and by analogy competence frameworks – are best seen as indicative and not prescriptive, not directives for action but guidance that should be interpreted in order to arrive at the best action to take. But identifying *how* this is done is quite a challenge, especially if we are to do so without resorting to portmanteau phrases such as "flair" that promise much but actually mean very little – after all, we can't train people to show "flair" unless we know what this comprises.

What would be helpful is to define the sort of steps that amount to (or are associated with) this sort of therapeutic capacity, aiming to identify and explicate the skills that differentiate the fluent from the struggling therapist, and by incorporating these into training make it more likely that these skills will be reproduced. This, of course, is the *raison d'être* of this book. Students of psychological therapy often complain about the gap between what they are taught and what happens in the clinic. Few clients they see are like those described in text books, and what seems straightforward on paper is challenging in practice, sometimes overwhelmingly so. This book directly addresses this gap between theory and practice by making more explicit the thinking and judgment that is required to translate CBT theory into CBT practice, focusing on the necessary twists and turns in which therapists need to engage if the outcomes their clients seek are to be achieved.

Reference

Roth, A. D., & Pilling, S. (2007). *The competences required to deliver effective cognitive and behavioural therapy for people with depression and with anxiety disorders.* London: Department of Health.

I
The Foundations

1
The Foundations

1

Mastering Metacompetence
The Science and Art of
Cognitive Behavioural Therapy

Adrian Whittington and Nick Grey

In a professional kitchen, recipes are essential to creating consistent food, so that everyone takes the same path to the same place. But cooks who rely only on strictly codified formulas miss out on what is really important. Are the carrots more or less sweet, more or less tender? Is the ginger very strong, so that less should be used, or too weak for the amount specified? Or the thorniest problem: How long does it take something to cook, in a specific oven, on a specific day, with a certain set of ingredients?

Daniel Patterson, Head Chef, Coi, San Francisco[1]

Introduction

Cognitive Behavioural Therapy (CBT) has grown up in a scientific tradition, which has been highly productive in the development of effective therapy. Research trials have given us a firm foundation for expanding the delivery of CBT, with the approaches delivered in the trials being reproduced in routine care to help a lot of people a lot of the time.

However, these trials can seem a long way from the consulting room when as a therapist you sit down with a unique client who has a unique set of difficulties and strengths. As a therapist you face a seemingly infinite range of options in your moment to moment decision making about what to do next as you try to deliver CBT in the most helpful way with this client at this point in time. A lot of the time you probably cannot be sure of the best options and have to proceed in the hope and faith that by working collaboratively with your client you will be able to negotiate a helpful way forward. This can feel more like an art than a science. Abilities required to apply therapy artfully, in a flexible and individually tailored way, have been named "metacompetences" in Roth and Pilling's competence framework for CBT (Roth & Pilling, 2007).

How to Become a More Effective CBT Therapist: Mastering Metacompetence in Clinical Practice, First Edition. Edited by Adrian Whittington and Nick Grey.

There are significant pitfalls on the path between the science of CBT and its artful delivery. These include the risk of rejecting the research base because of a sometimes imperfect fit with routine practice, the risk of drifting away from effective methods in the belief that you are being helpfully flexible, and the risk of being overly rigid in your approach in an attempt to adhere to protocol.

We believe that the science and art of CBT can and should be brought closer together to help avoid these risks, and that the concept of *metacompetent adherence* gives us a framework for bridging this gap. Metacompetent adherence means making your therapy decisions based on evidence that clearly supports the practice and on a sound theoretical rationale where the evidence is less clear. Mastering metacompetence is a process of making explicit and enacting the if–then procedural rules of therapy adaptation and where possible drawing on the evidence base. These rules will not take away all uncertainty, however. The experience of not knowing is inevitable and perhaps desirable for therapists – human experiences require you to respond with humility, compassion and openness to learning as you deliver the best evidence-based intervention that you can.

The Science of CBT: Efficacy, Effectiveness and Evidence-Based Practice

Thousands of research trials have been conducted to address the question of whether and for whom CBT is useful, and how it can be most effective. The research base of CBT includes efficacy studies that test treatment in carefully controlled experimental conditions and effectiveness studies that test the interventions in routine care settings, as well as a plethora of other approaches including dissemination trials, single case research, dismantling studies and experimental designs. Of these approaches randomized control trial (RCT) evidence has traditionally been viewed as the "gold standard" methodology for establishing whether an intervention works (Kaptchuck, 2001).

This scientific effort has been more intensive than for any other form of psychotherapy. Analysis of "what works for whom" clearly indicates CBT's wide utility (Roth & Fonagy, 2005). As a consequence of this evidence, CBT has been recommended in evidence-based treatment guidance for a wide range of psychological difficulties (e.g., National Institute for Health and Clinical Excellence, 2009, 2011) and has become more widely available. In the United Kingdom, a national programme to increase access to psychological therapies for depression and anxiety disorders has seen an unprecedented expansion in the provision of CBT (Clark, 2011).

Both efficacy and effectiveness research shows that CBT works for many people with many types of difficulties and that research-based interventions can be applied in routine practice without dramatic reduction in effect. However, trial-based evidence will never resolve all of your dilemmas as a therapist about exactly what works for whom in which situations. This has led to a movement towards evidence-based practice (EBP) as an approach to guide clinical decision making, drawing on a combination of research evidence, clinical expertise and client preferences (Lillienfeld, Ritschel, Lynn, Cautin, & Latzman, 2013).

Efficacy of CBT

Efficacy studies are those in which the treatment is carefully studied under "ideal" experimental conditions in a randomized controlled trial (RCT). Most reviews and meta-analyses have examined how CBT treatments have performed in efficacy studies.

These have themselves been examined in a larger review of meta-analyses of CBT RCTs across a wide range of disorders (Butler, Chapman, Forman, & Beck, 2006). Overall large effect sizes for CBT were seen for unipolar depression, generalized anxiety disorder, panic disorder, social anxiety disorder and post-traumatic stress disorder; moderate effect sizes for working with pain and anger; and CBT was as effective as behaviour therapy for obsessive compulsive disorder.

The degree to which results from RCTs translate into routine practice is a contentious issue (e.g., Westen, Novotny and Thompson-Brenner, 2004). RCTs typically have a single therapeutic focus (i.e., a particular psychiatric diagnosis/disorder), have an associated treatment manual, and are usually of a relatively brief fixed duration. This all makes sense scientifically, maximizing internal validity of the study, but has led to critiques of the evidence, suggesting that RCT conditions are too divorced from the realities of routine practice.

Effectiveness of CBT

Effectiveness studies measure the outcome of interventions provided in "routine" care settings. Effectiveness research indicates that it is possible to reproduce CBT RCT interventions in routine care settings with fewer controls and without greatly reducing their effects, although this is not guaranteed. A meta-analytic review of effectiveness trials of CBT for anxiety disorders showed that mean effect sizes were comparable to those in benchmarked RCTs (Stewart & Chambless, 2009). A similar meta-analytic review of effectiveness trials of CBT for depression showed a dilution of mean effect size in routine care, although the effect remained large (Hans & Hiller, 2013). Some effectiveness trials have even shown *larger* effects than in comparable RCTs (Ost, 2013). At one-year follow-up CBT for anxiety disorders in routine care has produced results almost equal to those of RCTs, whereas CBT for depression has not (DiMauro, Domigues, Fernandez, & Tolin, 2013; Gibbons et al., 2010).

The differences in effect of CBT in RCTs and routine care are not uniform and are likely to differ across the variety of treatments badged as CBT. Reasons for dilution of effect are not clear where these have been observed. Possible differences between RCTs and routine care include client characteristics, therapist and therapy characteristics. All may be relevant, but there is evidence that poorer quality control of therapy in routine settings may be at least as important in reducing effects as differences in the clients seen (Stewart & Chambless, 2009; Stirman, DeRubeis, Crits-Cristoph, & Rothman, 2005).

Despite the demonstrable value of CBT in routine settings as well as in RCTs, the evidence is currently insufficient to provide a comprehensive guide to the flexible, individually adapted delivery of CBT. The areas where research cannot be the only guide include numerous areas of complexity such as how best to intervene with co-morbid conditions (Shafran et al., 2009) and how best to deliver "flexibility within fidelity" (Kendall, Gosch, Furr, & Sood, 2008).

Evidence-based practice

There will never be enough research to tell you definitively what will work best for any particular individual client, and there will always be those who seek therapy from you who are "beyond the guidelines" developed during RCT trials. This situation leaves you unable to rely solely on RCT evidence to guide your practice as a therapist.

Evidence-based practice (EBP) offers the beginnings of a solution. EBP has been proposed in the United States as an approach to clinical decision-making, drawing on the "three-leg stool" of research evidence, clinical expertise, and client preferences (Spring, 2007). EBP has been distinguished from empirically supported treatments (ESTs) based on RCT evidence, which do not offer explicit specific guidance on adaptation and flexibility (Lilienfield et al., 2013). In the United Kingdom the concept of empirically grounded clinical interventions (EGCIs) also highlights the need for a broader approach to evidence-based practice than can be derived from RCT evidence alone; EGCIs are said to be derived from the sequence of clinical observation, experimental study and theory development, followed by treatment efficacy and effectiveness trials (Salkovskis, 2002). This approach values the role of experimentally derived theory as part of an evidence-based approach to intervention in the absence of specific evidence for what to do next.

As a therapist, EBP and EGCIs offer you a more comprehensive framework for making clinical decisions than trial evidence alone. However, both stop short of defining in detail the nature of the clinical expertise that you will need to draw upon and how you should put this into action.

The Art of CBT: Metacompetence

To be an evidence-based practitioner does not mean that you will always find yourself following a defined course of action or sequence of steps. In fact this is likely to feel like the exception rather than the rule in your therapy sessions. Much of the time you will base your actions on a combination of fundamental CBT therapy competences, your knowledge of specific CBT techniques and models, and an informed negotiation with your client about a way forward. The competences to enact this combination of factors into a coherent and effective therapy for anxiety disorders or depression have been defined very helpfully, drawing on an expert reference group and the manuals used in RCT trials that showed CBT to have a positive effect (Roth & Pilling, 2007).

Roth and Pilling (2007) identified five specific aspects of competence (see Figure 1.1). The first four outline competences of increasing levels of specificity to CBT and to CBT for particular problems, as follows:

Generic therapeutic competences: Required for the delivery of any psychological therapy, which include knowledge about mental health, ability to engage and assess clients, manage a therapeutic relationship and make use of supervision.
Basic CBT competences: The foundations of all CBT interventions, including knowledge of core CBT principles and abilities to agree goals collaboratively, jointly manage session structure and introduce a basic formulation using a cognitive-behavioural maintenance cycle.
Specific CBT techniques: A set of core cognitive and behavioural technical interventions, delivered within the context of Socratic dialogue and including, for example, the use of thought records, behavioural experiments, exposure and activity scheduling.
Problem-specific competences: The competences to deliver specific CBT intervention packages for particular disorders, for example the Clark intervention for panic disorder (Clark, 1986) or the Jacobson behavioural activation intervention for depression (Jacobson, Dobson, Truax, Addis, et al., 1996).

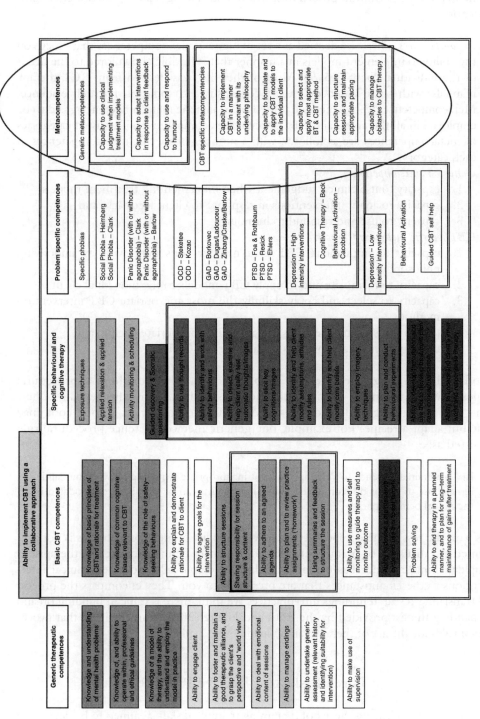

Figure 1.1 Competences for the effective delivery of CBT for depression and anxiety disorders (Roth & Pilling, 2007). © Crown Copyright (2007).

In addition, recognizing that skilled psychological therapy must be more than a combination of technical procedures, Roth and Pilling (2007) identified a fifth category:

Metacompetences. These are defined as a set of higher order competences that "focus on the ability to implement models in a manner that is flexible and tailored to the needs of the individual client" (p. 9). Most of their list was derived from RCT therapy manuals, with some based on expert consensus and some on research evidence. Metacompetences were generated in two areas: generic metacompetences, said to be employed in all therapies, and CBT-specific metacompetences. The listed categories of metacompetences are as follows, with a number of specific metacompetences in each category:

Generic metacompetences:
  1. capacity to use clinical judgement when implementing treatment models
  2. capacity to adapt interventions in response to client feedback, and
  3. capacity to use and respond to humour.

CBT specific metacompetences:
  1. capacity to implement CBT in a manner consonant with its underlying philosophy,
  2. capacity to formulate and to apply CBT models to the individual client,
  3. capacity to select and apply skilfully the most appropriate CBT intervention method,
  4. capacity to structure sessions and maintain appropriate pacing, and
  5. capacity to manage obstacles to carrying out CBT.

Roth and Pilling suggested that metacompetences may be thought of as procedural rules by which therapists can apply the methods of therapy in a theoretically coherent, but appropriately adapted and individually tailored way, as a good cook may use but adapt a recipe. For example, one generic metacompetence procedural rule is listed as:

> [to] maintain adherence to a therapy without inappropriate switching between modalities in response to minor difficulties (i.e., difficulties which can be readily accommodated by the model being applied).

As with the rest of the competency framework the list of metacompetences is not presented as exhaustive or permanent. Metacompetences define your art as a therapist in implementing evidence-based practice, adapting empirically grounded clinical interventions to the circumstances that are presented to you. They encompass the process of translating research findings into practice. We think there is value in building on and expanding the list provided by the Roth and Pilling (2007) framework so that procedural rules for the art of therapy can be made more explicit.

Three Risks to Effective Practice

There are risks in leaving the art of therapy as an implicit skill, assumed to be developed through experience or supervision, rather than something that is at least worth trying to define and make explicit. Without definition, lots of different forms of unhelpful practice can be labelled as appropriate flexibility or adaptation. Therapist resistance to research-based evidence can provide fertile ground in which such anomalous practice can grow. Even those committed to evidence-based practice may drift away from effective approaches or become overly rigid in their approach and not recognize that what is happening is far from artful.

The risk of rejecting research evidence

Many therapists hold research evidence as a highly valued guide in practice, and CBT therapists are likely to value it fairly highly. However, this is by no means universal. A qualitative study of US practicing psychologists found that most ranked research evidence as lower than clinical experience and intuition in guiding their practice (Stewart, Stirman, & Chambless, 2012). In the United Kingdom, therapist disquiet about applying research-based evidence is highlighted by the active debate on the subject in the UK Clinical Psychology professional literature (e.g., Smail, 2006).

Scott Lilienfield and colleagues (2013) have provided a thoughtful and constructive review and commentary on the "resistance" shown by some therapy practitioners to evidence-based practice. They highlight the risks of rejecting research evidence, citing harmful medical practices in mental health such as the prefrontal lobotomy, which gained currency through the reliance on clinical expertise in the absence of research data. Without research evidence, as a therapist you are unable to tell the difference between therapeutic effectiveness and placebo effect or spontaneous remission. This opens the way to a proliferation of spurious treatments.

There are numerous therapist beliefs that may interfere with the delivery of EBP, including a belief that what seems to be the evidence of your own eyes is more valuable than the evidence of RCTs (Lilienfield et al., 2013). Beliefs that we have found to be particularly relevant that could impede the dissemination of effective CBT treatments include beliefs that the clients who enter RCTs are not representative of the population seen in routine care and that treatments derived from RCT manuals are prescriptive and inflexible (Shafran et al., 2009). These beliefs are examined in the light of the following evidence.

Belief 1: Clients entering RCTs are not representative of those seen in routine care,
where there are more severe or co-morbid presentations
Co-morbidity is very common, with axis 1 conditions co-morbid with other axis 1 or axis 2 disorders in the range of 50 to 90 per cent (e.g., Kessler, Nelso, McGonagle, & Liu, 1996). It is true that RCTs do sometimes exclude participants with co-morbidity or as a result of severity, for example, if the client is actively suicidal. However, analyses of clients that are seen in routine care suggest that only 5 per cent would have been excluded from an RCT (Stirman et al., 2005). The most common reasons for exclusion in this routine care population would not have been more severe or complex presentations, but the clients in routine care not meeting minimum severity or duration criteria. More recent trials allow extensive co-morbidity without great reduction in outcome (DeRubies et al., 2005; Duffy, Gillespie, & Clark, 2007). Furthermore, a recent study of CBT for PTSD in routine care suggests that the majority of client characteristics that would have led to exclusion from an RCT made no difference to outcome of therapy. Large effect sizes were demonstrated even for clients that would have been excluded from an RCT (Ehlers et al., 2013).

Table 1.1 Likely differences between trials and routine practice

	RCTs	Routine practice
Resources	Usually better resourced	Resources restricted
Assessment	More structured, detailed and regular	Procedures to identify focal problems and diagnoses less common
Therapists	More likely to be expert in administration of a particular treatment	Covering a wider range of main problems
Caseloads	Usually smaller	Usually larger
Therapy	Protocol controls duration and number of sessions	Often service provider controls duration and number of sessions
Engagement	Sometimes greater efforts made to maintain engagement	Sometimes less emphasis on reducing attrition rates given the often large numbers waiting for treatments
Quality control	Adherence monitoring and high quality supervision	Adherence monitoring may be limited and supervision of less consistent quality

Belief 2: Interventions delivered in RCT manuals are prescriptive and inflexible
Clinical guidelines used in RCTs have been developed for diagnostic categories, which can be limiting in complex cases. However, interventions within RCTs are usually based on an individualized formulation, based tightly on a specific model for the problem that is the focus of the trial. Flexibility is in fact inherent in RCT treatments using manuals and the use of manuals must always involve "flexibility within fidelity" (Kendall and Beidas, 2007). Even in trials participants will "strain the paradigm" (Markowitz et al., 2012).

In reality there are likely to be significant differences between trial conditions and routine care, and also some differences on dimensions of resourcing, therapist expertise and quality control (Roth, Pilling, & Turner, 2010; Stewart and Chambless, 2009) (see Table 1.1).

These differences in context, therapy and therapist factors suggest that rather than RCTs needing to be more like routine practice in order to provide realistic outcomes, we should endeavour to make routine practice become more like the conditions established in RCTs in order to achieve the best outcomes.

The risk of therapist drift

In a similar vein, there is evidence that therapist "drift" from adherence to evidence-based protocols can lead to poorer responses to treatment. Glenn Waller has observed that therapists commonly "drift" away from pushing for behavioural change (a core element in component analyses of successful treatment) to a more discursive approach (Waller, 2009). This drift may be driven by a number of factors including therapists' own beliefs, emotional reactions and safety behaviours. Waller proposed that the same factors may lead clinicians to rush to implement newer "third wave" therapies even when the best evidence-based therapy has never been tried.

A detailed analysis of video recordings of CBT for anxiety, confirmed that therapists frequently switched away from core methods such as exposure (Schulte and Eifert,

2002). Therapists explained that they perceived a need to do something different when they faced relational difficulties in the session. More frequent switches in this direction were associated with more negative outcomes of therapy, whereas more frequent switches of direction towards implementing core methods were associated with more positive outcomes. Changes in treatment direction were not triggered by a lack of progress, but by therapists feeling less positive about their relationship with their client. In light of these findings it will be important for you to distinguish metacompetent flexibility and adaptation in your practice from drift or unhelpful changes of direction.

The risk of rigid application of technique

Lack of flexibility is another risk. Whereas therapists may sometimes switch away from core strategies when therapeutic alliance starts to deteriorate, therapists may equally sometimes be tempted to push even harder on rigid application of technique at these times, with negative effects on outcome (Castonguay, Goldfried, Wiser, Raue, & Hayes, 1996). There is emerging evidence that flexing the structure of interventions in a planned way (including providing more sessions) and the focus of sessions (including "stressor sessions" when the focus of session is primarily on current life events) can help to maintain good outcomes in effectiveness studies (Galovski, Blain, Mott, Elwood, & Houle, 2012). However, there is little data on whether particular variations on the structure of therapy (e.g., duration or frequency of sessions) are superior to others (Haaga, 2004; Westen et al., 2004). You will need to walk a tightrope between adherence and flexible adaptation and avoid straying into drift, or overly rigid practice.

Bringing the Science and Art Together: Metacompetent Adherence

Telling the difference between unhelpful drift and helpful flexibility or between unhelpful rigidity and helpful adherence is highly challenging. This book aims to help with this. It does not propose an "anything goes" approach, but rather a way of introducing appropriate adaptation and flexibility in a measured and evidence-based way, when faced with particular circumstances. Metacompetence is not all about flexing or changing "normal" CBT. It is about knowing when and what to flex within the principles and theoretical underpinnings of CBT. Often metacompetence will guide a practitioner to stay on course with the usual evidence-based method rather than divert into less well-tested methods.

We make a distinction between (1) *principles* of CBT, including its conceptual underpinning and core methods such as formulation and collaborative empiricism, (2) *tactics* such as deciding how to set up opportunities for cognitive change or which problem to tackle first, and (3) *techniques* such as the use of thought records or behavioural experiments. A sporting analogy can be helpful here. In tennis, for example, principles are the rules of the game, tactics refer to how different game situations are approached when responding to a particular opponent, and techniques include the application of forehand, backhand, volley and serve.

In considering how to apply CBT to each unique circumstance you should consider these as a hierarchy of levels for adaptation. Technique can be adapted in a myriad of unique ways to suit individual needs and it will be appropriate to do this in every session with every client. Tactics may be reconsidered in the light of evidence that the usual

	Tactics and technique: *Tight*	Tactics and technique: *Loose*
Principles: *Tight*	**Competent Adherence** Tactics and techniques applied in the standard way as in RCTs. Suited to learning CBT and to specific problem types with specific protocols. Likely to be effective if there is a good fit between the specific approach and the specific problem/case. Practitioners with less experience should aim to practice in this manner.	**Metacompetent Adherence** Appropriate adaptation of tactics and techniques using fundamental CBT principles. Suited to CBT for cases that don't fit the usual guidelines. Different to therapist "drift"; as motivation to adapt is theory and evidence-based. May be effective, more likely to be needed with complex cases and easier with greater clinical experience.
Principles: *Loose*	**Rigid Practice** Tactics and techniques applied rigidly without recourse to principles. When first learning CBT treatments practitioners may find themselves practicing in this manner – just thinking about what to do next without properly basing this on a formulation. Can be aversive for clients and have negative impact on outcome.	**Unfocused Practice** Unfocused tactics and erratic use of technique, without recourse to principles. This is the culmination of therapist "drift". Does not resemble CBT and likely to be less effective.

Figure 1.2   Different styles of CBT practice associated with loose/tight application of CBT principles, tactics and technique. © Adrian Whittington and Nick Grey (2013).

tactics are unsuitable, but principles should be held firm in all cases, except where there is evidence that another form of therapy or intervention may be more helpful.

How closely we hold to each of these aspects of CBT may be "tight" (more rigidly held) or "loose" (more flexibly held). These ideas are partly inspired by Cory Newman's excellent book on core competencies in CBT (Newman, 2012). Various degrees of tight/loose alignment to principles, tactics and technique can occur and can explain different styles of practice commonly encountered (see Figure 1.2).

According to this framework therapists aim to provide competent CBT, and then further to adapt and flex it as appropriate, by employing metacompetences. Some therapists, particularly when inexperienced, may fall into the trap of rigid practice, and others, however experienced, can drift into unfocused practice, sometimes mistaking this for metacompetence.

Many commonly occurring complexities add to the challenge of providing CBT (e.g. Westbrook, Mueller, Kennerley, & McManus, 2010). These include:

1. A mismatch between how client and therapist understand the problem (e.g., a client who assures you they do not have a drink problem despite objective signs that they are alcohol dependent).
2. Co-morbid Axis I problems (e.g., PTSD with depression)
3. Co-morbid Axis I and Axis II problems (e.g., Depression in the context of Borderline Personality Disorder)

4. Client factors (e.g., memory problems associated with learning disability or physical health problems associated with older age)
5. Client context factors (e.g., client's relatives inadvertently act in ways that maintain the problem, or social circumstances such a loss of employment)
6. Therapist–client interaction factors (e.g., client acts in ways that triggers counterproductive cognitions and behaviours in the therapist)
7. Therapist factors (e.g., therapist holds beliefs about CBT that do not reflect the evidence, for example, that straightforward application of CBT cannot provide long–term resolution of difficulties)
8. Therapist context factors (e.g., the provider rations the "dose" of CBT to below the level where effectiveness would be expected)
9. Therapy is not helping (e.g.,"usual" protocol is leading to no change, deterioration or client disengagement)

Metacompetence will be especially important in addressing these complexities, which often take us beyond the typical textbook application of CBT.

Conclusion

Providing CBT is inevitably both a science and an art. Metacompetence offers a framework for defining and helping to make explicit some aspects of the artistry of CBT. Metacompetent adherence is a way of bringing science and artistry together to deliver more effective therapy. This approach can reduce the risk of drift or unhelpful rigidity in practice and help you to resolve dilemmas that you will face in delivering CBT every day.

Metacompetence consists of numerous procedural rules for applying CBT in different specific circumstances. Roth and Pilling (2007) identified a number of desired outcomes from implementing these rules (e.g., "formulate and apply CBT models to the individual client"). In this book we attempt to uncover some of the specific rules by which these outcomes might be achieved, based on best evidence and the experience of experts in the field. The book reviews the foundations of CBT competence on which metacompetence must be built, establishes how you should adapt and flex the delivery of CBT in the face of complex presentations of anxiety and depression, and serves as an introduction to ways of meeting the additional needs of other specific client groups. It also guides you in how you might continue to learn additional procedural rules as you go forward in your practice.

Procedural Rules

- Always look first to whether you are competently delivering evidence-based approaches before you attempt variations on these.
- Do not get thrown off course by myths that evidence-based practice and evidence from randomized controlled trials is not relevant. Use this evidence as a starting point for competent practice.
- Beware the risks of therapist "drift" from proven approaches. Where you adapt or flex CBT, do so based on the principles of CBT and evidence-based practice.

- Avoid overly rigid adherence to particular techniques in the face of difficulties.
- Aim for metacompetent adherence, adhering to the principles and conceptual underpinnings of CBT while allowing appropriate flexibility in tactics and techniques of therapy.
- Set about collecting explicit "procedural rules" for metacompetent practice. You can start by reading this book and attempting to put the rules you read about into practice.

Acknowledgements

Many thanks to Helen Curr, Ben Smith and Kerry Young for comments on an earlier version of this chapter.

Note

1   Reproduced courtesy of www.foodandwine.com, by permission of Daniel Patterson

References

Butler, A.C., Chapman, J.E., Forman, E.M., & Beck, A.T. (2006). The empirical status of cognitive behaviour therapy: a review of meta-analyses. *Clinical Psychology Review, 26,* 17–31. doi: 10.1016/j.cpr.2005.07.003

Castonguay, L.G., Goldfried, M.R., Wiser, S., Raue, P.J., & Hayes, A.M. (1996). Predicting the effect of cognitive therapy for depression: A study of unique and common factors. *Journal of Consulting and Clinical Psychology, 64,* 497–504.

Clark, D.M. (1986). A cognitive approach to panic. *Behaviour Research and Therapy, 24,* 461–470.

Clark, D.M. (2011). Implementing NICE guidelines for the psychological treatment of depression and anxiety disorders: The IAPT experience. *International Review of Psychiatry, 23,* 375–384. doi: 10.3109/09540261.2011.606803

DeRubies, R.J., Hollon, S.D., Amsterdam, J.D., Shelton, R.C., Young, P.R., Salomon, R.M., . . . Gallop, R. (2005). Cognitive therapy vs. medications in the treatment of moderate to severe depression. *Archives of General Psychiatry, 62,* 409–416.

DiMauro, J., Domingues, J., Fernandez, G., & Tolin, D. (2013). Long-term effectiveness of CBT for anxiety disorders in an adult outpatient clinic sample: a follow-up study. *Behaviour Research and Therapy, 51,* 82–86. doi: 10.1016/j.brat.2012.10.003

Duffy, M., Gillespie, K., & Clark, D.M. (2007). Posttraumatic Stress Disorder in the context of terrorism and other civil conflict in Northern Ireland: randomized controlled trial. *British Medical Journal, 334,* 1147–1150.

Ehlers, A., Grey, N., Wild, J., Stott, R., Liness, S., Deale, A., . . . Clark, D.M. (2013). Dissemination of cognitive therapy for PTSD in routine clinical care: Effectiveness and moderators of outcome in a consecutive sample. *Behaviour Research and Therapy, 51*(11), 742–752. doi: 10.1016/j/brat.2013.08.006

Galovski, T.E., Blain, L.M., Mott, J.M., Elwood, L., & Houle, T. (2012). Manualized therapy for PTSD: flexing the structure of cognitive processing therapy. *Journal of Consulting and Clinical Psychology, 80,* 968–981. doi: 10.1037/a0030600

Gibbons, C.J., Fournier, J.C., Stirman, S.W., DeRubeis, R.J., Crits-Cristoph, P., & Beck, A.T. (2010). The clinical effectiveness of cognitive therapy for depression in an outpatient clinic. *Journal of Affective Disorders, 125*, 169–176. doi: 10.1016/j.jad.2009.12.030

Haaga, D.A.F. (2004). A healthy dose of criticism for randomized trials: comment on Westen, Novotny and Thompson-Brenner (2004). *Psychological Bulletin, 130*, 674–676. doi: 10.1037/0033-2909.130.4.674

Hands, E., & Hiller, W. (2013). Effectiveness of and dropout from outpatient cognitive behavioral therapy for adult unipolar depression: a meta-analysis of nonrandomized effectiveness studies. *Journal of Consulting and Clinical Psychology, 81*(1), 75–88. doi: 10.1037/a0031080.

Jacobson, N.S., Dobson, K.S., Truax, P.A., Addis, M.E., Koerner, K., . . . Prince, S.E. (1996). A component analysis of cognitive-behavioral treatment for depression. *Journal of Consulting and Clinical Psychology, 64*(2), 295–304.

Kaptchuck, T.J. (2001). The double-blind, randomized, placebo-controlled trial:Gold standard or golden calf? *Journal of Clinical Epidemiology, 54*, 541–549.

Kendall, P.C., & Beidas, R.S. (2007). Smoothing the trail for dissemination of evidence based practice for youth: flexibility within fidelity. *Professional Psychology: Research and Practice, 38*, 13–19. doi: 10.1016/j.cbpra.2009.11.002

Kendall, P.C., Gosch, E., Furr, J.M., & Sood, E. (2008). Flexibility within fidelity. *Journal of the Academy of Child and Adolescent Psychiatry, 47*, 987–993. doi: 10.1097/CHI.0b013e31817eed2f

Kessler, R.C., Nelson, C.B., McGonagle, K.A., & Liu, J. (1996). Comorbidity of DSM-III-R major depressive disorder in the general population: results from the US National Comorbidity Survey. *British Journal of Psychiatry, 168*, 17–30.

Lillienfield, S.O., Ritschel, L.A., Lynn, S.J., Cautin, R.L., & Latzman, R.D. (2013). Why many clinical psychologists are resistant to evidence-based practice: root causes and constructive remedies. *Clinical Psychology Review, 33*(7), 883–900. doi: 10.1016/j.cpr.2012.09.008

Markowitz, J.C., Kaplowitz, M., Eun-Jung, S., Meehan, K.B., Neria, Y., Jonker, H., . . . Lovell, K. (2012). Treating patients who strain the research psychotherapy paradigm. *Journal of Nervous and Mental Disease, 200*, 594–597. doi: 10.1097/NMD.0b013e31825bfaf4

National Institute for Health and Clinical Excellence. (2009). *The treatment and management of depression in adults.* NICE clinical guideline 90. Retrieved from http://guidance.nice.org.uk/cg90

National Institute for Health and Clinical Excellence. (2011). *Generalised anxiety disorder and panic disorder (with or without agoraphobia) in adults. Management in primary, secondary and community care.* NICE clinical guideline 113. Retrieved from http://guidance.nice.org.uk/CG113

Newman, C.F. (2012). *Core competencies in cognitive behavioural therapy: becoming a highly effective and competent cognitive behavioural therapist.* New York: Routledge.

Ost, L.-G. (2013, July). *One-session treatment, ACT, and implementation of research findings in clinical practice.* Paper presented at British Association for Behavioural and Cognitive Psychotherapies 41st Annual Conference, London.

Roth, A., & Fonagy, P. (2005). *What works for whom? A critical review of psychotherapy research* (2nd ed.). New York: Guilford Press.

Roth, A., & Pilling, S. (2007). The competences required to deliver effective cognitive and behavioural therapy for people with depression and with anxiety disorders. Improving Access to Psychological Therapies (IAPT) Programme. Retrieved from www.ucl.ac.uk/clinical-psychology/CORE/CBT_Competences/CBT_Competence_List.pdf

Roth, A., Pilling, S., & Turner, J. (2010). Therapist training and supervision in clinical trials: implications for clinical practice. *Behavioural and Cognitive Psychotherapy, 38*, 291–302.

Salkovskis, P.M. (2002). Empirically grounded clinical interventions: Cognitive-behavioural therapy progresses through a multi-dimensional approach to clinical science. *Behavioural and Cognitive Psychotherapy, 30*, 3–9. doi: 10.1017/S1352465802001029

Schulte, D., & Eifert, G.H. (2002). What to do when the manuals fail? The dual model of psychotherapy. *Clinical Psychology Science and Practice, 9,* 312–328.

Shafran, R., Clark, D.M., Fairburn, C.G., Arntz, A., Barlow, D.H., Ehlers, A., . . . Wilson, G.T. (2009). Mind the gap: improving the dissemination of CBT. *Behaviour Research and Therapy, 47,* 902–909. doi: 10.1016/j.brat.2009.07.003

Smail, D. (2006). Is clinical psychology selling its soul (again)? *Clinical Psychology Forum, 168,* 17–20.

Spring, B. (2007). Evidence-based practice in clinical psychology: what it is; why it matters; what you need to know. *Journal of Clinical Psychology, 63,* 611–631. doi: 10.1002/jclp.20373

Stewart, R.E., & Chambless, D.L. (2009). Cognitive-behavioral therapy for adult anxiety disorders in clinical practice: a meta-analysis of effectiveness studies. *Journal of Consulting and Clinical Psychology, 77,* 595–606. doi: 10.1037/a0016032

Stewart, R.E., Stirman, S.W., & Chambless, D.L. (2012). A qualitative investigation of practicing psychologists' attitudes toward research-informed practice: Implications for dissemination strategies. *Professional Psychology: Research and Practice, 43,* 100–109. doi: 10.1037/a0025694

Stirman, S.W., DeRubeis, R.J., Crits-Cristoph, P., & Rothman, A. (2005). Can the randomized controlled trial literature generalize to non-randomized clients? *Journal of Consulting and Clinical Psychology, 73,* 127–145. doi: 10.1037/0022-006X.73.1.127

Waller, G. (2009). Evidence-based treatment and therapist drift. *Behaviour Research and Therapy, 47,* 119–127. doi: 10.1016/j.brat.2008.10.018

Westbrook, D., Mueller, M., Kennerley, H., & McManus, F. (2010). Common problems in therapy. In edited by M. Mueller, H. Kennerley, F. McManus & D. Westbrook (Eds.), *Oxford Guide to Surviving as a CBT Therapist* (pp. 1–40). Oxford: Oxford University Press.

Westen, D., Novotny, C.M., &Thompson-Brenner, H. (2004). The empirical status of empirically supported psychotherapies: assumptions, findings and reporting in controlled clinical trials. *Psychological Bulletin, 130,* 631–663. doi: 10.1037/0033-2909.130.4.631

2

The Central Pillars of CBT

David Westbrook

Introduction

CBT has grown and developed in many different directions as it has been adapted to different populations, to an ever-increasing range of problems and to new forms of delivery. Many of the other chapters in this book will tell you about the fruits of this constant evolution of CBT. However, this chapter highlights some of the fundamental ideas and skills of CBT that you should be competent in using with relatively straightforward problems before you try adapting them to more complex situations. In terms of the Roth and Pilling (2007) competence framework, the focus here is on "basic" and "specific" CBT competences, as opposed to the "metacompetences" that feature in many of the other chapters.

The purpose of presenting this outline is: (a) to remind you of some of CBT's core features and strategies that remain applicable across a wide range of problems and modes of delivery; and (b) to encourage you to review whether you need to develop any of these further. You might want to use this chapter as a framework for reviewing your grasp of these basic skills and approaches.

So, what are these fundamental building blocks of CBT?

Core Principles of CBT

There are several assumptions about the nature of psychological problems and the best ways of approaching them through psychological therapy that together might be said to characterize CBT.

Valuing empirical evidence

CBT recognizes that all therapy is both art and science (see Chapter 1) and that scientific evidence cannot fully determine what we do in therapy. Nevertheless, CBT tends to value a scientific, evidence-based approach, both in the therapy delivered in the clinic and as a school of therapy in the wider world.

How to Become a More Effective CBT Therapist: Mastering Metacompetence in Clinical Practice,
First Edition. Edited by Adrian Whittington and Nick Grey.
© 2014 John Wiley & Sons, Ltd. Published 2014 by John Wiley & Sons, Ltd.

In the clinic, clients are encouraged to regard their thoughts and beliefs as "opinions, not facts". In other words, like opinions they may or may not be true, and we should look at the available evidence – or gather new evidence, for example, through behavioural experiments – in order to decide whether or not they are true in any particular case. Another version of the same sentiment that has become popular in recent years is the motto "Don't believe everything you think!" Both these mottos are based on the notion that our thoughts and beliefs may mislead us, and may need correction through empirical evidence.

The same approach characterizes CBT as a school of therapy. From its earliest roots in behaviour therapy, CBT has had a strong commitment to a scientific approach to developing and testing both CBT theories and the effectiveness of treatments based on those theories. Scientific research has been central to the way CBT has grown and developed and, many would argue, has contributed significantly to CBT's current status as a therapy of choice in many areas.

Interacting systems

Many CBT approaches find it useful to conceptualize psychological processes as the result of interactions between several systems within an individual, and between that individual and the external world. Four systems are commonly distinguished:

- *Cognition*: thoughts, beliefs, images, for example;
- *Affect*: emotions;
- *Behaviour*: overt behaviour and speech, which is observable by others;
- *Physiology*: bodily changes such as autonomic arousal in anxiety or anger, or the so-called "biological" symptoms of depression, such as changes to sleep patterns, appetite and so forth.

These different systems are seen as constantly interacting in all possible ways: thoughts may influence behaviour or affect, affect influences thoughts and physiology, and so on. This view of interacting systems is often illustrated with the diagram sometimes known as the "hot cross bun" (presented in Padesky & Mooney, 1990, although they did not use the term "hot cross bun" to describe it: see Figure 2.1). For example in a panic attack, anxiety (*affect*) is accompanied by symptoms of autonomic arousal (*physiology*), which are then misinterpreted by the person as indicating some catastrophic threat

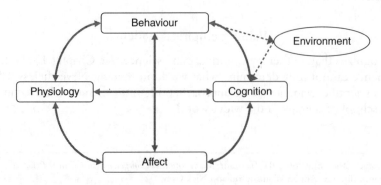

Figure 2.1 Interacting systems.

(*cognition*); then this perceived threat may drive the person to safety behaviours (*behaviour*), one of the consequences of which is to block corrective information that might have changed the *cognitions*.

Identifying which interactions are important in a particular problem is a central part of the process of developing CBT theories to understand a problem, and is also crucial in the process of *formulation* for a specific client's problems (see below); treatment is then aimed at modifying the interactions identified.

As well as these interactions between systems *within* the person, it is important to remember that interactions *between* people and their environment can also play an important role, as shown in Figure 2.1. "Environment" here is taken to include a wide range of external factors, including other people, situations, cultural factors and so on. As with other interactions, these go both ways: people influence their environment and are influenced by it.

Although changes in the cognitive and behavioural systems are usually the central pillars of CBT, and it is those systems that give the therapy its name, it is important to remember that the focus on them is a means to an end, not a goal itself. The ultimate goal of CBT is usually to change affect, that is, how patients *feel* – it is just that intervening through cognitions and behaviour helps us achieve that goal.

Continuum with "normal" processes

Within the CBT model, problems are usually seen as resulting from the excessive or dysfunctional operation of *normal* processes, rather than as being qualitatively distinct from normality. We are all subject to those processes, whether we have problems or not, and all CBT's concepts regarding cognitions and behaviour apply to us as therapists just as much as they do to our clients. It is just that for some people unhelpful processes get out of control and come to dominate their lives.

Formulation based

Most CBT is based on a *formulation*, that is, an individual model (often in the form of a diagram) of what a patient's problems are, how they developed and how interactions between the four systems and with the environment work to maintain the problems. The formulation (or "case conceptualization") serves several important functions:

- It helps both you and the client to understand the problems better.
- It guides you in applying CBT treatment strategies to the particular individual you are working with and helps you target those strategies in ways that will be most effective for this client.
- It may help to start the process of reducing negative thinking, by providing an explanation of what is going on that (as noted above) rests on normal processes, rather than on some fundamental defect in the client.

The formulation is developed collaboratively by therapist and client using information from assessment interviews, self-monitoring homework, questionnaires or other sources of information. Where there is a reasonably well-established CBT model for a relevant disorder then you will usually develop the formulation by individualizing that model: for example, if you have a client with obsessive-compulsive disorder (OCD), your formulation will be based on one of the CBT models of OCD (e.g., Rachman, 2003 or

Salkovskis, Forrester, Richards, & Morrison, 1998). Where there is no well-established model, or the available models do not adequately account for your client's problems, you may need to develop a formulation based more on generic CBT principles. See Chapters 5–7 for more detailed discussion of formulation in complex cases.

A slightly embarrassing fact for CBT is that the empirical evidence on the benefits of a formulation-based approach is actually not very clear at present – indeed, there is some evidence that formulation-based CBT may sometimes be *less* effective than strict protocol-driven therapy (Schulte, Kuenzel, Pepping, & Schulte, 1992). However, this is a complex matter to research, so general conclusions cannot yet be drawn. See Kuyken, Padesky, and Dudley (2009) for further exploration of these issues.

Types of cognition

Finally, it is common to distinguish between different kinds or levels of cognition. Perhaps the most common "Beckian" scheme distinguishes negative automatic thoughts, dysfunctional assumptions and core beliefs, as follows:

Core beliefs (CBs)

These are seen as the most general and long-lasting ideas one has about oneself, other people, or the world in general, which operate across a wide range of situations. They are typically learned early in life and are expressed in absolute terms: "I *am*...", or "The world *is*...", for example "I am unlovable/worthless/incompetent etc."; "The world is a dangerous place"; "Other people are hostile/critical etc."

Dysfunctional assumptions (DAs)

DAs are sometimes called "rules for living", which conveys an important aspect of their nature. They are seen as secondary beliefs arising from CBs, giving us guidelines for how to cope with life in the face of unhelpful CBs. They typically take the form of conditional, "ought/must", or "if–then" statements, for example, "If anyone does not like me then that's a disaster" (because it reveals my basic unlovability), or "I must always do everything perfectly" (otherwise my basic worthlessness will be revealed).

Negative automatic thoughts (NATS)

NATs are the frequent, often fleeting, negative thoughts that go through our minds in specific situations and contribute to our experience of negative emotions. To a greater extent than DAs or CBs, NATS are, or can easily become, conscious: most people are already aware of them or can become aware of them with a little practice. For example "I'm boring her", "I've messed that up", "I might have a serious illness", "My family are fed up with me" and so on.

One final point of caution here: it is easy to fall into the trap of thinking that CBs or DAs are "more fundamental" or "deeper" than NATs, and that therapy is therefore incomplete or unsatisfactory if it does not include direct work with this kind of cognition. For most common mental health problems, there is little or no evidence to support such a view. Pretty much all the evidence supporting the effectiveness of CBT for such problems is based on CBT that focused on NATs (and sometimes DAs), not CBs. There is some evidence that working with CBs may be beneficial in certain very specific cases (e.g., "schema-focused therapy" for borderline personality disorder: Giesen-Bloo et al., 2006) but there is no evidence that it is necessary in most cases.

Core Framework of Therapy

Having looked at the core principles of CBT, let us review some of the key therapeutic strategies, beginning with four fundamental ideas that provide an over-arching framework for most CBT: structure, collaboration, use of the Socratic method and the importance of homework.

Session structure

"Standard" CBT has a clear structure to its sessions. A typical session might look like this:

1. Agenda-setting: both you and your client suggest topics for discussion in the session, and jointly agree on prioritizing topics if there are too many to cover them all. You only depart substantially from the agenda if both of you agree that is appropriate.
2. A (usually brief) review of the client's week; of the last session (what was useful, what was learned etc.); and of homework (how did it go, what was learned, problem-solving any difficulties etc.).
3. Covering the main topics for the day, which might be any of a wide range of areas: a difficult event in the client's life, a therapeutic strategy you want to introduce, a difficulty that arose during homework, developing the formulation, for example.
4. Collaboratively deciding what might be useful homework to take forward or further develop themes from the current session.
5. Asking your client for feedback on the session: what was helpful, what was not, was there anything difficult or upsetting, and so on.

This structure helps to keep sessions focused on what is most important to your client, and also open up channels to communicate about the general process of therapy, which may help to prevent it getting blown off course by misunderstanding or other relationship problems. There is some empirical support for the importance of session structure, for example, part of the famous Treatment of Depression Collaborative Research Program (which compared CBT for depression to interpersonal therapy and medication) assessed CBT therapists using the Cognitive Therapy Scale to see whether therapist competence predicted outcomes (Shaw et al., 1999). They found that the strongest association with outcome came from the "therapy structure" items (agenda setting, pacing of the session and the use of homework).

Collaborative approach

One of the most important characteristics of CBT is the attention paid to developing and maintaining a *collaborative* therapeutic relationship between you and your client. (See Chapter 3 of this book for more substantial discussion of some of the issues involved in maintaining a good therapeutic relationship.)

CBT is not something you do *to* your client, and it does not see you as the all-wise guru who will enlighten clients about how to solve all their problems – still less tell them the meaning of life! CBT sees therapy as involving two people who are as far as possible equal partners, each with their own area of expertise. The client is the world authority on his or her own experience of the target problems, while you hopefully bring some expertise on how to understand and reduce such problems. There are always two heads in the room and we want to make use of both of them.

Of course, it would be naïve to imagine that the relationship can always be completely equal. At a very basic level, only one of the people in the room is getting paid to do this; and clients will often attribute a degree of authority to the therapist no matter how hard you strive to be collaborative. But this just means you need to try harder to encourage clients' active participation, to take seriously their ideas and to respect their independence.

In general, we see the client as the ultimate authority. For example, if there is a difference of opinion about some aspect of the formulation, or about how to apply a therapeutic strategy, in most cases you will work with the client's view – while retaining the option to revisit the question if it does not seem to be working out well. CBT's empirical approach can be useful here, because you can test out such differences of opinion using *behavioural experiments* (see below): "Rather than have a lengthy debate, let's try it out and see what happens …".

A corollary of this collaborative approach is that CBT therapists tend to have an open attitude to sharing goals, hypotheses, and information about problems and therapeutic strategies. Our ultimate aim is to make ourselves redundant by helping clients to become their own therapists.

Socratic method

Socratic method has been described as "the cornerstone of cognitive therapy" by Padesky in a pivotal conference speech on this approach (Padesky, 1993). Socratic method refers to therapists' use of questions to help clients broaden their perspective and consider a wider range of alternatives to their original view of an event or situation. Instead of simply offering the client a different thought – or even worse, *telling* the client how to think – the CBT therapist usually tries to ask questions that will help clients to find their own alternatives. Common kinds of question involve helping clients shift their view in *time* (e.g., "Imagine that in a year's time, I'm looking back at this situation – what advice would I be giving myself?"); in *person* (e.g., "What would I say to a friend who was in the same situation?"); or in *emotion* (e.g., "How would I see this if I was not depressed?")

Again, we have to confess to an embarrassing lack of empirical evidence for the central role of the Socratic method in CBT. That role is based on informed opinion rather than any substantial research (and as always, such opinion might turn out to be wrong once we have more evidence). Nevertheless there are some plausible reasons for using Socratic method despite it being based on common sense or clinical intuition rather than solid evidence. These reasons include:

• Socratic method helps get clients actively involved in thinking about their problems and therefore promotes collaboration.
• It helps clients start to consider their thoughts as "just thoughts", rather than necessary truths.
• It helps to avoid imposing therapist views on clients: we can make sure we explore and work with *their* thoughts, rather than assuming our own thoughts are relevant or useful.

- By working through their own thinking, clients are more likely to find new perspectives that make sense to them, and are also more likely to "own" those alternatives.
- It assists the goal of clients becoming their own therapists: instead of just giving them "answers", Socratic method helps them learn how to find their own answers.

It is also clear that there are risks in Socratic questioning, especially if it is not done skilfully. Clients may feel interrogated, or as if they are being "caught out" by a clever cross-examination, or simply that they are being led around a very circuitous path towards what the therapist wants them to say. At its most obvious, Padesky (1993) pointed out that there is no point in asking anyone a Socratic question if they lack the information to answer. (I probably would not get far with most readers if I asked you Socratic questions about, say, quantum mechanics!)

Given these risks, as well as the lack of research evidence about its benefits, we need to be clear that Socratic method is not a fetish and there are no grounds for saying it is universally applicable. Sometimes a blind insistence on doing everything Socratically may just make therapy much more long-winded than it needs to be. There will be times when you need to give your clients information in a more straightforwardly didactic way, or give them direct advice about how to proceed in a therapeutic task. For example, you know – but many clients do not – that exposure needs to be reasonably prolonged to be effective. There is unlikely to be any great benefit in trying to arrive at that conclusion Socratically.

Use of homework

Homework (clients' doing tasks related to therapy in the time between therapy sessions) is generally considered another core feature of CBT (although of course other forms of therapy may also use homework tasks). Homework can consist of many different kinds of activity, such as:

- therapeutic reading (e.g., self-help or educational materials);
- self-monitoring (e.g., diaries, thought records or activity schedules);
- practising a therapeutic strategy (e.g., verbal testing of thoughts, or increasing rewarding activity); and
- carrying out behavioural experiments

In contrast to the above discussion about the relatively sparse empirical support for the use of formulations or Socratic method, there is reasonably good evidence that doing homework is indeed associated with improved outcomes in CBT. In a recently updated meta-analysis based on 46 original studies, Kazantzis, Whittington, and Dattilio (2010) concluded that homework has a significant positive effect on the outcome of CBT ($d = 0.48$ in the subgroup of controlled studies).

Core Therapeutic Strategies

Perhaps the central goal of CBT is to help clients reconsider and re-evaluate the negative cognitions associated with their negative mood states. As the name of CBT suggests, there are two main ways we try to do that: cognitively (helping our clients through discussion and reasoning), and behaviourally (helping our clients through changing what they do in action in the world).

Verbal testing of thoughts

Looking for evidence
The first main method for testing thoughts is to help clients think systematically about what evidence there is that either supports or contradicts their negative thoughts. Usually it is best to start by considering evidence in favour of the thoughts, since that will often be easier for the client. Then move on to looking for evidence that may *not* fit with the thought. This is one of the areas where Socratic questions may be useful, by helping clients to consider evidence that is currently outside their awareness, for example, questions like "What has actually happened in the past when I thought I was about to die?", or "Have there been any times when you *have* successfully coped with this situation? If so, how?"

It is often important to remind clients that, in most cases, feelings are not good evidence. The kind of evidence we are looking for is more like the standard of objective evidence that a court of law would be looking for. The prosecution lawyer would not get very far if his only evidence against the accused was "Well, I just *feel* he's guilty, your honour"! In the same way, if we are trying to evaluate the idea that "I'm a bad mother", then "I just *feel* that I am" does not count as evidence.

Weighing pros and cons
Some thoughts or beliefs are not easily evaluated in terms of truth or accuracy. An obvious example is the old cliché that an optimist sees the glass as half full while a pessimist sees it as half empty. Neither of those two views is more *truthful* than the other, and there is no objective evidence that could support one of them rather than the other. But it might well be that different *consequences* follow from the two views. For example, perhaps the optimist's view leads to different emotional states than the pessimist's one.

Thus, an alternative to looking at truth or accuracy is to look in a more pragmatic way at consequences. Put aside for the moment whether this cognition is true; let's just think about how it affects you (or others who are important to you). This approach involves looking in systematic way at both the pros and cons of holding the cognition. What advantages/benefits does it give you? But also what disadvantages or costs does it have?

As always, you as therapist have to be honest in exploring this, and accept that it is always possible that your client will conclude that it is more advantageous to continue believing what seems to you like an unhelpful cognition. Your job is to make sure that your client has thought it through as thoroughly as possible, not to dictate the conclusion.

Working with imagery
Although CBT has always been aware that negative cognitions can take the form of images as well as verbal thoughts, interest in working with images has grown in the past few years. There are many variations on therapeutic work with images, but most involve:

- Identifying troublesome images and getting a detailed description of them.
- Developing alternative images. This can be done in different ways, including the use of fantasy (e.g., constructing an image of a rescuer intervening for someone

troubled by images of abuse), realistic corrective information (e.g., using video feedback to construct a more realistic self-image for someone with social anxiety); or changing the structure of the image(s) (e.g., imagining the image on a TV screen and then making it smaller, or more distant).

- Practising use of the new image, first in sessions and then later in real-life situations.

See Hackmann, Bennett-Levy, and Holmes (2011) for a comprehensive exploration of imagery work.

Behavioural methods

Both the original forms of behaviour therapy (BT), originating in the 1950s and 1960s, and the later developments of the "cognitive revolution" in the 1970s, gave a prominent role to treatment strategies that focus on making changes in the behavioural system. They agree that changing what you *do* is often a particularly powerful way of changing how you think and feel. The main difference in approach is the conceptual framework around behaviour change, which in turn influences some of the details of how behavioural work is carried out.

Within traditional BT, the main therapeutic strategy for anxiety disorders is *exposure*, that is, instead of trying to escape or avoid feared stimuli, approach them, either in reality (*in vivo* exposure) or in imagination. Exposure will generally be most effective when it is *prolonged* (e.g., long enough for anxiety to decline) and *frequent* (e.g., practised at least daily).

In more cognitively oriented therapy we have the concept of behavioural experiments, defined as:

> planned experiential activities, based on experimentation or observation, which are undertaken by patients in or between cognitive therapy sessions. Their design is derived directly from a cognitive formulation of the problem, and their *primary purpose is to obtain new information.* (Bennett-Levy et al., 2004, p. 8, emphasis added)

These procedures may look very similar from the outside, for example, both might involve a client with OCD in leaving his house without checking, but they are distinguished by the underlying rationale, their hypothesized mode of operation and their applicability. Table 2.1 summarizes some of these differences in the treatment of anxiety.

Both are well-established approaches, with good evidence for their effectiveness. There is currently not enough evidence to say whether one is more effective than the other, but a recent review suggested that, although conclusions are limited by the small number of studies and their methodological problems, the available data for anxiety disorders provides "some evidence that behavioral experiments were more effective than exposure alone" (McMillan & Lee, 2010, p. 467).

The other behavioural strategy commonly used in CBT is activity scheduling in depression. Like the above discussion of behavioural methods in anxiety, activity scheduling can be conceptualized as a straightforward behavioural procedure, in which reinforcing activities lead to improvements in mood, or as a series of behavioural experiments designed to test out the client's negative cognitions about himself, about activities, etc. (Fennell, Bennett-Levy, & Westbrook, 2004).

Table 2.1 Behavioural strategies: exposure compared to behavioural experiments

	Exposure	*Behavioural experiment*
Conceptual model	Behavioural	Cognitive
Fundamental idea	Works through repetition/ duration leading to habituation	Works through testing out predictions arising from thoughts/beliefs; may not need as much repetition
Illustration (for OCD)	Repeatedly walk out of the house without checking and the anxiety will gradually die away	Walk out of the house without checking and you can find out whether your feared disaster actually happens
Applicability	Mainly in anxiety (habituation is not supposed to work with depression, for instance)	Any kind of problem (can work anywhere there is a negative thought that generates testable predictions)

Focusing on activity has in a sense come full circle in recent years. Following Jacobson et al.'s (1996) "dismantling" study of Beck's cognitive therapy for depression, which showed that the purely behavioural, activity-based components of CT for depression seemed to be as effective as the full package, these behavioural components were developed into a new CBT treatment for depression that has come to be known as *behavioural activation* (Martell, Addis, & Jacobson, 2001).

Working with assumptions/beliefs

Finally, let us consider some of the strategies that have been developed specifically for working with DAs and/or CBs. As noted above, beware of assuming that all CBT *must* tackle such longer-term beliefs. However, there are times when progress seems to be blocked by such cognitions, and therefore they may need to be tackled directly. Of course all the methods already covered – weighing up the evidence, looking at the pros and cons, and behavioural experiments – will also be useful for DAs/CBs, but in this section we focus on some commonly used additional strategies.

Historical review
As noted earlier, CBs and DAs typically develop early in life, and one strategy based on this is to do what is sometimes called a *historical review*. The aim here is to put the cognitions in perspective by helping your client review what experiences might have led to their learning these ideas, to understand their origins and also to understand how the context may be very different now, so that although the beliefs once made sense, they are less applicable now. The idea is that examining what led to these ideas may help the client realize that they were *learned* (and are not simply absolute truths) and also that it is therefore possible that they could have learned, and still might learn, something different.

Continuum work
The aim of this technique (Padesky, 1994) is to re-evaluate DAs and CBs that often take extreme, "black-and-white" forms: "Either I do everything perfectly or I am a complete failure"; "If I snap at my children once then I am a bad mother"; or "No-one cares about me".

Continuum work is a way of trying to help clients think about such evaluations along a dimension, or continuum, rather than as one extreme or the other: not "I am terrible" versus "I am perfect", more like "I am somewhere on a continuum between terrible and perfect"; somewhere in the shades of grey, rather than either black or white.

You help your client draw up a dimension along a line between the two extremes, and rate their starting belief (which is typically towards the extreme negative end of the dimension – e.g., "I am 100 per cent bad"). Then you collaboratively draw up criteria for both ends of the continuum as well as some of the "shades of grey" in between. This can be done either by constructing abstract criteria (e.g., 50 per cent on the scale of "good motherhood" includes "regularly feed and dress children"); or it can be done by using actual people your client knows or has heard of (e.g., 100 per cent on the scale of a "bad person" is Hitler). These procedures often help clients to re-evaluate their extreme beliefs and move towards a more moderate view (e.g., "I don't like myself much but I'm not a mass murderer, so I guess I can't be 100 per cent bad").

Positive data log
This technique, also described by Padesky (1994), is essentially a specialized form of collecting evidence. Its focus is on negative beliefs about the self, and it can be used once your client has begun to develop a possible alternative, less negative, belief. The well-known biased perception and recall of negative versus positive information makes it hard for clients to notice or remember relevant evidence that might contradict their negative beliefs or support their new beliefs. The positive data log is therefore designed to help them focus more on such evidence. It is explicitly *not* designed to be balanced, on the grounds that your client will likely have spent years collecting evidence that appears to support their negative beliefs. What is needed to get a balanced view is to spend some time focusing on evidence that supports the new belief. Clients are therefore asked to keep a record focused only on such information, which they are to try to update daily, and bring along to every session for discussion. Although simple in conception, this is usually a very difficult task for clients, and needs a great deal of therapist support and encouragement as well as a long period of time – it may well need to continue after the end of therapy.

"Third wave" Cognitive Behavioural Therapy

The outline above has focused on "classical, Beckian" CBT, but for the sake of completeness it should be noted that the past 10 years have also seen the growth of what have been called "third wave" CBT approaches (Hayes, 2004). There is not much agreement about which models should be classified under that label, but the candidates include Acceptance and Commitment Therapy (ACT: Hayes, Strosahl, & Wilson, 1999), Mindfulness-Based Cognitive Therapy (MBCT: Segal, Williams, & Teadale, 2002), Dialectical Behaviour Therapy (DBT: Linehan, 1993) and Rumination-Focused CBT for Depression (Watkins et al., 2011). These therapies are by no means all the same, but they have in common a shift away from the classical Beckian approach of examining and testing the *content* of cognitions, towards an increased interest in cognitive *processing styles* and in the *relationship between* people and their cognitions: less disputing of one's thoughts and more disengaging from them, recognizing that they are "just thoughts" that can be calmly accepted rather than avoided or argued with.

There is some disagreement about the extent to which this shift is truly novel. For example, it has been argued that classical CBT has always contained an element of "distancing", or separating oneself from one's thoughts (Hofmann, Sawyer, & Fang, 2010), and indeed one might say that such an approach is suggested by the motto "Don't believe everything you think" described earlier in this chapter. Nevertheless there is no doubt that these new models are producing some interesting alternatives to, and perhaps may lead to enhancements of, traditional CBT – even though at present much more research on their effectiveness is needed.

Conclusion

In this chapter we have tried to give a brief survey of some of the "central pillars" of CBT – the foundations of the approach, on which adaptations to more complex problems or specific client groups rest. The rest of this book will take you on a journey through some of those more specialized topics.

Procedural Rules

- Be sure that you have a thorough grounding in this chapter's basic competences before moving substantially beyond them.
- Do not assume that complex or difficult problems necessarily mean you need to work with schemas or core beliefs.
- Consider checking out your "basic and specific" CBT skills more formally. You might think about using the self-assessment tool developed for the Roth and Pilling competences (Centre for Outcomes Research and Effectiveness, 2007), and/or having a therapy session rated by an experienced supervisor on a measure of CBT skills such as the CTS-R (Blackburn et al., 2001).
- Even experienced therapists often consider making good formulations to be one of the most difficult skills to learn in CBT. Supporting this idea, Eells, Lombart, Kendjelic, Turner, and Lucas (2005) found that only highly selected experts were rated as producing higher quality formulations than experienced or novice therapists (in fact on some measures, experienced therapists were rated lower than novices!). Make it a rule to practise by developing formulations for all your clients, review them with your supervisor, and consider looking for further specialist training in formulation skills – the same study suggested that "the learning of a systematic formulation method may be …[one of the specific skills differentiating experts from other therapists]" (Eells et al., 2005, p. 587).
- Linked to the first point above, do not be too quick to abandon "standard" CBT. There are several arguments suggesting that, when difficulties arise in therapy, therapists sometimes abandon well-tried basic CBT methods when actually it may be better to focus on implementing those methods as thoroughly and carefully as possible (Schulte & Eifert, 2002; Waller, 2009).

- In particular, do not forget the "B" in CBT. In other words, remember that behavioural methods – whether exposure tasks or behavioural experiments, weekly activity schedules or behavioural activation – remain some of our most powerful methods for achieving cognitive and affective change. Always look for ways to reinforce verbal discussion through trying things out in action in the wider world outside the therapy room.
- Finally, take seriously the evidence about the importance of homework. Leave time in sessions for collaboratively setting up homework tasks that develop naturally out of the session's work, and *always* follow up in the next session to see what happened, reflect on the results, and so on. Nothing will extinguish your client's doing homework quicker than your unilaterally setting homework and then never mentioning it again.

References

Bennett-Levy, J., Butler, B., Fennell, M., Hackmann, A., Mueller, M., & Westbrook, D. (Eds.). (2004). *The Oxford guide to behavioural experiments in cognitive therapy*. Oxford: Oxford University Press.

Blackburn, I.M., James, I. A., Milne, D. L., Baker, C., Standart, S., Garland, A., & Reichelt, K. (2001). The revised cognitive therapy scale (CTS-R): psychometric properties. *Behavioural & Cognitive Psychotherapy, 29*, 431–446.

Centre for Outcomes Research and Effectiveness (CORE) (2012). *Assessing competences against the cognitive behaviour therapy framework: self-assessment tool*. Retrieved from www.ucl.ac.uk/clinical-psychology/CORE/CBT_Framework.htm#assess

Eells, T. D., Lombart, K. G., Kendjelic, E. M., Turner, L. C., & Lucas, C. P. (2005). The quality of psychotherapy case formulations: a comparison of expert, experienced, and novice cognitive-behavioral and psychodynamic therapists. *Journal of Consulting & Clinical Psychology, 73*, 579–589.

Fennell, M., Bennett-Levy, J., & Westbrook, D. (2004). Depression. In J. Bennett-Levy, B. Butler, M. Fennell, A. Hackmann, M. Mueller & D. Westbrook (Eds.), *The Oxford guide to behavioural experiments in cognitive therapy* (pp. 205–224). Oxford: Oxford University Press.

Giesen-Bloo, J., van Dyck, R., Spinhoven, P., van Tilburg, W., Dirksen, C., van Asselt, T., … Artz, A. (2006). Outpatient psychotherapy for borderline personality disorder: randomized trial of schema-focused therapy vs transference-focused psychotherapy. *Archives of General Psychiatry, 63*, 649–658.

Hackmann, A., Bennett-Levy, J., & Holmes, E., (Eds.). (2011). *The Oxford guide to imagery in cognitive therapy*. Oxford: Oxford University Press.

Hayes, S. C. (2004). Acceptance and commitment therapy, relational frame theory, and the third wave of behavioral and cognitive therapies. *Behavior Therapy, 35*, 639–665.

Hayes, S. C., Strosahl, K., & Wilson, K. G. (1999). *Acceptance and commitment therapy: an experiential approach to behaviour change*. New York: Guilford Press.

Hofmann, S.G., Sawyer, A. T., & Fang, A. (2010). The empirical status of the "new wave" of cognitive behavioral therapy. *Psychiatric Clinics of North America, 33*, 701–710

Jacobson, N. S., Dobson, K. S., Truax, P. A., Addis, M. E., Koerner, K., Gollan, J. K., … Prince, S.E. (1996). A component analysis of cognitive-behavioural treatment for depression. *Journal of Consulting & Clinical Psychology, 64*, 295–304.

Kazantzis, N., Whittington, C., & Dattilio, F. (2010). Meta-analysis of homework effects in cognitive and behavioral therapy: a replication and extension. *Clinical Psychology: Science & Practice, 17*, 144–156.

Kuyken, W., Padesky, C., & Dudley, R. (2009). *Collaborative case conceptualization*. New York: Guilford Press.

Linehan, M. M. (1993). *Cognitive-behavioural treatment for Borderline Personality Disorder: the dialectics of effective treatment*. New York: Guilford Press.

McMillan, D., & Lee, R. (2010). A systematic review of behavioral experiments vs. exposure alone in the treatment of anxiety disorders: a case of exposure while wearing the emperor's new clothes? *Clinical Psychology Review, 30*, 467–478.

Martell, C. R., Addis, M. E., & Jacobson, N. S. (2001). *Depression in context: strategies for guided action*. New York: Norton.

Padesky, C. A. (1993). *Socratic questioning: changing minds or guiding discovery?* Keynote address for European Association of Behavioural & Cognitive Therapies Congress, London. Retrieved from http://padesky.com/newpad/wp-content/uploads/2012/11/socquest.pdf

Padesky, C. A. (1994). Schema change processes in cognitive therapy. *Clinical Psychology & Psychotherapy, 1*, 267–278.

Padesky, C. A., & Mooney, K .A. (1990). Clinical tip: presenting the cognitive model to clients. *International Cognitive Therapy Newsletter, 6*, 13–14.

Rachman, S. J. (2003). *The treatment of obsessions*. Oxford: Oxford University Press.

Roth, A., & Pilling, S. (2007). *The competences required to deliver effective cognitive and behavioural therapy for people with depression and with anxiety disorders*. London: Department of Health. Retrieved from www.ucl.ac.uk/clinical-psychology/CORE/CBT_Competences/CBT_Competence_List.pdf

Salkovskis, P. M., Forrester, E., Richards, H. C., & Morrison, N. (1998). The devil is in the detail: conceptualising and treating obsessional problems. In N. Tarrier, A. Wells, & G. Haddock (Eds.), *Treating complex cases: the cognitive behavioural therapy approach* (pp. 46–80). Chichester: Wiley.

Schulte, D., & Eifert, G. H. (2002). What to do when manuals fail? The dual model of psychotherapy. *Clinical Psychology: Science & Practice, 9*, 312–328.

Schulte, D., Kuenzel, R., Pepping, G., & Schulte, B. T. (1992). Tailor-made versus standardized therapy of phobic patients. *Advances in Behaviour Research & Therapy, 14*, 67–92.

Segal, Z. V., Williams J. M., & Teasdale, J. D. (2002). *Mindfulness-based cognitive therapy for depression: a new approach to prevent relapse*. New York: Guilford Press.

Shaw, B. F., Elkin, I., Yamaguchi, J., Olmsted, M., Vallis, T. M., Dobson, K. S., … Imber, S. D. (1999). Therapist competence ratings in relation to clinical outcome in cognitive therapy of depression. *Journal of Consulting & Clinical Psychology, 67*, 837–846.

Waller, G. (2009). Evidence-based treatment and therapist drift. *Behaviour Research and Therapy, 47*, 119–127.

Watkins, E. R., Mullan, E., Wingrove, J., Rimes, K., Steiner, H., Bathurst, N., … Scott, J. (2011). Rumination-focused cognitive-behavioural therapy for residual depression: phase II randomised controlled trial. *British Journal of Psychiatry, 199*, 317–322.

3

Developing and Maintaining a Working Alliance in CBT

Helen Kennerley

Stewart was frustrated – he'd stuck to the protocol, his CTS-R ratings were satisfactory and still therapy wasn't going smoothly. His supervisor kept prompting him to attend to the relationship, to create the right interpersonal context to carry out the tasks of CBT – but Stewart wasn't sure what this meant.

Much early work concerning the working alliance (WA) was generated from a psychodynamic perspective, and this almost certainly influenced Beck in his consideration of the necessary therapeutic relationship to promote CBT – after all he began his practice as a psychoanalyst, albeit an empirical one. The term working alliance or "therapeutic collaboration" as Beck, Rush, Shaw, and Emery described it in 1979 (p. 45), is used to describe a particular interpersonal dynamic within CBT.

There is a good deal of evidence that the quality of the therapeutic relationship is an important element of successful treatment, predicting compliance and outcome (Orlinsky, Grawe, & Parks 1994). Its relevance has long been recognized by the British Association for Behavioural and Cognitive Psychotherapies (BABCP) as one of its accreditation criteria stipulates that a practitioner should: "Demonstrate knowledge and understanding of the therapeutic relationship and competence in the development, maintenance and ending of such relationships" (British Association for Behavioural and Cognitive Psychotherapies, n.d.). The working alliance is an important aspect of the therapeutic relationship.

Meta-analytic reviews suggest a consistent relationship between strong therapeutic alliance and better psychotherapy treatment outcomes (e.g., Martin, Garske, & Davies, 2000), even with Internet-based treatment (Knaevelsrud & Maercker, 2007). However such findings should not be taken to indicate that a good therapeutic relationship alone is sufficient to promote good outcome. Beck, himself emphasized that "The general characteristics of the therapist that facilitate the application of cognitive therapy ... include warmth, accurate empathy and genuineness", but he also believed that "these characteristics in themselves are necessary but not sufficient to produce optimum therapeutic effect" (Beck et al., 1979, p. 45). Although many studies do find the therapeutic alliance is as relevant to CBT as other treatment approaches (e.g., Wilson et al., 1999), there are

How to Become a More Effective CBT Therapist: Mastering Metacompetence in Clinical Practice,
First Edition. Edited by Adrian Whittington and Nick Grey.
© 2014 John Wiley & Sons, Ltd. Published 2014 by John Wiley & Sons, Ltd.

findings that suggest that the quality of the therapeutic alliance might be less important in a structured approach like CBT (Krupnick et al., 1996; Carroll, Nich, & Rounsaville, 1997). Indeed, if the alliance were all, then we would be hard pressed to understand the successful application of bibliotherapy or computer-based CBT (see Williams & Martinez, 2008 for a critical review of CBT self-help models).

Nonetheless, the quality of the WA is repeatedly found to relate positively to therapeutic outcome, both to therapy adherence (e.g., Keller, Zoellner, & Feeny, 2010), and to improved remission rates (e.g., Wilson et al., 1999). Wilson and colleagues (1999) also found that symptom change over the course of treatment may have as much of an impact on patient ratings of alliance as the reverse – which then poses the interesting question: which comes first? Whatever we conclude – the quality of the working alliance remains empirically relevant.

It has also been addressed from the angle of actively managing therapy difficulties, or "ruptures", and it seems that a therapeutic relationship that is put to the test and withstands it offers the best prognosis (Bordin, 1979; Muran et al., 2009; Safran & Muran, 2000). Thus, developing a sound collaboration demands the therapist not only be aware of, and cultivate, the characteristics of a good alliance but also be prepared to be assertive in broaching difficulties.

To help you get the most out of your working alliance, this chapter addresses its nature, reflects on how you might develop and maintain a good alliance, and then considers how you can address therapeutic challenges that arise.

What is the Nature of the Working Alliance in CBT?

Beck and colleagues (1979) contrast CBT with "supportive" or "relationship" therapy stating that the relationship within the therapy is not simply an instrument to alleviate suffering but a vehicle to facilitate a common effort in carrying out specific tasks and achieving particular goals. They promote the notion of therapist and patient working as a team, each bringing their own expertise and sharing responsibility for change – but it is more than a business-like, practical arrangement as it requires "the same subtle therapeutic atmosphere that has been described explicitly in the context of psychodynamic psychotherapy … relationship involves both the patient and the therapist and is based on trust, rapport and collaboration."(p. 50) Empathic collaboration is key to establishing a working alliance in CBT.

Bordin (1979) conceptualized the WA comprising three parts:

- Goals: what the patient and therapist hope will be gained from therapy.
- Tasks: what needs to be done in therapy to achieve the goals.
- Bond: a positive therapist–patient relationship formed from trust and confidence that will support the tasks that will, in turn, bring the patient closer to his or her goals.

He suggested that balancing these three components, combined with genuine agreement on goals and tasks, is necessary for a successful WA.

This framework fits CBT well as factor analysis of the alliance in CBT has shown clear distinctions between the therapeutic relationship and the agreements of therapy (Andrusyna, Tang, DeRubeis, & Luborsky, 2001). Goal setting with a view to establishing mutually acceptable goals has always been fundamental to CBT (Beck et al., 1979) as has overtly discussing the means to achieve those goals (tasks), and we have already seen that Beck et al. (1979) recognized the importance of a sound therapeutic bond.

As noted earlier, in CBT the therapeutic alliance is seen as necessary but not suffi-cient to enhance prognosis, and treatment trials typically demonstrate a beneficial effect from CBT over and above that of being in a therapeutic relationship (Roth & Fonagy, 2005). Indeed, evidence indicates that it may be the nature of the patient's participation in treatment that is the strongest predictor of outcome: thus the *working alliance* is an active, dynamic relationship. As previously mentioned, an alliance that experiences problems that are resolved is linked with better outcomes than one with no ruptures, or a rupture that is not repaired (Bordin, 1979). In successful cases of brief therapy, the working alliance has been found to follow a "high-low-high" pattern over the course of the therapy, that is, the relationship is put to the test and grows from it (Stiles et al., 2004).

Indeed, in CBT we have known for some time that active, "working" patients do best; those who are engaged with the therapeutic task and consistently carry out between-session assignments make better progress (Burns & Nolen-Hoeksema, 1991). This also fits very well with Beck et al.'s (1979) suggestion that we should view the relationship as a "laboratory" for change, an interpersonal environment for collabora-tive thought and action.

Several scales have been developed to assess the patient–professional relationship in therapy. The first and most widely used is the Working Alliance Inventory (WAI), (Horvath & Greenberg, 1986), which is based on Bordin's concept. This has been shown to be valid (Horvath, 1994) and reliable in both its long and short forms (Hanson, Curry, & Bandalos, 2002) – although there have been suggestions that, in CBT, the concept of working alliance should not be assumed to be a single notion (a general "alliance" factor) as task and goal appear to co-vary and can seemingly act independently of bond (Andrusyna et al., 2001). As with so many elements of the CBT process, things are often more complicated and interesting that they first might seem.

Developing a Good Working Alliance

This begins with transparency in the relationship. As therapists we "socialize" patients to the CBT model and way of working, overtly building an understanding of their difficulties using them as key informants. The resulting formulation lays the foundation for working together by providing a rationale and a direction we pursue together. We agree the therapeutic goals and tasks. In short, we co-opt our patients as collaborators.

We then set out to coach them to become their own therapist by sharing our knowl-edge, combining it with theirs, encouraging them to develop and test out new ideas, being there to debrief and help them progress towards their goal. It is an active, shared experience.

In Chapter 2, Westbrook defines "The central pillars of CBT": developing a working alliance is not established independently of these key features of CBT, but is integrated into your practice of them. These strategies, with which you are already familiar, can contribute greatly to developing and maintaining the working alliance. The following sections illustrate how you can interweave process work as you implement the "central pillars" of CBT:

- conceptualization,
- agenda setting,
- Socratic method,
- collaborative empiricism,
- using feedback and capsule summaries, and
- homework.

Conceptualization

This fundamental framework for understanding your patient's difficulties is at the heart of your working alliance. Your *shared* formulation gives you an agreed "route-map" for therapy on which you will work together. It suggests the goals and tasks of therapy: it is this understanding of your patient's inner world and behavioural vulnerabilities that will help you plan your dialogues and interventions with care so that you engage and enable your patient (the bond). Do not be tempted to "shoe-horn" your patient's problem into a pre-existing model unless your assessment reveals that this really is the best representation of their difficulties; and do not fall into the trap of constructing a formulation and then putting it to one side – keep it in mind, update it, refer to it to guide you in your therapeutic choices and help you understand obstacles you encounter when working together. Here is an opportunity to communicate an authentic understanding that can enhance your working relationship.

Agenda setting

This is more than simply a necessary routine, it is fundamental to fostering collaboration and to helping patients develop the skill of problem solving. Therefore, share a rationale, make it genuine teamwork, and respect patients' contributions. Guidelines can be found in several texts (Beck et al., 1979; Westbrook, Kennerley, & Kirk, 2011) but it is worth reiterating that a non-judgemental stance and transparency, in particular, serve to bolster an open, working relationship.

THERAPIST (TH):	Ok, so shall we think about what we need to cover today?
PATIENT (PT):	I'm not sure
TH:	While you are thinking, perhaps I could put something on the agenda. I'd like to find out how your homework went and because you are having some health problems right now, I'd like to briefly catch up on your physical state.
PT:	OK – my doctor said that the blood tests won't come through until next week and until then he can't really give me anything strong for the pain – which makes it hard for me. I struggle when I'm in pain and then everything gets on top of me.
TH:	It sounds as though that does need some space on today's agenda then. So before we get into it in detail, let's write it down and consider what else we might need to find time for. Is there anything else you think we need to address this session: so far we have the review of your homework and an update on your health.
PT:	Oh I don't know. What do you think?

TH: Before I hijack the agenda and risk getting it wrong, I wonder if you can think of anything you'd hoped to have achieved by the end of today's session.

PT: (silent)

TH: Imagine it was the end of the session – would you be disappointed if there was a particular thing we had not discussed?

PT: Well if we still hadn't done anything about me not being able to drive to work, I'd feel pretty frustrated.

TH: So let's put that on the agenda – addressing your difficulties driving to work – I'm just wondering what you mean by that. Do you mean beginning to get a plan together or actually getting you driving?

PT: I'd like to be driving by the end of the session, of course, but being realistic I suppose I meant having a plan that I could get started on.

TH: That's helpful to know. So now our agenda has another item – to begin to develop a plan for getting you back to driving. Anything else?

PT: I can't think of anything – if we cover my health, my feeble attempt at homework and we work on a plan for driving I think I'll be stretched to my limit....

TH: That's a really good point. So how about we leave it at that and quickly think how we might allocate time to each of these agenda items?

Here you see teamwork – throughout, the therapist invites the patient to contribute to the agenda, when the patient struggles the therapist simply models using an agenda and contributes an item. When the patient gets caught up in a premature account of physical illness, the therapist gently brings the focus back to the agenda (modelling again) while emphasizing the importance of the patient's contribution. The therapist uses Socratic enquiry to facilitate the patient playing an active part in setting the agenda and uses positive reinforcement and is respectful throughout.

Socratic method

The now well-worn phrase "The cornerstone of cognitive therapy" (Padesky, 1993) captures the position held by Socratic methods in CBT, and rightly so as constructive Socratic questions can both reveal the nature of problems and point to solutions. It also presents an opportunity to enhance your working alliance. It requires more than just asking "what's so bad about that?" and, "what do you make of that?" – it is an exploratory, *facilitative* endeavour that embraces enquiry and experiential method that encourages the patient to feel involved and able. The therapist simply gives patients the lead, or prompt, that helps them generate a new conclusion, as you can see in the example of agenda setting. This shared role illustrates a "working alliance" beautifully as long as the therapist genuinely listens and is open-minded. We all know that Socratic methods should be hypothesis driven, that is, the therapist should be exploring a reasoned "hunch", but the therapist should also remain curious about the outcome. For example, in the earlier agenda setting scenario, when the therapist asks: "would you be disappointed if there was a particular thing we had not discussed?" the underlying hypothesis is that the patient has unvoiced concerns. Like all good hypotheses, it can be refuted – the patient could have said "No". If that had happened the therapist would revise his or her hypothesis in line with the new information. Questions that are asked with a view to *leading* the patient to a conclusion are neither Socratic nor in the spirit of fostering a genuine working alliance – however well meant the motives of the therapist.

Of course, Socratic methods are only one of a CBT practitioner's tools and direct questions have a place in information gathering and didactic methods have a place in patient education. The working alliance will best be served if you are sensitive to the needs of your patient and use direct and didactic methods appropriately, for example, if you are simply collecting background data and need to know if the patient is married and has children, use direct questions or if the patient does not have the knowledge to answer a Socratic enquiry you can be didactic in helping them expand their knowledge base. Being solely Socratic in these instances would be frustrating and thus contribute little to a sense of alliance.

Collaborative empiricism

This is very often an example of Socratic method in action: the patient develops hypotheses (guided by the therapist's Socratic enquiry) and evolves ways of testing them and debriefing (similarly guided by Socratic questions and didactic methods). This is clearly a joint task, with an overt goal and both parties bring knowledge and expertise to their part in it. This teamwork (the bond) can strengthen the working alliance as therapist and patient progress towards achieving the patient's goals; without this teamwork the over-arching goal of the patient becoming autonomous can be compromised.

THERAPIST: That's an interesting conclusion – that you don't always feel quite so bad. What do you make of that? (Socratic enquiry, encouraging the patient's ideas).

PATIENT: I suppose my mood does go up and down, even though I often think it is always down. (Hypothesis).

TH: Yes, and that's really interesting. Any ideas what influences that? What links with the ups and with the downs? (Socratic enquiry).

PT: Not really, no.

TH: How we might we go about discovering more about the links? Any thoughts on that? (Socratic enquiry to elicit patient's ideas about testing the hypothesis).

PT: I suppose I could try to remember my experiences better – but that's hard because my memory lets me down a lot. (Beginning to devise an experiment but identifying obstacles).

TH: Is there any way in which you could keep a record? (Socratically prompting problem solving).

PT: (looks worried) How do you mean?

TH: Well, could you keep a written account for a while – some form of log to help you remember? That's quite a common practice in CBT. (Prompting problem solving didactically).

PT: That might make it easier to remember things but you see I'm not a good writer.

TH: Not to worry – people find other ways – for example, several of my patients speak into their mobile phones. Could that be something for you? (Prompting problem solving didactically)

PT: Yes – mine records and I carry it everywhere. Sounds like a good idea. (Collaborative problem solving).

This then provides the basis for negotiating what sort of log would be most relevant (another collaborative task): a modified weekly activity schedule (WAS) or an adapted thought diary, for example. Together, therapist and patient evolve a "bespoke" behavioural experiment. In this case you see the therapist mixing Socratic enquiry with direct questions, sensitive listening and outright suggestions in order to foster the sense of empathic teamwork. The therapist is clearly contributing an understanding of behavioural experiments to the structure of therapy and practical knowledge to problem solving the patient's literacy difficulties, but is at the same time using the patient as the informant, building the session content around the patient's needs. Quite a juggling act, but one that actively balances goal, task and bond.

Using feedback and capsule summaries

These relatively simple techniques are powerful means of clarifying goals and tasks while attending to the "bond" of therapy. They enable us to check that therapist and patient are both "singing from the same hymn sheet" and present opportunities to take stock, pause for planning, review where we are and where we are going – collaboratively. Because it is a shared experience it can strengthen the working alliance. Regular capsule summaries ensure that both parties are clear about the rationale for an intervention, that a between-session task is clear, that goals are shared. For example:

> Let's just pause there and review what we hope to gain from this intervention.

> So let's just recap on what you are going to do between now and next session.

> Can I just check out my understanding of the problem/just what your goals are?

Thus, these very simple interjections not only shape up and clarify your therapy but fuel the two-way process that is crucial to therapeutic collaboration. You can further enhance this by following summaries or feedback with Socratic questions such as: "What do you make of that?" "How might you take this forward?" "How might we check that out?" and so on. Failure to reflect on such questions can result in passive involvement on the part of the patient and thus compromise your active working relationship.

Homework

Homework compliance not only correlates with good outcome (Burns & Nolen-Hoeksema, 1991) but evolving assignments also offer an opportunity to foster the message that you share the responsibility for progressing in therapy and that your patient will be active and involved. Your contribution will be supporting the evolution of the homework task by listening to your patient's needs and marrying this with your knowledge of theory so that assignments are meaningful and motivating – your patients are more likely to work *with* you if the task "speaks" to them. You also have an important role in debriefing assignments, thus enhancing the learning experience and promoting autonomy. You risk squandering opportunities to deepen your active, working relationship if you fall in to the traps of simply assigning homework and/or neglecting to review it. Therefore, ensure that you have "Homework review" on your agenda and throughout your session make the most of homework possibilities by asking questions such as: "What else do we need to understand this problem?"; How can you build on what you have done so far?"; and "How can we check this out?" These sorts of questions will help you both keep your minds open to *relevant* assignments (goal), while sharing expertise (task) and responsibility (bond).

Addressing Challenges in Maintaining
a Working Alliance

Every therapist experiences challenges that are inherent in the relationship itself. For example, a patient's confusions or unspoken fears of change can undermine cooperation, as can fears of abandonment or failure. Regular Socratic enquiry such as: "How is this sounding to you?" or "How do you feel right now?" will help you tune into the patient's difficulties or misconceptions – as will noting what is *not* said in therapy (Padesky, 1993). Watson and Greenberg (2000) distinguish two types of ruptures in the alliance and it is important to recognize each. They propose that ruptures can relate to:

- *The goals or tasks of therapy* (perhaps when the patient does not agree with or understand the purpose of a strategy or when a goal is not truly shared). Watson and Greenberg suggest such problems be tackled directly through discussing the issue, clarifying procedures and using honest negotiation to resolve the rupture. Although it will impinge on your working alliance such ruptures do not necessarily have to be dealt with by focussing on process. For example, a patient might not carry out an assignment and you, in reviewing the obstacles, might discover that she believes that her safety-seeking behaviours are essential to her well-being. Clearly, she has not fully understood the disadvantages of maintaining safety-seeking behaviours and you can revise the rationale for dropping them. You and she might then negotiate modifying rather than abandoning safety-seeking behaviours if letting go of them is too big a step. In short, openness and empathic negotiation of tasks can resolve many ruptures in the WA.
- *The patient–therapist bond* (for example, a patient does not trust the therapist or is overly dependent on the therapist). Ruptures relating to Bordin's "bond" are sometimes covert, only becoming apparent over time. In CBT, it has been suggested that when they are identified, they should first be addressed *within* the therapeutic relationship and not presumed to be characteristic of your patient's interpersonal functioning (Safran & Segal, 1990).

Bond-related ruptures often become apparent because they trigger responses within the therapist – responses that are clearly undermining of a respectful, collaborative alliance. These might include anger, revulsion, boredom and so on. Harder to spot are the ruptures that do not give rise to awkward or unpleasant feelings, for example, when the therapist and patient become too friendly and too conversational, or when the therapist enjoys the positive feedback from "fixing" the client's problems. These situations just as powerfully undermine a focussed, working relationship and the rupture needs to be identified and addressed. It is in these cases, when the problem in the alliance is less easy to see, that it is crucial not only to receive supervision but that supervision is, at least in part, "live".

In his 2001 text, Leahy explores patient resistance, or non-compliance, in cognitive therapy. He not only cites underlying processes within the patients, but highlights ways that the therapist's own responses may impede change. We need to formulate ruptures, embracing our own role in the scenario.

Safran and Segal (1990) offer guidelines for working with ruptures that can threaten the WA – guidelines that fit well with the notion of a working *alliance*.

Here I can only give a brief précis of their approach and would urge you to look at their original text in order to appreciate their very elegant strategy. In essence – apologies to the authors for the simplification – Safran and Segal define a series of steps to follow once the therapist has a hypothesis that there is something amiss within the WA.

1. Observe and develop an inter-personal hypothesis.
2. Begin to test the hypothesis by further observation. Monitor and look for patterns.
3. If there are clear interpersonal patterns linked to the rupture, first look for explanations nearest home – ask yourself if your own issues are intruding into the session. If they are, take them to supervision or your own therapy.
4. If you have enough reason to consider that there is an issue that is maintained by your patient's actions, then formulate what is happening, all the while appreciating your reciprocal role in this.
5. Focus on the issue embedded in the rupture and translate this into the genuine dilemma that *you*, the therapist, are facing.
6. Put the issue of your dilemma on the agenda and elicit help from your patient to resolve it.
7. Do not assume that the particular interpersonal pattern happens outside the therapy setting but facilitate the patient considering this.

There are several advantages to this approach: it is hypothesis driven – the therapist checks out assumptions before acting; it avoids implying that the patient is to blame – which could lead to straining the relationship: it further endorses the WA because the therapist elicits the patient's help. However, the dilemma must be authentic, not a euphemism for a criticism of the patient. An example of using Safran and Segal's approach is outlined in the following section.

Scenario

Sara's therapist felt nervous before each session. He had noticed this for several weeks and felt sure that it was not a "one-off". He had spoken with his supervisor and together they had identified therapist assumptions: "Sara will be aggressive and angry again;" "I can't deal with this level of hostility;" "This is no way to treat a therapist – I'm only trying to help – it's not fair!" "I feel helpless."

First they tried to understand what was happening by revisiting Sara's formulation and seeing how her behaviour made sense – once her therapist again appreciated how abused Sara had been and how afraid she now was, he was able to feel compassion towards Sara – this is essential to maintaining a sound WA.

Next they derived an interpersonal formulation that tracked the unhelpful interaction that had developed. Sara's fear of being emotionally abused led her to try to protect herself through anger. This triggered fear in her rather unassertive therapist who then became preoccupied with his own fears and discomfort. Therapist and supervisor speculated that Sara would be sensitive to this disengagement and her fears would escalate, as would her angry defence.

Next they addressed therapist unhelpful assumptions: "This is no way to treat a therapist – I'm only trying to help – it's not fair!" disappeared once they reminded themselves of the origin of Sara's behaviour – but "I can't deal with this level of hostility; and "I feel helpless," remained and these were tackled through role playing handling angry encounters until the therapist felt more confident and less helpless. This done, the rupture still needed to be addressed with Sara.

Her therapist felt that the issue was not that "Sara made him nervous," *his dilemma* was that *he* could not maintain the proper level of engagement throughout the session and as a result Sara was not getting effective treatment. This put no blame on Sara, it simply recognized what her therapist knew. Had he told her that she made him nervous, it would have been all too easy for her to interpret this as a criticism and this could have jeopardized the WA. So, the next session began:

> THERAPIST (TH): As usual, we need to set our agenda. There is something I want to put at the beginning if that's ok with you.
>
> SARA (S): Suppose so – do what you like.
>
> TH: I'd like to review how we've been working together and look at how I might offer you a better service.
>
> S: Eh?
>
> TH: I've been thinking about our therapy sessions, discussing them with my supervisor, and we both think that I sometimes sort of disengage and then I'm not able to work with you and support you as well as I would like. I'd like to see if we can't do something about that.
>
> S: OK (but not angry).

They finished setting the agenda, took this item and explored it further. The therapist explained that he noted a pattern in himself, namely that he sometimes jumped to the conclusion that Sara was angry and then he tended to "pull back". He realized that he had never checked this out with Sara and maybe Sara could help him better understand these less productive times and then he could make them more productive. This approach engaged Sara – it preserved the working alliance. Her therapist was very aware of Sara's formulation and, in his choice of words, took care not to trigger her fears of being misunderstood, abused and abandoned. He was also aware of his own fears and concerns and held these in mind as they explored their therapeutic rupture. Eventually Sara was able to summarize what they had discovered:

> S: Because of my past I come in here looking for trouble....
>
> TH: Sorry to interrupt, but what might be another way of looking at that?
>
> S: Okay, okay, I come in here a bit scared and I try to look after myself by being a bit aggressive. This pushes your buttons and you pull back from me and then you are not such a good therapist. I'm pleased to learn that this bothers you, but it's not good for my therapy. I think if I am less defensive, you might be able to do your job better.
>
> TH: Yes, and if I keep your formulation in mind and remember just how threatening it can be just being here, I can understand your reactions and focus more on you and your needs. I wonder – if we do lapse into our old pattern, what shall we do about it – what's the best way of rescuing the situation?
>
> S: Well you should say something – that's your job.
>
> TH: I agree. What if I simply said that I wondered if we were getting into the old pattern again? Then if you were of the same opinion, we could try to resolve it and move on?
>
> S: Sure

TH: And if you feel me pulling away I'd be grateful if you'd let me know – could you do that?

S: I think that now we've had this conversation I could.

Together they agreed that either of them could say "old pattern" if they felt a strain on the relationship and they found that this was a powerful way of de-centring and they did indeed learn to manage the odd rupture – although they were fewer. Sara's therapist then explored one final hypothesis – that this pattern might be played out outside the therapy sessions. He did this by simply asking: "this pattern, this trap that we get caught up in – does it just happen here or have you noticed it at other times?" Sara had in fact noted similar interpersonal interactions outside the sessions and they discussed this and how she might now use her insight to make changes. However, the way that the question was framed gave her the option of saying no, it gave her an opportunity to refute the therapist's hypothesis. This is important as in some instances the problem interaction will simply be a product of the patient being in an unusual and taxing setting, namely that of a patient in therapy.

Where Next?

By now you will have an understanding of what the WA is, how to establish it and how to maintain it even in the face of ruptures. You may find that you need to begin thinking about how you can use the principles and guidelines in this chapter when working with couples or groups or even when carrying out supervision (because the CBT supervisory alliance shares many qualities of the working alliance). Each therapist reading this chapter will have different needs, you will work in different specialities, you will have differing degrees of experience and different levels of access to supervision. Whatever your current position, you can continue developing the quality of your working relationships through self-reflection, peer supervision, "expert" supervision, reading and attending training opportunities. The onus is on you to be aware of your needs and resources and to build on the knowledge you have gained. Consider how *you* will take it forward and what *you* will need in order to do this, but ensure that you secure supervision of your work.

Summary

- The concept of the working alliance has been important to CBT since its inception. However, it is viewed as necessary but not sufficient in achieving good outcomes in CBT.
- It refers to a crucial interpersonal dynamic – that of a collaborative, active and respectful working relationship that comprises of goals, tasks and bond.
- Many CBT approaches and strategies can enhance the WA but there is an onus on the therapist to make the most of the relevant techniques – it isn't a simple matter of going through the motions.
- Ruptures can arise within the WA and these need to be addressed so as to strengthen the alliance.
- Supervision is paramount.

Procedural Rules

- Invest in your working alliance from the outset – it's not just something to consider when things get tricky.
- Construct a dynamic formulation that reflects your patient's inner world and difficulties. This will enhance your understanding of your patient and you can then use the opportunities to communicate a genuine understanding throughout the course of therapy.
- Balance Socratic method with direct enquiry, and balance Socratic and didactic teaching so that your patient feels enabled by your work together, never pressured or cornered into saying or doing something.
- Genuine "teamwork" will strengthen your working alliance, so make the most of it.
- Be aware of your own role in the session and track your feelings and thoughts. This might give you valuable pointers for deepening your understanding and developing your working alliance and will help you deal with therapy ruptures.

References

Andrusyna, T. P., Tang, T. Z., DeRubeis, R. J., & Luborsky, L. (2001). The factor structure of the working alliance inventory in cognitive-behavioral therapy. *The Journal of Psychotherapy Practice and Research, 10*, 173–178.

Beck, A. T., Rush, A. J., Shaw, B. F., & Emery, G. (1979). *Cognitive therapy of depression*. New York: Guilford Press.

Bordin, E. S. (1979). The generalizability of the psychodynamic concept of the working alliance. *Psychotherapy: Theory, Research, and Practice, 16*, 252–260.

British Association of Behavioural and Cognitive Psychotherapy. (n.d.). BABCP Accreditation. Retrieved from http://www.babcp.com/Accreditation/Accreditation.aspx

Burns, D., & Nolen-Hoeksema, S. (1991). Coping styles, homework compliance, and the effectiveness of cognitive-behavioral therapy. *Journal of Consulting and Clinical Psychology, 59*, 305–311.

Carroll, K. M., Nich, C., & Rounsaville, B. J. (1997). Contribution of the therapeutic alliance to outcome in active versus control psychotherapies. *Journal of Consulting and Clinical Psychology, 65*(3), 510–514. doi: 10.1037/0022-006X.65.3.510

Hanson, W. E., Curry, K. T., & Bandalos, D. L. (2002). Reliability Generalization of working alliance inventory scale scores. *Educational and Psychological Measurement, 62*(4), 659–673.

Horvath, A. O. (1994). Empirical validation of Bordin's pantheoretical model of the alliance: The Working Alliance Inventory perspective. In A. O. Horvath & L. S. Greenberg (Eds.), *The working alliance: theory, research, and practice* (pp. 109–128). New York: Wiley.

Horvath, A. O., & Greenberg, L. (1986). The development of the Working Alliance Inventory. In L. Greenberg & W. Pinsoff (Eds.), *The psychotherapeutic process: a resource handbook* (pp. 529–556). New York: Guilford.

Keller, S. M., Zoellner, L. A., & Feeny, N. C. (2010). Understanding factors associated with early therapeutic alliance in PTSD treatment: Adherence, childhood sexual abuse history, and social support. *Journal of Consulting and Clinical Psychology, 78*(6), 974–979. doi: 10.1037/a0020758

Knaevelsrund, C., & Maercker, A. (2007). Internet-based treatment for PTSD reduces distress and facilitates the development of a strong therapeutic alliance: a randomized controlled clinical trial. *BMC Psychiatry, 7*, 13. doi: 10.1186/1471-244X-7-13

Krupnick, J. L., Sotsky, S. M., Simmens, S., Moyer, J., Elkin, I., Watkins, J., & Pilkonis, P. A. (1996). The role of the therapeutic alliance in psychotherapy and pharmacotherapy outcome: findings in the National Institute of Mental Health Treatment of Depression Collaborative Research Program. *Journal of Consulting and Clinical Psychology, 64,* 532–539.

Leahy, R. (2001). *Overcoming resistance in cognitive therapy.* New York: Guilford Press.

Martin, D. J., Garske, J. P., and Davis, M. K. (2000). Relation of the therapeutic alliance with outcome and other variables: a meta-analytic review. *Journal of Consulting and Clinical Psychology, 68,* 438–450.

Muran, J. C., Safran, J. D., Gorman, B. S., Samstag, L. W., Eubanks-Carter, C., & Winston, A. (2009). The relationship of early alliance ruptures and their resolution to process and outcome in three time-limited psychotherapies for personality disorders. *Psychotherapy: Theory, Research, Practice, Training, 46*(2), 233–248.

Orlinsky, D., Grawe, K., and Parks, B. (1994). Process and outcome in psychotherapy. In A. Bergin and S. Garfield (Eds.), *Handbook of psychotherapy and behaviour change* (4th ed.). New York: Wiley.

Padesky, C. (1993). *Socratic questioning: changing minds or guiding discovery? Keynote address delivered at the European Congress of Behavioural and Cognitive* Therapies, London.

Roth, A., & Fonagy, P. (2005). *What works for whom?: A critical review of psychotherapy research* (2nd ed.). New York: Guilford Press.

Safran, J. D., & Muran, J. C. (2000). Resolving therapeutic alliance ruptures: diversity and integration. *Journal of Clinical Psychology, 56*(2), 233–243.

Safran, J. D., & Segal, Z. V. (1990). *Interpersonal process in cognitive therapy.* New York: Basic Books.

Stiles, W. B., Glick, M. J., Osatuke, K., Hardy, G. E., Shapiro, D. A., Agnew-Davies, R., … Barkham, M. (2004). Patterns of alliance development and the rupture-repair hypothesis: are productive relationships U-shaped or V-shaped? *Journal of Counselling Psychology, 51*(1), 81–92.

Watson, J. C., & Greenberg, L. S. (2000). Alliance ruptures and repairs in experiential therapy. *Journal of Clinical Psychology, 56*(2), 175–186.

Westbrook, D., Kennerley, H., & Kirk, J. (2011). *An introduction to Cognitive Behaviour Therapy: skills and applications* (2nd ed.). London: Sage.

Williams, C., & Martinez, R. (2008). Increasing access to CBT: stepped care and CBT self-help models in practice. *Behavioural and Cognitive Psychotherapy, 36*(06), 675–683.

Wilson, G. T., Loeb, K. L., Walsh, B. T., Labouvie, E., Petkova, E., Liu, X., & Waternaux, C. (1999). Psychological versus pharmacological treatments of bulimia nervosa: predictors and processes of change. *Journal of Consulting and Clinical Psychology, 67,* 451–459.

4

Working with Diversity in CBT

Sharif El-Leithy

There are not more than five primary colours, yet in combination they produce more hues than can ever be seen. There are not more than five cardinal tastes, yet combinations of them yield more flavours than can ever be tasted.

Sun Tzu, *The Art of War*

Every client who comes through your door varies in their biological make-up, life experiences, and ways of thinking, feeling and behaving. In turn you vary, and potentially differ, in all of these ways. Each aspect can also vary from day-to-day and in response to different contexts, including the context of working together in therapy.

We know that the CBT model is effective for treating a range of emotional difficulties, particularly anxiety and depression. However, we do not yet know how client variations and therapist-client differences affect CBT outcomes, although common sense and clinical experience would suggest that they can and do.

Some variations, like language, may seem immediately obvious in their implications; others, like spiritual beliefs, far less so. Some differences may pose barriers that you and your client need to overcome. Others might be strengths that you can draw on. Many of the differences may ultimately have little impact on the effectiveness of your joint CBT enterprise.

This chapter addresses three issues:

- How individual client and client-therapist differences impact on the outcome of CBT.
- How to identify and conceptualize these differences, and their effect on working with the CBT model.
- How can to adapt your practice to these differences, so that you and your client can still work effectively with the CBT model.

How to Become a More Effective CBT Therapist: Mastering Metacompetence in Clinical Practice,
First Edition. Edited by Adrian Whittington and Nick Grey.
© 2014 John Wiley & Sons, Ltd. Published 2014 by John Wiley & Sons, Ltd.

What is "Diversity"?

Diversity, at its simplest, is the variety in people and the differences between them. Some differences tend to be more apparent than others; and their multiplicity also means that it helps to classify them into groups. For example, Hays (2008) suggests a framework with the acronym ADDRESSING:

Age – including shared generational influences and experiences.
Dis/abilities, developmental – including physical, sensory and intellectual.
Dis/abilities, acquired – including injuries, health conditions.
Religion and spirituality – including mainstream and folk.
Ethnic and racial identity – including broad groups and cultures within them.
Socioeconomic status – income, occupation, education, social mobility.
Sexual orientation – heterosexual, lesbian, gay and bisexual.
Indigenous heritage – including status within their homeland.
National origin – including language, and also immigrant status, for example, refugees.
Gender identity – including gender roles, and those identifying as transgender.

Hays (2008) recommends using the ADDRESSING framework to develop a rich "cultural sketch" of each client, to identify how they are diverse and what cultural influences affect them. Diversity and culture are often used interchangeably in this way, to mean the "values, beliefs, norms, and life practices of a particular group that guide thinking, decisions, and actions in patterned ways" (Leininger, 1988, p. 156).

It is important to remember that grouping people by categories does not mean that they necessarily have the same needs or expectations – it gives a guide, not a rule. People are not simply the sum of their ethnicity, their age, or their nationality and any categorization risks obscuring the enormous potential for within-group variability, and for competing influences on people.

For example, compare a doctor and a farmer from the same ethnic group. Having fled their country as refugees, they may nevertheless have faced very different adversities, and differ in their needs, resources and expectations. They may share more in common, in terms of values, with similarly educated people of the host country than they do with each other. For the doctor who has escaped with their family, the loss in status as a refugee may be far more significant a stressor; while for the farmer who has fled alone, it may be both isolation and adjustment to living in a city. Each is also likely to approach working with the same highly acculturated, well-educated bilingual therapist very differently.

So, having general knowledge about these groups can help you generate hypotheses about an individual's experiences, beliefs and behaviour but these then need to be investigated and tested. Differences are also not necessarily salient by their *topography*, but rather by their *context, function* and *meaning*, for example, what it means to be born deaf in a deaf family, a hearing family, a superstitious family or a rich family. In this respect it can often be more helpful to consider *themes that vary across these diversity groups* but which share a similar function, for example, valued social roles or beliefs about illness.

Diversity has also become closely linked to inequality and social justice (Levinson, 2010). In every diversity category, there will be dominant and minority groups, for example, men, the physically-able, the well-educated, secularists, heterosexuals. In turn, dominant groups tend to have more resources, more power to decide societal values and greater status; while minority groups conversely suffer disadvantage.

Minorities are also more likely to be exposed to negative experiences as a result of their identity, including discrimination, harassment, adversity and trauma.

Despite this, it is important not to view diversity as necessarily meaning different, "special" or disadvantaged – to do so is itself a bias towards seeing the dominant group as "normal". Rather, you should see it as a factor to be explored further, guided by what you already know about the kinds of adversity that population have faced. Diversity may also bring particular strengths and resources with it, for example, being involved in political activity, playing a traditional musical instrument or going to the local temple. These are also important to explore if you are to understand your client's day-to-day experience.

How is Diversity Relevant to CBT Practice?

Theoretical issues

CBT is grounded in basic processes of learning and behaviour change that have received widespread empirical support. Given this theoretical foundation, there is every likelihood that CBT treatment principles apply across a wide range of populations (Pantalone, Iwamasa, & Martell, 2010). CBT also emphasizes understanding each individual's day-to-day experiences, the unique sense they make of them and how they respond. As such, CBT formulations already have flexibility built into them to accommodate idiosyncratic beliefs and behaviours.

CBT is based on principles that may also be particularly relevant to disadvantaged populations. It encourages you to develop an individualized case conceptualization, and to share this understanding with the client in a transparent way. It emphasizes collaborating – doing CBT with the client rather than doing it to them – and tailoring your methods to each individual. It has an explicit focus on empowering people through education and skills building, so that they can become their own agent of change.

However, CBT also makes assumptions about cognition that might not generalize outside the Western culture in which it arose. For example, CBT traditionally emphasizes thinking empirically, balancing observations and logical evidence to come to a single conclusion. This may devalue people who turn to folklore, collective experience and spiritual ideas to create meaning.

While apparently advocating a non-judgemental stance, CBT may also emphasize particularly Western values, such as autonomy rather than dependence, change rather than acceptance and asserting needs rather than subjugating them for the collective. People from cultures that do not ascribe to these values risk being framed in dysfunctional terms.

Empirical evidence

Most CBT outcome studies have been conducted on white, middle class, educated and verbal adults (Bernal & Scharró-del-Río 2001). The vast majority of studies only report basic demographics and do not control for diversity. Minority ethnic groups tend to be underrepresented, as are children and older adults. Those who do not speak English, have learning disabilities or sensory impairments are usually excluded from research trials altogether (Pantalone et al., 2010). We therefore do not know whether many of the most common forms of diversity affect outcome.

Encouragingly there are a number of studies that have shown CBT to be effective when adapted to particular groups. For example, an adapted form of CBT was effective for ethnic minority clients with psychosis (Rathod et al., 2013), Cambodian refugees with panic disorder (Hinton et al., 2005), and African-American women with agoraphobia (Carter, Sbrocco, Gore, Marin, & Lewis, 2003).

Only two studies have compared the effectiveness of a standard versus adapted CBT program for a particular population. Kohn, Oden, Munoz, Robinson, and Leavitt (2002) found a manualized CBT intervention for depressed African-American women was more effective when adapted by changing the language used to describe CBT techniques, and by including culture-specific content (e.g., African-American family issues). An adapted CBT was also more effective for Hispanic American clients when clinicians were trained to interact in a warmer, more personalized way, in keeping with Hispanic norms of relating (Miranda et al., 2003).

Clinical guidelines

There are numerous descriptions and case studies of adapting CBT for particular diversity groups (e.g., Hays and Iwamasa, 2006; Naeem & Kingdon, 2012). These serve an important starting point for treatment planning. A review of the literature on psychotherapy adaptation (Sue, Zane, Hall, & Berger, 2009) also reveals a wide range of possible procedural rules for if and when to adapt, including:

- Always adhere as closely as possible to "standard" evidence-based practice.
- Explicitly consider and adapt for every client's diversity issues from the outset.
- Achieve a balance between selecting interventions that are empirically rigorous and flexibly adapting their delivery.
- Adapt where a client's problems are influenced by membership of a specific diversity group.
- Adapt where there is evidence of a group's poor response to standard treatment, or when encountering obstacles in therapy.
- Adapt on the basis of an idiographic assessment of how a client's diversity issues relate to the development and maintenance of their problem.

Ultimately there is a lack of empirical data to help you decide when to implement adaptations, or indeed which adaptations to choose for any individual, multiply diverse client. This means that while you can use the available literature as a guide, there are no evidence-based procedural rules for you to follow.

Adapting CBT for Diversity:
A Case Conceptualization Framework

Given these limitations, a sensible starting point when working with diversity is doing what you know works: maintaining fidelity to the pillars of the CBT model (Westbrook, Chapter 2, this volume), and to evidence-based CBT approaches.

Simultaneously, however, you can develop and refine an individualized case-conceptualization of how diversity may impact on undertaking "standard" CBT. In this respect Westbrook, Mueller, Kennerley, and McManus (2010) suggest a helpful framework for conceptualizing the interacting factors that affect the outcome of a course of

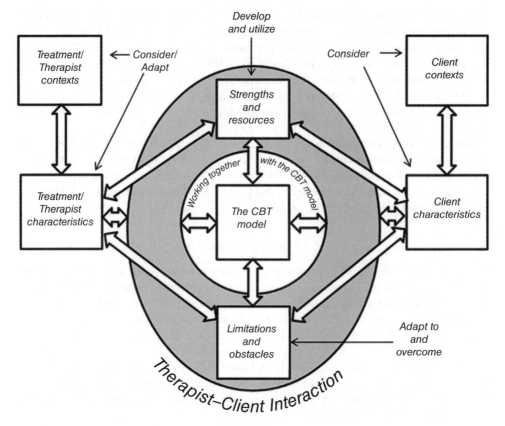

Figure 4.1   A framework for adapting CBT for diversity.

CBT. These include: the therapist's and client's characteristics; the therapist–client interaction; features of the CBT model itself; and how the therapist and client relate to, and work with, the CBT model. An adapted version of this framework can be applied to working with diversity issues in CBT (Figure 4.1).

You can use this framework from the outset to help you consider your client's diversity characteristics and associated cross-group themes. You can generate hypotheses about how these features might be relevant to your CBT formulation and to working together with the CBT model. The framework then gives you a structure for applying both the adaptation literature and your own experiences to these hypotheses, to systematically guide modifications to your formulation or treatment delivery.

You can apply this framework when first considering a referral, at the assessment and initial formulation stage, when encountering treatment obstacles or when reflecting on treatment failures. In this way you can provide high quality CBT that holds closely to the principles that we understand underlie its effectiveness, but delivered in a flexible and personalized manner.

The framework includes the following interacting factors:

- *Client characteristics:* cross-group themes arising from client diversity (see ADDRESSING) – language, models of illness, models of help-seeking, expressions of distress and symptoms, ways of relating, physical and neurocognitive issues.

- *Treatment/therapist's characteristics:* the therapist's own diversity characteristics, identity and therapeutic "style". Knowledge, beliefs and attitudes toward the client and their contexts.
- *Client contexts:* the client's historical, cultural, familial and social background. The adversity experiences and resources arising from the client's contexts.
- *Treatment/therapist contexts:* the therapist's personal/social contexts and those of the therapy service, such as how the service organizes treatment, the available resources, what treatments can be offered, where and how it is provided.
- *The CBT model:* fundamental aspects of CBT including using structure, developing a collaborative alliance, model/method selection, psycho-education and socialization, effective communication, Socratic dialogue and cognitive restructuring.

Rather than viewing diversity as exclusively a client characteristic, this framework suggests that diversity is primarily relevant in the way it affects the *therapist–client interaction*. This is a function of both therapist and client characteristics, and in turn both the therapist and client are potentially affected by their contexts. These interactions are ultimately important in how they affect *working together with the CBT model,* in that there may be particular *limitations and obstacles,* or indeed *strengths and resources.* Both of these may become a focus for adaptation, or "cultural bridging" (Hwang, 2006) by creatively finding ways to overcome the obstacles and build on strengths.

At the same time, these *limitations* and *strengths* are only a subset of the total therapist–client interaction (the shaded ring in Figure 4.1). Hence, regardless of your differences, there will typically be many aspects of therapy where you and the client can work together with the CBT model "as normal", and without the need to adapt your approach.

The potential for adaptation is also restricted: by the need to stick to the model of CBT as closely as possible; and by the limitations to adaptation that come from the therapist (their personal characteristics, the flexibility of their service) and similarly client characteristics. This means that adaptation must always be a process of meeting the client "halfway"; and through socializing to the CBT model, helping the client to meet you "halfway" too, so that you both stay as close to the CBT model as possible.

Overcoming Obstacles and Building: Applying the Adaption Framework in Clinical Practice

You can apply this framework clinically in four steps:

1. Assess your client's diversity characteristics and their contexts using the ADDRESSING framework, considering any themes that may be important to the therapist–client interaction and to working with the CBT model.
2. Consider your own therapist characteristics and your contexts, and how these may affect the therapist–client interaction. Make adaptations here to "meet the client halfway".
3. Generate ideas about where there may be limitations or obstacles in working together with the CBT model, and areas of strength or resources.
4. Use these ideas to help you create bridges – systematically adapting delivery of your treatment in a flexible manner while keeping faithful to the core principles of the CBT model. Apply both available literature and clinical experience, and collaboratively create solutions to overcome limitations and utilize areas of strength.

The example in Box 4.1 illustrates using this framework for adaptation

---

Box 4.1   Using the framework for adaption: scenario

A 70-year-old Tamil woman has been referred to you for depression. Your service typically uses a focused brief CBT including behavioural activation and cognitive restructuring elements. However you are struggling to implement any of these strategies with her – her attendance is sporadic; she focuses on discussing her physical complaints, and tends to withdraw when you ask her about her emotions. She also seems unwilling to consider keeping an activity schedule.

Using the framework you identify the following issues:

- *Client contexts* – she originates from rural Sri Lanka and living in the United Kingdom, is now isolated from friends and family. She lives a long way from the therapy clinic.
- *Client characteristics* – you suspect that like other Tamil people you have met, and also many in her age cohort, she has a tendency to express emotional distress through physical symptoms. However, she also suffers from arthritis. She speaks English as a second language. She has no previous experience of psychological treatments and seems to struggle with naming her emotions.
- *Therapist characteristics* – you are a 25-year-old white British woman and you do not speak Tamil. You live nearby with your family.
- *Treatment/therapist contexts* – you work in a busy primary care psychology service offering brief manualized treatments.
- *Client–therapist interaction* – you are working in the client's second language, which limits communication, as she is reluctant to use an interpreter. You wonder if your age affects how she relates to you and what problems she is comfortable to disclose.
- *CBT model* – you struggle to work together within the structure of brief treatment. Your client does homework sporadically. When you try to discuss your client's thoughts and feelings she reverts to discussing physical issues.

You develop the following hypotheses about potential *limitations and obstacles* to *working with the CBT model* and implement adaptations to overcome them:

- *Using structure*: she may struggle to attend regularly due to pain from arthritis. However, you are restricted by your service context in meeting elsewhere. *You explore arranging hospital transport for her. You offer the option of having a telephone session when she cannot travel.*
- *Collaborative alliance*: she may relate to you as she would a medical doctor and wants you to provide her with a "cure". You may not have fully appreciated how hard it is for her to travel to sessions or the impact of living alone. You suspect there are cultural barriers to disclosing her feelings, including the stigma of mental illness, and because you are her junior. *You focus the next session on validating her difficulties. You decide to explore the cultural issues around disclosure with her, and to explain the differences between how medical doctors and CBT therapists work.*

- *Model/method selection*: you wonder if the service's usual CBT approach may seem impersonal to her. A focus on thoughts/feelings and activity levels may not match her beliefs about the cause of her symptoms or of what constitutes acceptable treatment. *You agree with your supervisor to adapt the usual approach, initially focusing on engagement and coping skills, while giving time each week to discuss her physical symptoms, then gradually connecting them to her thoughts and feelings. You introduce the concept of stress to bridge physical and psychological explanations of her symptoms.*
- *Socialization*: as a result of her cultural background and age, she has limited experience of psychological treatment or concepts. She may have struggled to relate to standard metaphors for CBT such as "learning to drive a car with a driving instructor". *You explore examples from her own background of learning a skill and elaborate on them as a metaphor for the process of CBT.*
- *Communication*: she may have rejected using an interpreter because of her fears of stigma. Your treatment depends on language and literacy skills that may be difficult for her in a second language. *You offer to have some materials translated into Tamil including an activity schedule and a list of emotion words. You also learn a couple of Tamil emotion words from her, and focus on simplifying your communication style.*

You also identify some potential *strengths and resources* that you try to utilize.

- As you are outside her community, your client may be more willing to discuss mental health issues with you if she is assured of privacy. *You decide to have an explicit discussion about this.*
- You are aware there is a Tamil temple near her house where an Elders group meets every week. *With her consent you make contact and arrange for someone to accompany her to her first meeting. You explore and encourage her use of traditional meditation practices as a coping skill.*

The remainder of the chapter provides further suggestions and examples across each of the core areas of the adaptation model: clients' contexts, client characteristics, therapist characteristics and contexts, and working with the CBT model.

Clients' contexts

Clients from minority groups frequently present with emotional difficulties in the context of external stressors, such as poor housing, financial, legal or social problems. There may be discrimination, deprivation, isolation and exposure to criminality. Others may suffer caregiver stress, loss of friends from ageing, and exposure to war and trauma. Some stressors may be historical, others current. The client may also be actively seeking your help in solving these difficulties.

It is particularly important to devote time early in your work to explicitly discuss the presence and impact of these issues, and to validate your client's emotional reactions. However, it can sometimes be hard to judge how much your client's descriptions reflect realistic appraisals of the situation, as opposed to cognitive distortions typical of mood disorders. For example, are they really being picked on at work because their workmates are homophobic? Is it really not safe to walk around their housing estate?

Often the external stressor and some cognitive distortion will overlap, making these judgements even more complicated; and particularly where they reflect your client's minority membership of a diversity group, and you are a dominant member. Where you recognize such differences, you should be especially cautious in making these judgements using your own experiences. Instead, by exploring examples of the problem in detail, you should aim to develop an accurate functional analysis linking the external (stressor) and internal (meanings, reactions), considering how each might affect the other, and if there are any "vicious circles".

Where you identify real adversity, you may be able to signpost your client to possible solutions, or problem solve ways to tackle it. Within the limits of your role, you may agree to contribute directly, for example by writing a letter. However, you will often be limited in how much you and your client can change a particular issue in a relatively short time. Teaching your client problem-solving skills, helping them develop support networks and cultivating adaptive perspectives on their problems can be more effective in influencing contexts in the longer term. This can be balanced with developing emotion-focused coping skills for issues that cannot be changed, for example, if there is ongoing uncertainty about being granted asylum.

Client characteristics

Language

Language is the principle therapeutic tool in CBT, so obstacles potentially impair your ability to engage, understand or collaborate with your client. Cognitive techniques are particularly sensitive to language issues, for example, when eliciting beliefs, using guided discovery to explore abstract ideas such as responsibility or conveying therapeutic metaphors. Standard CBT protocols are also heavily reliant on reading and writing, which in turn are affected by educational level and developmental disabilities.

Some potential obstacles include:

- Speaking a different language altogether, requiring you to either use an interpreter or work in your client's (or your) second language.
- Receptive and expressive obstacles, for example, clients with sensory impairments, literacy problems or a lack of knowledge of psychological terms.
- Culture-specific language, for example, military terminology, youth slang or cultural tendencies to talk in analogies.
- Language dysfluencies affecting structure and intelligibility, for example, tangential speech in psychosis or following head injury.

Models of illness

Dysfunctional negative appraisals of physical and psychological symptoms are at the heart of many CBT models. Cultural differences in models of mind and body can affect these interpretations, examples include:

- Culture-specific models of the body, for example, in Cambodian culture, the interpretation of anxiety symptoms as blockages of vapour-like *Wind* believed to travel through vessels in the body, which in turn indicate life-threatening outcomes such as rupture of the blood vessels in the neck (Hinton & Otto, 2006).
- Spiritual or religious models of psychological symptoms, for example, nightmares as indicative of a spiritual or psychic attack.
- Preferences for physiological or biomedical explanations of symptoms, perhaps because of differences in mental health awareness.

- Stigma arising from cultural beliefs about physical and mental illness, for example, a belief that mental illness is an inherited weakness that affects the prospects of the whole family; that HIV is a highly contagious and fatal "plague" with sufferers morally responsible for their illness.

Models of help seeking

Aspects of your client's contexts can affect how they view help seeking. You may encounter these issues in the early stages of CBT, particularly in establishing the working alliance.

- People who have lived under authoritarian regimes may distrust professionals in general because of experiences of state control and surveillance.
- People who lack a concept of health services, or who have very poor social networks, may understand your role as more as a friend, sibling or parent.
- Some groups may have specific fears about engaging with psychiatric services arising from collective experiences, for example, Afro-Caribbeans in the United Kingdom as a result of associations with the police and forced hospitalization; or gay and lesbian clients who may fear attempts to "treat" homosexuality, given its previous classification as a psychiatric disorder.
- Expectations about the therapist's role may be in tension with CBT's collaborative approach, for example, that you will tell the client what to do, give medicines, "cure" or "heal" the problem'.

Expression of distress and symptoms

CBT treatments tend to rely on identifying psychological symptoms and matching them to diagnosis-specific treatment models. However, people may not express their distress in ways that are easily reconciled with typical symptom descriptions, making this matching more difficult. A good example is depression, which varies considerably between cultures in how symptoms present and how they are described (Tsai and Chentsova-Dutton, 2002).

A common issue can be clients who present with somatic complaints or medically unexplained symptoms rather than emotional or psychological distress. These presentations may be more common when:

- the client has difficulty interpreting or expressing their emotional states, for example, young people, older adults, people with sensory or learning disabilities;
- the client is less literate in Western psychological concepts such as worry or panic;
- there are barriers to disclosing psychological symptoms, such as feeling stigma, or fearing hospitalization; and
- psychological descriptions clash with cultural models of illness and healing traditions.

Ways of relating

Differences in cultural norms of social interaction can affect your working alliance, through mismatches in what you each expect of an acceptable therapeutic encounter. These differences also mean you need to be cautious in making assumptions about your client from observing how they relate to you. Examples include:

- Norms of eye contact, for example, Western cultures may interpret direct eye contact as a sign of trust and honesty, while Eastern cultures may see it as disrespectful.

- Norms of formality and personal disclosure, for example, clients viewing a refusal by the therapist to answer questions about family background as coldness; perceiving Socratic questions as rude or confrontational.
- Differences in emotional expression potentially affecting interpretations of emotional state, for example, viewing a client shouting or swearing as a sign of aggression; perceiving a client's acquiescence as indicating low self-esteem.
- Different expectations of social relationships, for example, gift giving, going to a client's house, contact outside of therapy sessions, and the importance ascribed to these acts.

Physical and neurocognitive issues

Illness, medical conditions, physical and learning disabilities may make it harder for your client to work within the structure of standard CBT – getting to sessions, engaging during sessions, remembering them afterwards and doing homework.

Both illness and disability may also be associated with negative views of the self that contribute to distress, and may be relevant to your CBT formulation (see Hutton et al., Chapter 11). Often these beliefs are partly accurate or reflective of societal attitudes, but have become over-general or over-valued. They may also motivate maladaptive coping responses, such as withdrawal or selective attention to rejection.

Traditional CBT makes considerable demands on cognitive functions such as memory, attention, problem solving, abstract reasoning, and pattern matching. Difficulties in these areas may mean the exercise of CBT becomes one of frustration for both client and therapist (Glickman, 2009). Hence it is important to identify and adapt therapy to these problems as early as possible, to avoid potentially providing your client with a further experience of failure.

Therapist characteristics and contexts

Your own diversity characteristics will naturally affect how your client relates to you. Minimizing your differences can conceal important mismatches that might affect treatment, whereas being open with your client about your differences, and spending some time reflecting on their implications, can help you find ways to overcome potential obstacles together.

In evaluating the impact of these differences, it can also be helpful to reflect on *who you are*; and how your beliefs and ways of relating are grounded in your cultural contexts. Hays (2013) describes a number of exercises to help you apply the ADDRESSING framework to yourself, and to undertake an honest self-assessment of the beliefs and experiences that arise from your own diversity. One example is to complete the sentence "I am …" as many times as you can and reflect on the answers.

We are all prone to making stereotyped assumptions that may bias how we assess and conceptualize our client's issues. These blind spots can lead to making mistakes in interpreting aspects of your interaction with your client. A lack of knowledge about a diversity issue may also mean we assume the client thinks or behaves in a similar way to ourselves. Becoming aware of these "holes" in your understanding is often a case of trial-and-error, so use supervision to reflect periodically on this process.

It can be helpful to learn more about the different client groups you more frequently work with in your context, although treat this knowledge as a guide and not a rule. Examples include reading news and historical accounts, watching documentaries, consulting group members and attending cultural events. Engaging with these activities can help you develop cognitive templates into which you can incorporate client-specific information.

Working together with the CBT model

Using structure

- Early in therapy be explicit about the role of structure in CBT, and how this may seem very different to other relationships. Be transparent about what you wish to cover in a session, and ask the client how you can best do that in a way they are comfortable with.
- Within the limitations of your context, it may be helpful to agree modifications to the standard structure, for example, shorter and more frequent sessions for people struggling with pain or concentration difficulties; less frequent sessions with a telephone or email "catch up" in between to review homework progress where there are obstacles to attending weekly.
- Where the client's style of talking is unstructured or wide-ranging, try to agree "stop" signals and use mini-summaries to add "scaffolding". Frequent reflections and drawing links between disparate statements can also help.
- Try to identify homework tasks that would be relatively normal in the client's context, so they fit into their normal social roles. Homework tasks may be stigmatizing if they fall too far outside or if they require too much help.
- In many cultures it would seem abnormal to simply stop a positive and personalized relationship so consider offering more flexible endings such as to drop-in or email you in the future, and offering limited booster sessions if required.

Box 4.2   An example of using CBT structure

Shaun had suffered a head injury in a motorbike accident, which left him with perseveration problems. In sessions he tended to talk at length, often moving between topics and was difficult to interrupt, meaning that often the agreed agenda got lost. After several meetings his therapist pointed out that they often seemed to end up off topic, and asked Shaun if he had noticed this too. He immediately responded that he knew he tended to "go on", and that it frustrated him. Problem solving this together, Shaun suggested that the therapist give him a clear "stop signal" with his hand when he felt they were going off topic, to help them return to the agenda.

Model and method selection

Where possible, try to match your client's presenting problems to a specific treatment model as a starting point, either a standard or one previously adapted for the relevant diversity issues. If you are unsure how to proceed, undertake a functional analysis of the symptoms to generate relevant clinical information. Often you will be able to recognize familiar processes underlying an unusual presentation, for example, rumination, avoidance, thought blocking or safety seeking.

Where your client presents with somatic symptoms, avoid the temptation to bring the focus back to psychological symptoms too soon. Rather, concentrating on physical complaints and behaviours will be crucial both to engaging your client while formulating their problems psychologically. It is also important to consider any interaction with physical illness, particularly in at-risk groups such as older adults or people with learning disabilities, and to exclude potential medical causes.

Coping-skills based interventions, such as Meichenbaum's (1985) stress inoculation training, are often easier to implement with diverse groups than meaning-change interventions. CBT as skills training has a practical emphasis that can have broad appeal and is more accessible to those less well versed in ideas of therapy for healing. Using the frame of skills learning demystifies the therapy process and also provides a template of how to relate to you collaboratively as "coach".

A skills training approach also easily accommodates culturally valued activities into a CBT frame, for example, meditation, mindfulness and acceptance in clients from Buddhist or Hindu backgrounds. Skills training can nevertheless facilitate meaning change, by drawing the learning and outcomes of implementing skills back to the understanding of the problem. As such, all skills training can also be constructed as a behavioural experiment that you can use to tackle dysfunctional meanings about symptoms, the self and the world.

Developing a collaborative alliance
The working alliance is the cornerstone to all CBT interventions, so your first step in adaptation may involve bridging obstacles arising from your client's ways of relating and models of help seeking.

- You may need to establish your credibility as a help giver – that you are able to help, that you have been helpful to similar clients before. One method is to achieve early gains, for example, by teaching a simple coping skill, or attending to a practical issue, so try ensure to your client leaves the first session feeling they have got something useful from your meeting.
- Conversely, remember the central role of empathy and validation, particularly where there are real adversities, and focus on these techniques until the client feels you have fully understood the difficulties they are bringing. Avoid focusing on change strategies too early.
- Consider the meanings your client attaches to being asked questions directly, for example, whether it feels like an interrogation or violates norms about intrusiveness, and switch to more flexible approaches such as open discussion or choosing social topics until you have established some trust. Balance informality and warmth with keeping to your CBT structure.
- Try to "meet halfway" in expectations of the relationship by being flexible with boundaries, but only within the limits that you are comfortable with, for example, answering personal questions about your family background or where you are going on holiday, in order to increase rapport. Disclosing a little to your client will often be met with far more in return.

Psycho-education and socialization
The CBT model may propose a very different understanding of symptoms to that of your client. You may have to work harder to present this alternative in a way that shifts your client's beliefs about the best way to think about, and respond to, their symptoms. This means you may need to spend more time than normal on the psycho-education phase, and on socializing to the CBT model.

A client's model of their symptoms will determine what they consider is an acceptable treatment, including how they view the CBT treatments you offer. This is important when considering how to socialize your client to a CBT model, and what kinds of interventions may be more acceptable to them, for example, using a "stress" rather than a "depression" model.

You can routinely provide accessible information about the prevalence of mental health difficulties and their symptoms, in order to tackle common myths and stigma. Also consider giving written or video testimonies from previous clients, relating what brought them into treatment and their experiences of CBT. This is particularly helpful where there is some match to your present client or their circumstances, so try to build up a library of different clients with specific diversity issues

It is usually inappropriate to challenge culturally-held illness beliefs directly. Instead, by simply exploring these beliefs you can help your client test out what might be taken-for-granted ideas, and in this way potentially reappraise both their own distress and others reactions to them.

Box 4.3   Psycho-education and socialization: an example

Issa was suffering with nightmares, but he seemed very reluctant to describe them to his therapist. Eventually he described how he repeatedly dreamt of an old woman sitting on his chest and choking him. The therapist recognized this as a common stress-related sleep disorder called "Old Hag syndrome", but asked Issa what he thought caused these dreams. He explained that a traditional healer had told him he was being haunted by a Jinamizi, or evil spirit, and that if he told anyone, it would haunt them too. They agreed to test this by seeing if either the therapist or interpreter had the same dream over the next two weeks. When they did not, Issa felt less sure it was a Jinamizi. Feeling less fearful going to sleep, he also noticed the dream occurred less often.

Enhancing communication

Diversity can create obstacles in communicating information and ideas that can make standard CBT approaches inaccessible to your client. Overcoming these obstacles often requires both creativity and flexibility.

- Combine verbal/written and visual materials where you can, to aid recall and understanding, and to overcome the mechanics of any disability (see Glickman, 2009). Figure 4.2 shows an example of two pictorial exposure tasks developed with a Spanish speaking client with limited literacy.
- Routinely use a whiteboard in sessions to enhance your communications, by drawing, writing and illustrating ideas. The act of jointly focusing on a whiteboard can increase the alliance by reducing the discomfort some clients feel in direct face-to-face interaction, especially when discussing personal topics.
- Try to use language taken from the client's own experience to name and describe CBT ideas, as these terms will "stick" far better than technical CBT terms.
- Stories, analogies and metaphors are particularly helpful in building "cognitive bridges" between you and your client (Stott, Mansell, Salkovskis, Lavender, & Cartwright-Hatton, 2010). Try to build up a library of metaphors or cultural

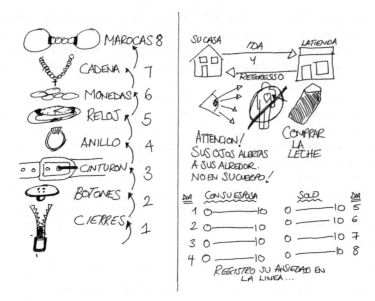

Figure 4.2 Pictorial graded exposure tasks, developed in session then photographed from a whiteboard to support homework. On the left, a hierarchy for exposure to trauma-related cues. On the right, repeated exposure task for panic disorder, with instructions to leave the house and buy milk daily while deploying attention externally: "Attention! Your eyes focused on your surroundings and not on your body!"

Box 4.4   An example of using meaningful client-oriented language

Harry was putting flashcards together with his therapist, to remind him how to cope with panic attacks. He commented it reminded him of similar cards they would carry when he was in the army, which would tell you what steps to take in a particular incident such as discovering a bomb. He laughed that soldiers called them "flap cards" because you used them to stop you getting in a flap. Subsequently whenever they used a new CBT technique, they tried to think of a similar military term to describe it, such as Ops Briefs for behavioural experiment sheets.

Box 4.5   An example of using client stories, analogies and metaphors

The therapist was trying to explain to Farhad how feared situations can generalize in PTSD, by telling him a story of a client who had been bitten by a big dog, and had come to fear all dogs afterwards, even small docile ones. Farhad remarked that in Iran they have a saying that "he who has been bitten by a snake fears a piece of rope". Subsequently they used this idea to formulate a flashcard to use when he felt anxious. The card prompted him with questions to help decide if a given situation was a "snake" or a "rope"; in other words, a real threat or a reminder of an upsetting memory.

analogies from each of your clients, to use with subsequent clients with similar backgrounds. When you suggest a metaphor or proverb, ask your client if there is anything similar in their culture as a client's own analogy will often aid understanding better than a stock metaphor.

Socratic dialogue and cognitive restructuring

A cornerstone of cognitive models is helping clients re-evaluate distressing or dysfunctional beliefs using Socratic conversations. However, this process can seem somewhat artificial or confrontational to clients from some populations. It can sometimes help to avoid more formal Socratic methods, such as completing thought records and identifying thinking errors, in favour of a more narrative CBT approach. This approach combines the teaching of CBT *skills* with helping the client generate alternative more positive *stories* about themselves, through discussing their efforts and successes in implementing these skills.

Where you are struggling to restructure a particular belief, check that the techniques you are using match your client's way of reasoning. So if the client's belief arises from spiritual ways of thinking, then it is better to adopt this framework to rethinking it, rather than trying to use standard "logical" approaches.

Box 4.6 An example of restructuring by matching a client's way of reasoning

Abdul was struggling with guilt over the death of his brother, who had been shot helping him escape from a prison camp. His therapist had unsuccessfully tried several methods to help him reappraise his responsibility, including Socratic enquiry and completing responsibility pie charts. Abdul explained that nothing could change his mind because in Islam, God gave man free will, so man is responsible when good and bad things happen by his actions.

The therapist acknowledged he did not know much about Islam, and was perhaps not the best person to help Abdul think about this issue. He suggested they try to find out more about what Islam teaches about free will, blame and destiny. Abdul agreed to speak to his local Imam at the mosque. When he returned he told the therapist how the Imam had sympathized with his feelings, and had shown him passages from the Koran. He had reassured him that in Islam man is only to blame for those things he can control; and that God himself chooses when everyone lives and dies. Abdul said this helped him to see what had happened as God's will, and that he felt more at peace.

Conclusion

This chapter summarized some of the ways in which diversity may be relevant to your CBT practice, and provided suggestions for how to think about and respond to the challenges it brings.

Procedural Rules

- Use a structure such as the ADDRESSING framework to routinely integrate diversity issues into your assessments and formulations.
- Develop knowledge about the diversity groups you work with, but use this as a guide not a rule. Remember to balance group and individual characteristics, and consider competing influences.
- Think about diversity in terms of the similarities and differences between you and your client, and their impact on working together with the CBT model. Be aware of your own diversity and what that may mean to your client, and to how you think about them.
- Aim to provide high-quality CBT that holds closely to the principles that we understand underlie its effectiveness, but delivered in a flexible and personalized manner. Start with doing what you know works, while developing an individualized case conceptualization to systematically guide modifications to your formulation or treatment delivery.
- Don't assume diversity necessarily means having to adapt your CBT approach – what you do together may not look very different from normal.
- Where there are obstacles to working with the CBT model, pay close attention to engagement, socialization and validation, and try to meet your client half-way in expectations about the nature of your working relationship. Be as flexible as your context allows in the way you deliver your interventions, while holding the structure and principles of your CBT.
- Focus on building skills as well as changing meanings, and tailor your interventions to be understandable, memorable and empowering. Focus on developing strengths and resources that arise from diversity, and overcoming obstacles using creative and collaborative solutions.

References

Bernal, G., & Scharró-del-Río, M.R. (2001). Are empirically supported treatments valid for ethnic minorities? Toward an alternative approach for treatment research. *Cultural Diversity and Ethnic Minority Psychology, 7*(4), 328–342.

Carter, M.M., Sbrocco, T., Gore, K.L., Marin, N.W., & Lewis, E.L. (2003). Cognitive-behavioral group therapy versus a wait-list control in the treatment of African American women with panic disorder. *Cognitive Therapy and Research, 27*(5), 505–518.

Glickman, N.S. (2009). Adapting best practices in CBT for deaf and hearing persons with language and learning challenges. *Journal of Psychotherapy Integration, 19*(4), 354.

Hays, P.A. (2008). *Addressing cultural complexities in practice: assessment, diagnosis, and therapy.* Washington, DC: American Psychological Association.

Hays, P.A. (2013). *Connecting across cultures: the helper's toolkit.* New York: Sage.

Hays, P.A., & Iwamasa, G.Y. (Eds.). (2006). *Culturally responsive cognitive-behavioral therapy.* Washington, DC: American Psychological Association.

Hinton, D.E., Chhean, D., Pich, V., Safren, S.A., Hofmann, S.G., & Pollack, M.H. (2005). A randomized controlled trial of cognitive-behavior therapy for Cambodian refugees with treatment-resistant PTSD and panic attacks: A cross-over design. *Journal of Traumatic Stress, 18*, 617–629.

Hinton, D.E., & Otto, M.W. (2006). Symptom presentation and symptom meaning among traumatized Cambodian refugees: Relevance to a somatically focused cognitive-behavior therapy. *Cognitive and Behavioral Practice, 13*(4), 249–260.

Hwang, W.C. (2006). The psychotherapy adaptation and modification framework: Application to Asian Americans. *American Psychologist, 61*(7), 702.

Kohn, L.P., Oden, T., Munoz, R.F., Robinson, A., & Leavitt, D. (2002). Adapted cognitive behavioural group therapy for depressed low-income African American women. *Community Mental Health Journal, 38*, 497–504.

Leininger, M.M. (1988). Leininger's theory of nursing: Cultural care diversity and universality. *Nursing Science Quarterly, 1*(4), 152–160.

Levinson, M. (2010). Working with diversity. In A. Grant, M. Townend, R. Mulhern, & N. Short (Eds.), *Cognitive behavioural therapy in mental health care* (pp. 181–191). London: Sage.

Meichenbaum, D. (1985). *Stress inoculation training.* New York: Pergamon Press.

Miranda, J., Chung, J.Y., Green, B.L., Krupnick, J., Siddique, J., Revicki, D.A., & Belin, T. (2003). Treating depression in predominantly low-income young minority women: A randomized controlled trial. *Journal of the American Medical Association, 290*, 57–65.

Naeem, F., & Kingdon, D. (Eds.). (2012). *Cognitive behaviour therapy in non-Western cultures.* Hauppauge, NY: Nova Science Publishers.

Pantalone, D.W., Iwamasa, G.Y., & Martell, C.R. (2010). Cognitive-behavioral therapy with diverse populations. In K.S. Dobson (Ed.), *Handbook of cognitive-behavioral therapies* (3rd ed., pp. 445–464). New York: Guilford Press.

Rathod, S., Phiri, P., Harris, S., Underwood, C., Thagadur, M., Padmanabi, U., & Kingdon, D. (2013). Cognitive behaviour therapy for psychosis can be adapted for minority ethnic groups: a randomised controlled trial. *Schizophrenia Research, 143*(2–3), 319–326.

Stott, R., Mansell, W., Salkovskis, P., Lavender, A., & Cartwright-Hatton, S., (2010). *Oxford guide to metaphors in CBT. Building cognitive bridges.* Oxford: Oxford University Press.

Sue, S., Zane, N., Hall, G.C.N., & Berger, L.K. (2009). The case for cultural competency in psychotherapeutic interventions. *Annual Review of Psychology, 60*, 525–548.

Tsai, J.L., & Chentsova-Dutton, Y. (2002). Understanding depression across cultures. In H. Gotlib & C.L. Hammen (Eds.), *Handbook of depression* (pp. 467–491). New York: Guilford Press.

Westbrook, D., Mueller, M., Kennerley, H., & McManus, F. (2010). Common problems in therapy. In M. Mueller, H. Kennerley, F. McManus, & D. Westbrook (Eds.). *Surviving as a CBT therapist* (pp. 1–40). Oxford: Oxford University Press.

II
Handling Complexity

5

Working with Co-Morbid Depression and Anxiety Disorders
A Multiple Diagnostic Approach

Adrian Whittington

I was a driven, ambitious person until five years ago when I broke my back. After that, things I used to think were important weren't any more. I had to give up work and was in hospital for months. The doctors said that I had been millimetres away from being paralysed. When I left hospital I felt very low. I didn't know what to do with myself. I felt like the old me was gone. I'm waking a lot in the night with pain and constantly tired. Then I had my first panic attack. These have been going on for a year now. I don't see how I can build up any kind of life for myself – I just can't go anywhere outside the house any more. I feel like an attack could strike at any time, even more so when I am tired or feeling miserable. Brian (aged 51)

Introduction

Co-morbidity of depression and anxiety disorders is very common, yet the development of CBT has been marked by the definition and evaluation of interventions focused on single disorders. The interventions with the most robust evidence base have tended to highlight and target a "primary" problem that is the focus of the treatment (although co-morbidity is common in trial populations too). As a result, single-focus specific treatments have been widely disseminated and effective treatment has been provided to large numbers of people with depression and anxiety disorders.

Trainee CBT therapists are often encouraged to learn the application of these approaches with relatively "straightforward" cases where co-morbidity is not significant. However, in routine practice after qualification, co-morbid presentations may not resemble closely these training cases. This can contribute to therapists feeling uncertain about how best to conceptualize, plan and intervene when a client has difficulties with two or more conditions. Co-morbidity can be associated with reduced treatment effectiveness, but is not always, suggesting that some adjustments to single-condition CBT may be more helpful than others.

How to Become a More Effective CBT Therapist: Mastering Metacompetence in Clinical Practice,
First Edition. Edited by Adrian Whittington and Nick Grey.
© 2014 John Wiley & Sons, Ltd. Published 2014 by John Wiley & Sons, Ltd.

This chapter reviews the epidemiology and CBT outcome data regarding co-morbid depression and anxiety and suggests procedural rules to apply at assessment, conceptualization and intervention phases of therapy when depression and anxiety disorders occur together. It provides a guide to decision making at each phase, drawing on the evidence base and illustrated with a composite case study of Brian, a 51-year-old man with depression and panic disorder. The chapter focuses on a *multiple diagnostic* approach to conceptualization, treatment planning and intervention, which for each case applies a combination of disorder-specific conceptualizations and adapts disorder-specific interventions to address multiple problems sequentially. This is distinguished from *transdiagnostic* approaches to working with co-morbidity, which combine conceptualization and treatment elements into a coherent single approach for application across different combinations of disorders (see Chapter 6 and Chapter 7 in this book). The present chapter makes tentative recommendations about when each approach should be used.

Co-morbid Depression and Anxiety Disorders: Epidemiology and Therapy Outcomes

Co-morbid depression and anxiety disorder is commonplace in the population as a whole, and those seeking treatment. In a large scale US epidemiological survey, 57.5 per cent of those meeting diagnostic criteria for major depressive disorder also met criteria for an anxiety disorder within the same year (Kessler et al., 2003). An English epidemiological study found that the presence of depression was highly correlated with nine other conditions including generalized anxiety disorder (GAD), obsessive compulsive disorder (OCD), post-traumatic stress disorder (PTSD), panic disorder and phobias (McManus, Meltzer, Brugha, Bebbington, & Jenkins, 2009). It was also striking that mixed anxiety and depressive disorder (an ICD-10 diagnosis requiring a disabling level of anxiety and depression symptoms but not meeting full criteria for any other disorder) was more common than all other mood and anxiety disorders put together (McManus et al., 2009). Of those using clinical services, 64 per cent of depressed attenders at a US outpatient clinic also had an anxiety disorder (Brown, Campbell, Lehman, Grisham, & Mancill, 2001). At the same clinic 43 per cent of patients had more than one current anxiety disorder. In addition, multiple co-morbidities of mood and anxiety disorders with other difficulties such as substance misuse, personality disorder or psychosis occur in 2.6 per cent of the population (McManus et al., 2009).

The present chapter focuses on depression and anxiety rather than wider co-morbidities, in order to achieve a manageable scope and as this is where there is the greatest prevalence. People with a combination of depression and anxiety disorder(s) tend to have more severe difficulties, may have increased risk of suicide, and be more likely to relapse than those with depression alone (Andreescu et al., 2007; Keller & Hanks, 1995), yet there has been little attention to designing effective treatments specifically for these types of mixed presentations (Fawcett, Cameron, & Schatzberg, 2010).

A comprehensive review of CBT outcome for treatment of anxiety disorders with co-morbid depression has suggested that co-morbidity can negatively impact outcome, although this effect is by no means universal or total (Bauer, Wilansky-Traynor, & Rector, 2012). This review shows that panic disorder responds well to treatment even when depression is also present, whereas treatment for social anxiety disorder and

Table 5.1 Conclusions based on Bauer et al.'s (2012) review of CBT outcomes for anxiety disorders with depression

Target disorder	Co-morbid depression as a predictor/moderator of anxiety treatment outcomes	Effect of CBT on co-morbid depression diagnosis and/or symptoms
Panic disorder with/without agoraphobia	Similar *rates of improvement* regardless of co-morbidity, although some studies show more residual panic symptoms when there is co-morbid depression.	CBT for Panic Disorder can lead to a reduction or remission in depression, although long-term maintenance of these gains is uncertain.
Social anxiety disorder	Higher levels of depression predict lower benefit of CBT for social anxiety including lower likelihood of maintaining gains at follow-up.	CBT for social anxiety disorder can lead to a reduction in depressive symptoms.
Obsessive compulsive disorder	Severe depression hinders treatment gains in CBT for OCD, while milder depression may have a limited impact.	CBT for OCD can lead to a reduction in depressive symptoms, with stronger indications that cognitive therapy can have this effect than behaviour therapy.
Generalized anxiety disorder	Mixed findings – some suggesting that depression predicts a reduced effect of CBT for GAD, others showing no impact and some showing apparent improved outcomes when depression is also present.	CBT for GAD can lead to a reduction in depressive symptoms and reduction in number of co-morbid mood and anxiety disorders.
Post-traumatic stress disorder	Only one case series is reported. A subsequent large UK study not reported in the review found that co-morbid mood disorder was a moderator of PTSD treatment outcome (Ehlers et al., 2013).	CBT for PTSD also leads to reductions in and remission in depression, maintained up to 12 months later.

OCD can be less effective in the presence of co-morbid depression. Evidence is mixed or insufficient to reach any clear conclusion in the case of CBT for GAD and PTSD in the presence of depression. Overall, the evidence does not suggest that disorder-specific approaches to anxiety disorders should be abandoned in the presence of co-morbid depression, but implies that some modifications may be necessary to maximize benefit. There are also consistent findings across disorders that treating a target anxiety disorder is likely to lead to reductions or sometimes remission in the co-morbid depression. A summary of the results of the review across disorders is presented in Table 5.1.

Treating one anxiety disorder can also impact on the severity of symptoms of other co-morbid anxiety disorders (Brown, Antony, & Barlow, 1995; Tsao, Mystkowski, Zucker, & Craske, 2005) although it appears that such effects can be incomplete, with benefit usually falling short of remission in the co-morbid conditions (McManus, Shafran, & Cooper, 2010).

Co-morbidity shows similar mixed effects on outcome where the treatment focus is depression. Higher levels of anxiety symptoms can impact on the success of either CBT or pharmacological treatment (Farabaugh et al., 2012). However, treating depression can be successful in the presence of co-morbid social anxiety disorder (Kashdan & Roberts, 2011) and effective treatment of depression can be associated with reductions in anxiety symptoms (Gibbons & DeRubeis, 2008).

Evidence concerning helpful and unhelpful adaptations of CBT in the context of co-morbid conditions is extremely limited, although as examined later in the chapter, there are indications that switching tack too vigorously within the therapy can be less helpful for both the primary problem and the co-morbid condition than sticking to the treatment plan for the primary problem (Craske et al., 2007; Gibbons & DeRubeis, 2008).

Where there is not a good fit with a disorder-specific approach with good evidence base, generic or transdiagnostic CBT conceptualization and intervention offer alternative approaches with a theoretical basis and some empirical support (Dudley, Kuyken, & Padesky, 2011).

A Multiple-Diagnostic Approach

Although disorder-specific approaches to CBT treatment of depression and anxiety disorders have a robust theoretical and evidence base, their use presents a number of challenges. These include (1) how best to apply such an approach with an individual with multiple conditions or diagnoses, and (2) how multiple differing treatments can be disseminated effectively.

These challenges have led to the development of alternative transdiagnostic approaches to conceptualization or treatment (See Chapters 6 and 7). These have drawn together core features of a range of conditions and use CBT principles to understand maintenance and to intervene by targeting common processes. One such approach combines CBT for depression and anxiety disorders into a unified protocol that allows the flexible application of a number of distinct modules of treatment depending on need (Barlow et al., 2011). This unified protocol has shown promising results in early trials (Ellard, Fairholme, Boisseau, Farchione, & Barlow, 2010; Farchione et al., 2012).

Transdiagnostic approaches build on generic CBT principles that allow formulation of the maintenance of cognitive-behavioural-emotional cycles of difficulty (e.g. Beck, 1995; Padesky & Mooney, 1990). While these approaches show promise, the evidence base for transdiagnostic intervention remains at an early stage of development.

The present chapter focuses instead on a multiple-diagnostic approach – the adaptation of empirically supported disorder specific approaches in order to tackle multiple conditions. This multiple-diagnostic approach is the way that multiple problems have typically been tackled in trials of disorder-specific treatments. This chapter proposes when this approach might be applied and when other approaches should be considered. Procedural guidance at each stage of assessment, conceptualization, treatment planning and intervention is outlined.

Assessment

Assessment methods for CBT have been outlined in detail elsewhere (Sanders & Wills, 2005; Westbrook, Kennerley, & Kirk, 2011), and form a cornerstone of effective therapy. Assessment needs to be holistic and comprehensive, including a broad social and occupational history, current relationships, drug and alcohol use, strengths and aspirations. From a multiple-diagnostic perspective, where there are co-morbid disorders accurate identification of these disorders will be a fundamental requirement as part of this assessment. This has been reflected in research trials of disorder-specific interventions, which have typically employed structured diagnostic screening in order to match interventions to primary presenting problems. However, formal diagnostic screening is less common in routine practice of CBT. Possible reasons for this include limitations of time and of therapist competence as well as potential reluctance among therapists to adopt a diagnostic frame.

Some clients find that naming their experience using a diagnostic label is helpful, allowing the problems to be externalized and differentiated from their personal identity. Others, however, find a diagnostic label constricting or stigmatizing, for example, if it carries meanings associated with biological illness that could limit belief in personal agency to effect change.

To apply a disorder-specific approach to multiple disorders, however, therapists do need to understand the different symptom patterns (i.e., diagnoses) that guide differing CBT treatments. The purpose here is not to shoe-horn clients into diagnostic categories that may not of themselves explain what is happening, but to recognize the specific maintenance factors implicated within the different disorder-specific CBT models. This will enable the most relevant (and therefore helpful) explanatory formulation model(s) to be applied. The identification of different types of difficulty or disorder can be explored at assessment while also recognizing the limitations of a diagnostic frame and language to make sense of an individual's experiences.

Having completed a thorough assessment a therapist well versed in the problem specific competencies for treatment of specific anxiety disorders and depression (Roth & Pilling, 2007) then faces a matching task to determine whether one or more particular disorder-specific CBT models for anxiety and/or depression offer a good fit with the client's difficulties for which they are seeking help. The "treatment choice decision tree" presented in Figure 5.1 proposes the most appropriate courses of action in the event of a good enough match to a single disorder, to multiple disorders, a poor or no match to a recognized CBT model, or a better match to a non-CBT model. Across each of these scenarios informed client choice of intervention should be treated as paramount.

Good enough match – single disorder
Where there is a single disorder that matches a proven disorder-specific approach well, the best evidence currently is to pursue disorder-specific treatment according to the usual protocol (Dudley et al., 2011; McManus et al., 2010).

Good enough match – multiple disorders
To date, research has not adequately addressed the question of the best sequencing or adaptation of disorder-specific treatment when there is co-morbidity. Typically research trials have identified and targeted a "primary" problem, although how this is identified is often not clearly defined. Evidence-based treatment guidance in the United Kingdom makes some initial recommendations regarding sequencing of treatment where there is co-morbid anxiety and depression, as shown in Table 5.2. These recommendations are tentative and vary in sophistication and detail, but together propose a sequential approach to disorder specific treatment. A variety of factors are suggested

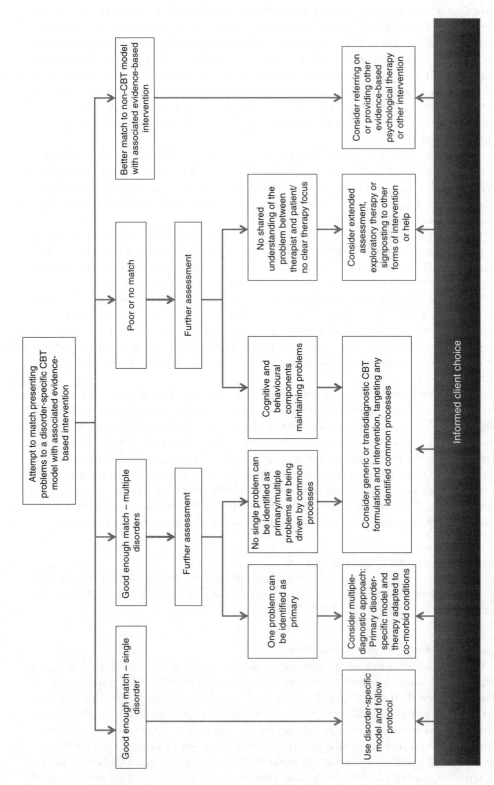

Figure 5.1 Treatment choice decision tree. © Adrian Whittington (2013).

Table 5.2   Recommendations from UK anxiety and depression treatment guidance regarding sequencing of treatment with co-morbid depression and anxiety (National Institute for Health and Care Excellence (NICE), 2005a, 2005b, 2009, 2011, 2013)

NICE guideline topic	Published	Recommended to consider for sequencing of treatment
Depression	2009	For depression accompanied by *symptoms* of anxiety – treat depression first.
		For anxiety *disorder* and co-morbid depression or depressive symptoms, consult the relevant anxiety guideline and consider treating anxiety disorder first as effective treatment of this can lead to improvement in depression.
Generalised anxiety disorder	2011	Treat the primary disorder first (the one that is more severe and for which it is more likely that treatment will improve overall functioning)
Panic disorder with or without agoraphobia	2011	Identify treatment priority by drawing up a timeline of when the different problems developed.
Obsessive compulsive disorder	2005	No guidance on sequencing
Post-traumatic stress disorder	2005	For PTSD and depression – treat PTSD first as effective treatment of this can lead to improvement in depression.
		With severe depression that makes initial psychological treatment of PTSD very difficult (for example, with extreme lack of energy and concentration, inactivity, or high suicide risk), treat the depression first.
Social Anxiety Disorder	2013	If depression started before social anxiety disorder, treat depression first. Treat the social anxiety when improvement in depression allows.
		If social anxiety disorder started before depression, ask the client whether they would still be depressed if the social anxiety disorder was successfully treated.
		• If they answer "no" – treat social anxiety disorder first (but if severity of depression prevents this, treat depression first)
		• If they answer "yes" – treat social anxiety and depression, taking account of client preference for what to treat first.

Note: This table covers the main NICE guidance on co-morbid anxiety disorders and depression in adults. NICE guidance also recommends how to manage other co-morbidities such as substance misuse and personality disorder

by the guidelines as important in determining the sequencing of treatment, including which disorder is:

- the most severe;
- the target for treatment that could most improve overall functioning;
- the greatest priority to the client; and
- the first to develop and therefore possibly driving the others.[1]

There is very little evidence to point to the relative importance of each of these factors or how they should be determined, but information should be gathered regarding each of these areas for building a conceptualization and to support treatment planning. Severity and impact of different conditions can be measured using disorder-specific scales (see Chapter 18) or using simple 0–10 scales for the distress and interference with life of the different problems.

Given the evidence that treating one condition often leads to improvement in others, there are good grounds for trying to identify the primary problem and tackling this first. This initial course of treatment can be adapted around secondary problems if necessary and these can be treated more directly if they remain at the end. This has been the approach used in most trials from which empirically supported treatments have been derived.

Even when there are multiple identifiable disorders, it is not always possible to identify one of these as clearly "primary". For example, this may occur when there are multiple problems that are maintaining one another, with roughly equal impact or when there are clear common processes underlying several disorders. These circumstances may be good reasons to consider the use of a generic or transdiagnostic CBT approach.

There is limited empirical evidence to guide this choice. However, multiple-diagnostic and transdiagnostic approaches are underpinned by a common principle – that identifying and reversing key maintaining cognitive and behavioural processes can relieve distress. The difference between them is in how this is achieved. A multiple diagnostic approach, by drawing on disorder-specific models, offers specific pointers as to which cognitive themes are of most relevance for particular conditions. Transdiagnostic approaches focus on the identification of shared cognitive themes that run across several different conditions.

Poor or no match

Naturally not all client experiences leading to seeking therapy will map onto disorder-specific models of conceptualization and treatment. In some cases, where the client can describe the difficulties in terms of maintaining cycles of cognition, behaviour and emotion, the use of a generic CBT formulation (e.g., Padesky & Mooney, 1990) may well be helpful in guiding the use of generic CBT techniques (e.g., activity scheduling, cognitive restructuring or behavioural experiments) to tackle the problems. While there is limited evidence supporting the efficacy of this approach beyond the treatment of depression, it has a sound theoretical rationale, aiming to target key maintaining cognitions and behaviours.

Sometimes therapist and client are not able to reach a consensus on the nature of the problem (e.g., the client sees the difficulty as others nagging him, whereas therapist believes client has a significant substance misuse problem), or the problems may be seem diffuse and hard to define. In either of these circumstances extended assessment and development of a shared idiosyncratic formulation can be powerful. Sometimes, more exploratory therapy may be indicated to allow time to develop an understanding of less clear issues or concerns.

Better match to a non-CBT model

Sometimes another model of therapy is a better fit than individual CBT. For example, couple therapy should be considered if the main focus of concern is a relationship issue.

Conceptualization and treatment planning

In the event of co-morbid problems with anxiety disorder and depression, conceptualization will be critical to determine how the multiple problems relate to one another and whether one problem can helpfully be seen as "primary" and driving the other(s). This section addresses how therapists can make decisions about how to proceed,

Box 5.1   Brian: assessment summary

Brian, a 51-year-old man, had worked for many years as a manager at a car fac-tory. He suffered multiple fractured vertebrae two years ago when he fell from a ladder while painting his house. Brian described a happy childhood and a good relationship with his wife. He had a son in his twenties. He had spent five months in hospital following the accident and had regained full function and mobility but suffered significant pain at night when lying down. He had agreed to an early retirement package as he felt he would never be able to return to his former work. After returning home from hospital Brian arranged several activities such as a holiday with his wife and son, and trips to sports events. He had his first panic attack on a holiday to Spain a year ago and another a few months later at a foot-ball match. On both occasions he felt faint and nauseous and was concerned he would pass out, so he sat down and put his head between his knees. He did not pass out. Brian had been reassured by paramedics on the second occasion that his symptoms were caused by anxiety but he had become gradually more withdrawn since then, and was no longer leaving the house for fear of having a panic attack. He was still concerned that in a bad attack he could pass out. Brian described feeling miserable and low all the time and often feeling unable to get out of bed in the morning because he was so tired. Brian met diagnostic criteria for both major depression (moderately severe) and panic disorder.

   In Brian's case there was therefore a clear match to two problems with proven disorder specific CBT treatments.

deciding with their clients what the primary problem is when there is a multiple match to disorder-specific models. This decision needs to be based on:

1.   your conceptualization of how the problems are related;
2.   the evidence base for the potential disorder-specific approaches and any evidence regarding implications of co-morbidity;
3.   your client's goals; and
4.   your client's choice.

These elements are core to any CBT treatment and allow the coverage and coherent organization of the various factors identified for consideration in treatment guidance as determinants of treatment sequencing. Severity, impact of problems, relative priority to the client and sequence of onset of different problems should all be taken account of when negotiating client goals, arriving at a conceptualization and reviewing the evi-dence base. Each of these elements is important, but it is an ethical imperative that informed client choice takes precedence over the others. Each element is reviewed below, illustrated with the implications for work with Brian (see Box 5.1).

Conceptualization
An understanding of how the problems are related will be critical for the decision about how to proceed. Drawing out idiosyncratic conceptualization diagrams for each disorder for your own use and for review in supervision can help with this. Look at the disorder-specific conceptualizations and consider how they may be linked. Are key cognitions,

behaviours, emotions or physical sensations implicated in one disorder triggering or maintaining another disorder? These can be good questions to explore with your client.

Producing complex diagrams of multiple problems *with your client* can feel overwhelming to them, however (Chadwick, Williams, & Mackenzie, 2003). Usually a simpler shared conceptualization will be more helpful, perhaps showing key maintaining cycles or just the primary disorder once this has been identified.

The following transcript is an example of a discussion early in therapy to explore the interplay between depression and panic for Brian:

THERAPIST (TH):	So, um, what ideas do you have about whether the depression and the difficulties with panic might be linked?
BRIAN (BR):	I don't know… I definitely felt very low before I had the first panic attack … but having panic attacks has just made the whole thing worse. It's all one big mess [looks upset].
TH:	I can see how anyone would feel a bit overwhelmed and that it feels hard to find a way out. Maybe we can work on this together?
BR:	I really would like to find a way out of it.
TH:	Ok, so let's look at how the two problems might be linked. If we were able to magic away the panic attacks tomorrow, do you think you would still be depressed?
BR:	I wish you could do that! [laughs] No, I think I would feel I had hope and could start to rebuild my life.
TH:	And what about if it was the other way round and we could take away the depression by magic – do you think you would still have panic attacks?
BR:	Um … that's hard to say. I don't really know because it seems to me they are caused more by not sleeping than the depression. When I've had a bad night with pain, that's when I am really aware of feeling on edge and like I'm going to faint.
TH:	Mmmm. I was wondering if feeling low sometimes makes your sleep worse too?
BR:	Yes, sometimes … definitely, I wake up early, full of worries about the day ahead.
TH:	Mmmhm … I see. So let me check out whether I have understood correctly – it seems to you that the panic attacks are keeping you feeling low, but that feeling low also affects your sleep, which makes you worry more about a panic attack?
BR:	It's a vicious cycle really isn't it?

Based on this sort of dialogue it is possible to identify maintaining links between multiple disorders. Idiosyncratic maintenance conceptualization diagrams for Brian are shown in Figure 5.2. These highlight the typical maintaining patterns within each disorder but also how the two appear to be linked and maintaining each other. Brian's therapist took this diagram to supervision and used it as a guide to decide how to proceed.

The conceptualization highlights the reciprocal relationship between depression and panic disorder for Brian. Panic is influencing depression by limiting the range of Brian's activities, whereas depression is influencing panic by exacerbating physical trigger sensations for panic. This presents two options from a multiple-diagnostic perspective: (1) treat the depression as primary and in the process reduce trigger sensations for panic, or (2) treat the panic as primary and thereby increase the range of potentially mood enhancing activity. Reducing trigger sensations is unlikely to represent a solution to panic because (1) sensations associated with tiredness would be likely to continue to

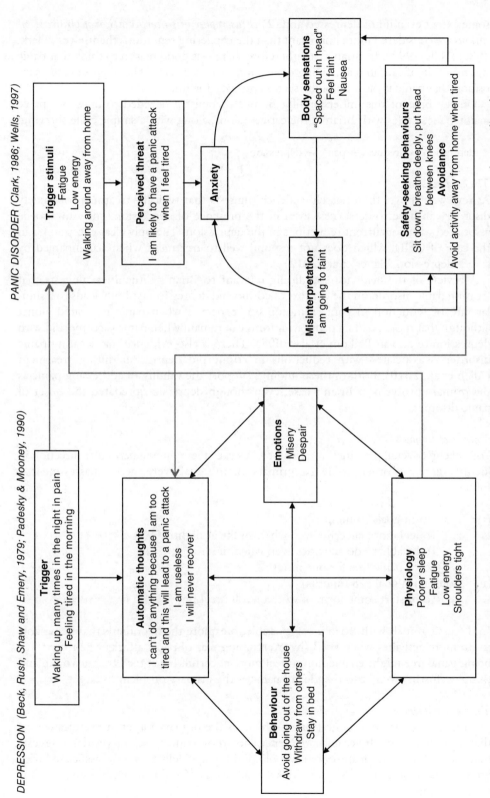

Figure 5.2 Brian's idiosyncratic conceptualization of depression and panic disorder, showing maintaining links between the two disorders.

some extent even if not depressed and (2) *catastrophic misinterpretation of physical sensations* are considered more important than the triggering sensations themselves (Clark, 1986; Wells, 1997). In Brian's case therefore there was good reason to think that panic was more significant in maintaining depression than vice versa. This supports the proposition that panic is most helpfully seen as primary for Brian.

On the basis of this understanding Brian's therapist proceeded to draw out panic maintenance cycles with Brian in the early sessions, along with a simple cycle showing:

depression → tiredness → panic → depression

The evidence base
As reviewed above, the research evidence suggests that typically treatment of anxiety disorder can have some success even in the presence of depression, and can also be associated with concurrent reductions in the depression. The only clear exception is in the case of OCD, which does not respond well to treatment when accompanied by severe depression (Bauer et al., 2012).

A review of the evidence specifically relevant to Brian's difficulties suggests that treating panic disorder in the context of co-morbid depression typically leads to a similar rate of reduction in panic symptoms as expected when panic is treated alone, although that more residual panic symptoms can remain when panic is co-morbid with depression (e.g., van Balkom et al., 2008). There is also evidence that treating panic disorder is associated with reductions in co-morbid depression during treatment (Allen et al., 2010). Both of these findings support the validity of addressing panic as the primary problem in Brian's case, even though depression predated the onset of panic disorder.

Your client's goals
Your client's overall priorities in terms of goals can steer you in a particular direction in identifying one or other problem as primary. Brian's goals were agreed at assessment as follows:

(i)   Short-term goals (6 months)
    a.   To feel more cheerful even when awake at night.
    b.   To be able to do activities even when tired.
    c.   To be panic free for one month.
(ii) Long-term goal (18 months)
    To re-start some form of work or volunteering.

In discussing goals with Brian it was possible to explore the hypothesis that being able to do more activities when tired (by overcoming fear of panic attacks when tired), or being panic free might enable him to feel more cheerful. He agreed that it would, and this gave further weight to the idea of panic as the primary problem to target.

Your client's choice
Even if all other factors suggest one problem as the primary target, it is ethically vital that informed client choice and preference should override these. Survey data suggests that client choice over features of psychological therapy delivery can be associated with improved outcomes (We Need to Talk Coalition, 2010), but much more research is needed in this area.

Informed choice is especially relevant where clients feel unable to tackle one or more anxiety difficulties directly at the time (e.g., through behavioural experiments, exposure or reliving of traumatic memories). In these circumstances it is necessary sensitively to inform clients of the potential limitations to progress that this will imply, but to offer other opportunities for treatment as relevant. For example, it may be possible to tackle depression in the context of ongoing anxiety difficulties.

Brian, understanding the rationale for behavioural experiments, was willing to pursue a treatment plan that he knew would involve creating situations that were likely to make him feel anxious, to test if he really would pass out. However, if he had not felt able to do this, it would still have been possible to treat his depression at least to some extent, with a focus on helping him to adapt to ongoing limitations imposed by his fear of passing out. He might have been helped to adapt cognitively (in terms of reviewing the true meaning of the ongoing limitations) and behaviourally (in terms of discovering what he could still do that would improve his experience of life). However, Brian was willing to undertake the proposed treatment plan, with panic disorder treated as a primary condition, and amendments made to the treatment to address the co-morbid depression.

Intervention

Where a primary problem has been identified, intervention can proceed largely according to the "usual" protocol for the primary condition, but there is also good evidence to suggest particular forms of adaptation to the therapy where there is co-morbidity. This section examines what adaptations should be avoided and how and when helpful adaptations can be made to maximize effectiveness, illustrated with reference to Brian's case.

Avoiding treatment dilution

When faced with multiple conditions it may be tempting for therapists to conduct a combined treatment simultaneously addressing targets across different conditions. This may sometimes occur in a haphazard fashion, with therapists switching tack to try to "cherry pick" targets for treatment from the different conditions as they crop up in therapy. This approach does not have a sound evidence base and may reduce the effect of CBT across the client's different problems.

Two trials illustrate the risks of treatment dilution in "straying" away from primary treatment. In one novel trial of CBT, clients with panic disorder and at least one other mood or anxiety disorder were either given group and individual CBT for panic disorder, or group CBT for panic disorder alongside individual CBT for the most severe co-morbid disorder. Those receiving therapy targeting two conditions, said to mimic therapeutic straying, made less progress on both panic outcomes and outcomes for the co-morbid condition, compared to those receiving the "pure" panic treatment (Craske et al., 2007). Similar results indicating the dangers of straying from a clear focus come from a trial of CBT for depression where some patients had high levels of anxiety symptoms. During the trial therapy recordings were analysed for the amount of focus by therapists in the sessions on either anxiety or depression. A more mixed focus was associated with reduced impact on both depression and anxiety, compared to a single, depression focus (Gibbons & DeRubeis, 2008). These trials suggest that within a limited time frame, sticking to a clear focus on treating a primary problem is desirable.

In Brian's case intervention focused on the treatment of primary panic disorder by re-evaluating the meaning of sensations of light-headedness that he experienced when tired, using both verbal reattribution and behavioural experiments. Temptation to stray into extended examination of Brian's negative cognitions about himself and the future ("I am useless" and "I will never recover") was resisted early in therapy, as it was hypothesized that powerful evidence regarding these cognitions would be derived from progress in overcoming panic disorder.

Addressing treatment interference from secondary conditions

While it will be important to avoid treatment dilution through unnecessary "straying", at times there will be a need to address hindrances to the primary treatment caused by interference from other co-morbid conditions. For example, depressive cognitions commonly interfere with anxiety disorder treatment by reducing hope and motivation. Anxious avoidance commonly interferes with depression treatment by reducing access to potentially rewarding activities and social support. In order to retain focus on the primary treatment in most situations these interferences are best addressed through collaborative problem solving, for example, by normalizing the obstacle (e.g., "it is really common for people to find that anxiety can make them want to avoid pursuing new activities even though these might help them to feel happier"), and discussing how the obstacle could be overcome in order to move forward (e.g., "how do you think we could find out whether going out with your friend would in reality be a helpful thing to do for your mood overall?").

The following excerpt illustrates how depressive cognitions presented an obstacle in Brian's treatment for panic disorder. It shows how these cognitions interfered with conducting a behavioural experiment for homework several sessions into the therapy. The proposed experiment followed some in-session behavioural experiments inducing faint feelings and involved getting up in the morning at the same time as his wife, even if tired, and going for a walk around his local neighbourhood – to see if he passed out.

THERAPIST (TH):	So shall we review the experiment we planned last time – you said there were some difficulties?
BRIAN (BR):	Well, I woke up when the alarm went off, but I'd had a really bad night and felt really bad – exhausted. I just couldn't get up and do it.
TH:	Oh, I'm sorry to hear that … sounds like it felt really hard. What was running through your mind after the alarm went off?
BR:	Just that I've got to get up and do this, but I'm too tired. And that I'm never going to get over this if I can't even walk round the block. I just felt useless.
TH:	I see … So those thoughts "I'm useless" and "I'm never going to recover" came up again for you?
BR:	Yes, I felt really low all day afterwards. In fact I stayed in bed most of the day.
TH:	Yes, I'm not surprised. I would also feel really low if I believed those things – and they are common things to believe when we get depressed. How much would you say you believe right now that you are useless?
BR:	About 70 per cent
TH:	And that you will never recover?
BR:	About 50.
TH:	Mmmm … What do you think would happen to those beliefs if you were able to get up and do something even when you are tired?
BR:	Er, maybe it would make them a little less powerful.
TH:	How do you think we could test that theory out?
BR:	Can we find something easier for me to try doing one morning, other than walking round the block?
TH:	That sounds like an excellent idea – something less challenging but that still tests that original idea that you will pass out if you do things when you feel those sensations of tiredness?

The depressive cognitions were normalized, measured as an important target for intervention, and explicitly revisited as part of the overall conceptualization and treatment plan. The planning of a new behavioural experiment was linked back to testing panic cognitions (primary treatment) while recognizing the potential value of this in testing interfering depressive cognitions. In this way diverting into cognitive restructuring of depressive cognitions was avoided, allowing immediate re-focus on the panic treatment.

Extending therapy if needed

It may be necessary to extend therapy to deal with residual symptoms of either depression or anxiety when treating co-morbid problems, as residual symptoms of both primary and secondary conditions are common (Bauer et al., 2012). This approach proved successful in a trial that added depression treatment after panic disorder treatment for patients presenting with both conditions. The depression treatment was equally effective for those who had recently completed CBT for panic disorder as it was for a depressed-only control group who had simply waited for the depression treatment (Woody, McLean, Taylor, & Koch, 1999). In a similar vein a dissemination trial of CBT for PTSD added more sessions of treatment for those with co-morbid conditions, and found that as a result co-morbid depression, alcohol abuse or panic disorder did not impact negatively on PTSD outcome (Gillespie, Duffy, Hackman, & Clark, 2002).

Brian's therapy was extended from 12 to 16 sessions, with the final four sessions having a focus on explicit activity scheduling and cognitive restructuring to improve mood further once the panic disorder was largely resolved.

Special attention to relapse prevention

The risk of relapse is higher when there is co-morbidity (Keller & Hanks, 1995). The reasons for this are not clear and could relate to a tendency for therapy to end due to time pressures or treatment dilution when treatment gains are incomplete. Extending therapy will address this possibility, but it is also wise to pay particular attention to relapse prevention with co-morbid cases, identifying relapse signatures and completing a thorough therapy blueprint.

Conclusion

Where there is a good match between client difficulties and multiple evidence-based CBT models of treatment, co-morbid depression and anxiety disorders can respond well to a multiple-diagnostic approach to CBT intervention. This involves identification and treatment for a single primary problem, using a disorder-specific treatment, possibly augmented by additional sessions to tackle residual symptoms. Treatment for a primary anxiety disorder will often lead to improvements in co-morbid depression, and treatment for primary depression can lead to reductions in co-morbid anxiety symptoms. However, there is a risk in switching tack to deal with secondary problems as it can lead to a dilution of the primary treatment and worse outcomes for both/all problems. Instead it can be appropriate to normalize interference from elements of other disorders in the primary treatment, identify the importance of these factors as targets for the therapy, problem solve to overcome interference and, if the conceptualization supports it, refocus on the primary treatment as a way to address them.

Procedural Rules

- Do a thorough assessment to determine which diagnoses or disorder-specific models may match the pattern of your client's difficulties. Then follow the "treatment choice decision tree" to decide how to conceptualize and intervene, taking full account of your client's informed choices:
  - i.   If there is a good match with a single disorder model, offer the "usual" disorder-specific approach.
  - ii. If there is a good match with more than one disorder-specific CBT model, decide whether one disorder can be identified as "primary" and if so offer a multiple diagnostic approach.
  - iii. If there are clear common processes underlying multiple disorders consider a transdiagnostic or generic CBT approach.
  - iv. If there is a poor or no match with disorder-specific CBT models consider using a generic CBT approach, other evidence-based intervention, extended assessment, referral or signposting.
- If embarking on a multiple diagnostic approach:
  - i.   Decide what problem might be considered "primary" based on:
    - a.   your conceptualization of how the problems are related;
    - b.   the evidence base for the treatments in the context of co-morbidity;
    - c.   your client's goals; and
    - d.   your client's choice.
  - ii. Stick to the treatment for the primary problem and avoid diluting this with haphazard forays into tackling secondary conditions.
  - iii. Address interference from secondary conditions by normalizing these, explicitly rehearsing their role in the conceptualization and treatment plan, problem solving, and where possible refocusing on the primary treatment as a means of also addressing these secondary problems.
  - iv. Extend therapy to address residual symptoms of the primary or secondary conditions.
  - v.   Pay special attention to planning for relapse prevention.

Acknowledgements

With thanks to Willem Kuyken, Roz Shafran, Helen Curr and Nick Grey who commented on earlier drafts of this chapter and to participants in a training workshop at the University of Sussex who reviewed an earlier version of the treatment choice decision tree.

Note

1   Caution should be applied in considering earlier onset as an indication of the primary disorder. While people with anxiety disorder(s) and depression often develop an anxiety disorder first (Andrade et al., 2003), this temporal relationship may simply reflect an earlier age of onset for anxiety disorders than depression that is also seen among those with only one condition (Brown et al., 2001).

References

Allen, L., White, K., Barlow, D., Shear, M., Gorman, J., & Woods, S. (2010). Cognitive-behaviour therapy (CBT) for panic disorder: relationship of anxiety and depression comorbidity with treatment outcome. *Journal of Psychopathology and Behavioural Assessment, 32*, 185–192.

Andrade, L., Bergland, P., Bijl, R., DeGraaf, R., Vollebergh, W., Dragomirecka, E., ... Wittchen, H. (2003). The epidemiology of major depressive episodes. Results from the international consortium of psychiatric epidemiology (ICPE) surveys. *International Journal of Methods in Psychiatry Research, 12*, 3–21.

Andreescu, C., Lenze, E., Dew, M., Begley, A., Mulsant, B., Dombrovski, A., ... Reynolds, C. (2007). Effect of comorbid anxiety on treatment response and relapse risk in late-life depression: controlled study. *British Journal of Psychiatry, 190*, 344–349.

Barlow, D., Farchione, T., Fairholme, C., Ellard, K., Boisseau, C., Allen, L., & Ehrenreich-May, J. (2011). *Unified protocol for the transdiagnostic treatment of emotional disorders. Therapist guide.* Oxford: Oxford University Press.

Bauer, I., Wilansky-Traynor, P., & Rector, N. (2012). Cognitive-behavioural therapy for anxiety disorders with comorbid depression: A review. *International Journal of Cognitive Therapy, 5*, 118–156.

Beck, A., Rush, A., Shaw, B., & Emery, G. (1979). *Cognitive therapy of depression.* New York: Guildford Press.

Beck, J. (1995). *Cognitive therapy. Basics and beyond.* New York: Guildford Press.

Brown, T., Antony, M., & Barlow, D. (1995). Diagnostic comorbidity in panic disorder: effect on treatment outcome and course of comorbid diagnoses following treatment. *Journal of Consulting and Clinical Psychology, 76*, 695–703.

Brown, T., Campbell, L., Lehman, C., Grisham, J., & Mancill, R. (2001). Current and lifetime comorbidity of the DSM-IV anxiety and mood disorders in a large clinical sample. *Journal of Abnormal Psychology, 110*, 585–599.

Chadwick, P., Williams, C., & Mackenzie, J. (2003). Impact of case formulation in cognitive-behaviour therapy for psychosis. *Behaviour Research and Therapy, 41*, 671–680.

Clark, D.M. (1986). A cognitive model of panic. *Behaviour Research and Therapy, 24*, 461–470.

Craske, M., Farchione, T., Allen, L., Barrios, V., Stoyanova, M., & Rose, R. (2007). Cognitive behavioural therapy for panic disorder and comorbidity: more of the same or less of more? *Behaviour Research and Therapy, 45*, 1095–1109.

Dudley, R., Kuyken, W., & Padesky, C. (2011). Disorder specific and trans-diagnostic case conceptualisation. *Clinical Psychology Review, 31*, 213–224.

Ehlers, A., Grey, N., Wild, J., Stott, R., Liness, S., Deale, A., ... Clark, D.M. (2013). Dissemination of cognitive therapy for PTSD in routine clinical care: effectiveness and moderators of outcome in a consecutive sample. *Behaviour Research and Therapy, 51*(11), 742–752. doi: 10.1016/j.brat.2013.08.006.

Ellard, K., Fairholme, C., Boisseau, C., Farchione, T., & Barlow, D. (2010). Unified protocol for the transdiagnostic treatment of emotional disorders: protocol development and initial outcome data. *Cognitive and Behavioral Practice, 17*(1), 88–101.

Farabaugh, A., Alpert, J., Wisniewski, S., Otto, M., Fava, M., Baer, L., ... Thase, M. (2012). Cognitive therapy for anxious depression in STAR*D: what have we learned? *Journal of Affective Disorders, 142*, 213–218.

Farchione, T., Fairholme, C., Ellard, K., Boisseau, C., Thompson-Hollands, J., Carl, J., ... Barlow, D. (2012). Unified protocol for transdiagnostic treatment of emotional disorders: A randomized controlled trial. *Behaviour Therapy, 43*(3), 666–678.

Fawcett, J., Cameron, R.P., & Schatzberg, A.F. (2010). Mixed anxiety-depressive disorder: an undiagnosed and undertreated severity spectrum? In D. Stein, E. Hollander and B. Rothbaum (Eds.), *Textbook of Anxiety Disorders* (2nd ed., pp. 241–257). Washington DC: American Psychiatric Publishing.

Gibbons, C., & DeRubeis, R. (2008). Anxiety symptom focus in sessions of cognitive therapy for depression. *Behavior Therapy, 39*, 117–125.

Gillespie, K., Duffy, M., Hackmann, A., & Clark, D.M. (2002). Community-based cognitive therapy in the treatment of post-traumatic stress disorder following the Omagh bomb. *Behaviour Research and Therapy, 40*, 345–357. doi: 10.1016/S0005-7967(02)00004-9

Kashdan, T., & Roberts, J. (2011). Comorbid social anxiety disorder in clients with depressive disorders: predicting changes in depressive symptoms, therapeutic relationships, and focus of attention in group treatment. *Behaviour Research and Therapy, 49*, 857–884.

Keller, M., & Hanks, D. (1995). Anxiety symptom relief in depression treatment outcomes. *Journal of Clinical Psychiatry, 56*, 22–29.

Kessler, R., Berglund, P., Demler, O., Jin, R., Koretz, D., Merikangas, K., ... Wang, P. (2003). The epidemiology of major depressive disorder. Results from the national comorbidity survey replication (NCS-R). *Journal of the American Medical Association, 289*, 3095–3105.

McManus, F., Shafran, R., & Cooper, Z. (2010). What does a "transdiagnostic" approach have to offer the treatment of anxiety disorders? *British Journal of Clinical Psychology, 49*, 491–505.

McManus, S., Meltzer, H., Brugha, T., Bebbington, P., & Jenkins, R. (2009). *Adult psychiatric morbidity in England, 2007: results of a household survey.* London: National Centre for Social Research.

National Institute for Health and Clinical Excellence. (2005a). *Obsessive-compulsive disorder: core interventions in the treatment of obsessive-compulsive disorder and body dysmorphic disorder.* NICE clinical guideline 31. Retrieved from www.nice.org.uk/cg031

National Institute for Health and Clinical Excellence. (2005b). *Post-traumatic Stress disorder (PTSD). The management of PTSD in adults and children in primary and secondary care.* NICE clinical guideline 26. Retrieved from www.nice.org.uk/cg026

National Institute for Health and Clinical Excellence. (2009). *The treatment and management of depression in adults.* NICE clinical guideline 90. Retrieved from http://guidance.nice.org.uk/cg90

National Institute for Health and Clinical Excellence. (2011). *Generalised anxiety disorder and panic disorder (with or without agoraphobia) in adults. Management in primary, secondary and community care.* NICE clinical guideline 113. Retrieved from http://guidance.nice.org.uk/CG113

National Institute for Health and Care Excellence. (2013). *Social anxiety disorder: recognition, assessment and treatment.* NICE Clinical Guideline 159. Retrieved from http://guidance.nice.org.uk/cg159

Padesky, C.A., & Mooney, K.A. (1990). Clinical tip: presenting the cognitive model to clients. *International Cognitive Therapy Newsletter, 6*, 13–14. Retrieved from http://padesky.com/newpad/wp-content/uploads/2012/11/v6no_1_2_present_model1.pdf

Roth, A., & Pilling, S. (2007). The competences required to deliver effective cognitive and behavioural therapy for people with depression and with anxiety disorders. Improving Access to Psychological Therapies (IAPT) Programme. Retrieved from http://www.ucl.ac.uk/clinical-psychology/CORE/CBT_Competences/CBT_Competence_List.pdf

Sanders, D., & Wills, F. (2005). *Cognitive therapy: an introduction.* London: Sage.

Tsao, J., Mystowski, J., Zucker, B., & Craske, M. (2005). Impact of cognitive-behavioural therapy for panic disorder on comorbidity: a controlled investigation. *Behaviour Research and Therapy, 43*, 959–970.

van Balkom, A., van Boeijen, C., Boeke, A., van Oppen, P., Kempe, P., & van Dyck, R. (2008). Comorbid depression, but not comorbid anxiety disorders, predicts poor outcome in anxiety disorders. *Depression and Anxiety, 25*, 408–415.

We Need to Talk Coalition (2010). We need to talk. Getting the right therapy at the right time. Retrieved from http://www.mind.org.uk/media/280583/We-Need-to-Talk-getting-the-right-therapy-at-the-right-time.pdf

Wells, A. (1997). *Cognitive therapy of anxiety disorders: a practice manual and conceptual guide.* New York: John Wiley & Sons.

Westbrook, D., Kennerley, H., & Kirk, J. (2011). *An introduction to cognitive behaviour therapy: skills and applications* (2nd ed.). London: Sage.

Woody, S., McClean, P., Taylor, S., & Koch, W. (1999). Treatment of major depression in the context of panic disorder. *Journal of Affective Disorders, 53*, 163–174.

6

Collaborative Case Conceptualization

Three Principles and Five Steps for Working with Complex Cases

Robert Kidney and Willem Kuyken

Rationale for Case Conceptualization

During an extended assessment session you agree with your new client, Mel, a list of presenting issues and goals to work on in therapy (see Box 6.1).

Further information supplied to you by Mel tells you that in her family of origin, her parents argued a great deal throughout her childhood and that both parents drank heavily. Mel's father, who was in the army, was verbally, physically and emotionally abusive to both Mel and her sister. Mel became a single parent at 16 after her mum refused to support her decision to have an abortion. Her younger sister, with whom Mel was quite close, left home to escape her father and lived on the streets as a sex worker using drugs during her teenage years. In adulthood, Mel has a history of making suicide attempts, often precipitated by a relationship conflict. She is divorced from her first husband with whom she had two children and lives with a partner. Her relationship with her partner is up and down and Mel has a tendency to withdraw whenever there is conflict.

As Mel's CBT therapist:

1. How do you conceptualize her presenting issues?
2. How do you begin to articulate a treatment plan that will help her move towards her therapy goals?
3. What CBT approaches do you use? If several seem appropriate, how do you integrate and/or sequence them?

The classic CBT protocols carefully characterize clients with particular disorders, set out a cognitive account of each disorder and then outline a treatment protocol that

How to Become a More Effective CBT Therapist: Mastering Metacompetence in Clinical Practice,
First Edition. Edited by Adrian Whittington and Nick Grey.
© 2014 John Wiley & Sons, Ltd. Published 2014 by John Wiley & Sons, Ltd.

Box 6.1   Mel's presenting issues and goals for therapy

Presenting issues:
A lifelong history of recurrent depression
Very up and down mood
Alcohol use at more than 40 units per week
Debt
Family conflict
Social anxiety

Goals:
Be a good mum (more shared positive time with my daughter)
Feel happier (go out with friends, smile, fun activities with partner, BDI-II
  scores down)
Reduce alcohol intake (within guidelines)

---

addresses the particular beliefs and behaviours that characterize that disorder. How do you conceptualize when clients present with several disorders? In Mel's case, for example, she presents with recurrent depression, alcohol dependence, self-harm and some evidence of longstanding interpersonal difficulties. In addition, what do you do when the issues clients present are life problems rather than disorders, such as in Mel's case where she has problems in her relationships and debt?

In short, how do you best use your training, experience and knowledge of CBT theory and protocols to help this person, at this stage in their life, with the particular issues and goals you agree to work with in therapy?

A New Model of Case Conceptualization

In this chapter, we set out a model of case conceptualization that therapists can use to develop an individualized description and understanding of a client's presenting issues. Case conceptualization is defined as

> a process whereby therapist and client work collaboratively to first describe and then to explain in cognitive-behavioural terms the issues a client presents in therapy. Its primary function is to guide therapy in order to relieve client distress and build resilience. (Kuyken, Padesky, & Dudley, 2009, p. 3)

The approach is described fully in the book, *Collaborative Case Conceptualization: Working Effectively with Clients in Cognitive-behavioral Therapy* (Kuyken et al., 2009), but is briefly summarized here before we describe how it can be used with clients presenting with complex and co-morbid presentations. The three principles identified in the book apply equally to enhance formulation and outcome when working with both a model specific and transdiagnostic approach. The adoption of the five steps described here may be particularly relevant when working with additional difficulty in terms of complexity, co-morbidity and issues that do not fall within clear diagnostic categories. It may be helpful for the therapist to consider three questions when making the decision whether to move beyond the use of a problem-focussed disorder-specific approach:

1. Is there an evidence-based disorder-specific theoretical model that can describe a primary presenting issue in cognitive behavioural terms?

    If the answer to this question is yes, then it would seem appropriate to adopt the disorder specific model. However, if there are common processes underlying co-morbid conditions, if no single disorder can be identified as "primary" or if there is significant difficulty with social or health issues, then the approach described here may offer additional benefits.

2. Which conceptualization model or descriptive approach is most likely to build collaboration, draw out client strengths and elicit hope in this key early stage of therapy?

    Clinical judgement and paying attention to client feedback is important in making this decision. In some instances it may be particularly important to work explicitly to elicit and develop a tangible sense of an alternative possibility or future through a resilience conceptualization. This may be true when clients are quickly overwhelmed by discussion of difficulties and find it hard to engage in treatment, or find it difficult to identify the possibility of change.

3. What is the simplest possible framework that provides a good enough level of description?

    A principle of parsimony may well apply in the face of co-morbidity. Clients and indeed therapists may feel overwhelmed by a number of different diagnostically specific formulations presented to account for different presenting issues. A single unifying formulation drawing out the transdiagnostic themes of both presenting difficulties and resilience may provide such a parsimonious approach. The intention here is to increase engagement though shared identification of the simplest possible formulation without the loss of essential information.

The clinical application of this approach was honed through clinical practice and supervision on a trial of CBT for treatment resistant depression (Wiles et al., 2013). This was a "real world" trial with clients with a primary presentation of treatment resistant depression, but who typically also presented with range of co-morbidities and complexities, as illustrated by Mel. A five step approach is outlined for working with complexity and co-morbidity in day-to-day clinical practice.

The metaphor of a crucible (Figure 6.1) can help illustrate how collaborative case conceptualization works. A crucible is a very strong container to which the therapist brings CBT knowledge and clinical experience while the client brings knowledge of his/her presenting issues and life experience. Case conceptualization is the process whereby an original and unique understanding of the client's presenting issues emerges like the product of a chemical reaction in a crucible.

The metaphor of a crucible illustrates three key features of the collaborative case conceptualization model. First, collaborative empiricism is the heat that enables the synthesis of CBT theory with clients' unique presentations and histories. Therapist and client work together to ensure that the right "ingredients" are brought to the crucible, that they are integrated in ways that make sense and that the process is experienced as useful in informing therapy. Empiricism refers first to a stance of developing hypotheses together. These hypotheses are then tested by the client as part of therapy discussion

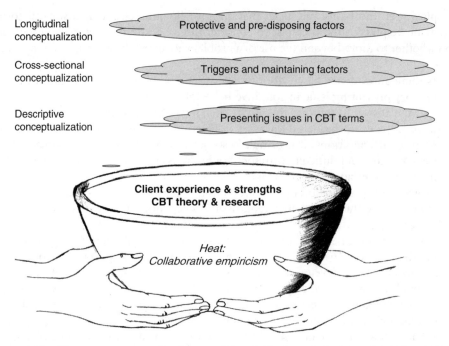

Longitudinal conceptualization

Cross-sectional conceptualization

Descriptive conceptualization

Figure 6.1 The case conceptualization crucible. © Kuyken, Padesky and Dudley (2009). Reproduced with permission of the authors.

and homework. It also refers to drawing on relevant evidence-based theory or protocols. CBT has an extraordinary repertoire of clinically informed theories and protocols that therapists need to weave into the evolving case conceptualization.

Second, like the chemical reaction in a crucible, a conceptualization evolves through several stages. Typically, it starts with a more descriptive cognitive-behavioural account of clients' presenting issues. In Mel's case, this started with describing how depression comprises thoughts (e.g., "When my therapist finds out all about me, s/he won't like me"), feelings (e.g., sadness), behaviours (e.g., tendency to withdraw) and bodily sensations (e.g., lethargy). It then tends to evolve into more explanatory models based on theoretical accounts of how the presenting issues are maintained. In Mel's case, this may be a behavioural account of how her tendency to withdraw at times of conflict negatively reinforces the withdrawal itself because it enables her to avoid facing the fear and distress that she experiences during conflict. Finally, a conceptualization of what maintains a person's presenting issues can be developed into a longitudinal conceptualization in which the person's history is used to understand vulnerability and resilience. For example, as a young child Mel had no choice but to withdraw in the face of her father's abusive behaviour. However, she learned that she and her sister could support each other emotionally. This became one way in which she would resiliently manage some of the more difficult periods of her upbringing.

Third, what emerges from a crucible is determined entirely by what ingredients are introduced. Typically CBT case conceptualization focuses primarily on clients' problems and the aspects of their context and history that predispose and maintain the problems. Collaborative case conceptualization proposes that to cultivate clients' resilience, it is important to highlight client strengths and aspects of their context and history that are protective and support their resilience. In Mel's case, she had several strengths, not least her ability to form strong relationships with female friends. In her later teenage years and in adulthood, her role as a mother, while also stressful, gave her a sense of purpose and reward.

In summary, collaborative case conceptualization emphasizes three key components in case conceptualization:

- Conceptualization requires a collaborative approach where both therapist and client are equally important in the process of developing and testing emerging understandings of the client's presenting issues.
- Conceptualization evolves throughout the course of therapy from simpler more descriptive accounts to more explanatory accounts that help reveal how presenting issues are maintained.
- Conceptualization will best support client's progress towards their goals and long-term resilience if the client's strengths and protective factors are explored.

Five Steps of Case Conceptualization

Moving towards conceptualization and intervention begins by asking clients about their SMART (Specific, Measurable, Achievable, Realistic/within Resource, Time limited) goals for treatment. By keeping a clear sense of the goals for treatment, the therapist and client can keep track of those things that are consistent with or develop resilience, and those things that deplete the client and perhaps maintain their presenting issues. This may be important when considering responses that may have been adaptive in the past, but are no longer optimal in meeting the client's goals. Goals are an important shared benchmark to measure the value of different strategies adopted to manage difficulties identified. This is particularly relevant when the steps necessary to begin the process of change are feared and unfamiliar. Having well-defined SMART goals is, therefore, critical for they enable the client and therapist to monitor the changing patterns of responses and determine their effectiveness.

Step 1: Making sense of chaos: collaborative development of a descriptive conceptualization of the target presenting issue(s)

When we first start to conceptualize with our client, we need to start at the simplest level of conceptualization. This is a simple descriptive conceptualization that articulates, for the client and therapist, the client's main presenting issues in cognitive and behavioural terms. In the illustrations provided here, we will use a simple model of depression (Beck, Rush, Shaw, & Emery, 1979), beginning with the five part model (Padesky & Mooney, 1990), as an example of how Mel's difficulties can be described in terms of her emotions, thoughts, behaviour and physical sensations. However, these first steps in conceptualization can apply to whatever cognitive behavioural model best describes the issues that your client is bringing to therapy (see Kuyken et al., 2009).

The first step in a collaborative case conceptualization, therefore, is a familiar one: to develop a descriptive conceptualization (Kuyken et al., 2009) of a typical example of the client's presenting issue. This level of conceptualization normally describes specific recent examples of the presenting issue(s) that are targeted for change. It seeks to understand how the different domains of CBT (cognition, affect, behaviour and physiology) interact to contribute to the creation of a specific situation in the context of the person's life.

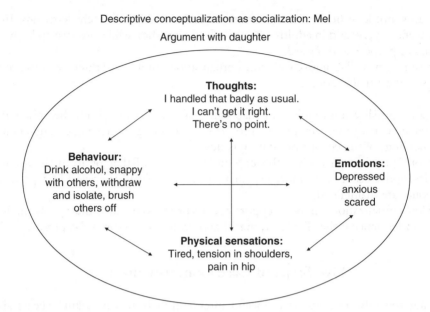

Figure 6.2　Descriptive conceptualization of a presenting issue.

Mel's initial priority for treatment was not a diagnostically driven one. She was aware of feeling at her worst when she was not getting on with her daughter. We began by considering specific examples of when Mel had been in conflict with her daughter, and developed descriptive conceptualizations of each example. One such descriptive conceptualization is illustrated in Figure 6.2. In this example, Mel noted that she was often aware of experiencing waves of strong emotions, which was typical for her. By breaking down her experience into the different domains, we were able to begin to develop a shared sense of how this feeling was sustained.

At this stage, we considered how this specific example fitted with Mel's goals and whether she wanted to consider alternative behavioural and cognitive responses to this trigger. Mel was able to identify clearly that cognitive and behavioural patterns identified in the descriptive conceptualization of her presenting issue were not how she wanted things to be. This was helpful for Mel in identifying the areas that needed to change. However, Mel's response to this was interesting. Although Mel thought that this described her well in this situation, she also felt somewhat flat, with a sense of "there, now you see how stuck things are".

A response of feeling stuck or beyond help and a corresponding drop in mood when conceptualizing difficulties is not uncommon in clinical practice (Chadwick, Williams, & Mackenzie, 2003). This response can be representative of clients who may have been struggling with difficulties for a long period of time. Clients may also have had one or more prior treatments for their difficulties, and could potentially be very aware of how stuck things are and why their difficulties continue. Clients may experience the problem-focused conceptualization alone as aversive, leading to the client becoming more withdrawn in the session. However, this formulation provides an opportunity for; increasing shared understanding of difficulties, the therapist to express empathy and validation of the difficulties that the client is experiencing, and ultimately, for the client to feel heard.

Of critical importance however, is what follows this very familiar first step. This is the point at which the therapist begins to develop a tangible alternative where change is possible. This is a step that first requires the client's difficulties to be heard, validated and conceptualized.

Step 2: The possibility of change: collaborative development of a descriptive conceptualization of resilience

Up to this point, the focus has been on understanding, tracking and identifying difficulties for the client. This would seem appropriate as these are the very reasons why our clients consult us. The application of evidence-based effective treatment models for specific diagnostic presenting issues is one of the strengths of CBT. Careful attention has been paid to understanding effective ingredients in treatment, training therapists to develop theory practice links and enabling therapists to collaboratively deliver bespoke intervention plans. However, the effectiveness of CBT can be enhanced further by going beyond an exploration of problems alone.

The next step in the approach is the incorporation and development of a descriptive conceptualization of resilience. This can help clients see the possibility of change and moving towards their goals through thoughts and behaviours that support positive change. Equal weighting and attention is placed on this descriptive conceptualization of resilience as it was for the descriptive conceptualization of presenting issues. Hence, one important factor in this step is taking the time to develop a good level of detail in the resilience conceptualization across and between all domains (cognitive, affective, behavioural and physiological).

Clear details of resilience patterns allow the therapist to move beyond a noble, but thin and fragile, description of a person's sense of resilience – which may represent a clear intention to respond differently, without a clear sense of how to do so (e.g. "I'll do something different") – to a well-developed narrative of the qualities of coping and resilience held by the client and the developing knowledge and skills of how to facilitate this.

We begin by seeking to develop a collaborative descriptive conceptualization of resilience or exceptions to the client's difficulties. It may be possible to develop this descriptive conceptualization based on a situation that the client has already experienced. These experiences may have occurred a time when the client was not, for some reason, able to enter into the familiar problem-focused pattern of thoughts and behaviour. Perhaps escape or avoidance was not possible on one occasion, or the client was in a situation where they had to act differently, or was in a situation that supported their strengths and resilience coming to the foreground. This is an opportunity to conceptualize an example of the presenting issue when things went differently. The exception sought here for conceptualization should be of the same presenting issue, but where the outcome was moderated, less intense, or more in line with the client's goals (as judged by the client).

Clearly, such an incident may not always have occurred or it may be something that the client finds difficult to bring to mind. In this instance, an initial intervention may be to try to create this alternative. The client and therapist will have developed a descriptive conceptualization of the presenting issue in step one and can Socratically consider whether this pattern fits with the goals for treatment. It is often useful to discuss with the client whether it would seem worthwhile to the client to do something differently. Having considered that an alternative pattern of behaviour may be more consistent with the goals for treatment, it becomes possible to collaboratively and empirically explore the resilience conceptualization in more detail. By testing out different behaviours or thoughts, an example of a response that is indicative of resilience, can emerge. This is then developed as a descriptive resilience conceptualization and tracked across the different domains of the conceptualization. Alternatives are explicitly considered in relation to SMART goals to increase the sense of hope, the possibility of change and to develop motivation for changing familiar patterns.

The exploration of exceptions or resilience may, therefore, be developed from prior experience or developed directly through experimentation and intervention. For example, thoughts such as, "changing behaviour won't make any difference," can be explicitly tested with activity-scheduling and behavioural experiments. For behaviour, the use of activity-scheduling in CBT may also be developed in response to the identification of avoidance, withdrawal, inactivity and rumination in the conceptualization of depression. Conceptualization of resilience reflects upon what it was that allowed the client to shift out of problematic reactions into a healthier and more productive response in line with the client's goals.

The behaviours that are both supportive of, and supported by, this alternative are developed and rehearsed. This can increase clients' understanding of the skills and behaviours that a person can purposefully enter into to develop resilience and step away from presenting issues. As with more standard problem-focused CBT conceptualization, the conceptualization of coping and resilience is developed collaboratively over time and revised in the light of new evidence.

Clients may well have styles of thinking or beliefs about themselves that make it difficult for them to identify their strengths and resilience. Moderation in levels of difficulty, shifts in posture or tone, partially attempted alternative strategies and problem-free areas of life all provide areas of resilience. For example, Mel's decision to contact her GP and request help is a skill that could be considered to include several layers of resilience, including: the identification of a problem; the recognition of the need to do something about it; taking action to access help; managing all challenges (emotional, physical and practical) to attend the session; and then to discuss this with a previously unknown person. In the context of a difficulty like depression, these may not be easy steps, because negative thinking might quickly discount them. It is important therefore for therapists to be attentive to the small strands of resilience inherent in our clients and to support the identification of them (see Box 6.2).

With Mel, the possibility of resilience began at assessment through seeking out information consistent with exceptions and identifying variations in coping. Through this process, it was possible to consider with Mel that she had survived a number of extremely challenging situations. We were able to identify that things were not currently 100 per cent bad,

---

Box 6.2   Key skills in identifying resilience

- Reflecting on the challenges survived
- Seeking exceptions to difficulties
- Drawing out positive experiences
- Considering vulnerability/resilience as a dimension that is fluid and changing (things were not this tense 100 per cent of the time)
- Discussing and formulating exceptions
- Planning an experiment *to create* the exception
- Drawing on strengths from problem-free areas of life
- Noting variations in presentation in session

100 per cent of the time, giving a sense of variation. By considering exceptions or through deliberately planning to create these, the notion of resilience became more tangible and real to Mel. These notions then begin to provide a template for alternative patterns of response judged by her to be more consistent with her goals.

Specifically, Mel and her therapist were able to uncover some strands of resilience when she identified a time when she had been able to offer a different response to her daughter's requests to go out, which went better. We considered what this specific response was and what had made it possible in terms of her thoughts to be able to respond more constructively. Mel initially had a tendency to dismiss any sense of resilience, but by considering this through the same conceptualization-based approach, she was able to see how the behavioural changes that she had made impacted upon other domains of her experience. This marked the event as a good exception to the problems she wished to address in therapy. Crucially, because it was also more in line with her goals, it was therefore to be enhanced and repeated.

The transcript illustrates this work with Mel and Figure 6.3 shows the diagram that Mel and her therapist co-created.

MEL: I was shouting at the kids again, it can't be good for any kid to be shouted at like that.

THERAPIST (TH): Mel, I was thinking about what you were telling me about how things are for you, and I was trying to put two things together. On the one hand, you have this idea or fear that you are like your Mum and Dad, and all the experiences that you went through with that. On the other hand, you work really hard and are determined for things to be different for your children?

MEL: Totally, I want my kids to be able to wake up in the morning, go to school, come home and not be frightened of their parents.

TH: How do you try and make that happen, that different experience?

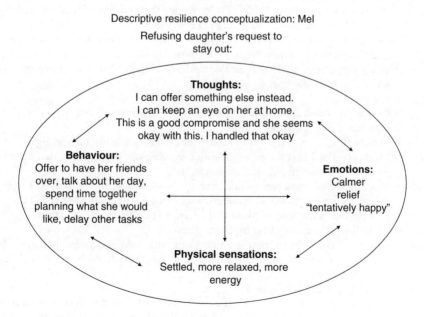

Figure 6.3 Descriptive conceptualization of resilience.

MEL: As kids we never had any family time. I think the only time they spoke to us was to shout at us. We weren't allowed to have friends around or go out and have fun. I want to be interested in my kids, to know what they're doing, how they're getting on, to feel able to have friends over.

TH: These things that you mentioned about having friends over, having family time, and being interested in them; are they things that are consistent with your goal about being a good mum, the kind of parent that you want to be?

MEL: I guess so, but I can do more than I am, be more like other people.

TH: These behaviours that you identified in terms of being interested in your kids, spending time together, are these behaviours things that you're able to do from time to time?

MEL: I make sure that we always spend time at dinner together when we can talk.

TH: Okay, so there's something about spending time together, but it's also about talking together? Is that a time when you can show that you are interested in them?

MEL: When my daughter came home in tears the other day because she was teased about her trainers … I know I can't afford the latest ones for her, but I can at least spend time with her and show I understand what that's like for her, to hear her out.

TH: So you were listening and showing that you understood how that was like for her?

MEL: Yes.

TH: Can you write that behaviour down? How would you put it in your own words?

MEL: Listening to my daughter. I guess I was thinking about her thoughts and feelings, and to sympathize.

TH: What was the impact of that, when you spent time together to listen to her and are being supportive of her? It seemed like a different experience to the other example we drew out?

MEL: Although I felt sad about not being able to buy her everything, I was pleased at being able to talk with her. I didn't have that painful awful feeling I get after shouting at her, where I'm a rubbish parent. I didn't have the awful pain in my hip and shoulder.

TH: There was also a different physical sense?

MEL: It was just an absence of pain in my body, it felt calmer. I could write that down.

TH: That sounds like a good idea. It's really interesting that you had a different experience.

MEL: Okay, so when I did this I had no pain in my body.

TH: So what we've got so far is that this was a difficult situation, but you were being together, eating together, you were interested in her, thinking about her feelings, being supportive, working to understand what things were like for her, and that seemed to feel different physically?

MEL: Yes, it did.

TH: What did you think about doing this? Was there a different thought process about how that was, about how it went?

MEL: I thought that it was better that I hadn't shouted at her or got into an argument.

TH: What do you think that meant about your parenting and your goals in that situation where you hadn't ended up shouting at her?

MEL: I guess it showed I was able to understand where she was at. She needed to know that there was someone who understood, cared for her and wanted to be there for her. That's the kind of Mum that I want to be able to be, you know?

TH: Okay let's write some of these thoughts down.

MEL: I think it's that I need to show her that I care, that I do understand her, and I listened to her without shouting. I handled it okay. I could do better though, can I put that down?

TH: It was okay but I can do better?

MEL: Yes. I think that this was much better for me, and perhaps I can do this more consistently or keep this going in other ways and it seems that this is much more helpful for me.

TH: How did it feel emotionally to respond in this way to her?

MEL: I think in how I handled it, I felt … I was frustrated that I couldn't just buy her what she wanted, but in terms of how I handled it, it was a nicer feeling. I felt more contented and happier.

TH: Okay, let's try and capture some of these feelings here too. Let's try to see if we can join up these different areas in the same way as we did when we were looking at some of your difficulties, and see how this fits with your goals. Maybe there are things that we can learn from here that will help us to move towards your goals? If you were feeling more contented, did that have an impact on how you were feeling physically?

MEL: Absolutely, when I am feeling tense, the pain I get in my hip is at its worst. But I didn't get any headaches, like when we argue, I was feeling better. I think that this went better with how I'd like things to be.

I could have gone down the old road and ended up arguing, feeling awful, drinking and just thinking that I'm the worst Mum in the world. But I didn't. And doing things differently really helped in that situation. This other pattern is much better for me.

Step 3: Bringing it together: explicitly linking the presenting issue and resilience descriptive conceptualizations

The problem and resilience conceptualizations are presented alongside each other and linked at the most appropriate domain of the five-part model, though all domains are identified as inter-connecting (see Figure 6.4). The inter-connecting conceptualization can however be rotated to join together at any of the domains, but is most likely to be at cognitive or behavioural domains (e.g., thoughts to thoughts, behaviour to behaviour).

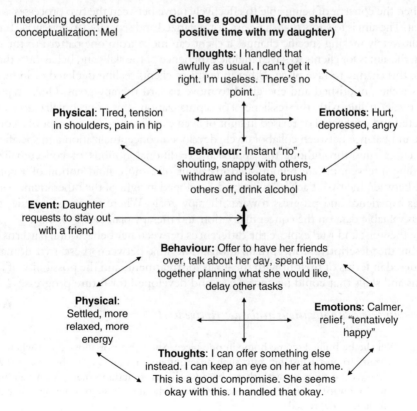

Figure 6.4 Inter-connected descriptive conceptualization (connected at behavioural domain).

Box 6.3   Key skills in connecting descriptive
conceptualizations together

- Link different conceptualizations to the client's SMART goals
- Consider which domain (cognitive or behavioral) had the biggest impact on change in the exception explored. In other words, where does it make most sense conceptually to link the two formulations?
- Join the two conceptualizations at this stage
- Track the impact of the different patterns of response and consider which fits with the client's goals
- Emphasize the possibility of using resilience skills to move from difficulty to preferred outcomes
- See resilience as agency
- Strengthen the possibility of an alternative through the check and balance between conceptualization and the outcome of skills use
- Set up further behavioral experiments to strengthen resilience

---

Joining the conceptualizations together in this way has a number of aims. First, it gives equal weighting to the descriptions of processes that promote the presenting issue and those that promote resilience in line with the client's goals. Second, by connecting the two together, the concept of being able to effectively move between the two processes is made explicit. The aim is to show that these are not polarized and separated experiences, but that by deliberately making specific changes a client can move from one pattern to the other. Third, the aim is for clients to have tangible experience of the skills and behaviours that will enable this change to take place, either in terms of clients feeling depleted or in terms of clients feeling nourished and energized to move toward therapy goals. Once steps have been made in line with the resilience conceptualization, this conceptualization can be evaluated and confirmed or revised in light of lived experience. This concept of a constant check and balance between collaboratively developed conceptualization and specific daily experiences runs throughout the approach. Traditional notions of conceptualization preceding intervention are relinquished in favour of a more fluid notion of a constant dance between the two. Each is revised and developed in light of the other in line with the client's experience and progress towards therapy goals. Where progress is made, this is used as valuable data on the conceptualization and therapy plan (see Box 6.3).

The therapist and Mel explore the differences between her behavioural patterns identified in the descriptive conceptualizations. The link between these two domains is considered in terms of their fit with the goals for treatment, and the possibility of future actions and skills that could be considered and developed for future progress.

Interlocking conceptualizations at the descriptive level

MEL: Will she be bullied, come home in one piece. She's just not allowed out when she wants to and I just get into such an argument. I want her to be able to have friends and meet up with them, because that is something that I wasn't allowed to do. I want to find a way to manage that without ending up shouting at her and feeling so depressed.

TH: If you were able to find a way to help her spend time with her friends, and for that to feel okay, would that be in line with your goals?

MEL   I think so, because all kids need to have friends.

TH: So if we take this example?

MEL: Yes

(Looking together at descriptive conceptualization of presenting issue developed)

TH: When we look at this conceptualization, in that situation when she wanted to go out with friends, you noticed the thoughts, "I handled that awfully as usual, I've done it again, I can't get it right, I'm useless, there's no point". Were those the kind of thoughts that you noticed going through your mind?

MEL: After I'd said "no," then shouted at her, yes.

TH: So it sounds as though what happened first was the shouting.

MEL: Yes, that instant "no" that I gave without thinking about why I said no, and then the argument. That's the problem.

TH: Okay, so if that behaviour feels like an important area to look at, if we were to bring in some of these skills from this conceptualization where things went well (looking at the descriptive conceptualization of resilience) is there anything here that you think might be helpful from this example?

MEL: I guess one thing that may be helpful from here is about asking and listening before I say anything. She just asked, "Can I go out?" and I just said "no," I didn't even know what she wanted to do.

TH: It was like an automatic response, and it felt that this started the whole process off?

MEL: Yes, absolutely.

TH: Are we saying that when she makes a request that there's something about making sure that you are listening and understanding?

MEL: Yes, she's probably only going to be walking around the street talking to her friends, but I don't think that straightaway, I worry that something awful will happen or that she will need money for something.

TH: Okay, so these are the kind of thoughts that lead you to immediately say no, but lead into conflict?

MEL: Yes.

TH: So if you were to take some of the skills from your resilience over here, and to move them into this situation what would that look like? (Places the conceptualizations side by side)

MEL: I'd like to ask her what she wants to do.

TH: Okay, so can you write that down. Then what would you do?

MEL: Well, if I think it's too dark, or too late or something, then maybe I can think about alternatives and to negotiate, so I can put down talking about how else she can be with her friends and talking it through, she's not so little any more.

TH: So this seems in line with this emerging alternative resilience response we identified, and that might look like listening to her, talking with her, being supportive, asking what she wants and negotiating an alternative with her if, as her parent, what she wants is not seen as safe. Is this different from the instant no, shouting and drinking pattern?

MEL: Yes.

TH: What would it mean if you were able to carry out this alternative pattern?

MEL: I think it shows that I'm trying to understand her.

TH: If you're trying to understand her, what does that mean about the goal of trying to be a good enough parent?

MEL: That I'm trying to keep her safe, that I'm a caring parent.

TH: How would that feel if you were able to respond in that way, to be asking, understanding, negotiating, how would that feel?

MEL: I wouldn't feel so anxious, I'd be calmer.
TH: Okay, let's make a note of these. How would you be feeling differently physically?
MEL: Less tired.
TH: Let's find out. In the same way all of these areas join up together. Thinking about this now; if you were to respond in this way tonight when she comes home, by behaving differently when the request comes in by listening and negotiating. If you did all these things how would that fit with your goals to be a good parent, starting with this shift in behaviour?
MEL: If I could do that a bit more often, then that would help me feel that I wasn't always shouting and that I can be a good mum.

The domain at which the conceptualizations are linked together highlights the different responses to a trigger in that particular domain, by explicitly seeing the impact of a response in one domain and how it links to the rest of the conceptualization. For example, a problem-focused behavioural response to a trigger (e.g., withdrawal and avoidance) can be seen to increase problem-focused responses in other domains (e.g., cognitively "I can't cope."). By contrast a behavioural response to a trigger from the resilience conceptualization (e.g., engaging in social activity, talking to friends) is seen as linking to resilience-focused responses in other domains (e.g., cognitively, "I seemed to cope okay") (see Figure 6.4).

The first three steps described above may be repeated with clients early in treatment, as a number of typical examples are identified and descriptively conceptualized. In another example, Mel identified a shift in outcome in line with her goals as a result of a shift in behaviour. By moving away from isolating herself and drinking alcohol, and moving instead towards sharing her difficulties with a trusted friend, maintaining a social contact and reducing her drinking; Mel identified that she had experienced reduced emotional vulnerability through not drinking. From a position of sobriety, she was able to feel a different kind of vulnerability in sharing her difficulties with her friends, and at the same time also experiencing a feeling of support and contentment.

This conceptualization could also have been rotated to connect at cognitive domains. At this stage, Mel began to use the experience of her behavioural experiments to challenge unhelpful cognitions related to making changes in behaviour ("I must cope alone"). For example, she was able to identify that she had been able to challenge her desire to withdraw after a period of conflict, and had contacted a friend. This had led to her drinking less and gave her a different emotional experience, though she still experienced strong emotions. She was able to consider the patterns of response that she had fallen into and a sense of how she might change these. This was linked to the resilience thought that talking to close friends was helpful for coping.

Mel was able to begin to move towards her goals through having a clear sense of a resilience conceptualization, how to move towards this in behavioural terms, and the lived experience of this being effective.

Step 4: "It's always like this": cross-sectional conceptualization of presenting issues and resilience, and the inter-connection between them

In this step, the client and therapist review the descriptive conceptualizations of the client's presenting issues and resilience that have been developed in steps one and two to identify recurring themes. A number of examples of different but specific situations will have been developed up to this point. Client and therapist work together to identify the themes that show up repeatedly, across presenting issues, situations and time. This process is referred to by Kuyken et al. (2009) as cross-sectional conceptualization.

Identifying repeating maintaining patterns and themes brings several anticipated benefits. A broad and varied range of presenting issues can come to feel more defined and manageable, as recurring themes identify the lynchpin beliefs and behaviours that maintain the presenting issues. Specific skills identified and learnt in the (specific) descriptive resilience conceptualizations can be generalized to other contexts and times, as part of a cross-sectional (general) conceptualization. This increase in accessibility of resilience skills can also help the client to experience presenting issues as more manageable because the skills that they hold are identified as being effective in different contexts. This conceptualization may therefore help with the explicit transition of the skills and knowledge of the client, increasing the possibility for change, as well as continued relapse prevention.

A cross-sectional conceptualization of both Mel's presenting issues and resilience was carefully and collaboratively developed in sessions. Reviewing Mel's descriptive conceptualizations of presenting issues identified a number of recurring themes across different situations, contexts and time. There were many instances when she would feel depressed and report thoughts that she was "unable to cope" and that she was "no good/worthless". This was often triggered by thoughts that she was being criticized or rejected, and typically she would respond behaviourally through avoidance and withdrawal. This in turn impacted upon her emotional and physical vulnerabilities. Often she would seek further avoidance through self-soothing strategies of substance misuse and self-harm. This cross-sectional conceptualization is seen within the interlinked cross-sectional conceptualization (Figure 6.5).

Equal emphasis on her descriptive resilience conceptualizations began to identify some themes in resilience. A cross-sectional resilience conceptualization was co-created through the same process of reviewing resilience across difficulties, time and context. Mel identified patterns of resilience linked to being with others, discussing difficulties with trusted others, spending quality time with her children and maintaining her sobriety. Alternative thoughts consistent with her goals supported the idea of "strength in numbers" through sharing her concerns with trusted others.

Sharing her concerns with others was a challenging idea for Mel and she was initially quite sceptical and frightened by the proposed changes she would need to make. It was important therefore to link patterns of behaviour and their outcome to her SMART goals for treatment. Through this process, Mel was able to identify that "strength in numbers" had been useful across different examples and was consistent with her goals.

The two cross-sectional conceptualizations are then connected together, as before, at the most appropriate domain as determined in collaboration with the client. Added value is gained by explicitly linking the cognitive and behavioural skills in each domain that help move the client from a problem-focused to a resilience-focused response.

For example, when identifying a pattern of behaviour consistent with the problem conceptualization, the client can use the cross-sectional conceptualization to:

- identify the pattern of behaviour;
- link its impact on feelings, thoughts and body sensations as well as the situation itself;
- understand the impact of this pattern in terms of the goals for treatment;
- have a clear sense of skills to use at this point to move towards the resilience conceptualization (matching domains of the conceptualization and CBT skills);

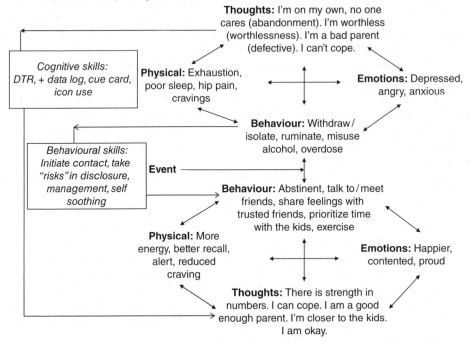

Goals: Be a good Mum (more shared time with my daughter)
Feel happier/worthwhile (out with friends, smile, positive times within relationships, BDII score down)
Reduce alcohol intake (within guidelines)

Figure 6.5   Cross-sectional inter-linked conceptualization.

- have a clear understanding of how the resilience conceptualization impacts upon the goals for treatment; and
- identify vulnerabilities and high-risk patterns.

Cross-sectional conceptualization represents a kind of "dance" between the general and the specific. That is to say, the therapist moves skilfully back and forth between prototypical specific situations that are typical of the descriptive conceptualization and the higher-level themes and rules that make up the cross-sectional conceptualization. The former are grounded in meaningful day-to-day examples and the latter have higher order learning, which clients can apply in their lives. Both the specific and general are considered as to whether they take the client towards or away from his/her goals. It may be helpful to consider, with your client, working explicitly at these two levels. This means considering how resilience applies in the day-to-day challenge that the client is facing (specific), and how this relates to the themes of resilience identified (general). The goal is to develop a cross-sectional resilience conceptualization that clients can use to work towards their therapy goals and will be useful beyond the end of therapy.

Step 5: Deepening resilience: linking the cross-sectional conceptualization back to underlying assumptions

In line with Beck et al. (1979) cognitive therapy progresses from focusing upon the "raw data" of automatic thoughts, to exploring assumptions underlying the predisposition to difficulties. Underlying assumptions are identified as providing "a personal matrix of meaning and value, the backdrop against which every day events acquire relevance, importance and significance" (Beck et al., 1979, p.244). Exploration, identification and modification of underlying assumptions are seen as important for a number of reasons, including: increasing understanding of the strategies adopted by clients; facilitating alternative coping; and the prevention of relapse.

Work within this approach has therefore progressed towards developing a collaborative understanding of the underlying assumptions (if... then ...) or rules held by clients that are seen to maintain target presenting issues. These assumptions and rules have been identified as underpinning the cross-sectional patterns maintaining problems, and in turn the responses identified in descriptive conceptualizations developed. Once assumptions have been explicitly named and identified, clients are invited to consider their usefulness. Again, their usefulness can be helpfully measured in light of the goals for treatment and the client's preferred future. Therapist and client consider together what rules or assumptions may support identified cross-sectional patterns of resilience and whether it is worth trying out these alternatives. This involves: increasing awareness of patterns of behaviour though the identification of these rules; noticing when they are active; recognizing their impact; and considering alternative adaptive resilience-focused responses.

When considering underlying assumptions or rules it is important to consider the context in which they were developed, as this can be validating for clients. For example, anyone growing up with parents who expected perfection might develop unrelenting standards, as a reasonable response to coping with the environment in which they grew up. These rules may have been essential and effective ways of coping with situations at the time of origin to try to prevent criticism. However, it is considered that in the current context, there may be alternative rules that could support cross-sectional patterns of resilience. Identification of alternative rules or "new systems" (Padesky & Mooney, 2012) is more commonplace in CBT and can be traced back to Beck et al. (1979) who identified that cognitive challenging of belief systems is more effective when it is linked to alternative adaptive assumptions. However, there are several less commonplace adaptations presented here. Adaptations include collaborative development of the conceptualization from descriptive to cross-sectional levels and explicitly linking the two together. This is developed further in identifying conditional levels of belief to underpin cross-sectional resilience.

The resilience rule (or conditional assumption supportive of resilience) is identified though discussion and experimentation based upon resilience conceptualizations up to this point. This could be developed though behavioural experiments, paradoxical application of the old rule, or considering "icons" of a person's goal for therapy. This involves helping the client to think of someone they know that shows a high level of achievement of their goal. Therapist and client then work to consider the possible rules that this icon may hold that allow him/her to achieve this goal. A new rule may be tried out "as if" it were the rule held by the client. This rule is then tracked in terms of how it maps on to the resilience cycle. The client is asked to review which rule would be supportive of the resilience cycle developed and adoption of this rule this is rehearsed.

In working with Mel, the therapist had been able to identify that Mel's old rule for living was supportive of her behavioural isolation, cognitive and emotional avoidance and sense of being on her own. This old rule was identified as "strength is coping alone and not letting others know what is going on". She was able to take a position against the impact of this rule to create the alternative rule "strength is letting other people in to help me". This came to be described in sessions as comparing notions of "standing alone as a tower of strength" versus "strength in numbers" (see Figure 6.6).

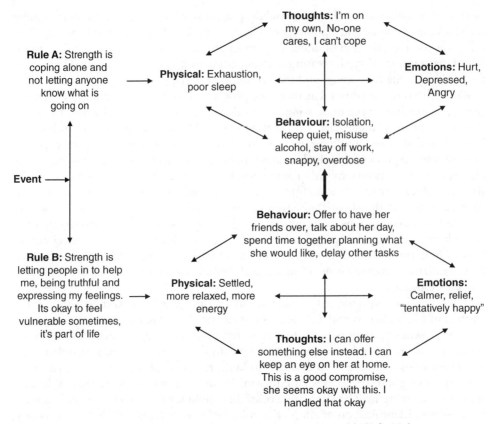

Figure 6.6 Cross-sectional conceptualization linked to conditional beliefs: Mel.

In certain circumstances the therapist may need to link the conceptualization further to the level of unconditional beliefs (core beliefs or schemas). In this instance, the same approach of conceptualizing resilience with as much care and attention as the conceptualization of presenting issues continues to be applicable. If presenting difficulties are linked back to early experiences and core beliefs, then core beliefs supporting the underlying assumptions of resilience may equally be considered and established in the conceptualization. This final step, therefore, may be repeated to the level of unconditional belief where this is necessary to support clients in moving towards their therapy goals.

Conclusion

Within the five-step approach there is a deliberate and explicit weaving of resilience and relapse prevention throughout the intervention. Rather than viewing relapse prevention as an important activity for the final phases of treatment, it is much more integrated. It is central to the entirety of treatment in the form of explicit and clear patterns of resilience, which may be understood both in general terms and in the application of resilience skills in any given moment. Relapse prevention can be facilitated through the principles of collaboration, empiricism and the incorporation of resilience. Furthermore, it should be adopted from the beginning and continued through the entire work and beyond.

The approach outlined here is considered to offer a number of benefits:

- Facilitating a sense of hope and the possibility of an alternative future.
- Developing a clear sense of agency and creating an alternative preferred way of coping in line with goals.
- Having a clear sense of the patterns of responding that maintain or create presenting difficulties.
- Increasing understanding of the skills used to create change and how to apply these skills.
- Understanding how to deal with lapses and unexpected life events.
- Developing skills for resilience across a range of presenting issues.
- Increasing the ability to maintain and build resilience into the future.

Procedural Rules

Step 1. Making sense of chaos: collaborative development of a descriptive conceptualization of the target presenting issue(s)

Beginning the process together

- Outline together a list of presenting issues.
- Develop clear SMART goals for treatment. Record these, give a copy to the client and keep them handy for reference.
- Complete CBT assessment, with exploration of strengths and resilience.
- Identify a typical example of the main presenting issue. Use this to work on socialization to the model through a descriptive conceptualization of the presenting issue being addressed.
- Socratically explore how each domain of the conceptualization impacts upon each other and review the impact of this in the client's identified goals.

Step 2. The possibility of change: collaborative development of a descriptive conceptualization of resilience

Seek exceptions to the influence of the presenting issue and times when the problem was less influential.
   Skills here include:

- reflecting on the challenges survived,
- empathic listening for changes and variation,
- considering changes in resilience (things were not this tense 100 per cent of the time),
- discussing and formulating the exception,
- planning an experiment to create the exception, and
- drawing skills from problem-free areas of life.

Step 3. Bringing it together: explicitly linking the presenting issue and resilience descriptive conceptualizations

Connect the descriptive conceptualizations of the presenting issue and resilience together at the most appropriate domain.

- Identify explicit skills that help to move from the presenting issue to the resilience conceptualization.
- Practice these skills (enhanced skills use in the specific area of difficulty).
- Track the impact of the different patterns of response and consider how these fit with the client's goals.
- Emphasize the possibility of using resilience skills to move from the difficulty to the preferred outcomes. Also emphasize the promotion of agency through creating interlinked descriptive conceptualizations.
- Set up behavioural experiments to strengthen resilience.

Step 4. "It's always like this": cross-sectional conceptualization of presenting issues and resilience, and the inter-connection between them

Develop cross-sectional conceptualizations of presenting issues and resilience and connect these at the most appropriate domain.

- Review descriptive conceptualizations developed to date.
- Seek themes in responses across events, time and presenting issues. Use descriptive conceptualizations of presenting issues to develop a cross-sectional conceptualization.
- Repeat this process for the descriptive conceptualization of resilience to develop a cross-sectional conceptualization of resilience.
- Join the two cross-sectional conceptualizations at the most appropriate domain.
- Review the impact of different themes in response (specific instances to the general theme) in relation to the agreed SMART goals.

Step 5. Deepening resilience: linking the cross-sectional conceptualization back to underlying assumptions

Identifying the underlying assumptions supporting both presenting issues and resilience

- Link the cross-sectional conceptualization of the presenting issues to the underlying assumptions or rules for living that underpin this pattern of response.
- Link the cross-sectional conceptualization of resilience to new underlying assumptions or rules that underpin this pattern of response.
- Track the impact of the different assumptions or rules upon the SMART goals for treatment.
- Deliberately test out new rules or assumptions through behavioural experiments.

- Identify new rules in action (general) and the application of these in the moment (specific) and back again (the dance between the general and the specific).
- If appropriate, consider linking both presenting issues and resilience back to the level of unconditional belief and track the impact of old schemas and possible new schemas in line with the SMART goals for treatment.
- Road test new rules to prevent relapse and build resilience.

Acknowledgements

We are grateful to Halley Cohen for her editorial assistance. The model of case conceptualization from which this chapter builds is described in Kuyken, Padesky and Dudley (2009). *Collaborative case conceptualization*. New York: Guildford Press.

References

Beck, A. T., Rush, A. J., Shaw, B. F., & Emery, G. (1979). *Cognitive therapy of depression*. New York: The Guilford Press.

Chadwick, P., Williams, C., & Mackenzie, J. (2003). Impact of case formulation in cognitive therapy for psychosis. *Behaviour, Research and Therapy, 41*, 671–680.

Kuyken, W., Padesky, C. A., & Dudley, R. 2009. *Collaborative case conceptualization: working effectively with clients in cognitive-behavioral therapy*. New York: Guilford Press.

Padesky, C. A., & Mooney, K. A. (1990). Clinical tip: Presenting the cognitive model to clients. *International Cognitive Therapy Newsletter, 6*, 13–14.

Padesky, C. A., & Mooney, K. A. (2012). Strengths based cognitive behavioral therapy: a four step model to build resilience. *Clinical Psychology and Psychotherapy, 19*, 283–290.

Wiles, N., Thomas, L., Abel, A., Ridgway, N., Turner, N., Campbell, J., … Lewis, G. (2013). Cognitive behavioural therapy as an adjunct to pharmacotherapy for primary care based patients with treatment resistant depression: results of the CoBalT randomised controlled trial. *Lancet, 381*(9864), 375–384.

7

Transdiagnostic Approaches for Anxiety Disorders

Freda McManus and Roz Shafran

The term "anxiety disorders" refers to a group of psychiatric disorders that is characterized by a disabling overestimation of threat and danger, heightened physiological arousal and behavioural avoidance. The Diagnostic and Statistical Manual of Mental Disorders, 4th Edition (DSM-IV-TR; American Psychiatric Association (APA), 2000) specified 11 different anxiety disorder diagnoses including panic disorder, agoraphobia, specific phobias, social phobia, obsessive compulsive disorder, post-traumatic stress disorder, generalized anxiety disorder and "anxiety disorder not otherwise specified"(ADNOS). DSM-V, has reduces this to nine different anxiety disorders with panic disorder and agoraphobia separated and post-traumatic stress disorder and obsessive compulsive disorder moving out of the category of "anxiety disorders" (American Psychiatric Association, 2013). Lifetime and 12-month prevalence rates of anxiety disorders have been reported to be the highest of all the psychiatric disorders, at rates of almost 30 per cent and 18 per cent respectively (Kessler et al., 2005; Kessler, Chiu, Demler, & Walters, 2005). Anxiety disorders have a profoundly negative impact on quality of life (Saarni et al., 2007), and impose a substantial economic cost on society (Greenberg et al., 1999). Given the prevalence and impact of anxiety disorders, there is a need for them to be conceptualized and treated as effectively and efficiently as possible.

Cognitive-behavioural therapy (CBT) protocols have demonstrated efficacy in treating the main anxiety disorder diagnoses (for a meta-analysis see Hofmann & Smits, 2008). These diagnosis specific protocols have developed from programmes of research that have (i) specified a cognitive-behavioural model of the processes hypothesized to maintain a specific anxiety disorder, and (ii) devised a cognitive-behavioural treatment designed to reverse the putative maintaining processes. Such approaches have been rigorously evaluated in randomized controlled trials with predominately positive results (Butler, Chapman, Forman, & Beck, 2006). However, such protocols were developed with patients fitting the diagnostic criteria for one specific anxiety disorder, rather than for patients with more than one anxiety disorder. This is a significant limitation since 40–80 per cent of patients with an anxiety disorder meet criteria for two or more anxiety disorders (Brown, Campbell, Lehman, Grisham, & Mancill, 2001; Kessler et al., 2005).

How to Become a More Effective CBT Therapist: Mastering Metacompetence in Clinical Practice,
First Edition. Edited by Adrian Whittington and Nick Grey.
© 2014 John Wiley & Sons, Ltd. Published 2014 by John Wiley & Sons, Ltd.

While individuals with co-occurring anxiety disorders may be successfully treated for their "primary" anxiety difficulty using a diagnosis-specific protocol, the impact of the intervention on the secondary anxiety disorder is variable and often limited (e.g., Brown, Antony & Barlow, 1995; Newman, Przeworski, Fisher, & Borkovec, 2010; Tsao, Mystkowski, Zucker, & Craske, 2002). A clinically intuitive approach to co-occurring anxiety disorders is to administer sequential interventions to address the difficulties concurrently or in turn. However, recent findings suggest that this approach may be less effective than an equivalent duration of a single diagnosis-specific treatment (Craske et al., 2007; Randall, Thomas, & Thevos, 2001). Thus, while the move towards disorder-specific treatments has brought with it enormous benefits, diagnosis specific protocols for treating anxiety disorders have limitations, and may not be the ideal for patients with more than one anxiety disorder. Furthermore, Ellard, Fairholme, Boisseau, Farchione, and Barlow (2010) suggest that "recent scientific advances suggest that there may be more that unites anxiety and mood disorders then previously conceived, potentially making the need for numerous diagnosis specific treatments obsolete and opening the possibility of a more parsimonious application of evidence-based treatments in clinical practice" (p. 88).

The Need for a Transdiagnostic Approach to Treating Anxiety Disorders

Given that there are specific protocols with demonstrated efficacy in treating most of the individual anxiety disorder diagnoses, what areas remain to be addressed? We suggest that two important challenges for the effective treatment of anxiety disorders remain. First, there is a need to develop interventions for patients with more than one (co-existing) anxiety disorder, and for those who do not fit neatly into any given diagnostic model, that is, they have an "anxiety disorder not otherwise specified" (ADNOS). The second challenge is to ensure that evidence-based treatments are effectively disseminated to routine clinical practice as specific protocols are currently significantly underused (Shafran et al., 2009). Farchione et al. (2012) note some of the disadvantages of the diagnosis-specific approach including difficulties with dissemination and high co-morbidity in routine clinical practice. The approach suggested here arises from the common clinical dilemma of how to (i) parsimoniously conceptualize co-occurring anxiety disorders/ADNOS and (ii) how to decide where to focus time limited interventions (typically 6–12 sessions) with such patients. The transdiagnostic treatment for anxiety disorders described here does not include any new techniques. Instead it is an attempt to structure standard CBT interventions such that they can be applied to any individual presenting with anxiety difficulties, regardless of the specific diagnosis.

Transdiagnostic Approaches

"Transdiagnostic" approaches to the understanding and treatment of psychopathology are those that transcend the diagnostic boundaries set out by classification schemes such as DSM-IV-TR (APA, 2000). They can completely transcend such boundaries, as exemplified by interventions such as Acceptance and Commitment Therapy (Hayes, Strosahl, & Wilson, 2004) and Mindfulness-based Cognitive Therapy (Segal, Williams, & Teasdale, 2002) or they can apply to specific categories of diagnosis such as the transdiagnostic approach to eating disorders (Fairburn, Cooper, & Shafran, 2003). Given our starting point as clinicians trained in the use of diagnosis specific CBT protocols for specific anxiety disorders, and the strong evidence for their effectiveness in treating a variety of individual anxiety disorders (National Institute for Clinical Excellence (NICE), 2004; 2005a; 2005b), the approach we propose here has arisen from the single disorder protocols and been applied only within the category of "anxiety disorders". The transdiagnostic approach described below is modelled on the approach used in the treatment of eating disorders which has been shown to be effective (Fairburn et al., 2009). The transdiagnostic approach to eating disorders arose from the observations that eating disorders have common distinctive clinical features that appear to be maintained by shared mechanisms, and that the same patient receives multiple diagnoses over time depending on the particular presentation of symptoms at that time (Fairburn et al., 2003). Unlike anxiety disorders, the diagnostic criteria are structured to prevent a patient from having multiple eating disorder diagnoses at the same time. The approach is not generic, it is applied only within the general diagnostic category of "eating disorder". The theory is concerned with the processes that maintain eating disorder psychopathology and the treatment aims to target this psychopathology rather than any particular diagnosis. Thus, within this approach, binge eating is addressed in the same way regardless of whether the patient has a diagnosis of anorexia nervosa, binge eating disorder, bulimia nervosa or an eating disorder not otherwise specified.

Transdiagnostic Approaches to Anxiety Disorders: Theory

A similar argument to that made for a transdiagnostic approach to eating disorders can be applied to anxiety disorders. First, anxiety disorders share common clinical features and second, these features appear to be maintained by common processes.

Common clinical features

The hallmark of anxiety disorders is the overestimation of the likelihood of threat and its potential consequences (Beck, 1976). The content of the threat varies according to the specific disorder. For example, the threat posed by intrusive thoughts is overestimated in obsessive-compulsive disorder (OCD); the threat presented by the occurrence of bodily sensations is overestimated in panic disorder and health anxiety (hypochondriasis) and in social phobia, both the probability and potential cost of the threat of negative evaluation by others are overestimated. Across the anxiety disorders the appraisal of threat is accompanied by both somatic symptoms of arousal and a desire to avoid or otherwise mitigate the threat. While these clinical features are common across the various anxiety disorders, they are unique to the category of "anxiety disorder" (Beck, 1976; Salkovskis, 1996).

There is also a range of common symptoms that occur across anxiety disorders. Panic attacks are not specific to panic disorder but can occur in all anxiety disorders, as well as in those without a psychiatric disorder (APA, 2000). OCD and PTSD are both characterized by unwanted persistent thoughts, images or impulses that are perceived as intrusive and cause marked anxiety (Huppert et al., 2005). The repeated checking that is a hallmark of obsessive compulsive problems also occurs in GAD (Schut, Castonguay, & Borkovec, 2001) and health anxiety (Rachman, 2012). Similarly, almost two-thirds of patients with panic disorder have at least one symptom of OCD (Torres, Dedomenico,

Crepaldi, & Miguel, 2004). To a large extent it is unsurprising that there are shared symptoms across the anxiety disorders as the disorders themselves are difficult to differentiate at a conceptual and diagnostic level (e.g., Goldstein, 1987).

Common maintaining processes across anxiety disorders

Clark (1999) identifies six processes that maintain anxiety related beliefs across anxiety disorder diagnoses: safety-seeking behaviours, attentional deployment, spontaneous imagery, emotional reasoning, memory processes, and the nature of the threat representation. There is empirical support for many of these (see Harvey, Watkins, Mansell, & Shafran, 2004; Mansell, Harvey, Watkins, & Shafran, 2009).

Neither aetiological data nor treatment outcome data can provide direct evidence that anxiety disorders are maintained by common processes, however, the findings from both are consistent with the idea. For example, biological data suggest a shared general biological vulnerability across anxiety disorders (Etkin & Wager, 2007; Hettema, Prescott, Myers, Neale, & Kendler, 2005) with Eley (2001) concluding that genetic influences account for approximately one-third of the variance in childhood anxiety. Similarly, the most effective pharmacological and psychological interventions for the different anxiety disorders are the same: selective serotonin reuptake inhibitors (Bandelow, Zohar, Hollander, Kasper, & Moller, 2002) and CBT (Nathan & Gorman, 2002; Roth & Fonagy, 2005). Furthermore, the data reviewed above showing some (albeit not total) improvement in co-morbid anxiety when the primary anxiety disorder is targeted (e.g., Newman et al., 2010) suggests that the anxiety disorders share some common processes. In summary, the conceptual overlap among the anxiety disorders, their shared clinical features, and the data supporting the existence of common maintaining processes suggest that a "transdiagnostic" approach may be an appropriate way of conceptualizing and treating anxiety disorders.

Transdiagnostic Approaches to Anxiety

Researchers have begun exploring transdiagnostic CBT approaches that aim to address common maintaining mechanisms across the anxiety disorders. Most notably Barlow and colleagues have developed a "unified protocol" for treating both anxiety and mood disorders (Barlow, Allen, & Choate, 2004), which is gaining empirical support for its efficacy (Farchione et al., 2012). Similarly Norton and colleagues have proposed a "transdiagnostic" group CBT protocol (i.e., treating a heterogeneous group of patients using a single treatment protocol) (Norton, 2012). Michelle and Peter Roy-Byrne have implemented a transdiagnostic treatment termed "CALM" (Coordinated Anxiety Learning and Management) for anxiety disorders in primary care and found it to be more effective than usual care for principal anxiety disorders and, to a lesser extent, co-morbid anxiety disorders (Craske et al., 2011). Both this intervention and mindfulness-based stress reduction were effective at reducing the principal anxiety diagnosis severity (Arch et al., 2013).

It is beyond the scope of the current chapter to provide a detailed review of these approaches but Craske (2012) and Mansell, Harvey, Watkins, and Shafran (2008, 2009) provide recent reviews. Here we will outline one transdiagnostic approach, based on the model applied in eating disorders, which attempts to provide the flexibility to incorporate the specific interventions developed within evidence-based diagnosis-specific approaches. It draws primarily on UK based approaches to the treatment of specific disorders, has a clear hypothesized maintenance cycle (McManus, Shafran, & Cooper, 2010) and preliminary support from a case series (McManus, Clark, Muse & Shafran, submitted). The approach prioritizes addressing the common maintaining mechanisms across anxiety disorders but has the flexibility for symptom specific interventions to be incorporated. The goal is to achieve a balance between adopting a standardized approach across all anxiety patients, while ensuring that the intervention remains personalized to the extent that it addresses the idiosyncratic presenting difficulties of a given individual. As has been shown to be effective in the treatment of eating disorders and disorders in childhood (Weisz et al., 2012), this can be done by utilizing a modular design with "core" treatment modules across all patients, to address universal maintaining factors, with additional "optional" modules employed according to the individual's presentation.

Transdiagnostic Protocol for Anxiety Disorders

The transdiagnostic treatment outlined here contains both "core" and "optional" treatment modules to address respectively (i) the processes common to all anxiety disorder diagnoses and (ii) other maintaining mechanisms that are specific to a given individual's presentation. The protocol is based on a transdiagnostic model developed by the authors in collaboration with Dr Zafra Cooper and Dr Gavin Clark. The model (see Figure 7.1) was derived from a cognitive-behavioural analysis of maintaining mechanisms in anxiety disorders and the original cognitive conceptualization proposed by Beck and Emery (1985). It suggests that the misinterpretation of benign stimuli as threatening is maintained by a number of common cognitive processes, and by the performance of counter-productive strategies that prevent disconfirmation of the erroneous threat appraisals. Specific beliefs and assumptions interact with and contribute towards the process of misinterpretation of (i) triggers/fear-objects (e.g., beliefs about the nature and personal meaning of the occurrence of a trigger such as intrusive thoughts or a phobic stimulus), (ii) anxiety sensations (e.g., beliefs about the nature, course and consequences of anxiety, as well as personal meaning/self-evaluation of the occurrence of anxiety), and (iii) counter-productive strategies (e.g., the relationship of counterproductive strategies with threat and the personal significance of their performance – escape/avoidance) that serve to maintain and exacerbate the perception of threat.

Treatment Overview

The purpose of the formulation is to guide the focus of the intervention. Following the model outlined, interventions will focus on the conceptual links between the patient's anxiety disorders and the commonalities between diagnosis-specific approaches to anxiety disorders (e.g., misinterpretations of anxiety sensations as dangerous, the use of avoidance or other counter-productive strategies to manage threat). In accordance with the patient's presentation, a combination of core and optional modules is utilized to address the presenting difficulties. The intervention components have their basis in current empirically validated cognitive-behavioural theory and treatment-protocols. Core modules aim to address maintenance processes conceptualized as maintaining

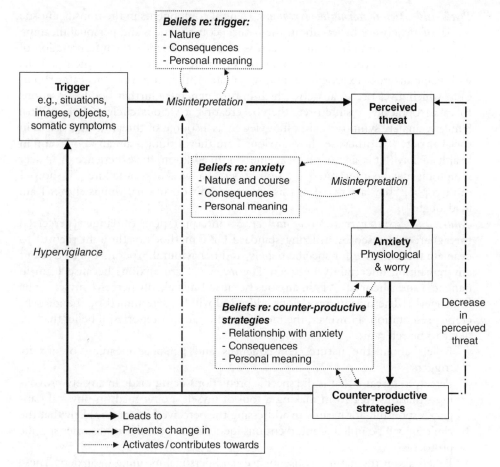

Figure 7.1   Transdiagnostic cognitive behavioural model of anxiety disorders. © Freda McManus and Roz Shafran 2013.

anxiety across *all* anxiety disorder diagnoses, thus forming the basis of the intervention with all anxiety patients. In contrast optional modules are employed selectively according to the nature of the difficulties identified within the individual's formulation.

Core modules are:

- *Collaborative formulation and socialization to the CBT model.* This involves collaboratively developing an individualized transdiagnostic formulation (as shown in Figure 7.1) and socializing the patient to the cognitive behavioural understanding of their anxiety. With more than one anxiety disorder it is useful to review examples of the different types of anxiety. Once the formulation is derived, socialization to the cognitive-behavioural understanding of anxiety can begin. A useful way of setting up the socialization is to regard therapy as a test of Theory A ("I am anxious because I am in danger") vs. Theory B ("I am anxious because I misperceive myself to be in danger"). In this way the course of therapy can be structured as a test of which of these two accounts represents a better fit with reality. The final stage of socialization involves collaboratively identifying and specifying SMART goals for the course of therapy, in relation to the patient's anxiety difficulties.

- *Psycho-education to normalize symptoms.* Central components in the transdiagnostic model of anxiety are beliefs about the nature, consequences and personal meaning of anxiety. One common symptom across anxiety disorders is the interpretation of anxiety symptoms themselves as a source of danger. For example, when patients with panic disorder experience a bodily sensation, they interpret this catastrophically, which gives rise to anxiety, which in turn generates further bodily sensations to catastrophically misinterpret, thereby creating a vicious circle (Clark, 1986). Similarly anxiety symptoms are often viewed as a source of threat in themselves in social anxiety ("if others see how anxious I am they'll think I am an idiot") and in health anxiety ("it is sign of physical illness"). In addition, the experience of anxiety symptoms may be interpreted as a sign of personal weakness or failure ("it shows I can't cope", "the fact that I'm this anxious/can't do normal things shows I am inadequate").

- *Addressing misinterpretations of danger.* Misinterpretations of danger (perceived threat) are addressed by utilizing standard CBT methods of thought records to evaluate the evidence for specific beliefs, and behavioural experiments to test out any remaining uncertainty between Theory A ("I am anxious because I am in danger") and Theory B ("I am anxious because I mistakenly perceive myself to be in danger"). The misinterpretations addressed will be determined by the idiosyncratic presentation. However, the model specifies four categories of belief that are likely to be relevant:
  ○ Beliefs about the nature, consequences and personal meaning of anxiety triggers.
  ○ Perceived threat – that is the specific predictions being made in anxiety provoking situations (e.g., I'm making a fool of myself/going mad/in physical danger/responsible for harm). In addressing the perceived threat it is likely that the clinician will be utilizing interventions identified as effective in disorder specific protocols.
  ○ Beliefs about the nature, consequences and personal meaning of anxiety. These may be that anxiety is in itself dangerous, or that it is interpreted as a sign of personal failure or weakness.
  ○ Beliefs about counter-productive strategies. These may relate to the patient's relationship with anxiety or to the perceived consequences or personal meaning of anxiety.

- *Addressing avoidance and counter-productive safety strategies.* A common maintenance cycle across anxiety disorders is avoidance and the use of safety-seeking behaviours (Salkovskis, 1991). Such behaviours prevent the patient from finding out that their anxiety related beliefs are not realistic. An essential component of CBT for any anxiety problem will be the careful identification and testing out, usually in behavioural experiments, of the consequences of not engaging in avoidance or safety behaviours, that is, testing out specific predictions about what is likely to happen in the feared situations if avoidance/safety behaviours are not used. This may be challenging for patients as using avoidance and safety-seeking behaviours may be the main way that they have coped with their anxiety thus far. Thus, it can be useful to do a formal cost benefit analysis of changing from their old strategy of, for example, doing everything they possibly can to avoid the threat, to a strategy of using anxiety symptoms as a trigger to check out whether what they are afraid of is likely to occur/whether it will be as bad as they fear.

Addressing avoidance and safety-seeking strategies is a theme throughout the intervention. Avoidance and safety-seeking strategies must be incorporated into testing perceived threats. The client's safety behaviours need to be dropped when testing out perceived threats in order for the perceived threat to be fully tested. Similarly, addressing beliefs about counter-productive strategies leads into changing the use of those strategies. Again, interventions shown to be effective in disorder specific protocols are likely to be utilized when addressing avoidance and safety seeking strategies (e.g., exposure and response prevention in OCD or reducing self-focussed attention in social anxiety (McManus et al., 2009)).

- *Modifying cognitive biases.* As discussed above, anxiety is associated with typical cognitive biases such as selective attention to threat, for example, monitoring for feared bodily sensations or scanning for phobic stimuli. Such biases maintain anxiety by increasing the perceived likelihood of threat and thus need to be addressed in treatment. This should begin with a review of the helpfulness (or otherwise) of the processes. Many patients are actively using the strategy as an attempt to manage their difficulties. For example, in social phobia patients may engage in anticipatory processing (Clark & McManus, 2002) prior to feared social events whereby they review all their past social failures in an attempt to prevent them from happening again. Looking at the advantages and disadvantages of such strategies should lead to the conclusion that it is comparatively unlikely to be helpful and almost guaranteed to increase anxiety. Similarly patients with PTSD may constantly scan for danger in an attempt to keep themselves safe from further catastrophes and it may be helpful to review the comparative advantages and disadvantages of such strategies.

- *Relapse prevention planning.* As with any course of CBT it is important to collaboratively construct a "blueprint" to summarize what the patient has learned in therapy, and to specify a plan for dealing with anxiety symptoms on an on-going basis. This is especially important in dealing with patients with multiple anxiety disorders as it is likely that they will have suffered from anxiety symptoms thought their lives and it is not realistic to expect to have no anxiety in the future, not matter how successful the intervention.

At around session 8, progress should be reviewed and a decision made about how to use any remaining sessions. It may be that implementing the core modules described above has set the patient on the road to recovery, and all that is required is more of the same. However, there may be factors maintaining the patient's anxiety that have not been addressed by the core modules (e.g., poor problem-solving, low self-esteem, perfectionism). If so then one or more optional modules may be needed according to the individual presentation. We have identified some optional modules below that may be required according to the idiosyncratic presentation:

- *Addressing low self-esteem.* Low self-esteem may contribute to the patient's anxiety in that if the patient has strongly held general negative self-evaluative beliefs (e.g., "I'm not good enough", "I'm inadequate") then these will drive anxious predictions in that if you perceive yourself as not good enough then it follows that you are unlikely to perceive yourself as able to cope with what life throws at you. Thus an optional module using CBT techniques to address low self-esteem (Fennell 1997; Waite, McManus, & Shafran, 2012) can be used to attenuate low self-esteem.

- *Problem-solving.* If the patient lacks problem-solving skills this may maintain their anxiety in that they will be anxious when they are presented with life problems that they feel unable to solve. Thus an intervention to strengthen the patient's problem-solving skills may be useful (e.g., Nezu, Nezu, & Perri, 1989)
- *Addressing perfectionism.* Perfectionism has been shown to negatively impact outcomes across different forms of treatment and thus may impair progress in CBT for anxiety disorders (Egan, Wade, & Shafran, 2011)
- Other issues such as intolerance of distress can be addressed within this protocol on an ad-hoc basis using evidence-based interventions such as those described by Linehan for the treatment of borderline personality disorder (Linehan, 1993).

In many clinical settings there are limits on treatment duration and/or the number of session available. Thus, when implementing optional modules it may be helpful to use bibliotherapy or other self-help materials to aid progress.

Structure of Treatment

The intervention was devised with treatment duration limits in mind and thus is intended to be delivered over 12 one-hour treatment sessions, according to the following schedule: the first six sessions at twice a week, the following four sessions weekly, and the penultimate and final session occurring at fortnightly intervals. Flexibility according to individual needs is, of course, recommended.

Case Example

Clare was referred for treatment with a combination of symptoms of OCD, social phobia and PTSD. She was particularly struggling with the OCD symptoms. She experienced intrusive images of her house or workplace catching fire or flooding and responded with extensive neutralizing (checking all sources of electricity and water repeatedly). Consequently it took her up to two hours to leave her house and she went to great lengths to avoid being the last person to leave the building at her workplace. In addition, she was anxious about social situations, feeling that others would be able to see her anxiety symptoms and think badly of her. Clare worried a lot about what other people thought of her and felt that she lacked confidence and generally "was not good enough". She also experienced intrusive images relating to a previous traumatic experience in which she was violently assaulted by an acquaintance. She avoided all reminders of this event and tried to make sure she was in complete control in all social interactions so as to prevent anything similar happening again. Clare tried to cope with her difficulties using safety behaviours, avoidance and other compensatory strategies (e.g., always looking her best and having a perfectly tidy house in order to "compensate" for her perceived inadequacies). She strove to conceal her anxiety difficulties from those around her as she didn't want to burden them with her troubles and she feared they would think badly of her if they knew how "weird" she was.

The first two sessions were used to gain a detailed assessment of Clare's anxiety difficulties, and to collaboratively draw up the transdiagnostic formulation shown in Figure 7.2 by going through several recent incidents of high anxiety. Socialization to the CBT model began by constructing the idea of Theory A ("I am anxious because

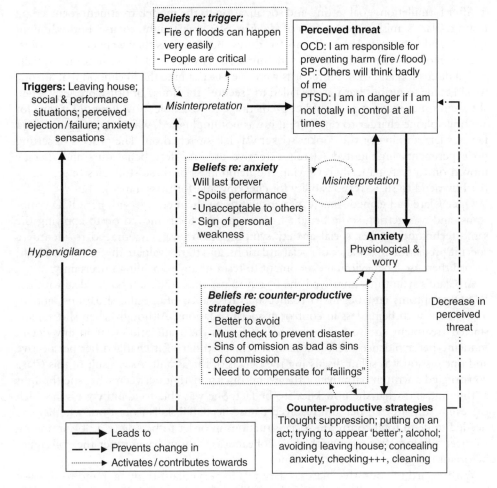

Figure 7.2 Transdiagnostic formulation of Clare's difficulties.

I am in constant danger") versus Theory B ("I am anxious because I mistakenly perceive myself to be in constant danger"). The therapist took care to normalize Clare's anxiety difficulties by giving information on the frequency of anxiety disorders, and on the incidence of intrusive thoughts and checking behaviours in the general population. SMART goals were set for therapy and included:

- Being able to leave the house having only checked taps, sockets etc., once.
- Spending only 15 minutes tidying up before guests arrived.
- Being only 20 per cent anxious in informal social situations (a reduction from the current 50–90 per cent).
- Not using alcohol to manage social situations, that is, being able to attend social situations without drinking alcohol.
- Being able to be last to leave the building at work.
- Being able to tell at least two close friends about some of her anxiety difficulties.
- Not having to be in complete control in all social situations, for example, not to have to know exactly where she was going/with whom but instead to be able to meet a friend and decide then where they would go.

After formulation, goal setting and socialization to the model, treatment focussed on testing Clare's misinterpretations of danger. She was taught to use both thought records and behavioural experiments to address her fears. As they were currently causing her most distress and disability, the initial focus was on OCD symptoms. Initially verbal discussion and thought records were used to examine the likelihood that anyone would come to serious harm if she failed to "secure" the house or office properly. Then she went on to test out some of her predictions, for example, how long did it take for a mobile phone charger to catch fire if it was not unplugged, what happened if a basin tap was left running or the cooker socket was left switched on. The process of setting up experiments highlighted Clare's extensive use of safety behaviours and therapy moved on to systematically reviewing the helpfulness of these strategies (e.g., asking her boyfriend to share responsibility for checking and for reassurance).

Once Clare had gained some experience in using the methods with her OCD symptoms, and was getting some benefit from them, the focus moved on to applying the same techniques to her social anxiety symptoms. She was encouraged to identify a specific prediction in advance of social situations, and to re-evaluate this using a thought record then use a behavioural experiment to test out any remaining uncertainty.

As Clare's symptoms improved she began to use the same methods to deal with her PTSD symptoms and began to reduce her avoidance of specific situations, and to experiment with being less in control in social situations. Although when she initially started treatment she had not wanted to discuss the traumatic event in any detail, reducing her avoidance of situations that reminded her of it changed her perspective and one session was spent discussing the details of the assault. As a result of this Clare constructed a written narrative of the event, discriminating between what she thought at the time and what she now knew to be fact. She was able to identify ways in which the event still affected her and resolved to use her CBT skills to test out whether she needed to be in total control in social situations in order to be safe (e.g., by arranging to meet a friend after work with their colleagues, without having met the colleagues before or being familiar with the venue).

With regard to cognitive biases, Clare was hypervigilant to danger and to signs of potential negative feedback from others. The advantages and disadvantages of this strategy were reviewed and Clare agreed to actively work against it by seeking out signs of social approval and safety. This was a struggle as when looking for signs of approval Clare felt that she couldn't help but notice the opposite. Instead she found it more useful to notice when she was scanning for danger/social disapproval and try to refocus her attention on her purpose in the situation, for example, enjoying spending time catching up with her friend, or getting her message across in a meeting.

After eight sessions progress was reviewed and Clare felt that she was able to continue to make progress with her remaining anxiety symptoms using thought records and behavioural experiments, and that she would like to spend the remaining sessions working on low self-esteem. The therapist agreed that Clare's beliefs about being inadequate, which had developed following the trauma, were likely to leave her vulnerable to anxiety in the future. Thus the remaining sessions utilized the module for low self-esteem and focussed on her negative self-evaluative beliefs. This work was enhanced by Clare having already developed a repertoire of CBT skills and by using self-help workbooks alongside the sessions (Fennell, 2006). Interventions included challenging the evidence for her negative self-evaluative beliefs, identifying positive qualities and reducing avoidance of situations that triggered negative self-evaluation (e.g., dating).

The final sessions were used to construct a blueprint of what Clare had learned in therapy and how she would apply it in situations that she identified and likely to trigger anxiety for her in the future.

Conclusion

To conclude, the approach described here is proposed as a transdiagnostic cognitive-behavioural protocol that can be used to effectively and efficiently formulate and treat individuals with multiple co-occurring anxiety disorders. Transdiagnostic approaches to treating anxiety are important since the appearance of multiple anxiety disorders is the clinical norm and there is little empirical data as to how they should be addressed. If multiple anxiety diagnoses may be efficiently formulated and treated within a single protocol, this may prove to be the most economical and effective method of delivering and disseminating cognitive-behavioural interventions for co-occurring anxiety disorders. The approach proposed here is not suggested to be superior to the evidence-based diagnosis specific protocols, but as an alternative for when a clinician is unable to utilize effectively a diagnosis specific protocol. It arose as an attempt to help clinicians formulate patients with multiple or atypical anxiety disorder presentations, and to identify what to focus on in limited session time. The preliminary data are encouraging but further investigation in large-scale controlled trials is needed before firm conclusions about the efficacy and efficiency of transdiagnostic approaches to treating anxiety disorders can be drawn.

Procedural Rules

- If a patient has anxiety difficulties fitting multiple diagnostic categories, or that don't clearly fit into any one anxiety diagnosis, and there are common processes maintaining them, consider using the transdiagnostic formulation and protocol.
- When following the transdiagnostic approach to treating anxiety outlined in this chapter:
  o Use the model as a template to formulate the common maintaining processes and counter-productive strategies.
  o Before you start intervening, ensure that the patient has bought into the idea that their anxiety difficulties may be a misperception of threat, and that they can test this out in a variety of ways.
  o Utilize the "core modules" to address key maintaining factors.
  o Review progress and if necessary additional "optional modules" to address other difficulties that may be contributing to the maintenance of the patient's anxiety, for example, low self-esteem, perfectionism or difficulties problem-solving.
  o Adapt the protocol to the presentation of the individual patient, as you would with any other approach, for example, if the patient doesn't appear to have counter-productive strategies, then don't place them at the heart of the formulation. If there is a clearly relevant traumatic event, then make sure it is included in the formulation (and also check whether the presentation isn't better accounted for by a PTSD model).

- o   With such patients it is easy to be a "Jack of all trades, and master of none". Thus, in a time-limited intervention it is a priority to maintain focus on the elements identified in the formulation as maintaining anxiety across the different aspects of the anxiety presentation.
- o   Maximize treatment gains by ensuring that any behavioural changes are embedded within a cognitive rationale (i.e., what did you learn from doing that? What does that tell you about how dangerous that situation is for you?), and that any cognitive changes are followed up with behavioural implementation (i.e., now that you know it is not as dangerous as you feared, what will you do differently?)
- o   When trying to address multiple anxiety disorders within a limited time, focus on ensuring the patient has learnt the CBT skills that they can employ across the range of their anxiety presentation. Your role is to teach the CBT skills, and then to problem solve the patient's independent use of the skills. Patients' learning of skills can be facilitated across and within sessions by making use of homework assignments, and by beginning and ending sessions by getting the patient to review both what has been learnt, and how they will implement this going forward.
- o   Ensure that therapy concludes with the patient and therapist drawing up a comprehensive blueprint covering what has been learnt as well as how the skills can be best used to tackle anxiety related difficulties in the future. For this purpose it is most useful if the patient is given a recording of each session – that way they have them available should they ever wish to refresh their memory of what they learnt during the sessions.
- •   If the patient's presentation clearly fits a disorder specific protocol, and the therapist has the skills to implement this protocol, then it is important to be aware that at the current time, the evidence base for the use of diagnosis-specific protocols is far greater than for the newer transdiagnostic approaches. Similarly, if service constraints permit, co-morbid presentations may also be addressed by implementing two or more disorder specific protocols in succession.

References

American Psychiatric Association. (2000). *Diagnostic and statistical manual of mental disorders* (4th ed., text revision). Washington, DC: American Psychiatric Publishing.

American Psychiatric Association. (2013). *Diagnostic and statistical manual of mental health disorders: DSM-5* (5th ed.). Washington, DC: American Psychiatric Publishing.

Arch, J. L., Ayers, C. R., Baker, A., Almklov, E., Dean, D. J., & Craske, M. G. (2013). Randomized clinical trial of adapted mindfulness-based stress reduction versus group cognitive behavioral therapy for heterogeneous anxiety disorders. *Behaviour Research and Therapy, 51*, 185–196.

Bandelow, B., Zohar, J., Hollander, E., Kasper, S., & Moller, H. J. (2002). World Federation of Societies of Biological Psychiatry guidelines for the pharmacological treatment of anxiety, obsessive-compulsive and posttraumatic stress disorders. *World Journal of Biological Psychiatry, 3*, 171–199.

Barlow, D. H., Allen, L. B., & Choate, M. L. (2004). Towards a unified treatment for emotional disorders. *Behavior Therapy, 35,* 205–230.

Beck, A. T. (1976). *Cognitive therapy and the emotional disorders.* New York: International Universities Press.

Beck, A. T., & Emery, G. (1985). *Anxiety disorders and phobias: A cognitive perspective.* New York: Basic Books.

Brown, T. A., Antony, M. M., & Barlow, D. H. (1995). Diagnostic comorbidity in panic disorder – effect on treatment outcome and course of comorbid diagnoses following treatment. *Journal of Consulting and Clinical Psychology, 63,* 408–418.

Brown, T. A., Campbell, L. A., Lehman, C. L., Grisham, J., & Mancill, R. B. (2001). Current and lifetime comorbidity of the DSM-IV anxiety and mood disorders in a large clinical sample. *Journal of Abnormal Psychology, 110,* 585–599.

Butler, A. C., Chapman, J. E., Forman, E. M., & Beck, A. T. (2006). The empirical status of cognitive-behavioral therapy: a review of meta-analyses. *Clinical Psychology Review, 26,* 17–31.

Clark, D. M. (1986). A cognitive approach to panic. *Behavior Research and Therapy, 24,* 461–470.

Clark, D. M. (1999). Anxiety disorders: Why they persist and how to treat them. *Behavior Research and Therapy, 37,* S5–S27.

Clark, D. M., & McManus, F. (2002). Information processing in social phobia. *Biological Psychiatry, 51,* 92–100.

Craske, M. (2012). Transdiagnostic treatment for depression and anxiety. *Depression and Anxiety, 29,* 749–753.

Craske, M., Farchione, T. J., Allen, L. B., Barrios, V., Stoyanova, M., & Rose, R. (2007). Cognitive behavioral therapy for panic disorder and comorbidity: More of the same or less of more? *Behavior Research and Therapy, 45,* 1095–1109.

Craske, M. G., Stein, M. B., Sullivan, G., Sherbourne, C., Bystritsky, A., Rose, R. D., ... Roy-Byrne, P. (2011). Disorder-specific impact of coordinated anxiety learning and management treatment for anxiety disorders in primary care. *Archives of General Psychiatry, 68,* 378–388.

Egan, S. J., Wade, T. D., & Shafran, R., (2011). Perfectionism as a transdiagnostic process: a clinical review. *Clinical Psychology Review, 31,* 203–212.

Ellard, K. K., Fairholme, C. P., Boisseau, C. L., Farchione, T. J., & Barlow, D. H. (2010). Unified protocol for the transdiagnostic treatment of emotional disorders: Protocol development and initial outcome data. *Cognitive and Behavioral Practice, 17,* 88–101.

Eley, T. C. (2001). Contributions of behavioral genetics research: Quantifying genetic, shared environmental and non-shared environmental influences. In M. W. Vasey & M. R. Dadds (Eds.), *The developmental psychopathology of anxiety* (pp. 45–59). New York: Oxford University Press.

Etkin, A., & Wager, T. D. (2007). Functional neuroimaging of anxiety: a meta-analysis of emotional processing in PTSD, social anxiety disorder, and specific phobia. *American Journal of Psychiatry, 164,* 1476–1488.

Fairburn, C. G., Cooper, Z., Doll, H. A., O'Connor, M. E., Bohn, K., Hawker, D. M., ... Palmer, R. L. (2009). Transdiagnostic cognitive behavior therapy for patients with eating disorders: a two site trial with 60 week follow-up. *American Journal of Psychiatry, 166,* 266–267.

Fairburn, C. G., Cooper, Z., & Shafran, R. (2003). Cognitive behavior therapy for eating disorders: a "transdiagnostic" theory and treatment. *Behavior Research and Therapy, 41,* 509–528.

Farchione, T. J., Fairholme, C. P., Ellard, K. K., Boisseau, C. L., Thompson-Hollands, J., Carl, J. R., ... Barlow, D. H. (2012). Unified protocol for transdiagnostic treatment of emotional disorders: A randomized controlled trial. *Behaviour Therapy, 43,* 666–678.

Fennell, M. J. V. (1997). Low self-esteem: a cognitive perspective. *Behavioural and Cognitive Psychotherapy, 25,* 1–25.

Goldstein, S. (1987). Three cases of overlap between panic disorder, social phobia and agoraphobia. *Journal of Clinical Psychiatry, 48,* 452–453.

Greenberg, P. E., Sisitsky, T., Kessler, R. C., Finkelstein, S. N., Berndt, E. R., Davidson, J. R. T., ... Fyer, A. J. (1999). The economic burden of anxiety disorders in the 1990s. *Journal of Clinical Psychiatry, 60*, 427–435.

Harvey, A., Watkins, E., Mansell, W., & Shafran, R. (2004). *Cognitive-behavioral processes across psychological disorders: a transdiagnostic approach to research and treatment.* Oxford: Oxford University Press.

Hayes, S. C., Strosahl, K. D., & Wilson, K. G. (2004). *Acceptance and commitment therapy: an experimental approach to behavior change.* New York: Guilford Press.

Hettema, J. M., Prescott, C. A., Myers, J. M., Neale, M. C., & Kendler, K. S. (2005). The structure of genetic and environmental risk factors for anxiety disorders in men and women. *Archives of General Psychiatry, 62*, 182–189.

Hofmann, S. G., & Smits, J. A. J. (2008). Cognitive-behavioural therapy for adult anxiety disorders: A meta-analysis of randomized placebo controlled trials. *Journal of Clinical Psychiatry, 69*, 621–632.

Huppert, J. D., Moser, J. S., Gershuny, B. S., Riggs, D. S., Spokas, M., Filip, J., ... Baer, L. (2005). The relationship between obsessive-compulsive and posttraumatic stress symptoms in clinical and non-clinical samples. *Journal of Anxiety Disorders, 19*, 127–136.

Kessler, R. C., Berglund, P., Demler, O., Jin, R., Merikangas, K. R., & Walters, E. E. (2005). Lifetime prevalence and age-of-onset distributions of *DSM-IV* disorders in the national co morbidity survey replication. *Archives of General Psychiatry, 62*, 593–602.

Kessler, R. C., Chiu, W. T., Delmer, O., & Walters, E. E. (2005). Prevalence, severity, and comorbidity of 12-month DSM-IV disorders in the national comorbidity survey Replication. *Archives of General Psychiatry, 62*, 617–627.

Linehan, M. M. (1993). *Skills training manual for treatment of borderline personality disorder.* New York: Guilford Press.

Mansell, W., Harvey, A., Watkins, E., & Shafran, R. (2008). Cognitive behavioural processes across psychological disorders: a review of the utility and validity of the transdiagnostic approach. *International Journal of Cognitive Therapy - Special Issue on Transdiagnostic Approaches to CBT, 1*, 181–191.

Mansell, W., Harvey, A., Watkins, E., & Shafran, R. (2009). Conceptual foundations of the transdiagnostic approach to CBT. *Journal of Cognitive Psychotherapy; An International Quarterly, 231*, 13–27.

McManus, F., Clark., D., Grey, N., Wild, J., Hirsch, C., Fennell, M., ... Manley, J. (2009). A demonstration of the efficacy of two of the components of cognitive therapy for social phobia. *Journal Anxiety Disorders, 23*, 496–503.

McManus, F., Clark, G., Muse, K., & Shafran, R. (submitted). Case series evaluating a transdiagnostic cognitive behavioural treatment for co-occurring anxiety disorders.

McManus, F., Shafran, R., & Cooper, Z. (2010). What does a "transdiagnostic" approach have to offer the treatment of anxiety disorders? *British Journal of Clinical Psychology, 49*, 491–505.

Nathan, P. E., & Gorman, J. M, (2002). *A guide to treatments that work* (2nd ed.). New York: Oxford University Press.

National Institute for Clinical Excellence (2004). *Anxiety: Management of anxiety (panic disorder, with or without agoraphobia and generalized anxiety disorder) in adults in primary, secondary and community care.* London: National Institute for clinical excellence. Clinical Guideline No. 22. Retrieved from http://www.nice.org.uk/nicemedia/pdf/cg022niceguidelineamended.pdf

National Institute for Clinical Excellence (NICE) (2005a). *Obsessive-compulsive disorder: core interventions in the treatment of obsessive-compulsive disorder and body dysmorphic disorder.* Clinical Guideline No. 31. London: National Institute for clinical excellence. Retrieved from http://www.nice.org.uk/nicemedia/pdf/cg031fullguideline.pdf

National Institute for Clinical Excellence (NICE) (2005b). *Post-traumatic stress disorder: the management of PTSD in adults and children in primary and secondary care.* Clinical Guideline No. 26. London: National Institute for clinical excellence. Retrieved from http://www.nice.org.uk/nicemedia/pdf/CG026fullguideline.pdf

Newman, M. G., Przeworski, A., Fisher, A. J., & Borkovec, T. D. (2010). Diagnostic comorbidity in adults with generalized anxiety disorder: impact of comorbidity on psychotherapy outcome and impact of psychotherapy on comorbid diagnoses. *Behaviour Therapy, 41*, 59–72.

Nezu, A. M., Nezu, C. M., & Perri, M. G. (1989). *Problem-solving therapy for depression: theory, research, and clinical guidelines.* New York: John Wiley & Sons.

Norton, P. J. (2012). A randomized clinical trial of transdiagnostic cognitive-behavioral treatments for anxiety disorder by comparison to relaxation training. *Behavior Therapy, 43*, 506–517.

Rachman, S. (2012). Health anxiety disorders: a cognitive construal. *Behaviour, Research and Therapy, 50*, 502–512.

Randall, C. L., Thomas, S., & Thevos, A. K. (2001). Concurrent alcoholism and social anxiety disorder: A first step toward developing effective treatments. *Alcoholism, Clinical and Experimental Research, 25*, 210–220.

Roth, A. & Fonagy, P. (2005). *What works for whom?* (2nd ed.). London: Guilford Press.

Saarni, S. I., Suvisaari, J., Sintonen, H., Pirkola, S., Koskinen, S., Aromaa, A., & Lonnqvist, J. (2007). Impact of psychiatric disorders on health-related quality of life: general population survey. *British Journal of Psychiatry, 190*, 326–332.

Salkovskis, P. M. (1991). The importance of behaviour in the maintenance of panic and anxiety. *Behavioural Psychotherapy, 19*, 6–19.

Salkovskis, P. (Ed.) (1996). *Frontiers of Cognitive Psychology* (pp. 48–96). New York: Guildford Press.

Schut, A. J., Castonguay, L. G., & Borkovec, T. D. (2001). Compulsive checking behaviors in generalized anxiety disorder. *Journal of Clinical Psychology, 57*, 705–715.

Shafran, R., Clark, D. M., Fairburn, C. G., Arntz, A., Barlow, D. H., Ehlers, A., ... Wilson, G. T. (2009). Mind the Gap: Improving the dissemination of CBT. *Behaviour Research and Therapy, 47*, 902–909.

Segal, Z. V., Williams, J. M. G., & Teasdale, J. D. (2002). *Mindfulness-based cognitive therapy for depression: a new approach to preventing relapse.* New York: Guilford Publications.

Tsao, J. C. I., Mystkowski, J. L., Zucker, B. G., & Craske, M. G. (2002). Effects of cognitive-behavioral therapy for panic disorder on comorbid conditions: replication and extension. *Behavior Therapy, 33*, 493–509.

Torres, A. R., Dedomenico, A. M., Crepaldi, A. L., & Miguel, E. C. (2004). Obsessive-compulsive symptoms in patients with panic disorder. *Comprehensive Psychiatry, 45*, 219–224.

Waite, P., McManus, F., & Shafran, R. (2012). Cognitive behaviour therapy for low self-esteem: a preliminary randomized controlled trial in a primary care setting. *Journal of Behaviour Therapy & Experimental Psychiatry, 43*, 1039–1044.

Weisz, J. R., Chorpita, B. F., Palinkas, L. A., Schoenwald, S. K., Miranda, J., Bearman, S. K., ... Research Network on Youth Mental Health (2012). Testing standard and modular designs for psychotherapy treating depression, anxiety and conduct problems in youth: a randomized effectiveness trial. *Archives of General Psychiatry, 69*, 274–282.

8

When and How to Talk about the Past in CBT

Gillian Butler

Introduction

An important assumption made by cognitive therapists is that the people with whom they work have good reasons for thinking the way they do. These good reasons are assumed to be based on experiences, which are the source of conclusions such as: "if you let yourself get close to others you will only get hurt", and of messages reflecting their meaning: "I don't matter", "You're never safe". In order to re-think such thoughts it helps to be able to talk about past experiences and to re-evaluate their meaning in the present. But talking about the past is not always easy or helpful. It may be painful, and especially for those who have suffered traumatic or abusive experiences earlier in life, it can provoke flashbacks, dissociation and self-harming behaviours. This chapter puts forward a set of ideas and principles to help clinicians decide when, and how, to talk about the past with people whose past histories have left them with complex, long-standing difficulties. Suggestions draw on the theory of CBT, research into fundamental processes, clinical research, and observations made during treatment of about 40 patients who had suffered abusive or traumatic experiences during childhood.

Beck et al. (1979) tell us "the content of cognitive therapy is focused on 'here-and-now' problems. Little attention is paid to childhood recollections except to clarify present observations" (p. 7). The extensive body of research demonstrating the effectiveness of CBT with Axis-1 disorders surely demonstrates that lasting benefit can often be achieved without talking extensively about the past. It is important to complete a thorough assessment of personal history, and of problem development, and for these to contribute to the formulation upon which the choice of interventions will be based. But the assumption is that it is only necessary to engage in detailed exploration of the past in special circumstances. Theoretically, when underlying beliefs and assumptions are predominantly functional it is sufficient to focus on present thoughts and behaviours. When people have sufficiently positive beliefs, or a balanced set of functional and dysfunctional ones, they can assimilate the implications of cognitive and behavioural changes into their existing belief system, and modify or strengthen their beliefs

How to Become a More Effective CBT Therapist: Mastering Metacompetence in Clinical Practice,
First Edition. Edited by Adrian Whittington and Nick Grey.
© 2014 John Wiley & Sons, Ltd. Published 2014 by John Wiley & Sons, Ltd.

without specific help, and without detailed exploration of the past. Indeed this can be a confidence-building discovery.

Therefore, the special circumstances that indicate when to focus on the past in more depth are theoretically defined by the presence and dominance of dysfunctional beliefs and assumptions, rather than by a particular diagnosis. Someone with a specific phobia may have such low self-esteem that cognitive and behavioural changes are easily dismissed, and changes are transient. If their underlying beliefs interfere with progress, further work on these, and on their origins, could be helpful. Someone who has suffered a single traumatic experience may recover quickly, and not need to talk about the past if the trauma has not shaken their beliefs, for instance about the safeness or dangerousness of the world surrounding them, or about themselves. People who have suffered extensive childhood trauma or neglect may also have experienced sufficient love and support to have built up some protective beliefs, especially about themselves, that provide a lasting degree of robustness. They may not need, or wish, to re-visit the past during therapy. So it can be argued, on grounds of efficiency, that therapists should focus on the present first, and only focus more extensively on the past when progress eludes their patients.

Material for this chapter is drawn from work with people who suffered the effects of prolonged childhood trauma and whose beliefs, about the world, other people and themselves were profoundly dysfunctional. In these cases, clinical judgment played a large part in making decisions about when, and how, to talk about the past as research has not yet enabled us to predict when doing so will have de-stabilizing, beneficial or minimal effects. Techniques available include cognitive restructuring, re-living past traumatic experiences, imagery re-scripting (Arntz & Weertman, 1999), up-dating old memories using imagery (Holmes & Hackmann, 2004), and re-visiting the past using imaginal methods such as the two-chair technique. Other methods have been developed from work with specific subsets of traumatized people such as adults or children living in war zones (Narrative Exposure Therapy; Schauer, Neuner, & Ebert, 2005), or combat veterans. There is also a large body of research done with students demonstrating the lasting value of writing about childhood traumas (Niederhoffer & Pennebaker, 2005; Pennebaker, 2000).

Theoretically important work on autobiographical memory and on working memory provides another source of ideas (see e.g., Conway & Pleydell-Pearce, 2000; Williams et al., 2007; Williams & Broadbent, 1986). One strand of this work explores the accessibility of specific versus general memories in people suffering from depression. Repeatedly depressed patients readily come up with general themes when thinking about the past, and find it harder to elaborate the details. In studies of the effectiveness of various methods of working with the past in depressed people Dalgleish has been able to differentiate more and less successful methods (Dalgleish, Hill, Morant, & Dunn, 2011). Memory specificity training mediated changes in mood, but accessing self-affirming memories, working on positive memories or training working memory (executive or "brain" training) did not. In contrast, Engelhard describes a particular focus on specific (rather than general) aspects of trauma memory in PTSD, and she found that taxing working memory could bring symptomatic relief. She suggests that EMDR may be helpful when it places demands on working memory: demanding tasks such as mental arithmetic or the computer game Tetris had similar effects (e.g., Van den Hout, Barelski, & Engelhard, 2013). So the specificity or generality of trauma memories seems to be linked to affective symptoms, but in different ways in depression, when memories tend to be over-general, than in PTSD, or anxiety, when specific and intrusive memories tend to persist. Interestingly, this focus on specificity in PTSD can be reduced to good effect: perspective broadening tasks reduce responses to distressing films as well as to autobiographical memories (Schartau, Dalgleish, & Dunn 2009). But this still does not tell us enough. Clinicians still do not know, for example, when it would be best to focus on specific details (as in re-living), or to focus on broader themes and more general meanings.

Clinical Starting Points

The material summarized here is drawn from clinical work with adults who had experienced severe, prolonged and usually multiple forms of traumatic experience during childhood. Most of them met criteria for Borderline Personality Disorder and described fluctuating degrees of anxiety and/or depression. Deciding to talk about the past is difficult (partly) because it is hard to know, in individual cases, whether this will "lay it to rest", "draw a line under it" and "complete the emotional processing", or whether it will increase the risk of self-harm, re-traumatization, or occasionally symptoms of Dissociative Identity Disorder. After years of unremitting pain and fear, when there are extensive gaps in memory, or when the truth about the past cannot be known, talking about the past can be clinically risky. If feelings run too high it is impossible to think straight, while intellectualizing and keeping feelings locked up achieves little or nothing. So both cognition and emotion should be accessed for people to change. Some preliminary guidelines about when to talk about the past and when not to, drawn from clinical observation and theoretical considerations, are provided in Figure 8.1.

More likely to be helpful when it:

- Provides distance, and enables reflection
- Involves validation and affirmation
- Elicits a (compassionate) response in the listener
- Helps to re-evaluate beliefs (e.g., about blame, or "badness")
- Helps to make sense, and links things up (contributing to formulation work)
- Re-calibrates normality (a lifetime of brutality does not make that behaviour normal)
- Starts the process of exploring different perspectives

Less likely to be helpful when:

- Subjectivity dominates
- The telling becomes ritualized
- The perspective gets stuck
- Detachment is too great, and emotion is lacking
- Accompanying emotions are too intense or uncontrollable
- It elicits confabulation, dissociation, self-harm or other signs of intense distress

Figure 8.1 Initial guidelines for talking about the past.

My aim here is to make these ideas more specific. One patient commented, after she had made significant improvement: "You've got to look backwards in order to look forward, but you can only do that from a position of strength". The questions addressed here arise from thinking about that position of strength. What does it consist of? How do we know if it is absent? And what should we do if it is? How do we help people to build, and to stabilize, that position of strength? How do we use it to make talking about the past useful for living in the present and for thinking about the future? Preliminary answers to these questions are provided below. The ideas are divided into three main sections focusing on meta-cognitive awareness, on building up a sense of self and on developing an identity (see also Butler, 2004; Butler and Holmes, 2009; Holmes and Butler, 2009).

There are common themes running through the points made below. First, the work described cannot be done "mechanically" – it depends for its success on building a good therapeutic relationship. Second, the style of cognitive therapy is particularly well-suited to this task. The open, collaborative, explicit and exploratory nature of the style, when used flexibly, makes it easier to focus attention on the meaning of all that goes on in therapy, as well as on the meaning of past experiences, and to bring that up for mutual reflection and feedback.

Meta-Cognitive Awareness

Meta-cognitive awareness here refers to the ability to reflect on thoughts, feelings and behaviours, and therefore on the actions and memories that form the fabric of past experience. Without the capacity for reflection people can become lost in subjectivity, and unable to step back from their feelings, and the interpretations upon which they are based, and are unable to think about their thinking (obviously, a necessary pre-requisite for benefitting from CBT). When talking about a recent distressing event, people who cannot use meta-cognitive awareness become stuck in describing what happened, focusing on their reactions to both internal and external events. Using the terminology of Bateman and Fonagy (2004), they have not yet developed "reflective self-function". When asked Socratic questions about how they made sense of what happened, or what they did, or might have wanted to do, they return repeatedly to the same, elaborated subjective reporting, as if unable to reflect as well as react. They may seem to be seeking comfort, or asking the therapist to take the pain away, as if they are unable to organize a coherent or functional response to distress. Their comments are often full of confusions, for example, between thoughts and feelings, or between different kinds of feelings, or between different kinds of pain. Physical and psychological pain may be hard to disentangle, so that mentioning feeling miserable, like feeling wretched, may be a way of referring to either kind of distress. For example, one patient confused affective distress with symptoms of septicaemia, and another with those of a serious urine infection. In both cases emergency treatment was needed, and there were numerous occasions when relatively minor symptoms, such as those of a cold or flu, were missed, on the assumption that they were part of "normal"' psychological distress. Accounts of past events, at times when people have no access to meta-cognitive awareness, are often tangential, disconnected, muddled or even incoherent, and possibly similar to those given by children who have experienced disorganized attachment styles of parenting (which may of course be a common history for adults traumatized as children).

I would suggest that talking about the past when someone is unable to use meta-cognitive awareness is not helpful. There are some adults who have not yet learned how to reflect as well as react, and others for whom the sense of being lost in subjectivity is episodic, and, for example, triggered by flashbacks or intense emotion. In either case, once therapists have recognized the repetitiveness of accounts, and the inability to engage reflection in response to Socratic questions, it will be more useful to turn attention away from the past and to focus instead on recent events, or on the current content of therapy.

Methods for developing the ability to reflect are outlined next, and understood here as necessary preliminaries to being able to talk usefully about the past. Assuming an extreme degree of difficulty, the first step is to segment the flow of experience into discrete events, so that both parties know what they are talking about. For example, during a muddled account of her previous week, a patient spoke about being taken by a friend to look at some local floods. This was put on the agenda as it had greatly upset her, and we labelled it "visiting the flood". Describing it she was frequently side-tracked, and the label helped to re-focus the discussion as well as to distinguish this event from numerous other issues. Assuming that the flood had some special significance, we tried to find out more about its meaning for her in the present. This appeared to be linked to a profound fear of showing distress.

Starting from the feelings is useful when people are not good at reflecting. The next step is to ask the patient what they needed in that situation. In this case the answer was clear: to get home – quickly. Then we could focus on how she could have brought this about: on taking appropriate action to meet her needs. The idea here, in bare outline, is:

- identify, and label, a specific and recent event;
- focus on feelings first;
- identify what the patient *needs* in that specific situation, to resolve those feelings;
- think together about what *action(s)* would help to meet those needs; and
- if possible, draw general conclusions from these to test out during homework assignments.

Going through these steps helped this patient to start to reflect about this recent incident, and to think about possible actions that might have been helpful and possible. After repeated practice with similar situations, in which feelings, needs and action plans were linked up, her ability to reflect improved, and she also became better able to take appropriate action when upset.

The background to this example has important implications. This person had suffered extensive physical and sexual abuse throughout her childhood, and as far as possible had been excluded from the life of the rest of the family. Almost any reference to the past during our initial meetings, or any inadvertent elicitation of a painful memory, led to episodes of dissociation during which she ceased to respond, and after which she was too exhausted to continue the session. Later, after focusing as described above, on the present, and learning to reflect as well as react, she was able to speak about the past without dissociating. She then revealed much that helped to make sense of her reaction to seeing the flood. In outline, she had been punished for showing feelings, and her brother had once tried to drown her when swimming in waters that resembled those of the flood. Talking about the past at a time when she was not able to reflect on it was not helpful, and risked causing further distress and/or damage.

This overall strategy has been generally useful, and the explicitness of cognitive therapy helps to clarify the steps involved. Patients can then use them (often creatively) as new situations arise. Someone who became increasingly fearful the closer and more intimate her relationships became, and who had learned to protect herself with violent aggression when feeling emotionally at risk (literally too close for comfort) said, after she had managed for the first time to control her violent impulses: "First I recognized what I needed, then I decided what to do, then I acted on it". For this to work well it is essential to select an emotionally salient, recent event, to keep attention focused on this and to explain the steps clearly. The ability to communicate well, the language used and the nature of interactions during therapy are likely to make a difference, as the following quotation from a therapy tape suggests:

> Having a word for something puts you in a different position. Then you can use language to work things out. Words provide some distance ... describing feelings rather than having them ... If you don't talk about things (or write about them) you remain caught up in it.

Helping people to reflect also helps them to find the words in which to talk about complex and painful things. It appears that people who remain "caught up in things", and unable to reflect on them are also unable to organize their behaviour to meet their needs – at least at that time. Starting from feelings in the present and focusing on recent episodes of distress without talking about the past fosters the capacity for self-reflection, and for self-organization. This starts the process of building that "position of strength" from which talking about the past may be more useful.

Building Up a Sense of Self

Being able to reflect should put people in a good position to talk about their past experiences. However, clinical observations suggest that difficulties persist, especially when the sense of self is poorly developed or unstable. Then, accounts of the past often reflect the valence of the sense of self, for instance as bad, evil or culpable: "I'm rotten to the core"; "I'm just a piece of shit". Or people talk about the past with a specific purpose in mind: to test out reactions, to shock or to find out if they will be believed. Sometimes they tell their stories in ways that reflect aspects of what the past means to them while omitting other aspects: as victims or as survivors for instance. Then they may describe experiences that fit with their current view, but still attempt to keep safe, or under control, by avoiding other facts or conclusions. One patient wrote: "I use a lot of protective vocabulary" and I "try to find a way to say all these things without being re-traumatized by feeling I will be disbelieved, rejected, abandoned, blamed or shamed". The resulting accounts are frequently inconsistent, incomplete, contradictory, disconnected or repetitive. Sometimes the telling appears ritualized, and from the point of view of a therapist searching for new ways of seeing things, it feels stuck.

Inconsistencies and contradictions are common for all of us of course, but in people with traumatic histories they can be quite destabilizing. Describing her abusive father a patient spoke about: "Feeling safe when he held my hand and terrified at other times", and being confused and upset by the contradiction involved. Remembering disparate experiences (safety and terror linked to the same person) can be like being pushed from one extreme to the other, (black and white thinking), and can feel intolerable: "Compromise is selling my soul, or losing my integrity". Finding a resolution, or middle ground is not only difficult, it means losing a part of oneself. Someone else, at the start of the process of talking about the past, came to disturbingly inconsistent conclusions: "I don't believe in punishment as a way of dealing with anything", and "I have to punish myself". Another said: "I value interdependence between people, but never want contact with my mother". This person then concluded that she must be a bad person as she could not apply her values to herself. It is perhaps a commonplace now to accept that our memories, the images in which they are embedded, and the ways in which we recollect past experiences play a significant part in defining who we are: our sense of self. When these memories do not cohere the sense of self feels fragile. Working to build a more robust sense of self would then theoretically be helpful, and having a stronger, more stable sense of self should contribute to the effectiveness of thinking, and re-thinking about the past and its meaning. Otherwise echoes of the past may send tremors through the sense of self. A patient who was subjected to the intense anger of others as a child noticed this when his partner got angry. Because someone who cared about him also became angry he was completely thrown, and said "I don't know who I am with him".

It follows that we should find more ways of helping people to build up a functional and robust sense of self before we can expect to make the most of talking about the past. Two of these will be discussed next: work on validation and work on values.

Validation work

People want to be liked, to have their good qualities appreciated, and to feel that others accept and approve of them. However attempts to validate people who believe that they are evil, or responsible for the bad treatment they received, or of no account, are frequently shrugged off as (more or less) polite, but wrong-headed, empty statements that you might expect from a well-meaning therapist. A patient explained to me why attempts at validation were meaningless to him: "If I matter, bad things won't happen. But they did. So I don't".

Pinel and Constantino (2003) point out that many clinicians are not clear about what is necessary for validation to be effective. They suggest that positivity alone is insufficient and easy to discount, as it fails to demonstrate that the person being validated has been seen for what they really are. They propose that effective validation should involve *verification* as well as positivity. Verification is achieved when people believe that their true selves have been seen, understood and accepted. So therapists should explore the negative views that people have of themselves, and learn how to validate their negative self-judgments, without labelling them as bad people. This may be achieved by recognizing someone's good reasons (based on their specific memories) for arriving at negative judgments about themselves. It might mean recognizing the bad things someone has done, and paying attention to their failures (perceived or otherwise). It might mean, together and collaboratively, gathering specific evidence from the past and considering its implications. Then, in the context of an accepting relationship, validation based on both positivity and verification contributes to the development of a stable sense of self.

The patient who was distressed by visiting the flood responded well to this more elaborated form of validation. She commented: "I have never had someone on my side before" and she started to talk about her past experiences without dissociating. At this stage she was still fragile, and felt safer if we focused on the past for relatively brief periods of time, on specific incidents and on their implications for her in the present. Bigger themes such as their meaning for her self-beliefs, or beliefs about the world and other people were addressed later.

Work on values

Our values help to define us: they tell us what we are for or against, and what matters to us. One patient said: "If I'm a non-person I don't see any need to hold values, or to apply them to my own life". At this stage his accounts of the past were largely analytical and unemotional (full of gaps and inconsistencies). Another spoke about the past using the values and attitudes that he had as an abused and threatened child. Describing the moment the abuse was discovered he said: "We were caught". The therapist's response was a question: "*Who* was caught?" He suddenly realized that he was rescued, not caught, and his previous account reflected the "childish" values that he no longer held. With little additional help he then re-thought his assumptions about having done wrong, being responsible for that and being to blame. I suggest that work on identifying values also contributes to creating the position of strength from which it is possible to look back usefully on the past.

There are many openings in therapy for working on identifying and clarifying values. Therapists can reflect back the implications of their observations, asking for example: "What does it say about you, that you … helped out your friend … enjoyed your sister's success … were angry when lied to?" They can work on identifying rules and assumptions revealed by patient's words: "You should never hurt a child … should always stick up for yourself … do what others want". It can be useful to ask people to list their values or guiding principles and to talk about which ones matter most, or need clarifying or contradict each other. The decisions that people make reveal their values, and help to define what matters to them. At times of uncertainty (should I take this job/move away from here/do what my neighbour has asked me to do) it is useful to help patients first to think about their values and then to think about what decision might fit with those values. In the words of another patient: If I matter, it matters what decisions and choices I make, and these help to determine my sense of who I am". So practice with decision making is also helpful.

The actions of others reveal their values: being treated with respect, being looked after when sick, and discovering that one shares others people's values brings with it a sense of connectedness. Exemplifying values provides a sense of valuing, not just of validating, the person one is working with in therapy. Bringing together the work on reflection with that on validation and values helps a person to develop a more coherent, consistent and organized sense of self. It helps them to hang on to that sense of consistency despite contradictions. A patient working on his values for homework wrote: Mattering helps me to recognize my needs. Values dictate the way I behave, the way I seek to meet my needs.

Many other methods for helping people to improve their self-opinion are to be found in work on self-confidence and self-esteem. Further ideas about validation can be found in Linehan (1993), and on values in Hayes, Strosahl, and Wilson (1999). Validation and values are given a central place here because the topics have obvious links with the attitudes and beliefs that influence the way people see themselves – with their sense of self – as well as with the ways in which they understand their experiences, and so far they have received relatively little attention from cognitive therapists.

Developing an Identity

With a more stable sense of self it becomes easier to talk about memories of specific incidents in the past, and to reflect on their meaning. Many questions arise. Do they make me a bad person? Or is it possible that I am an ordinary person to whom bad things happened? Are all other people untrustworthy? Or not? CBT, with its focus on individual perspectives, sensitivity to feelings, practical behavioural work and exploratory attitude towards evidence, now and then, is ideally placed for addressing these questions. Aspects of it can also be explained sufficiently simply for use as self-help material (Butler & Hope 2007, pp. 308–330). We have yet to think about how exactly to make the most of talking about the past and how to make decisions about what to do when.

Observations suggest that difficulties addressing the past often persist, and that these involve problems developing a sense of continuity, with making meaningful links over time, with planning ahead and with the sense of existing in an integrated way over time (Butler, 2004). I refer to these here as consequences of problems of identity. An example may help to clarify. A patient well on the road to recovery, attended a conference with a colleague. Together they met someone they both knew, who asked: How did you two meet? The patient was unable to reply, and hugely distressed. Later she said: "I can't tell a story about myself"; "I can't use the word 'I' in a story. I still don't know who I am". Of course one way of resolving these problems is to tell the story of the past, and try to link up disconnected fragments, thinking about the meaning of the various experiences that made up the past. But meaning is more than one thing. Explorations in therapy may stop short if patients are not asked about different aspects of the legacy of past experiences, such as their significance, the impact they had on them (interfering with their lives, reducing opportunities), and their implications (for self-worth, for developing intimate relationships). People may also have different intentions when talking about the past, such as to leave it behind, or elicit a particular reaction: perhaps one that was needed earlier. Such intentions will influence what people mean by what they say, and demand skilled listening from therapists. Examples of the types of questions that can help people to discover and to explore the different aspects of the meaning of the past to them are listed in Figure 8.2.

In order to talk usefully about the past three processes should be differentiated. First, patients need to find a way of representing it: of putting it out there so as to reflect on it. They may use any medium: written or spoken language, metaphor, imagery, drawings, music or artefacts. All of these have spontaneously been used by my patients when talking about the meaning to them of the past, and it helps if therapists encourage patients to express themselves in any way they wish (Butler & Holmes, 2009). The second process is that of conveying the meaning: being willing to tell the story or show the writing, drawing or object, and if necessary to explain it to a listener (or recipient). Therapists should check that what has been conveyed has been correctly understood. The final process is that of reflecting on meaning. Using the terminology of cognitive therapy this means exploring and re-examining it. It also means using the capacity for abstract as well as concrete thinking, making links between different times and experiences, and extracting meanings.

A difficult dilemma arises with this last process, concerning whether to focus on specific detail, possibly using re-living or another of the more fine-grained techniques, or to focus instead on generalities: on broad themes, including the different aspects of

General questions

What did that mean to you? What was that about? How do you understand that? Or make sense of it? What does it tell you? How do you fit it all together?

Content

What are you referring to? What actually happened? Which event are we focusing on?

Significance

How important was that for you then? ... or in your life? How much has that affected you? How big a part does that play in the decisions you make now?

Impact

What effect did that have on you? How did it affect ... schooling ... friendships ... your sense of who you are? ... confidence? ... Family life? Feelings? .... How you spend your time? ... Relationships? ... Sexuality? How has this interfered with your life?

Implications

What does that tell you about ... yourself? ... Other people? ... The world? What is likely to happen in x or y situations? How does it influence the choices you make?

Figure 8.2   Examples of questions about different aspects of meaning.

meaning. As a novelist and philosopher, Alain de Botton provides some interesting reasons for reducing, rather than elaborating, detail. He says:

> Memory (as the imagination) is ... an instrument of simplification and selection ... layers of experience settle into a compact and well-defined narrative ...
> The anticipatory and artistic imaginations omit and compress, they cut away the periods of boredom and direct our attention to critical moments and, without either lying or embellishing, thus lend to life a vividness and a coherence that it may lack in the distracting woolliness of the present. (2002, p. 15).

Condensing, instead of elaborating, can be extremely useful when talking about the past. The patient who could not tell her story when she met an acquaintance at a conference, who had spoken frequently in therapy about the past, and had used detailed re-scripting and re-living techniques at different times, later told her whole story in about 40 minutes. Here is her comment (from a session tape):

> I feel more like a person with a painful memory than having something inside you have to gouge out ... it was like integrating lots of different bits into one sort of narrative; making connections between things I hadn't pieced together before ...It made me realise that contradictions were OK: feeling safe when he held my hand and terrified at other times .... Before I just looked at things in discrete blocks.

Condensing provided a sense of continuity, clarifying meanings and integrating experiences into a single narrative. This person found that she could now use the sense of continuity for forward planning. Talking about the past had led her through the present and into the future: possibly a result of first developing a "position of strength".

Procedural Rules

- Do not talk about the past when someone appears "lost in subjectivity"; unable to reflect as well as react. Instead focus on the immediate present.
- Develop reflection skills by starting from an emotionally salient, specific incident. Find out what the patient needed, and discuss appropriate action. Make explicit links between feelings, needs and actions.
- When the sense of self is fragile or unstable, work to increase confidence, use effective validation and work on values.
- Validating includes both positivity and verification.
- Identify personal values, and encourage people to make decisions that fit with those.
- Help people to integrate different experiences, to develop a sense of continuity, and to focus on general meanings and themes as well as details.
- Meaning includes the significance, impact and implications of the past. Listen for what the person means by what they say.
- Respond differently when someone is representing, conveying or reflecting on the meaning of the past. Encourage any form of representation.
- Consider condensing, rather than elaborating, accounts of the past when working on broader, more general themes and meanings.

References

Arntz, A., & Weertman, A. (1999). Treatment of childhood memories: theory and practice. *Behaviour Research and Therapy, 37*, 715–740.

Bateman . A, & Fonagy, P. (2004). *Psychotherapy for borderline personality disorder*. Oxford: Oxford University Press.

Beck, A. T., Rush, A. J., Shaw, B. F., & Emery, G. (1979). *Cognitive therapy of depression*. New York: Guilford Press.

Butler, G. (2004). Clinical difficulties to revisit. In J. Yiend (Ed.). *Cognition, emotion and psychopathology: theoretical, empirical and clinical directions* (pp. 290–307). Cambridge: Cambridge University Press.

Butler, G., & Holmes, E. (2009). Imagery and the self following childhood trauma: observations concerning the use of drawings and external images. In L. Stopa (Ed.), *Imagery and the damaged self: Perspective on imagery in cognitive therapy* (pp. 166–180). London: Routledge.

Butler, G., & Hope, T. (2007). Dealing with the past. In G. Butler & T. Hope (Eds.), *Manage your mind: the mental fitness guide* (2nd ed., pp. 308–330). Oxford: Oxford University Press.

Conway, M. A., & Pleydell-Pearce, C. W. (2000). The construction of autobiographical memories in the self-memory system. *Psychological Review, 107*(2), 261–288.

Dalgleish, T., Hill, E., Morant, N., & Dunn, B. D. (2011). The structure of past and future lives in depression. *Journal of Abnormal Psychology, 120*, 1–15.

De Botton, A. (2002). *The art of travel*. London: Hamish Hamilton.

Hayes, S. C., Strosahl, K. D., & Wilson, K. G. (1999). *Acceptance and commitment therapy*. New York: Guilford.

Holmes, E., & Butler, G. (2009). Cognitive therapy and suicidality in post-traumatic stress disorder. In N. Grey (Ed.), *A casebook of cognitive therapy for traumatic stress reactions* (pp. 178–193). Hove, UK: Routledge.

Holmes, E., & Hackmann, A. (2004). Mental imagery and memory in psychopathology (Special Issue). *Memory, 12*(4).

Linehan, M. M. (1993). *Skills training manual for treating borderline personality disorder*. New York: Guilford.

Niederhoffer, K. G., & Pennebaker, J. W. (2005). Sharing one's story: on the benefits of writing or talking about emotional experience. In C. R. Snyder & S. J. Lopez (Eds.), *Handbook of positive psychology* (pp. 621–632). Oxford: Oxford University Press.

Pennebaker, J. W. (2000). Telling stories: The health benefits of narrative. *Literature and Medicine, 19*, 3–18.

Pinel, E., & Constantino, M. J. (2003). Putting self-psychology to good use: when social and clinical psychologists unite. *Journal of Psychotherapy Integration, 13*, 9–32.

Schartau, P. E. S., Dalgleish, T., & Dunn, B. D. (2009). Seeing the bigger picture: training in perspective broadening reduces self-reported affect and psychophysiological response to distressing films and autobiographical memories. *Journal of Abnormal Psychology, 118*, 15–27.

Schauer, M., Neuner, F., & Ebert, T. (2005). *A short-term intervention for traumatic stress disorders after war, terror or torture*. Ashland, OH: Hogrefe & Huber.

Van den Hout, M. A., Barelski, N., & Engelhard, I. M. (2013). On EMDR: eye movements during retrieval reduce subjective vividness and objective memory accessibility during future recall. *Cognition and Emotion, 27*(1), 177–183.

Williams, J. M. G., Barmhofer, T., Crane, C., Hemans, D., Raes, F., & Dalgleish, T. (2007). Autobiographical memory specificity in emotional disorder. *Psychological Bulletin, 133*(1), 122–148.

Williams, J. M. G., & Broadbent, K. (1986). Autobiographical memory in attempted suicide patients. *Journal of Abnormal Psychology, 95*, 144–149.

9

"Is it Them or is it Me?" Transference and Countertransference in CBT

Stirling Moorey

Introduction

John,[1] a 45-year-old unemployed man, had a diagnosis of major depressive disorder and was receiving a course of CBT. In sessions he would often jump to conclusions that the therapist was angry with him, particularly if he expressed a differing opinion. However, he quite often pointed out that the therapist was not quite getting it right when he tried to reflect back and summarize John's negative thoughts. The therapist found himself getting irritated that John interrupted so much, and also annoyed by the way he often followed up a disagreement with a placating statement like "I don't want you to think I'm not grateful for what you're doing". John was also finding it difficult to identify what he wanted to get out of treatment, and a few sessions into therapy they had still not agreed "SMART" goals. The more the therapist attempted to pin him down, the more vague he became and the more angry the therapist felt at this "resistant" patient. John had experienced sustained emotional abuse from both his parents. He was the one in the family who was always blamed for things that went wrong: he was subjected to a torrent of criticism and humiliation, particularly from his father who seemed to have been a bitter man, resentful he had not made more of his life and had possibly suffered from chronic depression himself.

It seemed very likely that John's behaviour in the session was influenced by his childhood experiences of criticism. Traditional psychotherapies would describe this as "transference" and the therapist's critical reaction to this as "countertransference;" but are these terms useful, or acceptable, in cognitive behaviour therapy? This chapter will explore the interface between CBT and psychodynamic thinking about the therapeutic relationship, and suggest a method for conceptualizing and working with these phenomena: developing the metacompetency of managing interpersonal schemas.

How to Become a More Effective CBT Therapist: Mastering Metacompetence in Clinical Practice,
First Edition. Edited by Adrian Whittington and Nick Grey.
© 2014 John Wiley & Sons, Ltd. Published 2014 by John Wiley & Sons, Ltd.

Transference in Analytic Thought

The concept of transference has developed since first introduced by Freud in the late nineteenth century. In classic Freudian theory transference was seen as derived from unresolved Oedipal conflict with the patient's mother and/or father. In *Case Studies in Hysteria* (Breuer & Freud, 1895) Freud wrote about how the patient *transfers* unconscious ideas about a figure from the past onto the therapist, and observed that these illusions disappeared with the conclusion of the analysis. Rather than a simple projection of feelings onto a neutral figure of the analyst, transference is *now* seen as a more interactive process and to some degree even co-constructed. Klein introduced the idea that not only was there projection onto the therapist, but the therapist might also respond to this in keeping with the patient's expectations: projective identification. For instance, a patient whose mother was critical and controlling might find this side of her own personality unacceptable and so "project" it into the therapist. The therapist then finds herself being directive and implicitly judgemental, and so unconsciously acting out the mother's role with the patient. This idea of the therapist's countertransference providing important information about the patient's inner world has become increasingly influential in subsequent analytic thinking. As we will see, two of the key features of transference in psychodynamic theory that distinguish it from more cognitive concepts are the ideas that it is conflict driven and motivated: "it originates from the patient's unresolved emotional conflicts with significant others in childhood" and it "is seen as motivated in the sense that the patient clings to transference perceptions and experiences, even in the face of contrary evidence, for a range of psychologically significant reasons" (Gelso & Bhatia, 2012, p. 385).

Accessible definitions of the psychodynamic concepts of transference and countertransference are as follows:

> *Transference* is the phenomenon whereby we unconsciously transfer feelings and attitudes from a person or situation in the past on to a person or situation in the present. The process is at least partly inappropriate to the present. (Hughes & Kerr, 2000, p. 58)

> Countertransference is the response that is elicited in the recipient (therapist) by the other's (patient's) unconscious transference communications. (Hughes & Kerr, 2000, p. 62)

Why CBT is Wary of Transference

Cognitive behaviour therapists have never embraced the term transference and have in the past been openly hostile to the concept. As they emerged as new approaches, behaviour therapy and then cognitive therapy needed to define themselves as distinct from the psychoanalytic and client-centred approaches that were prevalent in the 1950s and 1960s. An unequivocal, indeed provocative, way to do this was to jettison transference, one of the core concepts of traditional therapy. By contrast to the vague slightly mystical discourse of psychotherapy, these new therapies would be empirically based, dealing in hard facts, not untestable conjecture. There also seemed to be good clinical reasons for moving away from the relationship as the focus of therapy. Looking below the surface at conflictual interpersonal patterns had failed to deliver effective treatments for anxiety disorders, but simple behavioural techniques, which paid no attention to the transference, began to demonstrate outstanding results with phobias. Even more striking was the discovery that obsessive compulsive disorder, hitherto thought to be untreatable, responded to exposure with response prevention. Patients who had been disabled for years were dramatically liberated from the chains of obsessional rituals (e.g., Marks, Hodgson, & Rachman, 1975). Techniques such as flooding and graded exposure that focused on the patient's here and now problems directly without considering the relationship proved highly effective in randomized controlled trials. In the 1970s there was no evidence supporting psychodynamic psychotherapy for depression whereas Beck's cognitive therapy, focusing on thoughts rather than interpersonal process, was found to be as effective as medication (Rush, Beck, Kovacs, & Hollon, 1977). Behaviour therapy got by very well without paying much heed to the relationship between therapist and client, and cognitive therapy saw warmth, genuineness and empathy as necessary but not sufficient components of therapy. As we will see later, there are certain features of the structure and delivery of CBT that reduce the likelihood that transference will develop, and these may have contributed to the belief that it was a redundant concept. But as cognitive behaviour therapy has moved into the field of personality disorders it has become harder to ignore the phenomenon (Beck, Freeman, & Davies 2007; Bradley, Heim, & Westen, 2005).

Cognitive Models of Transference and Countertransference

The basic assumptions on which the traditional psychoanalytic concept of transference is based appear at first sight antithetical to behavioural and cognitive theory. The idea of purposive unconscious communication, the defensive function of projecting unacceptable feelings onto the therapist, and the word "transference" itself, which seems to assume a hydraulic model of transferring feelings from one person to another were not easy to accommodate within original theories of CBT. Psychodynamic theories appeared unscientific and based on outdated notions of the way the mind and brain functioned. Cognitive therapy espoused information processing theory and the cognitive psychology concept of "schema" as a more modern underpinning for its theories (Kovacs & Beck, 1978). But this dichotomy is a false one because some psychodynamic writers have also been interested in exploring how cognitive psychology can provide a paradigm for investigating psychopathology and also use the term schema.

From a cognitive perspective Beck (1967) defined a schema as "a cognitive structure for screening, coding, and evaluating the stimuli that impinge on the organism" (p. 283).

From a psychoanalytic perspective, Perlow (1995) defined a schema as

> An amalgamation of memories regarding an object, which functions as an anticipatory set for future interaction. As such, mental representation of an object refers to a "schema" which organises experience and provides a context both for present perceptions and fantasies, and for the recall of past memories. (p. 2)

As Louw and Straker (2002) note, cognitive therapists such as Beck and Freeman have tended to use the term schema to refer to largely cognitive structures while analysts such as Kernberg have emphasized schemas as cognitive-affective structures. This dichotomy has also appeared in the differential interests of the two camps in cognitive and affective neuroscience respectively. However, other cognitive therapists have recognized schemas as cognitive-affective units (Safran & Segal 1990, Young, Klosko, & Weishaar 2003). Young's concept of an Early Maladaptive Schema for instance includes cognition, affect, physiological response and underlying memories.

Bowlby (1988) was the first to develop a cognitive model of interpersonal relationships. His "internal working models" are models of the self, the world and the relationship between them, built on the basis of perceptions and experiences with significant attachment figures. They comprise a model of the world – who are the attachment figures, where may they be found, and how may they be expected to respond? – and a model of the self – how acceptable am I in the eyes of my attachment figures? Bowlby suggested these working models help the person perceive events, forecast the future and construct plans. Their existence may remain outside conscious awareness and multiple representational constellations can co-exist, based on the person's experience with different attachment figures. They can operate simultaneously despite being mutually incompatible, for example, both wanting to approach to receive care and support while at the same time fearing rejection. In Bowlby's model, transference can be understood as resulting from the misattributions the individual unconsciously makes under the influence of representational models of himself and others.

Bowlby used Piaget's concepts of assimilation and accommodation to explain transference. When transference occurs the patient–therapist relationship is being *assimilated* to a pre-existing model, because the patient's pre-existing model of caretakers has not been updated or *accommodated* to take account of how the therapist is actually behaving. Several other psychodynamically oriented theorists have proposed cognitive models of relationships. Horowitz (1988, 1998) termed working models "role-relationship models" and constructed a full cognitive model of psychodynamics. Cognitive analytic therapy (CAT) was strongly influenced by Horowitz's writings on role relationship models and self-states. Ryle refers to these interpersonal processes as "reciprocal role procedures" (Ryle & Kerr, 2002), again conceptualizing these as models of self and others and the procedures or scripts for how these relationships are maintained. These have in common the idea that repeated experiences of a phenomenon lead to the laying down, internalizing or extracting (the language used depends on the theoretical perspective) of cognitive structures. Stern (1985) provided empirical evidence that these generalizations of interactions can begin as early as infancy. This "implicit relational knowing" is a system of representation of the external world that develops within days of birth. Safran and Segal (1990) combined ideas from Sullivan's interpersonal psychiatry with cognitive therapy using the term "interpersonal schema".

Although the authors cited so far have different terminologies and slightly different emphases, a number of commonalities emerge. Interpersonal schemas are cognitive structures for interpreting and evaluating information about interpersonal relationships. They contain information about the self, the other and the relationship between them. They integrate cognitive, affective, memory, behavioural and somatic elements of the interaction and so constitute a script for predicting others' behaviour and your expected response to it. Interpersonal schemas can be seen as "programmes for maintaining relatedness" (Safran & Segal, 1990).

We all have these schemas in order to make sense of our relationships. Like much automatic processing they follow heuristic rules so we can make rapid decisions about what we should do in a given situation. When interpersonal schemas are too rigidly applied we can encounter problems. As Slap and Slap-Shelton (1994, pp. 691–692) put it:

> later life situations and relationships are perceived as being a repetition of aspects of its old templates without recognizing ... what is different. Thus insofar as this organization is active the neurotic goes through life remaking the same movie. Persons from current life are cast into roles originally created by parents, siblings, and other significant figures of

childhood; transference is the consequence of this mode of cognition. While the actors and sets may change, the characters, plot and affects remain the same.

Is it then true that the "tenets of tacit information processing and a feed-forward mechanism have opened the portal for dynamic theorising in cognitive therapy"? (Louw & Straker, 2002, p. 201)

Empirical Evidence

While it may be possible to explain the concept of transference in a language that is more acceptable to cognitive behaviour therapists, this does not mean that it exists. Over the past 20 years Susan Andersen has been leading a programme to investigate the misinterpretations we make in relationships from a social-cognitive perspective. The research uses a two-session paradigm (Andersen & Thorpe, 2009). In the first session participants describe a significant other, using self-generated sentences of positive and negative items. In a second session they learn about a new person who is described as either having similar qualities to the significant other or different qualities; the qualities of the significant other are mixed with filler descriptions so the participants are unaware of the origins of the descriptions. After learning about the new person participants then complete measures to assess their attitudes towards the new person. A yoked control condition is also used in which the information about the new person is derived from descriptions of another participant's significant other, so that all participants are actually exposed to exactly the same features.

Using a recognition-memory paradigm participants are found to "fill in the blanks" about the new person using their prior knowledge of their significant other (Andersen & Cole, 1990), and this applies even if the information is presented subliminally (Glassman & Andersen, 1999). Further research has demonstrated an effect on evaluation and facial affective response, expectations about interactions, and motives and goals (see Andersen & Thorpe, 2009). There is not only an effect on cognition and affect but also on interpersonal behaviour, and the behaviour of others. For instance, in a telephone conversation the new person will respond in a positive or negative manner in keeping with the participant's expectations of how their significant other would behave towards them (Berk & Andersen, 2000). If the new person is seen to be like a positive significant other this will evoke more openness and disclosure, whereas if the new person is like a negative significant other hostility will be evoked (Berk & Andersen, 2000). However, when the significant other is a close family member with whom there is a negative relationship, although hostility will be evoked, in the experiment the participant will try to gain acceptance from the new person (Berk & Andersen, 2008). This is compelling evidence for everyday evaluations being biased by the similarities of the people we meet to important people from our past. Although Andersen refers to this as "transference" there are differences: the finding is not limited to childhood relationships but applies to anyone who is significant in our lives, and there is not particular evidence for this being a defensive procedure. Nevertheless, it would suggest that these biases are at least as likely to occur in the clinical setting and provides support for the phenomenon.

Gelso and Bhatia (2012) cite a number of studies that have demonstrated that transference does occur in non-analytic therapies. For instance Bradley et al. (2005) found that ratings of transference by psychodynamic, eclectic and cognitive therapists treating patients with DSM-IV personality disorders were basically similar and on factor analysis yielded five dimensions: angry/entitled, anxious/preoccupied, avoidant/counterdependent, sexualized and secure/engaged.

Interpersonal Schemas

Bringing together this clinical, theoretical and empirical thinking, this chapter uses the term "interpersonal schema" as a label for a hypothetical structure for interpreting and evaluating information about interpersonal relationships. Interpersonal schemas contain information about the self, the other and the relationship between them and as such constitute scripts for predicting others' behaviour and directing the individual's response. These scripts may have a narrative quality as they describe a sequence of interactions. Interpersonal schemas integrate cognitive, affective, memory, behavioural and somatic elements of interaction. A range of cognitive processes are involved; in the context of schemas driving close relationships. Baucom and Epstein (1990) identified five: *selective attention* to events confirming beliefs, *attributions* about the causes of events in the relationship, *expectancies* about the probability of events occurring, *assumptions* about how relationships work, and *standards* for how relationships should be. Interpersonal schemas will be self-fulfilling in two ways: through cognitive biases that select information confirming the schema and through behaviours that elicit a confirming response from others. Through non-verbal and verbal methods the other person is recruited into a role that confirms the individual's beliefs about the relationship.

Like any schema, schemas that guide relationships will serve the function of simplifying the world so that it is more predictable. Again, like all schemas interpersonal schemas will be arranged in a hierarchical fashion: some will be shared beliefs and procedures for interacting within a given culture or sub-culture, beneath this there will be family schemas with expectations about how family members behave, and at the individual level, there will be assumptions derived from the person's unique experiences of relationships.

Transference occurs when an interpersonal schema leads to a set of misinterpretations of the therapist's personality or behaviour. This may be triggered by specific characteristics or behaviours of the therapist that consciously or unconsciously remind the patient of significant others in their past as described by Andersen. It may also be triggered by the setting of therapy itself, whereby features such as structure, the nature of the therapeutic relationship and the expectations of therapy remind the client of repeated interactions from the past.

Countertransference reactions can be understood as broadly coming from three sources. The first is the therapist's own transference to the patient, that is, a personal or idiosyncratic reaction to the patient on the basis of characteristics that remind the therapist of a significant other. The second can be termed empathic countertransference, where the therapist's cognitive and/or emotional reaction mirrors the patient's experience. The third type of countertransference is more of a reciprocal interaction with the patient's transference reaction to the therapist. The consequent relationship pattern that is played out in therapy can be seen as evidencing the degree to which there is a fit or mismatch between therapist and patient schemas. There can either be schema congruence, schema conflict or schema complementarity. *Schema congruence* occurs when there is a match between the therapist and patient's schema through empathic countertransference. Therapists may "buy into" the patient's negative worldview (Beck, Rush,

Shaw, & Emery, 1979, p. 59). The patient's sense of hopelessness activates hopeless-ness in the therapist. This is identical to that which Racker (1968) called a concordant countertransference, as the therapist is understood to have "tuned" to the patient's internal world, "from the inside" and is therefore also experiencing something of the hopelessness with which the patient is struggling. *Schema conflict* emerges when there is a mismatch between some of the patient's beliefs or behaviours and the therapist's beliefs. Therapists may view depressed patients as "wilfully passive, indecisive, and manipulative" (Beck, et al., 1979, p. 58). Again the therapeutic collaboration empha-sized in cognitive therapy "decreases these sorts of problems and frustrations" (Beck et al., 1979, p. 58). *Schema complementarity* is seen when the interpersonal beliefs and needs of patient and therapist fit together to create a self-perpetuating cycle. For instance, when a patient with a dependency schema meets a therapist with an unrelent-ing standards schema, the therapist may work hard but end up looking after the patient. A narcissistic patient with entitlement beliefs may get a therapist with a self-sacrifice or subjugation schema to treat them in a special way. Leahy (2003) describes some of the common schemas in therapists and patients that can interact in a toxic way to generate countertransference problems in CBT. As we have seen some countertransference can be recognized as "idiosyncratic" since it arises from the therapist's own schemas, other countertransference feelings might be termed "diagnostic" since they represent a reac-tion to the patient's schemas that may be unusual or unfamiliar in the therapist's emotional repertoire. These can give valuable information about the patient's cognitive-emotional world. However, because the therapist and patient are engaged in a complex interaction, the thoughts and feelings of both parties will frequently comprise states derived from their individual history and states emerging from the relationship itself.

A question arises about how the therapist can best prepare themselves so they do not fall into some of the pitfalls of countertransference reactions. The traditional method for doing this has been through personal therapy. There are some practical obstacles to personal therapy for CBT therapists. Because standard CBT is problem focused, it is best suited to working with discrete distressing problems, and therapists are more likely to find it of benefit when they are facing significant stress. If negative schemas are not currently active it may be more difficult to identify the sorts of assumptions that inter-fere with therapy. CBT therapists do not always feel comfortable with more psychody-namic therapies, which do address these issues. The advent of schema therapy may provide an acceptable model for conceptualizing and working with our blind spots. Personal therapy can help us to understand ourselves better and recognize the beliefs that lead to personal reactions to patients. The value of personal therapy in making us better therapists has yet to be established. There are also questions about the extent to which a knowledge of our idiosyncratic interpersonal schemas is generalizable to the therapy setting. What is important in that setting is an understanding of how schemas play out in the therapy relationship. For this reason, focusing on therapist beliefs may be as valuable as a course of personal therapy.

Why Transference Doesn't Appear in CBT

There are several aspects of CBT that discourage the development of a regressive *nega-tive* transference. Therapy is brief and time-limited, and though this does not preclude the patient's expectations, assumptions and first impressions from creating a strong reaction to the therapist, for many people the short-term nature of CBT means they do not invest as much emotional energy in the relationship. Therapy is structured: an agenda is set and a business-like manner often employed. In this way the problem is placed on the table between therapist and patient rather than located in the relational space between them. The relationship itself is explicitly collaborative, allowing the therapist to be more transparent than in analytic therapy, and even use judicious self-disclosure where appropriate. The relationship is not then singled out for special attention as it is in analytic therapy. The aim is to normalize rather than pathologize, to help the patient become their own therapist. The assumption is that the therapist may be an expert in the treatment but the patient is expert in their own problems and often has the solutions to those problems.

All this firmly places the relationship on a footing of adult to adult interaction and limits the opportunities for misconceptions to arise.

Where Transference Does Appear in CBT

The characteristics of therapy described will not, of course, prevent misinterpretations of therapist behaviour occurring. The place that these schemas often get played out is, paradoxically, in reaction to the very structure we have just been discussing. Right from the beginning of cognitive therapy (Beck et al., 1979) it was recognized that negative therapeutic reactions may occur to the structured, active nature of the therapy (p. 58). If a patient has beliefs about being controlled or dominated by other people, then being asked to do "homework" can be like a red rag to a bull. If they have beliefs that they are unable to cope alone and need help to survive, the expectation that they will do self-help assignment between sessions will seem too much: in fact, patients can feel not understood or attacked as the therapist is expecting them to do the very things that brought them to therapy in the first place. Transference reactions may arise from these interpersonal beliefs that are reflections of the patient's personality, but they may also arise from the mood disorder itself. So for instance, a depressed patient may believe that everything is hopeless and so not do their homework because they *know* they will not get better.

Transference in CBT may then sometimes be derived from schemas related to the Axis I disorder or from early interpersonal schemas often related to Axis II pathology. Some of the features of CBT (such as structure or pushing patients to experience strong affect during an experiment) may themselves activate the therapist's own personal schemas (e.g., if I upset people I'm a bad person).

The Interpersonal Schema Worksheet (ISW)

Interpersonal schemas and their effects in the therapeutic relationship can be understood using a conventional Beckian model of thoughts, emotions, behaviours and the rules for relating underlying them. The Interpersonal Schema Worksheet (Moorey, 2013) shown in Figure 9.1 offers a simple format for mapping these on a single A4 sheet. There are three main contexts in which this conceptualization can be developed. The safest is within supervision, where the therapist can explore his or her reactions with support from the supervisor who uses guided discovery to elucidate the interpersonal cycles being played out in the session. Since these reactions often arise because of

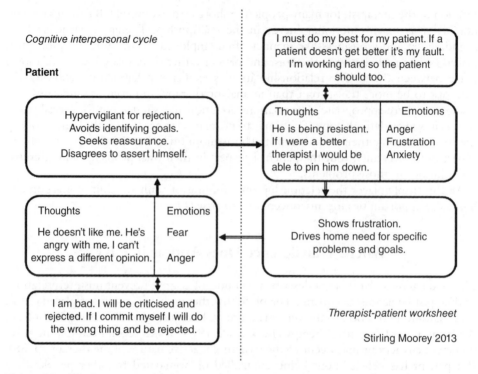

Cognitive interpersonal cycle

Patient

Hypervigilant for rejection.
Avoids identifying goals.
Seeks reassurance.
Disagrees to assert himself.

Thoughts	Emotions
He doesn't like me. He's angry with me. I can't express a different opinion.	Fear Anger

I am bad. I will be criticised and rejected. If I commit myself I will do the wrong thing and be rejected.

I must do my best for my patient. If a patient doesn't get better it's my fault. I'm working hard so the patient should too.

Thoughts	Emotions
He is being resistant. If I were a better therapist I would be able to pin him down.	Anger Frustration Anxiety

Shows frustration.
Drives home need for specific problems and goals.

Therapist-patient worksheet

Stirling Moorey 2013

Figure 9.1 The Interpersonal Schema Worksheet. © Moorey (2013). Reproduced with permission of the author.

our blind spots, it is helpful to have a supervisor to facilitate our understanding of them. The second context is the therapist working alone to use the worksheet as part of their own preparation for the session, and the third is developing the interpersonal conceptualization directly with the patient in the session.

When completing the sheet it is possible to start at any point in the cycle, but the patient's behaviour and therapist's thoughts and feelings in response to this is usually where most evidence is available. John, who we met at the beginning of the chapter, was doing a number of things in the session that upset his therapist. He was failing to identify goals, disagreeing over small details and then seeking reassurance after each disagreement. The therapist's automatic thoughts were:

He is being resistant. He's deliberately thwarting me.

If I were a better therapist I would be able to pin him down.

These were accompanied by the associated emotions of anger, frustration and anxiety. As a way to work with this, the therapist could use supervision and recordings of therapy sessions to identify his own in-session behaviour. In this case it was an over-emphasis on finding specific problems and goals, which was obvious from listening to the session recordings. Although he was trying to be professional, there was emotional "leakage" and his frustration was palpable.

The patient's automatic thoughts may be more difficult to identify, and in fact John was hiding what he actually thought and felt. In the supervision session the supervisor encouraged the therapist to role play John's "resistance". Playing John, the therapist began to feel anxious and slightly bullied, and a hypothesis emerged that John's rule for relating might be "If I commit myself I will do the wrong thing and be rejected", and that underlying this might be core beliefs that he was bad and others would reject him. These unconditional beliefs had already been identified as negative thoughts that John reported in the first few weeks of treatment. The experiment arising from supervision might then be to test this conceptualization by sharing it collaboratively and compassionately with John in the session.

The final component of the cycle is the therapist's beliefs which in this case were: "I must do my best for my patient. If a patient doesn't get better it's my fault. I'm working hard so the patient should too."

These are beliefs that the therapist can examine himself or with the help of his supervisor, using cognitive techniques and behavioural experiments to test their validity and helpfulness.

The worksheet can also be applied to relationships other than in the therapy setting. These include relationships with partners, family members or close friends.

A Stepped Model for Managing Transference and Countertransference

This section assumes the therapist is treating a patient with a DSM-IV Axis I disorder and that goals for therapy are symptom and problem focused. There may be co-existing characterological problems or personality disorder, but these are not the main focus of therapy. The assumption is that therapy is aimed at alleviating panic, OCD, depression and so forth, rather than personality change, because treatment for the latter would usually include work on the therapeutic relationship as one of the main foci of therapy. When therapy-interfering transference and countertransference arise in the setting of an Axis I disorder a stepped model can be adopted.

Step 1: Predicting and preparing for problems

The first step is to identify potential problems in the relationship before they occur. The therapist might talk to John about his sensitivity to criticism:

> From what you've been telling me about your family, it seems that you were criticized for virtually anything you did. When this happens to us over and over again it can leave us quite sensitive to anything that feels like criticism or rejection. Do you find that?

Adding

> It's possible I might say or do things that sometimes sound critical. We know from research that even tone of voice can trigger associations with memories of people who've treated us badly. So we might need to look out for times when I trigger your sense of rejection. Would you be able to tell me if this starts to happen?

It would be very important in this therapy to regularly ask for feedback and check how John is feeling about the therapist. It will also be important for the therapist to be aware of his own countertransference. This may be an empathic countertransference evoked by the depression e.g. feeling hopeless and low. As we have seen (Figure 9.1) it is also likely to be a reciprocal countertransference where John's interpersonal schema pulls a response of irritation and rejection from his therapist. The Interpersonal Schema Worksheet can help prepare for this.

Step 2: Managing alliance ruptures

If the potential for a break in the therapeutic alliance has been identified early and named it may be sufficient to note it when it occurs and get back on track with the focus of the session, for example, John might be helped to recognize he has fallen back into the pattern of disagreement followed by reassurance seeking, and this might allow him to let go of his need for reassurance in that moment. But sometimes the alliance rupture will need to be addressed in more depth, primarily through reality testing, in order to return to the agreed agenda item. These problems are not new to cognitive therapists and the occurrence of positive and negative transference towards the therapist is referred to in the original depression manual (Beck et al., 1979, p. 313).

The patient's thoughts and feelings about the therapist are elicited and the therapist apologizes if he or she has made a mistake. It will be very important in helping John to be completely honest if the therapist does make an error that John has noticed rather than becoming defensive, because denying it will simply confirm John's view that he will always be in the wrong. Any misinterpretations on the patient's part can be corrected through cognitive methods.

The therapist should not automatically assume that anything that interferes with the smooth course of therapy is due to transference. As with other problems the approach is to start with the simplest explanation and intervention and if that does not apply, only then move on to more in depth formulations. So when a therapist encounters an alliance rupture, the initial approach will be to look at what has gone wrong in the collaboration. For instance, if there is a problem with homework the therapist might ask themselves:

- Have I explained the homework properly?
- Have I set homework that is in some way too hard for the patient?
- Does the patient understand what the benefits of the self-help assignment might be?
- Is this a collaboratively agreed assignment, or am I imposing what I think the patient should do?

Asking for the patient's thoughts in relation to the difficulty may identify the misinterpretation as arising from the patient's disorder rather than transference, for example, hopelessness and failure to do homework because of level of depression. If these approaches fail, or if it is clear from the conceptualization that this is an issue of interpersonal schemas, then these will need to be addressed directly.

Step 3: Working with interpersonal schemas

The therapist working with John's depression will want to engage him so that he can learn the value of scheduling activities to gain a sense of pleasure and mastery, and to learn to recognize and test negative thoughts arising from his depressive illness. Steps 1 and 2 will be important in keeping the collaborative relationship going at crucial times for John to learn to manage his depression. However, the depression will probably be integrally connected with John's beliefs that he is bad and that everyone will reject him. Transference issues will be present at key points in the therapy. The developmental formulation or the ISW are invaluable in providing a framework for understanding what is going on and helping patient and therapist to get a little metacognitive awareness and decentring. This serves the same function as the Sequential Diagrammatic Reformulation in Cognitive Analytic Therapy (Ryle & Kerr, 2002). Each time the feelings of anger and rejection come up in relation to the therapist they can be recognized and named and then worked with in a number of ways. Many of these techniques are taken from work with personality disorders (Arntz, 2011; Beck, Freeman, & Davies, 2007; Ryle & Kerr, 2002; Young, Klosko, & Weishaar, 2003) but can be adapted an incorporated into short-term therapy:

1. Empathically attuning to John's feelings of rejection and linking them to his early experiences. Here the message given by the therapist is that John was hurt and humiliated through his childhood so it is not surprising that he will be sensitive to anything that resembles this in therapy.
2. Helping John distinguish between the genuine, valid feelings of hurt triggered by the memories from the past associated with the schema, and the present situation.
3. Linking this reaction to other times he has felt this way in therapy and outside.
4. Cognitive restructuring to help John reality test what is actually happening in the therapy session.
5. From the cognitive restructuring, developing a flashcard summarizing the reasons his interpretations are unhelpful or incorrect (Young, Klosko, & Weishaar, 2003).
6. Imagery re-scripting of early childhood memories associated with rejection (Arntz, 2011, Young, Klosko, & Weishaar, 2003).

The extent to which these methods can be used in a short-term therapy will vary, and the extent to which therapists feel comfortable and skilled in using them will also vary. As longer term evidence-based therapies for personality disorder become established, the challenge will be to find ways to incorporate some of their active ingredients into short-term CBT for complex cases without losing its focus and efficacy.

Summary

Transference and countertransference are terms that have a distinguished pedigree in psychodynamic thinking but have understandably been viewed with suspicion by cognitive behaviour therapists. Whatever the terminology, there is both clinical and empirical evidence that some patients relate to their therapists as they relate to significant others in their lives, often with associated misinterpretations of the real character of the therapist. The characteristic features of CBT damp this down but do not eliminate it. The concept of an Interpersonal Schema is a way to conceptualize transference and countertransference as products of the cognitive unconscious, rather than necessarily a dynamic unconscious. This chapter has described how an Interpersonal Schema Worksheet can be useful in formulating these phenomena. A stepped approach to managing unhelpful transference has been outlined: first, reducing its potency through judicious use of the conceptualization to predict problems; second though managing alliance ruptures to retrieve a collaborative relationship; and third through working directly with interpersonal schemas with selected patients. Longer term CBT-based approaches for personality disorders are increasingly dealing with these aspects of the therapeutic relationship and the incorporation of some of their techniques into standard CBT practice is an exciting line of future development.

Procedural Rules

- Patients relate to their therapists as they relate to significant others in their lives, often with associated misinterpretations of the real character of the therapist.
- The concept of an Interpersonal Schema is a way to conceptualize transference and countertransference as products of the cognitive rather than dynamic unconscious.
- Conceptualizing interpersonal schemas early in therapy can help to predict and prevent alliance ruptures.
- Conceptualizing interpersonal schemas can help in the management of alliance ruptures so that a collaborative relationship can be re-established.
- In certain patients working directly with transference as a sign of interpersonal schemas in action can foster understanding and provide opportunities for behavioural experiments to promote interpersonal learning.

Acknowledgements

Much of my thinking on interpersonal schemas has been shaped by the cognitive rendition of transference in Cognitive Analytic Therapy (CAT). I would like to thank Antony Ryle, Hilary Beard, Mark Dunn and Annie Nehmad for their CAT teaching and supervision. I have also incorporated some ideas from Schema Therapy into the section on interventions for interpersonal schemas and would like to thank Arnoud Arntz, Marjon Nadort, Arnie Reed and Chris Hayes for their teaching of these techniques.

Note

1 This clinical description is taken from experiences with various patients and supervisees, and so is a composite rather than specific case description.

References

Andersen, S. M., & Cole, S. W. (1990). "Do I know you?": The role of significant others in general social perception. *Journal of Personality and Social Psychology, 59*, 383–399.

Andersen, S. M., & Thorpe, J. S. (2009). An IF-THEN theory of personality: significant others and the relational self. *Journal of Research in Personality, 43*, 163–170.

Arntz, A. (2011). Imagery rescripting for personality disorders. *Cognitive and Behavioral Practice, 18*, 466–481.

Baucom, D., & Epstein, N. (1990). *Cognitive behavioral marital therapy*. New York: Bruner Mazel.

Beck, A. T. (1967). *Depression: clinical, experimental and theoretical aspects*. New York: Hoeber.

Beck, A. T., Freeman, A., & Davies, D. D. (2007). *Cognitive therapy of personality disorders*. New York: Guilford Press.

Beck, A. T., Rush, A. J., Shaw, B. F., & Emery, G. (1979). *Cognitive therapy of depression*. New York: Guilford Press.

Berk, M. S., & Andersen, S. M. (2000). The impact of past relationships on interpersonal behaviour: Behavioral confirmation of the social-cognitive process of transference. *Journal of Personality and Social Psychology, 79*, 546–562.

Berk, M. S., & Andersen, S. M. (2008). The sting of lack of affection: chronic goal dissatisfaction in transference. *Self and Identity, 1*, 393–412.

Bowlby, J, (1988). *A secure base*. London: Routledge.

Bradley, R., Heim, A. K., & Westen, D. (2005). Transference patterns in the psychotherapy of personality disorders: an empirical investigation. *British Journal of Psychiatry, 186*, 342–349.

Breuer, J., & Freud, S. (1895). Studies in hysteria. In J. Strachey (Ed.), *The standard edition of the complete psychological works of Sigmund Freud* (Vol.2). London: Hogarth.

Gelso, C. J., & Bhatia, A. (2012). Crossing theoretical lines: the role and effect of transference in nonanalytic psychotherapies. *Psychotherapy, 49*, 384–390.

Glassman, N. S., & Andersen, S. M. (1999). Activating transference without consciousness: Using significant-other representations to go beyond what is subliminally given. *Journal of Personality and Social Psychology, 77*, 1146–1162.

Horowitz, M. (1988). *Introduction to psychodynamics: a new synthesis*. London: Routledge.

Horowitz, M. (1998). *Cognitive psychodynamics: from conflict to character*. London: John Wiley & Sons.

Hughes, P., & Kerr, I. (2000). Transference and countertransference in communication between doctor and patient. *Advances in Psychiatric Treatment, 6*, 57–64.

Kovacs, M., & Beck, A. T. (1978). Maladaptive cognitive structures in depression. *American Journal of Psychiatry, 135*, 525–533.

Leahy, R. L. (2003). *Overcoming resistance in cognitive therapy*. New York: Guildford Press.

Louw, F., & Straker, G. (2002). Borderline pathology: an integration of cognitive therapy and psychodynamic therapy. *Journal of Psychotherapy Integration, 12*, 190–217.

Marks, I. M., Hodgson, R., & Rachman, S. (1975). Treatment of chronic OCD 2 years after in vivo exposure. *British Journal of Psychiatry, 127*, 349–364.

Moorey, S. (2013). The interpersonal cycle worksheet. *Cognitive Connections*. Retrieved from http://cognitiveconnections.co.uk/wp-content/uploads/2014/01/Cognitive-Interpersonal-Cycle-Worksheet.pdf

Perlow, M. (1995). *Understanding mental objects*. London: Routledge.

Racker, H. (1968). *Transference and countertransference*. New York: International Universities Press.

Rush, A. J., Beck, A. T., Kovacs, M., & Hollon, S. (1977). Comparative efficacy of cognitive therapy and pharmacotherapy in the treatment of depressed outpatients. *Cognitive Therapy and Research, 1*, 17–37.

Ryle, A., & Kerr, I. (2002). *Introducing cognitive analytic therapy: principles and practice*. Chichester: John Wiley & Sons.

Safran, J. D., & Segal, Z. V. (1990). *Interpersonal process in cognitive therapy*. New York: Basic Books.

Slap, J. W., & Slap-Shelton, L. (1994). The schema model: a proposed replacement paradigm for psychoanalysis. *Psychoanalytic Review, 81*, 677–693.

Stern, D. N. (1985). *The interpersonal world of the infant: a view from psychoanalysis and developmental psychology*. New York: Basic Books.

Young, J. E., Klosko, J. S., & Weishaar, M. E. (2003). *Schema therapy: a practitioner's guide*. New York: Guilford Press.

10

What To Do When CBT Isn't Working?

Michael Worrell

Be like water making its way through cracks. Do not be assertive, but adjust to the object, and you shall find a way around or through it. If nothing within you stays rigid, outward things will disclose themselves. Be water my friend.

Bruce Lee[1]

Any honest reading of the available research literature will lead you to conclude that even if you were practicing all of your CBT interventions at an appropriate level of competence, you will have many experiences where the intervention does not work. There are two related questions that I would like to address in this chapter. First, what should you do when CBT *isn't* working? How can you develop metacompetencies for responding flexibly when you encounter stuck points in the process of an ongoing therapy? In the wider therapeutic literature this topic has been thought about as falling within the notion of "working with resistance in therapy". Second, what should you do when both you and quite possibly your client have done the best possible and yet CBT *hasn't* worked? How do you draw such unsuccessful interventions to some form of acceptable closure? This topic falls more broadly within the area of "managing endings".

It is probably true, that the more competent a CBT therapist you become, and the wider your base of theoretical and empirical knowledge, the less apparently "resistant" clients you will have. However, what if "treatment failures" remain a feature of your experience of working as a CBT therapist? I would like to draw your attention to an important text in the tradition of behaviour therapy, Foa and Emmelkamp's *Failures in Behavior Therapy* (1983). Foa and Emmelkamp state:

> Contact with clients has taught us that clinical practice is not as simple as that portrayed in textbooks. After thorough assessment and application of the appropriate techniques we still fail occasionally. What has made this realisation even more painful is the fact that failures have not often been openly discussed. This reticence fostered the belief that if one encounters a treatment failure, then one is a failure as a therapist. For, if the therapist has made a correct behavioural analysis and subsequently applied adequately the appropriate procedures, success would have been inevitable. (1983: 3)

How to Become a More Effective CBT Therapist: Mastering Metacompetence in Clinical Practice,
First Edition. Edited by Adrian Whittington and Nick Grey.
© 2014 John Wiley & Sons, Ltd. Published 2014 by John Wiley & Sons, Ltd.

Foa and Emmelkamp argue that the study of treatment failures is crucial for the advancement of behaviour therapy. I believe that it is also in the reflective and critical investigation of our own experiences of encountering apparent treatment failure, that we can support the development of metacompetencies. Crucial in this process, is that we remain aware of, and prepared to challenge, automatic thoughts along the lines of "If I encounter treatment failures this means I am a failure as a therapist"!

What Do We Mean by 'Treatment Failure'?

How should "treatment failure" be defined? Can it be defined simply as the client not demonstrating the attainment of defined goals within a specified time frame? In many instances of "successful therapy" (from the point of view of both client and therapist) some but not all of the clients goals will have been attained by the end of sessions. Most clinical outcome will in fact sit somewhere along the continuum between success and failure. Few outcomes are in fact so "black and white". A review of the research literature also reveals that there is no generally agreed upon definition of treatment failure (Lambert, 2011). There are, in fact, a range of interpretations that can be used including:

- The client not responding to treatment by the time it is terminated as assessed against a standardized measure.
- The client responds well to treatment, again with reference to a standardized measure, but then relapses once therapy is over.
- The client who responds "sub-optimally" to treatment whereby there may be some change but much less than hoped for or expected or where symptoms remain "clinically significant".
- The client who is considered a "refractory case" where there is little or no change in the presenting problems by the end of therapy and where the clinical problem itself is referred to as "complex" or "difficult to treat".
- The client who unilaterally terminates therapy early, and where the short- to long-term outcome remains unknown.
- The client who deteriorates such that it can be reasonably concluded that their clinical state has been made worse as a result of attending therapy.

As Lambert (2011) notes, there is considerable variation in these definitions and the client who ends therapy relatively "untouched" by the intervention is in a very different position to the one who may, from an ethical standpoint, have been "harmed" by the therapy or therapist.

Resistance is Futile?

Historically, many of the types of problems and difficulties that have been associated with treatment failure or drop out have been understood with reference to the concept of "resistance". The concept of "resistance", however, has also been one of the most problematic terms in the history of psychotherapy, as authors from a wide range of theoretical orientations have regarded it as essentially a form of blaming the client for a lack of progress. Lazarus and Fay (1982), for instance, argued that the concept of resistance represents an "elaborate rationalization" used by therapists to explain treatment failures.

Indeed, it can be a deeply pejorative and misleading term, and in most instances, if you are finding yourself having automatic thoughts about your client such as "they are just so resistant" or "clearly they don't want, or are not ready for change", this is best taken as an internal cue to engage in some deeper and wider reflection.

Turkat and Meyer (1982) attempted a behavioural analysis on the concept of resistance. They concluded that there are no client behaviours that can universally be labelled resistance and that the range of behaviours that could serve a resistant function is potentially infinite. They argue that resistance must be defined as "client behaviour that the therapist labels as anti-therapeutic" (1982, p.158). This is similar to the Dialectical Behaviour Therapy notion of "therapy Interfering behaviours" (Linehan, 1993), which is a far more usable concept from a CBT perspective, as this also highlights the fact that the therapy interfering behaviour may be displayed by the therapist as much as by the client.

A contemporary CBT view on the nature of therapeutic resistance strongly support a view of these phenomena as "understandable", "adaptive" and as "making sense" from the perspective of the client at some level. Resistance is indeed, neither necessarily futile nor irrational! Consistent with this perspective, clients are preferably not seen as "failing therapy".

Common Forms of Resistance

Keeping in mind Turkat and Meyers' (1982) analysis, what are some forms of resistance that are most likely to arise in CBT practice and be related to potential client drop out or failure? Consider the following examples:

Example 1: A lack of collaboration

Mary[2] is mid-way through a 12-session treatment contract for low mood and anxiety. She initially appeared to respond well to the therapist's efforts to collaboratively develop a shared formulation and treatment plan and seemed also to have been socialized well into the treatment model and liked the emphasis on structured sessions. In her most recent session, however, her therapist asked:

THERAPIST (TH):   And so Mary, what would you like to put on the agenda for today's session?

MARY: Umm. Well I don't know really, whatever you think would be good

TH: Right ... OK ... well if you consider how your week has gone, and how that exposure task went ... what do you think might be useful to address? (feeling slightly frustrated and impatient)

MARY: well ... umm, I'm not sure ... I think things are going well so I would be happy to talk some more about the exposure if you think that's a good idea

TH: (feeling increasingly impatient): OK well let's put the exposure task on the agenda and also look at how we might include a few new steps for homework then.

In this example the client appears to be avoiding actively collaborating with setting an appropriate agenda. This may be expressive of the client's experiential avoidance. The therapist however appears to have become increasingly frustrated and then effectively "gives up" and departs from a collaborative stance, potentially functioning to reinforce the client's passivity and experiential avoidance. The above interaction opens the possibility for the client to further disengage from the treatment as well as a weakening of the working alliance and increasing the risk for non-attendance or premature drop out.

Example 2: Responding to positives with increased negative emotional expression towards the therapist

David has been seen for 12 sessions of CBT for depression. He has had a long history of depression since his early adolescence and had a protracted episode of psychoanalytic treatment, which he reports was somewhat helpful. He has responded well to the Behavioural Activation elements in CBT and has been quite compliant with homework assignments to complete activity diaries and also to engage in a process of gradually increasing the range of activities including both pleasant events and activities focussed on competence or "mastery". A noted pattern has emerged, however, that was present from session one. For the first half hour of the session, David talks fairly insistently about how terrible he is feeling, how change is unlikely, how the CBT strategies he has learnt are entirely superficial and unlikely to work in the long term, and that he is just "a depressive character".

DAVID: Well you know ... I do think that really I am not getting anywhere ... I can't see how making these lists is really going to do anything for me ... my life is stuffed actually if you really look at things objectively ... just the energy it takes me to complete these forms for you is unbelievable

TH: David, I can really hear how rough you have been finding things, and you have certainly struggled with depression for many years. Looking at these scores on the PHQ though seems to show some overall improvement. You actually seem much improved since we first started working together.

DAVID: I think it's the complexity of my depression that really concerns me. It's been around so long and is so deep in me it's hard to see how that will ever change. I mean, sometimes I am just so low in mood it's like looking out of a long dark cave. Everything seems totally horrific and there is no real way out. How does making lists really address that?

TH: (noticing a familiar rise in irritable feelings and aware of the time passing and that an agenda has not been set): Yeah ... I can really see that the severity of depression has been pretty bad for you in the past. Again though ... it looks like some of the work you have done increasing the amount and range of your activity has paid off ... you are actually doing more and seem to be experiencing some improvement in mood. So I wonder how we can best take this forward today? What shall we focus on to make best use of our time?

DAVID: (raising his voice and looking away from the therapist): But why am I like this? Why has it got to this? You are not the first shrink I've seen you know! I have been at this for years and still no progress! Perhaps I need something else?

In this example the client appears to be responding to the therapist's attempts at focussing the session and noting positive changes with increased expressions of distress. The therapist also appears to be only superficially acknowledging and validating the client's distress leading to further escalation of client expressions of distress and hopelessness. The interaction above appears to fit well Leahy's (2001) descriptions of "Validation resistance".

Example 3: Not engaging with between-session tasks

Sally has been seeing her therapist for difficulties with social anxiety. She experiences social anxiety at work in relation to meetings and in particular if the meeting has been arranged at short notice and she has little time to engage in her safety behaviour of over preparing what she might say. She has responded well to in session video assisted exposure experiments, and her homework has been dropping safety behaviours at work.

> TH: So Sally I am wondering how you got on with the homework? Remind me what that was and how did it go?
>
> SALLY: Um well ... not sure really... not sure I really remembered what I had to do. I mean I know you wanted me to try and not over prepare for the next meeting and maybe see how that goes. I guess... I don't know
>
> TH: Um yes... my recollection was that we had agreed you would try out a behavioural experiment using that form I gave you that asked you to specify a prediction of what might happen if you didn't do that and then have a look at what actually happens.
>
> SALLY: Oh yeah. Um ... I basically didn't take that form to work really. I mean I think I did manage things better this week.
>
> TH: Ok ... well it's great to hear that overall you feel you are doing well. How did you go in terms of monitoring your anxiety level and triggers?
>
> SALLY: Right... there was that as well. I don't know really. I didn't do that writing down bit. I think I can remember how things went but no I didn't do any writing stuff down if that's what you wanted.

Difficulties around homework: either problems in establishing a collaborative process of homework design and review, or problems with a lack of carry through with home-work tasks are perhaps the most commonly occurring form of therapy interfering behaviour. They are also possibly the form of therapy interfering behaviours most deserving of careful therapist attention as there is good reason to predict that a lack of engagement with between session tasks will be associated with poor treatment response or early unilateral termination (Kazantzis & Shinkfield, 2007; Newman, 1994).

As is hopefully apparent from the above, it can be a mistake to identify resistance as something that can solely be located "within" the client as some form of consistent cli-ent feature. Resistance is best understood as expressing an interpersonal phenomenon and as such is responsive to client factors, therapist factors and contextual factors (including the demands of the therapy itself). Keeping this interpersonal and contextual perspective on resistance in mind, what steps can you look at when working with situ-ations of apparent resistance?

When CBT isn't working, ensure first that it is in fact CBT that has been delivered!

In the face of episodic forms of roadblocks and challenges, the most effective stance is likely to be therapist persistence and adherence. Rarely is a course of therapy consistently smooth and where there are persistent difficulties with homework completion, or difficulty with engaging in a collaborative and structured therapy process, the first issue to consider is the possibility of therapist error or as Waller (2009) has discussed, "therapist drift". There are many advantages to the term "drift" as opposed to "error" or "mistake", as looking for the latter perhaps biases you towards the identification of specific instances, whereas the idea of "drift" may point you towards the possibility that it is more a case of being off-course by a few degrees in a consistent fashion, which leads you to arriving at a destination quite far removed from the original intention.

The range of possible errors or points of drift is quite large. A few of the most important, that could potentially be related to client resistance, poor results and drop out include, but are not limited to:

1. Difficulties with initial engagement and forming a collaborative working relationship. There may have been a push to start active interventions prior to a strong working alliance having been established.
2. Problems with assessment and formulation. Difficulties can occur in terms of an incomplete or incorrect formulation leading to the application of a treatment strategy that is inappropriate to the presenting difficulties.
3. Problems with the delivery of interventions. There are wide arrays of difficulties that can occur, including an inconsistent and incomplete application of techniques, so that for instance, the therapist is not working with cognitions that are the most central to the client's concerns, or a failure to use a full range of techniques so that, for example, appropriate behavioural strategies are being neglected.

Reviewing audio or video tapes of your work in peer or expert supervision is the most effective means of identifying possible therapist drift and error. Having done so, it is important to also come to some formulation of what might be maintaining these errors. Possibly the issue is one of competence development, which can be appropriately addressed in supervision or further training. Often however, what might be indicated is that therapist drift is at least partly a response to features of the client's presentation (client characteristics), features of the context for treatment (service variables including pressures for quick through-put of clients) and aspects of the therapists beliefs and emotions (therapist factors). Identifying the interactional aspects of therapist drift seems important, as "blaming the therapist" is often as unhelpful as blaming the client.

When CBT "isn't working" try to define exactly what "not working" means and use CBT theories to formulate this!

You may often initially become aware that you are struggling with resistance through having some sense of being "stuck" or "blocked". As an initial step, consistent with the problem -solving orientation of CBT, it is important to attempt to define what the apparent resistance is, in clear behavioural terms. What is the client doing, or not doing, that the therapist experiences as in some fashion counter-therapeutic? The fact that the client only attends two out of every five offered sessions, arrives consistently 15 minutes late, or refuses to complete written self-monitoring forms, is far more useful and "workable" information than a general statement of client resistance. Attempting to define things in behavioural terms also allows us to address the possibility that there are indeed aspects of the client's presentation (possibly then interacting with therapist and context factors) that are functioning to block effective treatment, without this identification of client features constituting a form of blaming the client.

Once you have clearly defined what it is that appears to be present as an obstacle or roadblock to therapy, and that it appears that this is not primarily the result of an identifiable therapist error, a procedural rule that can be considered is as follows:

> If you encounter what appears to be a significant roadblock or obstacle in treatment, that appears to be primarily attributable to factors originating with the client, seek first to determine what the function of the resistance behaviours might be.

This procedural competence of being able to employ CBT theory to devise tentative hypotheses or formulations of what might be maintaining the resistance, I would argue, is an important aspect of developing appropriate flexibility and artistry as a CBT therapist. This can be contrasted with the possibility of responding to apparent client reluctance, ambivalence or non-cooperation with an increased "technical" focus and reiteration of the importance of complying or the value of the specific procedures. Or in other words therapist counter-resistance!

Castonguay, Goldfried, Wiser, Raue, and Hayes (1996) report on an intriguing study that appeared to show that therapist persistence with standard CBT interventions (specifically persisting with a focus on the effects of distorted cognitions in the maintenance of depressed mood), in a situation of client resistance, was associated with poor outcome in CBT for depression. They also propose that this increase in apparent client resistance may not be due to the use of an inappropriate strategy or intervention, but rather that the appropriate strategy may have been used in an *inflexible* manner that was not responsive to the client's feedback and concerns.

A significant step towards developing metacompetence as a CBT practitioner, is the ability to pause when apparent resistance is encountered, and, rather than persisting in an intervention that is not flowing, to attempt to think about what the roadblock might be indicating. In other words, in the face of apparent resistance, attempt to formulate rather than persist with the technical intervention.

As well as considering clients idiosyncratic beliefs about complying with treatment procedures, and the possibility that such beliefs are themselves implicated in the clinical problems the client is seeking help for, it may also be beneficial to widen your assessment of possible relevant factors to include influences from the client's natural environment (such as the presence of a spouse hostile to or threatened by the client's engagement in treatment, or struggling with their own substance misuse problem) as well as the possibility that the client's reluctance in fact is expressive of a skill deficit rather than being primarily the expression of interfering beliefs or emotions.

When CBT isn't working switch your focus from persisting with a change intervention and focus on acceptance and validation

Difficulties with resistance and therapy interfering behaviours often escalate to the point that a rupture in the working alliance occurs. Competencies for addressing ruptures once they have occurred are discussed in Chapter 3. How might you work to minimize their occurrence? One suggestion is that, once you have become aware that you are stuck (and are perhaps feeling increasingly frustrated or confused), cease following the intervention strategy for a moment and seek to collaborate with your client to mutually disclose how you are both experiencing the current interaction. This might involve you using a limited degree of self-disclosure in which you present the client with feedback about your sense that you are both potentially getting stuck and working at cross purposes. Here is how this might look with "David" a client described earlier who was responding to the therapist's noting of positive changes with an increase in negative expressed emotion and where there is a risk of a rupture forming.

DAVID: I think it's the complexity of my depression that really concerns me. It's been around so long and is so deep in me it's hard to see how that will ever change…

TH: OK … David I am just starting to wonder … (Speech becoming slower and more tentative) … I just want to slow us down just a bit … I guess I am having a feeling right now that we are kind of pushing against each other here … I am aware that we often seem to start our session this way ... not sure if you have noticed this too, but it seems like we often get into this pattern where I start to notice positive changes you are making, and when I do so you seem to then respond with an emphasis on how bad things feel ... do you notice anything like that?

DAVID: Well yeah ... it does feel sometimes like you don't really get how bad I feel ... I mean I know you do ... and actually I do value coming here ... it's just sometimes I am not sure if you get how much of a struggle this really is.

TH: Yes... I can see that must feel really invalidating. I think it is going to be important for us to somehow make it possible for you to let me know that things are feeling that way in here. I am also aware that this approach is at times pretty hard work. Seems like we need to find a way that we can both notice when some positive changes are happening, and not to let go of these, but for this not to be done in a way that seems to be ignoring the difficulties that you have and still do experience ... would you be willing to look at this?

This type of dialogue might be one that needs to occur more or less frequently, depending upon the degree of resistance that shows up. Leahy (2001) suggests that in situations such as this you might also explicitly negotiate with your client about how the session is spent. The first 15 minutes could be given over to validation before any change strategies are considered. This might also be done in the form of a behavioural experiment whereby the client is invited to compare and contrast the effect of sessions where there is primarily a focus on validation versus sessions that include a good degree of work on change strategies.

Consistent with much of the research examining the role of technical and process factors in therapy outcome (Castonguay & Beutler, 2006) it may be possible to state an important procedural rule as follows:

When you encounter significant forms of client resistance, your use of directive change strategies should be modified to inversely correspond with the level of resistance.

In other words, successfully working with resistance may require a *temporary* grading down of a directive change strategy and a focus instead on validation and maintaining engagement. The art involves doing so in a manner whereby you don't lose traction for change either! However, what should you do if these strategies prove themselves insufficient, and CBT is still not working?

When standard CBT isn't working try something else!

A number of authors, such as Waller (2009), have cautioned us against racing towards an embrace of some of the "newer" third wave or acceptance focussed versions of CBT. Leaving aside some of the heat that has been associated with this debate, however, it is the case that there is a growing body of evidence to suggest that such approaches indeed can be effective, and it is reasonable for a CBT therapist, working primarily within a standard Beckian framework, to seek to incorporate some of these, as well as other strategies, in cases where the standard approach appears to be failing (Federici, Rowa, & Antony, 2009). A detailed treatment of all of these is beyond the scope of this chapter, however, several possibilities are briefly described.

1.   *Focus on strategies to enhance "motivation"*: many CBT interventions can achieve good results relatively swiftly with clients who are well socialized to the model and willing to engage in treatment procedures. As outlined above however, many

clients may present with beliefs and anxieties about the dangers and risks of change and may be far more ambivalent about a sustained engagement with a programme of change. For clients who are in a state of considerable ambivalence regarding change, it may be beneficial to draw upon work that has focussed on identifying stages of change (Prochaska & DiClemente, 1992). Strategies adapted from motivational interviewing (Miller & Rollnick, 2002) may be integrated into the early stages of CBT in an effort to make it more likely that the active change strategies of CBT are introduced at a point at which the client is best prepared to make use of these.

2. *Teach strategies of mindfulness and acceptance*: Linehan (1993) has argued that clients presenting with challenging forms of therapy interfering behaviours need to be responded to by a therapist who can balance change strategies and acceptance strategies. A striking feature of many of the "third wave" approaches such as Acceptance and Commitment Therapy (Hayes, Strosahl, & Wilson, 1999) and Mindfulness based CBT (Fresco, Flynn, Mennin, & Haigh, 2011) has been the focus on teaching clients skills for "opening to" and "allowing" distressing psychological experiences. While at the present stage the available empirical evidence would suggest that you attempt to work within a standard Beckian framework wherever your assessment indicates that this is appropriate, it is also possible that adapting your intervention to include interventions and ideas drawn from ACT and other mindfulness-based approaches may be appropriate, particularly when dealing with more resistant clients.

3. *Teach emotional regulation skills*: effective CBT often requires clients to experience increases in affect. Many clients presenting with forms of therapy interfering behaviour and resistance demonstrate difficulties with regulating emotional experience. Clients can present as effectively phobic of their emotions, they may be experienced by the therapist as "experientially avoidant", as distracting themselves and their therapists from affective experience and as "blocking" or "pushing away" affect. A range of developments within contemporary CBT, such as Barlow's "unified protocol" for the treatment of mood and anxiety disorders (Barlow et al., 2011) highlight difficulties and deficits with emotional regulation as being a central maintaining factor across different psychological disorders and recommend directly targeting this in treatment. Chapter 7 on a transdiagnostic approach to anxiety disorders by McManus and Sharfran provides guidance for addressing emotional regulation problems.

4. *Target client perfectionistic standards and rules*: a further example of a potentially transdiagnostic process is the work that has been done on "clinical perfectionism". Many clients who present with high degrees of perfectionism may struggle with homework compliance due to the fact that they expect themselves to comply perfectly with the homework assignment, can experience high levels of anxiety and self-attack between the session when they struggle to achieve this high standard, and then avoid completing the homework assignment and come to experience their "failure" in therapy as further proof of their personal inadequacy or weakness. Garland and Scott (2007) provide an excellent case study where the work with a highly perfectionistic depressed client focussed on her difficulties with homework. It was apparent in this case that working on the client's non-compliance with homework, and the considerable efforts the therapist needed to make to maintain client engagement, *was the therapy*, rather than this issue being something that must be overcome before the therapy could proceed.

The above four areas of possible adaptation constitute possible lines of work where you find yourself having become stuck. Nevertheless, having attempted such, you will still, on occasion, be in situation where you must draw an unsuccessful therapy to a close. How might this best be done?

When CBT hasn't worked, draw your intervention to an acceptable close

The issue of "termination" or "ending therapy" has received far less attention in CBT as compared to other models. In part this reflects the emphasis in CBT that the ending phase is not necessarily inherently a problematic nor complex experience, as well as an emphasis on the client being assisted to become their own therapist and the aim of all interventions being the generalization of changes made in sessions to the client's wider life, and the maintenance of gains over time. Consistent with this model, the preferred process of ending is one where there is a gradual tapering off of sessions followed by one or a series of "booster sessions" that allows therapist and client to consider progress and problem solve any difficulties that may have arisen with generalization and maintenance.

Where goal attainment in CBT has been mostly successful, and the client has experienced a significant improvement in their mood and functioning, the termination phase is most likely to be experienced as unproblematic. A very useful strategy to employ at the termination stage is to jointly construct a "therapy blueprint" (Butler, Fennell, & Hackmann, 2008) that summarizes what the client has learned and will be carrying forward past the end of treatment. This blueprint, and any associated post-therapy homework tasks, might then form the foundation for subsequent booster sessions. Noting that clear criteria to help clinicians determine whether or not a client is "ready" to enter a termination phase of treatment has been unclear in CBT, Jakobsons, Brown, Gordon, and Joiner (2007), have outlined seven possible criteria that effectively can be regarded as the "gold standard" for termination readiness. These criteria are:

1. a decrease in symptoms as assessed by sound measures;
2. a decrease in symptoms that is stable and maintained for eight weeks;
3. a decrease in functional impairment;
4. observed evidence that the decrease in symptoms is not a spontaneous remission;
5. observed client usage of the new skills, particularly at times, or on themes, of former vulnerability;
6. client pride regarding their new skills, in contrast to initial doubt regarding whether the techniques would work; and
7. transfer of decrease in symptoms to other areas.

These seven criteria certainly appear to be of considerable worth, and in cases of relatively successful outcome are likely to support a clinician to come to an informed decision about client readiness for termination. What about those cases where a client does not display the observed positive signs outlined above? In these cases clinicians are perhaps more likely to fall into a number of common traps including delaying the termination phase, and offering prolonged treatment, in the absence of evidence that further treatment will result in substantial further gains. Therapists can find themselves effectively experiencing a form a "sunk cost" in their work with clients. The idea of "sunk costs" has been introduced by Leahy (2001) to describe the situation where resistant clients may be unwilling to move away from currently unworkable behaviours and commitments due to their perception that "I have invested so much in this way of being already" combined with the perception that to do so might result in the experience of shame and a correspondence degree of damage to their sense that they are capable of making good decisions in the future. It is understandable that CBT therapists, who may habitually and functionally approach their work with a high level of commitment and optimism, may experience the pull of sunk costs when treatment gets bogged down.

Several procedural rules may be helpful in approaching the ending phase of therapy with clients where there have been significant difficulties and/or poor results.

1. Attend to the termination phase at the beginning of treatment. This is a key point at which we can go wrong. A failure to address the ending at the beginning makes it more likely that either the ending will "drift" or that the ending phase will be vague and unsatisfactory for client and therapist. Attending the ending at the beginning may primarily involve attention to the clear specification of treatment goals and agreement on treatment procedures. The clearer the goals for treatment, the more likely it is that progress can be tracked and the decision made as to whether termination has been reached "naturally" or is necessary due the therapy being unsuccessful.

2. Attempt to clarify criteria for termination with your client, even if this is provisional. Termination criteria may be specified as in the seven areas identified by Jakobsons et al. (2007) or it may be anchored to such features as a set number of sessions (that is reviewed and monitored regularly) or a set point in time which is judged as "reasonable" as a test of the interventions utility for the client.

3. Have an ending session and record both positive and negative aspects of the therapy from the client's and the therapist's perspective. Clients may often avoid the ending session in the case of an unsuccessful therapy and particularly if the therapist has allowed the therapy to drift over time. Where it has been possible to avoid such drift, it is advisable to invite the client to attend a final review session, where, rather than drawing out a blueprint, what is noted down is a summary of where the client feels they have got to. This could include a summary of where they were at the start and at the end of the unsuccessful treatment, acknowledging in a straightforward manner the lack of change. Second, this could include a summary from the therapist of what their formulation was and what interventions the therapist considered may have been helpful for the client. It may also be useful to note what aspects of the intervention the client struggled with, and how the therapist understood this. This is essentially aimed at a compassionate yet clear description of where the client struggled such as "It seemed that although a graded exposure to being on public transport would be a useful way forward, you experienced this as particularly challenging and that this seemed to be related to a belief that any sign of impending anxiety is a bad sign and a sign that it is time to withdraw."

It may also be important both to note down what the client's emotional response and thoughts are about the unsuccessful therapy and for the therapist to validate these as understandable. Again, it is desirable to both acknowledge where specifically the client may have struggled with therapy but in a way that does not blame the client for treatment failure. Finally it may also be useful to note down any signs of client resilience or strength, including the resilience and the strength involved in the decision taken to risk entering therapy as well as noting possibilities for onward referral and future treatment. Equally, therapists may choose to acknowledge in a simple and direct fashion that they too have felt some disappointment at the outcome reached. While it is important to express this in a manner that does not blame the client, such a disclosure can also convey that the attempt at therapy has been a significant and important one for the therapist. My experience suggests that, even in cases where treatment has been experienced as a disappointment, an attempt at open and honest feedback from both parties has resulted in an acknowledgement (from both), that the attempt has been meaningful and valuable, and that this allows for the therapist to both validate the client's disappointment and reinforce their ongoing possibilities for constructive problem solving and change.

Procedural Rules

1. When clients are considering significant psychological change, expect the phenomenon of resistance to be present. Accept resistance as a natural, adaptive and potentially useful and informative aspect of working meaningfully with people.
2. When beginning therapy, as well as specifying clear goals for treatment and working hard to engage clients, consider how you would define "poor response" or "failed treatment".
3. When you encounter blocks to treatment, consider first the role of possible therapist drift and error.
4. When you encounter significant and persistent blocks to treatment, define in behavioural terms what the blocks consists of, and then seek to devise a formulation, with your client, about what might be maintaining this. Possibly, your work with your client on the resistance will become the focus of the treatment itself. Resolving the resistance may also be part of meaningful change for the presenting problem.
5. When you encounter significant and persistent blocks to treatment, look to vary your level of directiveness and focus on change in inverse proportion to the level of resistance. Higher levels of blocking and opposition may be responded to with lower levels of emphasis on change and higher levels of acceptance, validation and collaboration.
6. When standard treatment methods fail, consider strategies to enhance motivation, work with acceptance and mindfulness, as well as strategies to improve emotional regulation and reduce perfectionism. Ensure these strategies are consistent with your formulation of the case.
7. Anticipate difficulties around termination from the beginning of treatment, work to set clear criteria for termination from the start.
8. When ending unsuccessful cases, work to non-defensively elicit client feedback about their experience of therapy and also attempt to define where the therapy may have got stuck, without blaming the client (or yourself) for this.

Notes

1 BRUCE LEE® and the Bruce Lee signature are registered trademarks of Bruce
   Lee Enterprises, LLC. The Bruce Lee name, image, likeness, quotes, and all related
   indicia are intellectual property of Bruce Lee Enterprises, LLC. All Rights Reserved.
   www.brucelee.com
2 All client examples have had identifying information changed.

References

Barlow, D., Farchione, T. J., Fairholme, C. P., Ellard, K. K., Boisseau, C. L., Allen, L. B., &
    May, J. T. E. (2011). *Unified protocol for transdiagnostic treatment of emotional disorders.
    Therapist guide*. Buckingham: Open University Press.
Butler, G., Fennell, M., & Hackmann, A. (2008). *Cognitive-behavioral therapy for anxiety disorders:
    mastering clinical challenges*. London: Guildford Press.
Castonguay, L. G., & Beutler, L. E. (2006). *Principles of therapeutic change that work*. New York:
    Oxford.
Castonguay, L. G., Goldfried, M. R., Wiser, S., Raue, P., & Hayes, A. M. (1996). Predicting the
    effect of cognitive therapy for depression: A study of unique and common factors. *Journal
    of Consulting and Clinical Psychology, 3*, 497–504.
Federici, A., Rowa, K., & Antony, M. M. (2009). Adjusting treatment for partial or nonresponse to
    contemporary cognitive-behavioral therapy. In D. McKay, J. Abramowitz, & S. Taylor (Eds.),
    Cognitive-behavioral therapy for refractory cases: turning failure into success. Washington,
    DC: American Psychological Association.
Foa, E. B., & Emmelkamp, P. M. G. (1983). *Failures in behavior therapy*. New York: John Wiley
    & Sons.
Fresco, D. M., Flynn, J. L., Mennin, D. S., & Haigh, E. A. P. (2011). Mindfulness-based cognitive
    therapy. In J. D. Herbert and E. M. Forman (Eds.), *Acceptance and mindfulness in cognitive
    behaviour therapy: understanding and applying the new therapies* (pp. 57–82). New York: John
    Wiley & Sons.
Garland, A., & Scott, J. (2007). The obstacle is the path: overcoming blocks to homework
    assignments in a complex presentation of depression. *Cognitive and Behavioral Practice, 14*,
    278–288.
Hayes, S., Strosahl, K., & Wilson, K. G. (1999). *Acceptance and commitment therapy:
    An experiential approach to behavior change*. New York: Guilford Press.
Jakobsons, L. J., Brown, J. S., Gordon, K. H., & Joiner, T. E. (2007). When are clients ready to
    terminate? *Cognitive and Behavioral Practice, 14*, 281–230.
Kazantzis, N., & Shinkfield, G. (2007). Conceptualising patient barriers to nonadherence with
    homework assignments. *Cognitive and Behavioral Practice, 14*, 317–324.
Lambert, M. J. (2011). What have we learned about treatment failure in empirically sup-
    ported treatments? Some suggestions for practice. *Cognitive and Behavioral Practice,
    18*, 413–420.
Lazarus, A. A., & Fay, A. (1982). Resistance or rationalisation? A cognitive-behavioral perspective.
    In P. Wachtel (Ed.), *Resistance: psychodynamic and behavioral approaches* (pp. 115–132).
    New York: Plenum Press.
Leahy, R. (2001). *Overcoming resistance in cognitive therapy*. New York: Guilford Press.
Linehan, M. M. (1993). *Cognitive-behavioral treatment of borderline personality disorder*.
    New York: Guilford Press.
Miller, W. R., & Rollnick, S. (2002). *Motivational Interviewing: preparing people for change*
    (2nd ed.). New York: Guilford Press.

Newman, C. F. (1994). Understanding client resistance: methods for enhancing motivation to change. *Cognitive and Behavioral Practice, 1*, 47–69.

Prochaska, J. O., & DiClemente, C. C. (1992). The transtheoretical approach. In J. C. Norcoss, & M. R. Goldfried (Eds.). *Handbook of psychotherapy integration* (pp. 300–334). New York: Basic Books.

Turkat, D., & Meyer, V. (1982). The behavior-analytic approach. In P. Wachtel (Ed.), *Resistance: psychodynamic and behavioral approaches* (pp. 157–184). New York: Plenum Press.

Waller, G. (2009). Evidence-based treatment and therapist drift. *Behavior Research and Therapy, 47*(2), 119–127.

III
Adapting for Specific Client Groups

11

CBT with People with Long-Term Medical Conditions

Jane Hutton, Myra S. Hunter, Stephanie Jarrett and Nicole de Zoysa

Introduction

Depression is two to three times more common in people who have one LTC (long-term medical condition) and seven times more common in those with two or more (Department of Health, 2011). Chronic health problems can cause or exacerbate depression, and also complicate its identification and assessment, due to overlap of symptoms (National Institute for Health and Clinical Excellence (NICE), 2009). In the context of LTCs, depression is associated with reduced quality of life, greater disability, higher healthcare costs, poorer concordance with treatment and poorer health outcomes (NICE, 2009).

Psychosocial factors tend to predict level of functioning better than biomedical factors and there is growing evidence that psychological interventions can lead to improved quality of life, ability to cope with illness and medical outcomes, as well as reduced service use and costs, especially when implemented in primary care (Department of Health, 2009a). In a recent systematic review, outcomes of psychological interventions for depression were similar in people with and without medical disorders (Department of Health 2011; Van Straten, Geraedts, Verdonck-de Leeuw, Andersson, & Cuijpers, 2010).

The NICE guidance for depression and chronic illness (NICE, 2009) is based on a stepped care approach and has some differences from the NICE guidance for depression, for example:

- Caution is recommended in the use of medication for mild depression.
- Low-intensity interventions are recommended for mild to moderate depression and for sub-threshold depressive symptoms which are persistent or complicate medical treatment. Options include group-based peer support or physical activity, computerized CBT and guided self-help.

How to Become a More Effective CBT Therapist: Mastering Metacompetence in Clinical Practice,
First Edition. Edited by Adrian Whittington and Nick Grey.
© 2014 John Wiley & Sons, Ltd. Published 2014 by John Wiley & Sons, Ltd.

- High-intensity interventions are recommended for moderate depression. Options include individual or group CBT, behavioural couples therapy, and medication, with or without CBT. Collaborative care is recommended for those whose depression does not respond.

The United Kingdom Department of Health (2010) has published five helpful information sheets for healthcare professionals.

Assessment, Formulation and Finding a Focus

It is important to invest time to understand "the bigger picture" and develop a shared perspective on how physical and emotional problems might interrelate (Figure 11.1 and Figure 11.2).

It is helpful for clients to have a coherent understanding of their condition, and an opportunity to process associated emotional and cognitive reactions (Moorey, 1996). Personal meanings of illness have emotional and behavioural implications. For example, anxiety if threat is perceived, low mood for loss, social withdrawal for stigma and active coping for challenge. Beliefs about illness can be explored using the Illness Perception Questionnaire (IPQ, n.d.), which is based on the self-regulation model (Leventhal et al., 1997), and includes primary appraisal (of illness and its likely impact) and secondary appraisal (of ones coping abilities and resources). Discussion of the different strategies that are helpful in dealing with acute versus chronic illness can be useful.

Having developed a shared model, the next task is to agree a feasible focus for intervention. This may include addressing unhelpful symptom-related beliefs and behaviours (e.g., reducing avoidance and hypervigilance) and structuring daily activities, exercise and social engagement, with an approach of living with and accepting symptoms rather than fighting them (Furze, Donnison, & Lewis, 2008). It may be helpful to include a friend or relative, so they are aware of the model. Clients often

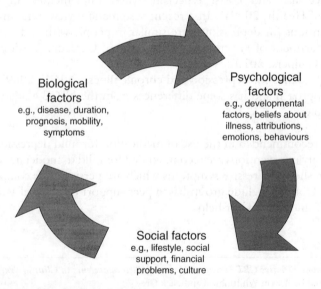

Figure 11.1   A biopsychosocial model.

Start with client's perspective on the problem
- What's your understanding of why you have been referred here?
- What are the main problems in your life?
- Is there anything which makes your symptoms worse? Or better? Anything you can do that helps? Or makes things worse?
- Can you tell me about your illness? What effect has it had on your life? (Ask about different domains and listen for cognitions)
- What's the worst thing about your situation? (Be aware of your own assumptions)
- If I'd met you before you were ill, what would have been different?
- Can you tell me about your strengths, and what you're good at?
- What are the things that are most important to you in life?

Impact on life and coping
Level of functioning, past and current coping strategies and help seeking

---

Cognitions
Explore personal and family experiences of illness and treatment, which will inform beliefs
Use downward arrow to explore assumptions (e.g., If I'm in pain, I can't do anything)
Listen for beliefs about:
- Illness and treatment (e.g., catastrophizing in the context of negative experience)
- Meaning of illness (e.g., being weak, a failure, unlovable)
- Own reactions (e.g., I should be in control of my feelings, I shouldn't upset my family, I should avoid thoughts about the future)
- Explore beliefs held by significant others. What does X think/do/say about that?

Explore relationships between illness and mood
- Time course of symptoms; physical and psychological moderating factors (consider timelines, diaries)
- May be difficult to tease out relative contributions of physical and psychological factors, for example, to impaired sleep; adopt hypothesis testing approach

---

Need confidence that appropriate investigations and interventions have been completed or are ongoing
Check with GP if any constraints to exercise and so forth.

Aim to develop a shared model
- Simple biopsychosocial model (Figure 11.1) may be useful starting point
- Build tailored CBT model linking thoughts, feelings, actions and physical symptoms and identify possible areas for intervention
- Outline relevant evidence base for CBT

Agree goals and treatment plan
Take account of client's values and physical limitations; consider longer/shorter sessions or telephone appointments as required; allow time for liaison with other health professionals

---

Figure 11.2 Assessment – areas to consider.

benefit from developing skills in negotiating the healthcare system, and careful feedback to referrers is a good way of communicating biopsychosocial perspectives. Individual formulation is crucial, as the degree of interplay between physical and psychological factors varies; some clients' psychological issues are quite independent of their physical illness.

In the remainder of this chapter, these general principles will be developed and illustrated using four common conditions.

Chronic Pain

Pain is a universal experience but is usually an acute problem, which resolves over time or with treatment. One in seven people in the United Kingdom experience chronic pain, defined as "continuous, long-term pain of more than 12 weeks or after the time that healing would have been thought to have occurred in pain after trauma or surgery" (British Pain Society, n.d.). Prevalence of pain report is slightly higher in women (depending on site of pain) and in older adults. However, interference by pain with daily activities does not increase with age and most people who seek help for chronic pain are between 40 and 60 years old (Department of Health, 2009b). Variations in pain report have been found between cultural and ethnic groups, but are often confounded by other factors, such as socioeconomic status.

While acute pain can usually be related to a physical cause and physical treatment, such as medication or rest, can help resolve it, chronic pain is more complicated, its exact cause is often unknown, and using a solely physical explanation is unhelpful. Although there may be signs of physical change in investigations such as x-rays and MRI scans, these correlate poorly with pain experience (Boos et al., 1995). There is no objective method of measuring pain: it can only be assessed through subjective report. Physical treatments aimed at relieving chronic pain can have limited efficacy and unpleasant side-effects (Jamison, 2011).

Based on previous experiences with acute pain, most clients expect a physical explanation and treatment for their chronic pain. This can lead to unhelpful cognitions that result in increased distress (see Table 11.1). In particular, the lack of a clear physical explanation and limited efficacy of medical interventions can make patients fear that their doctor doesn't believe them and thinks the pain is "all in my head". The belief that pain is *either* physical *or* psychological is not supported by current research, which demonstrates that *all* pain is affected by biological, psychological and social factors.

Advances in pain research have highlighted the importance of nervous system plasticity. The pain system can become sensitized and overreact to normal stimuli, such as touch or movement, by sending unnecessary pain messages. An oversensitive smoke alarm goes off when the toast is burning, making the same noise as if the kitchen were on fire. Similarly, someone can experience the same intensity of pain as if they had damaged themselves, although no damage is occurring and no changes are seen on investigations. This is important for someone with chronic pain to understand. Pain is normally viewed as a warning signal, but in chronic pain "hurt" no longer equals "harm".

Psychological factors are known to affect the pain system and play an important role in acute and chronic pain. They are more powerful predictors of outcome than demographic and physical factors (Main, Sullivan, & Watson, 2008). Consequently, psychological therapy can significantly improve outcomes for people with chronic pain. CBT is more widely researched in relation to chronic pain than to any other chronic medical problem (White, 2001). Meta-analyses have shown that CBT can have a significant impact on several biopsychosocial variables in chronic pain (Eccleston, Williams, & Morley, 2009).

Assessment and formulation

Beliefs regarding the cause of the pain, its future course and perceived control over it should all be assessed. It is useful to begin by hearing the client's story about how the pain began and the treatment they have received. Starting with the physical aspects of their pain experience (the site of pain, what it feels like, physical limitations) can help address fears of the pain being perceived as "all in their head".

Table 11.1 Unhelpful thoughts and possible interventions

Thoughts	Consequences	Intervention/accurate information
Chronic pain		
They haven't found anything yet – they must have missed something serious	Multiple investigations	Diagnostic investigations do not correlate with pain, changes to the way that pain nerves function do not show on x-rays, MRI
Pain is caused by damage – worse (chronic) pain is caused by more serious damage	Anxiety, search for physical explanation and cure	Clear information on chronic pain (different from acute pain), explanation of how "hurt" does not always mean "harm"
Pain as danger/warning signal		Pain as false alarm
The doctor has given me antidepressants, they must think I am depressed/the pain is psychological	Non-adherence to medication Difficulties in relationship with doctor	Information about how antidepressants have been found to have an effect on pain, in doses too low to target depression
I can't live a normal life until I get rid of this pain	Focus on pain and trying to get rid of it	Examine effect (behavioural experiment) of focussing on pain (= increased pain); change focus to improving quality of life despite presence of pain
There is nothing I can do to deal with my pain/nothing will help Inevitable deterioration If my pain continues I will end up in a wheelchair	Depression Feeling helpless/hopeless	Accurate information about course of chronic pain (deterioration depends on whether patient stays active) Periodic flare-ups Direct towards self-help information – ideas on what *can* be done "When my pain flares up I can cope by...." "What shall I try to improve my situation?"
Activity hurts so I had better limit what I do/ whether I go out	Reduced activity Avoidance	Pacing using behavioural experiments Active involvement
Diabetes		
If my blood test results are bad, I'm useless	Poor monitoring/recording	Explore using downward arrow Several factors affect blood glucose levels
I must avoid having a hypo/ complications at all costs	Deliberately running sugars high/low	Support engagement with health professionals and encourage more balanced view

(*continued*)

Table 11.1 *Continued*

Thoughts	Consequences	Intervention/accurate information
If I can't do it perfectly I might as well give up	Yo-yo dieting, unsustainable exercise plans, continued smoking	Realistic goal-setting
Nothing I do is working	Giving up on diabetes care	Realistic goal-setting, engagement with health professionals
I feel OK, so I don't see the need for medication/ changing my diet	Patchy adherence to medication regime and lifestyle change	Discuss concept of subjective reasoning and delayed consequences of behavior
CHD I've got heart trouble now and there's nothing I can do about it	Lack of motivation to change health-related behaviours	Lifestyle changes and medication significantly reduce re-infarction rates
I'm bound to have another heart attack	Hopelessness/depression	About 60 per cent of patients do not have another heart attack
If I get chest pain, it must mean something serious	Avoidance of potential triggers leads to maintenance of fears and reduced activity, which has impact on mood and prognosis	Discuss roles of anxiety and exertion
Angina is like a mini heart attack		Stable angina is a sign to slow down temporarily; it is a completely different process to a heart attack and does not damage the heart
I need to avoid getting stressed		There is no consistent evidence linking stress directly to heart attack; stress may contribute indirectly, via risk factors, such as smoking
I need to rest		Physical activity can make the heart stronger and too much rest makes the heart unfit
I have to stop all my pleasures in life	Low mood	Explore creatively new pleasures or more moderate, ways of enjoying existing ones
The doctors have cured me	Lack of adjustment and behavioural change	Treatment can be lifesaving and reduce symptoms, however, it does not "remove" the disease, which is progressive
COPD Breathlessness is dangerous	Avoidance of exertion leading to maintenance of fears, reduced fitness and low mood	Discussion of importance of exertion to the point of mild breathlessness, and of role of anxiety
I've brought this on myself by smoking	Low mood	Work on usefulness of thoughts, shame, stigma

Eliciting factors that can affect the pain will often provide useful information to draw up a biopsychosocial model. Patients are often aware that stress exacerbates their pain and this can be used to challenge the dualistic model of pain (*either* physical *or* psychological). The CBT maintenance model, which includes the same factors as the biopsychosocial model, can help explain the patients' experience.

Treatment

While therapy can result in reductions in pain report, this should not be the goal of treatment, as it cannot be guaranteed. Instead, therapists should set realistic goals of reducing distress and disability as well as improving self-confidence in dealing with pain. This can be assessed by the Pain Self-Efficacy Questionnaire (Nicholas, 2007).

These changes can be achieved by providing realistic information about chronic pain, specifically, how we can experience real pain without it being a sign of worrying pathology, and confirming that the client is not imagining or fabricating their pain. Good liaison with the local chronic pain service will help in the provision of this information. The focus can then be shifted away from searching for a cure and towards dealing with the problems that pain causes, such as social isolation, reduced activity and loss of role.

Unhelpful beliefs should be addressed using the standard repertoire of CBT techniques. Specific techniques such as relaxation, distraction and attentional focus retraining can be helpful, particularly when dealing with a flare-up in pain (see also Table 11.2)

Table 11.2 Special considerations in chronic pain, diabetes, CHD and COPD

Issue	*Intervention strategies*
Chronic pain	
Fear of not being believed	Psychoeducation regarding biopsychosocial model – *all* pain consists of physical, psychological and social factors
Fear that something serious has been missed	Exploration of fears and factors contributing to them (e.g., family member had undiagnosed cancer), liaison with hospital services to understand assessment, treatment and information received
Difficulty accepting limitations caused by pain	Focus on acceptance – changing factors that can be changed (e.g., activity) and accepting factors that are harder to change (e.g., pain)
Fear of movement	Exploration of fears, accurate information regarding pain and movement, pacing activity
Diabetes	
Emotional adjustment to diagnosis or other transitions, e.g., starting insulin	Psychoeducation about emotional adjustment
Poor treatment adherence or misuse of insulin	Expand on risk assessment
Not eating can put patients at risk of hypos, if they are taking insulin	

(*continued*)

Table 11.2 *Continued*

Issue	Intervention strategies
Diabetes "burn out" due to depressogenic thinking styles, e.g., black-and-white thinking leading to rigid and unsustainable attempts to control blood sugars	Realistic goal setting around blood sugars Promote engagement with health professionals
Poor glycaemic control can produce symptoms overlapping with those of depression	Check glycaemic control
Overlap between anxiety and hypo symptoms, e.g., sweating, dizziness	Refer to medical protocol for identifying and treating hypos
Effect of stress on blood sugar levels (up or down)	Particular importance of stress management
Excessive control/testing of blood sugars	Explore health beliefs, graded exposure
Reality of developing complications	Acceptance-based approaches, explore helpfulness of worry
CHD Emotional adjustment to changes in role, functioning, perception of immortality	Psychoeducation about emotional adjustment
Poor treatment adherence due to mood or beliefs	Support engagement with health professionals; prioritize exercise as protective for cardiac and emotional health
Unhelpful beliefs about asking for help, especially in women; important as social isolation predicts poorer prognosis	Explore potential "mind reading" and support social networks
Cardiac "invalidism", where disability exceeds that expected from illness severity	Explore health beliefs and helpfulness of worry; behavioural activation and pacing
COPD Relaxation can be helpful, as it reduces fast, shallow breathing and perceived obstruction of the airways	Balance carefully with exposure to breathlessness through paced activity, and reducing reliance on safety behaviours
Hyperventilation is highly aversive (although not dangerous)	Model hyperventilation, demonstrating how readily breathlessness can be induced independent of any respiratory condition
Sleep difficulties, related to discomfort of oxygen provision or fear of death	Tailored sleep hygiene strategies; explore fears

Behavioural activation is as important in chronic pain as in depression. However, it can be problematic, as activity is often associated with increased pain. This can be addressed using "pacing". It is important that pain is *not* used to guide when to stop an activity. Instead, other guides such as time or distance can be used to ensure a change of activity *before* the pain has increased. Pacing can include resting more frequently, but also involves changing the biomechanics of an activity before the pain increases. For example, pacing of gardening might entail sitting and pulling out a couple of weeds, before standing to prune a shrub for a couple of minutes, and then walking to fetch a garden tool, before sitting to weed again.

There are many online resources for people with chronic pain. A good starting point might be the pain tool kit (n.d.), which was created by, and for, people living with chronic pain and is regularly updated.

Group pain management programmes, run by a multiprofessional team incorporating psychology, physiotherapy and doctors or specialist nurses, have consistently been found to be effective in reducing distress and disability (Koes, Tulder, & Thomas, 2006). If you have a pain management programme in your area, it should provide a useful resource for support and advice. People with chronic pain with significant pain-related distress and disability should be referred to a multidisciplinary team where available. There are some national referral services.

Diabetes

Diabetes is a chronic, progressive condition in which blood sugar levels rise because the body cannot process glucose properly. Type 1 diabetes is an autoimmune disease, usually diagnosed in childhood or adolescence, where the body produces no or little insulin. In type 2 diabetes, cells cannot use insulin properly and insulin production may be reduced. It usually appears after the age of 40 and is often linked to being overweight. Common symptoms of untreated diabetes include increased thirst, urination, fatigue, weight loss, blurred vision, thrush or genital itching and slow wound healing. Type 2 diabetes has doubled in prevalence over the past decade and diabetes now accounts for 10 per cent of the NHS budget. Diabetes is particularly common in South Asian and Afro-Caribbean people in the United Kingdom; this appears to be due to a combination of social and genetic factors (Oldroyd, Banerjee, Heald, & Cruikshank, 2005).

In some cases, diabetes may be managed with lifestyle changes alone. These include healthy eating (eliminating sugar is not necessary), limiting alcohol consumption, keeping active, maintaining a healthy weight and not smoking. Other people may also require oral medication and/or insulin, delivered by self-administered injections or a pump attached to the body.

Good diabetes control can minimize or delay complications. Glycated haemoglobin, or HbA1c, is a marker of diabetes control during the first three months before the test. Current guidance (NICE, 2011) states a target of 6.5–7.5 per cent; a 1 per cent reduction is associated with significant risk reduction.

Long-term complications of diabetes include permanent damage to the eyes, kidneys, nerves, heart and major arteries. Short-term, but unpleasant and sometimes dangerous, complications include hypoglycaemia (acutely low blood glucose) and states known as DKA and HHS, which are related to chronically high blood glucose. The symptoms of hypoglycaemia vary between individuals but often include shakiness, sweating, pallor, palpitations, confusion and irritability. DKA (diabetic ketoacidosis) arises when the body has no insulin. Symptoms include vomiting, dehydration, confusion and gasping for breath. Symptoms of HHS (hyperosmolar hyperglycaemic state) include frequent urination, great thirst, nausea, dry skin, disorientation and drowsiness.

Depression is at least twice as common in people with type 2 diabetes as in the general population. This is of significant concern, as depression is associated with a two-to-five fold increased risk of mortality in diabetes (Zhang et al., 2005), due to a combination of direct physiological mechanisms and poorer motivation to engage in healthy behaviours. Anxiety is also common, and may present as needle phobia, or specific fear of having a hypoglycaemic episode or developing complications. Classical needle phobia may be a barrier to adherence for blood testing and insulin injections. However, negative feelings about diabetes and its treatment in general, may also be misinterpreted by professionals as needle phobia.

Assessment and formulation

Useful questions to ask a client or referrer include whether they have type 1 or 2 diabetes, their last HbA1c result, insulin or oral medication, and any recent change in their medication or development of complications. The Problem Areas in Diabetes Questionnaire (Joslin Diabetes Center, 1999) may provide pointers to areas of concern.

Table 11.1 lists some unhelpful thoughts and their likely impact on health-related behaviours. Therapists should also look out for specific cognitive distortions and misunderstandings. For example, it is untrue that blood sugar levels should be stable *all* the time. Fluctuations are normal and the emphasis should be on their frequency and magnitude. Relatedly, it is untrue that *any* high blood sugar reading will lead to complications. Rather, *chronic* exposure to high levels increases this risk. It is also untrue that blood sugar levels are *only* affected by the patient's actions. They are also affected by a variety of factors including, stress, hormones, illness and genetics.

Treatment

Table 11.2 lists special considerations for CBT with this client group. Clients' understanding of their diabetes may be greatly enhanced by an education programme, such as DAFNE (for type 1) or DESMOND (type 2), which are available in most of the United Kingdom. The website of the charity Diabetes UK (www.diabetes.org.uk) contains a wealth of useful information for therapists and their clients.

Coronary Heart Disease

Coronary heart disease (CHD) results from restriction of blood supply to the heart by blockage of the coronary arteries, usually by fatty deposits. It may be silent, or present with symptoms including chest pain. In stable angina, there is sufficient blood flow at rest, but not for a heart beating fast due to exertion or stress. This tends to result from stable narrowing of the arteries. It is a sign to slow down, but is not dangerous. In unstable angina, blockages are more susceptible to disturbance and episodes occur when a blockage shifts, triggering a coronary artery to become partly or completely blocked. It requires urgent medical review as it can lead to a myocardial infarction (MI or heart attack), in which blood flow to the heart is blocked for long enough to damage part of the heart muscle.

Known risk factors for CHD include poor diet, high BMI, smoking, excessive alcohol consumption, inactivity, high blood pressure, diabetes and genetics. Socioeconomic disadvantage is linked to higher cardiac mortality and morbidity, partly due to increased behavioural and medical risk factors (Skodova et al., 2008). Lack of social support is strongly and consistently related to development of CHD and worse prognosis once CHD is present. Mortality from CHD is significantly higher for people born in the Indian sub-continent. Biological risk factors do not fully account for this (Jafar et al., 2005) and an interaction has been found between activity, mood, emotional support and ethnicity (Williams, Kooner, Steptoe, & Kooner, 2007).

Investigations include angiogram, in which dye is passed into the coronary arteries, usually via the groin, and then observed via x-ray to visualize any blockages. The condition may be managed with medication or, in more severe cases, require surgery (coronary artery bypass graft or CABG), or angioplasty, in which a balloon is inserted into the artery and inflated to open a narrowed section. A stent, or short tube of mesh, may be inserted to permanently support the artery.

Cardiac rehabilitation programmes incorporate graded exercise, peer support and education about CHD and self-management, and are widely available (see http:// maps.cardiac-rehabilitation.net/). Exercise is protective for cardiac and psychological health, so supporting clients eligible for rehabilitation to engage with it may be a valuable component of therapy.

Depression is more common in people with CHD than in the general population. It is a strong independent risk factor for developing CHD, comparable to smoking. In the context of CHD, depression is independently associated with increased cardiac and non-cardiac mortality and other cardiac events. Depression is also associated with poorer quality of life and worse symptomatic, psychological, social and functional outcomes (Goldston & Baillie, 2008). This is partly related to its impact on adherence to treatment and lifestyle changes. Anxiety is particularly common in people who have had an MI. Findings are less consistent regarding mortality and morbidity than those for depression, but persistent anxiety seems to be predictive of disability.

The symptoms of anxiety, angina and MI, particularly chest pain, overlap, but there are some differentiating factors. Stable angina usually occurs during physical exertion or psychological arousal, lasts less than 10 minutes and wears off when the trigger is no longer present. It usually begins in the middle of the chest, but may spread out to the jaw, neck, shoulder or arm. It is responsive to medication, such as nitroglycerin (GTN spray) and relaxation. Anxiety tends to cause pain more concentrated under the left breast.

In more serious causes of chest pain, that is, unstable angina and MI, pain may occur during rest or appear suddenly during physical exertion. It is not relieved by GTN spray, relaxation or slowing down. In MI, pain usually lasts at least 20 minutes.

Assessment and formulation

Health beliefs predict numerous outcomes, including readmission to hospital, physical functioning and attendance at cardiac rehabilitation. In most cases, health beliefs are better predictors than clinical indices of severity. Unhelpful beliefs such as low perceived control over illness may contribute to depression. Interventions targeting beliefs are associated with improved outcomes, for example, level of symptoms, attendance at cardiac rehabilitation and return to work. Various beliefs and unhelpful thinking styles may underlie the same behaviour, and clients may hold misconceptions about their condition (see Table 11.1).

Treatment

In treating anxiety, the medical diagnosis, and whether chest pain due to CHD can be expected, should be clarified with a physician. If a patient's condition is stable and asymptomatic, it is more likely that chest pain is non-cardiac and that standard protocols, for example, for panic or health anxiety, can be followed. However, as CHD is progressive, any new onset of pain should be investigated. Therapists should check with a physician before conducting any behavioural experiments involving sudden onset of exercise or hyperventilation.

When a patient is expected to experience some cardiac chest pain, a different approach is required. This might include:

- Exploring whether their chest pain may sometimes be caused by CHD, and at other times by non-cardiac causes, such as anxiety, indigestion or hyperventilation
- Explaining the cyclical links between thinking, physiology and symptoms.
- Discussing benefits of reducing anxiety around chest pain.
- Challenging unhelpful health beliefs.
- Introducing the concept of appropriate concern, perhaps by analogy with a guitar string, which mustn't be too tight or too loose. Chest pain in CHD can't be ignored, but doesn't have to take over the client's life.
- Teach relaxation techniques to manage episodes of angina.
- Using pacing and behavioural activation to increase activity levels.
- Referring to the client's chest pain protocol (from hospital or cardiac rehabilitation teams).

Table 11.2 lists other considerations in CBT with this client group. Further information is available from the website of the British Heart Foundation (www.bhf.org.uk).

Chronic Obstructive Pulmonary Disease

Chronic obstructive pulmonary disease (COPD) is an umbrella term encompassing several conditions, including emphysema and chronic bronchitis. Its main symptoms are breathlessness, which can severely restrict everyday activities, and cough. Approximately 0.9 million people in United Kingdom are being treated for COPD and a further 2.8 million are thought to have the condition. It is most commonly caused by smoking, followed by exposure to pollutants. People who have COPD typically report stigma and lack of understanding. It is a progressive illness, and its course is marked by acute exacerbations associated with chest infections, which require treatment with antibiotics, sometimes delivered intravenously in hospital. COPD is strongly associated with socioeconomic status, especially for men, and social deprivation predicts worse prognosis, probably via a combination of chronic exposure to stress, lower self-efficacy and less healthy behaviour (Koster et al., 2004).

There is no cure, but much can be done to manage COPD. Smoking cessation is crucial. It is also important to keep active. This entails tolerance of moderate breathlessness, balanced with pacing of activities and careful planning to conserve energy. Pulmonary rehabilitation is recommended. Like its cardiac equivalent, it includes graded exercise, education and peer support.

COPD impacts significantly on quality of life, physical and social functioning, work, leisure and sleep. There may also be deficits in memory, frontal lobe functioning, processing speed and fine motor control, due to oxygen deprivation. Quality of life and disability are more strongly related to emotional functioning than to disease severity and can be improved by addressing psychological issues. Hynninen, Breitve, Wiborg, Pallesen, and Nordhus (2005) provide an excellent literature review. Anxiety and depression are much more common than in the general population. Depression is associated with shorter survival, longer hospital stays, poorer adherence to treatment, persistent smoking, poorer physical and social functioning and lower quality of life. Anxiety is associated with poorer functioning and more time in hospital and is the best single predictor of quality of life. Vicious cycles of breathlessness, catastrophic misinterpretations, anxiety, heightened attention, inactivity and reduced fitness commonly develop. Self-efficacy mediates the association of lung function and quality of life and predicts physical functioning. Lower self-efficacy predicts anxiety, depression and continued smoking.

Social support predicts quality of life and adherence to treatment. Physical limitations will impact on shared activities, including sexual relationships. Significant others have an important role to play and need accurate information to provide effective support, for example, by supporting the client to stop smoking and not encouraging rest as a response to mild breathlessness.

Assessment and formulation

Therapists should explore their client's beliefs about and understanding of COPD and how they can best manage it. Useful questions include "What's the worst thing about living with COPD?" and "Can you tell me about a time when you couldn't catch your breath?" The St George's Respiratory Questionnaire, especially the Impacts subscale, which assesses psychosocial function, can be used to gather information and as an outcome measure. The questionnaire and manual are freely available online at http://www.healthstatus.sgul.ac.uk/sgrq-c.

Treatment

Therapists should be mindful of a client's other appointments and physical limitations. Getting up and ready to go out in the morning is often particularly difficult. Special considerations and unhelpful thoughts related to COPD are listed in Tables 11.1 and 11.2. Work on shifting attentional focus and on assertive communication is also likely to be helpful. The latter might include making optimal use of medical consultations, and asking for and accepting help from family and friends, while maintaining autonomy.

Coventry and Gellatly's (2008) systematic review, describes the evidence for CBT, used in conjunction with exercise and education, as "limited but promising" in reducing anxiety and depression in COPD. Further good quality studies have been published since, notably that of Howard, Dupont, Haselden, Lynch, and Wills (2010), whose intervention consisted of four weekly group sessions for elderly patients with severe COPD, integrating CBT with physiotherapy. It significantly improved depression and health status and significantly reduced attendance at A&E. Further information about COPD is available on the website of the British Lung Foundation (http://www.blf.org.uk/Home).

Procedural rules

- Ensure that the CBT model fits well with the interaction of physical symptoms and psychological distress.
- At assessment and early in therapy, focus on engagement, and the client's understanding of how a psychological approach might be helpful for them.
- Share a biopsychosocial, cognitive-behavioural model of the client's situation and what they can do to improve it.

- Liaise with other healthcare professionals involved in the client's care to ensure that you have a good understanding of their medical condition and to share information about what you are doing in therapy.
- Look out for any misunderstanding or gaps in knowledge that the client may hold about their condition.
- Use Socratic questioning and the downward arrow technique to look for any distortions beyond the realities of the condition.
- Adapt CBT interventions to accommodate the condition.

References

Boos, N., Rieder, R., Schade, V., Spratt, K. F., Semmer, N., & Aebi, M. (1995). The diagnostic accuracy of magnetic resonance imaging, work perception and psychosocial factors in identifying symptomatic disc herniations. *Spine, 20*, 2613–2625.

British Pain Society (n.d.). Frequently asked questions. Retrieved from http://www.britishpainsociety.org/media_faq.htm

Coventry, P. A., & Gellatly, J. L. (2008). Improving outcomes for COPD patients with mild to moderate anxiety and depression: A systematic review of cognitive behavioural therapy. *British Journal of Health Psychology, 13*, 381–400.

Department of Health (2009a). *Psychological management of long term conditions, including medically unexplained symptoms.* Retrieved from http://www.evidence.nhs.uk/search?q=psychological+assessment+and+treatment+of+long+term+conditions

Department of Health (2009b). *2008 Annual Report of the Chief Medical Officer on the State of Public Health.* The full report can be downloaded at: http://webarchive.nationalarchives.gov.uk/20130107105354/http://www.dh.gov.uk/en/Publicationsandstatistics/Publications/AnnualReports/DH_096206

Department of Health (2010). *Improving care for people with long term conditions: "at a glance" information sheets for healthcare professionals.* Retrieved from https://www.gov.uk/government/publications/improving-care-for-people-with-long-term-conditions-at-a-glance-information-sheets-for-healthcare-professionals

Department of Health (2011). *Talking therapies: A four-year plan of action.* Retrieved from https://www.gov.uk/government/publications/talking-therapies-a-4-year-plan-of-action

Eccleston, C., Williams, A. C. D., & Morley, S. (2009). Psychological therapies for the management of chronic pain (excluding headache) in adults. *Cochrane Database of Systematic Reviews, 2.*

Furze, G., Donnison, J., & Lewin, R. G. P. (2008). *The clinicians guide to chronic disease management for long term conditions: a cognitive behavioural approach.* Keswick: M&K Update Ltd.

Goldston, K., & Baillie A. J. (2008). Depression and coronary heart disease: a review of the epidemiological evidence, explanatory mechanisms and management approaches. *Clinical Psychology Review, 28*, 288–306.

Howard, C., Dupont, S., Haselden, B., Lynch, J., & Wills, P. (2010). The effectiveness of a group cognitive-behavioural breathlessness intervention on health status, mood and hospital admissions in elderly patients with chronic obstructive pulmonary disease. *Psychology, Health & Medicine, 15*, 371–385.

Hynninen, K. M. J., Breitve, M. H., Wiborg, A. B., Pallesen, S., & Nordhus, I. H. (2005). Psychological characteristics of patients with chronic obstructive pulmonary disease: A review. *Journal of Psychosomatic Research, 59*, 429–443.

IPQ (n.d.). *Illness Perception Questionnaire.* Retrieved from http://www.uib.no/ipq/

Jafar, T. H., Jafary, F. H., Jessani, S., & Chaturvedi, N. (2005). Heart disease epidemic in Pakistan: women and men at equal risk. *American Heart Journal, 150*, 221–226.

Jamison, R. N. (2011). Nonspecific treatment effects in pain medicine. *Pain Clinical Updates, IASP, XIX(2)*.

Joslin Diabetes Center (1999). Problem areas in diabetes questionnaire. Retrieved from http://www.dawnstudy.com/News_and_activities/Documents/PAID_problem_areas_in_diabetes_questionnaire.pdf

Koes, B. W., van Tulder, M. W., & Thomas, S. (2006). Diagnosis and treatment of low back pain. *British Medical Journal, 332*, 1430–1434.

Koster, A., Bosma, H., Kempen, G. I., van Lenthe, F. J., van Eijk, J. T., & Mackenbach, J. P. (2004). Socioeconomic inequalities in mobility decline in chronic disease groups (asthma/COPD, heart disease, diabetes mellitus, low back pain): only a minor role for disease severity and comorbidity. *Journal of Epidemiology and Community Health, 58*, 10, 862–869.

Leventhal, H., Benyamini, Y., Brownlee, S., Diefenbach, M., Leventah, E. A., Patrick-Miller, & Robitaille, C. (1997). Illness perceptions: theoretical foundations. In K. Petrie & J. Weinman (eds.). *Perceptions of health and illness* (pp. 19–46). Amsterdam: Harwood.

Main, C., Sullivan, M., & Watson, P. (2008*). Pain management: practical applications of the biopsychosocial perspective in clinical and occupational settings* (2nd ed.). Edinburgh: Churchill Livingstone.

Moorey, S. (1996). When bad things happen to rational people: cognitive therapy in adverse life circumstances. In P. Salkovskis (Ed.). *Frontiers of cognitive therapy* (pp. 460–469). London: Guilford Press.

National Institute for Health and Clinical Excellence (2009). Depression in adults with a chronic physical health problem: treatment and management (CG91).

National Institute for Health and Clinical Excellence (2011). Quality standards for diabetes in adults (QS6).

Nicholas, M. K. (2007). The pain self-efficacy questionnaire: taking pain into account. *European Journal of Pain, 11*, 153–163.

Oldroyd, J., Banerjee, M., Heald, A., & Cruickshank, K. (2005). Diabetes and ethnic minorities. *Postgraduate Medicine Journal, 81*, 486–490.

Pain Tool Kit (n.d.). Home page, Retrieved from www.paintoolkit.org

Rubin, R. R., & Peyrot, M. (2001). Psychological issues and treatments for people with diabetes. *Journal of Clinical Psychology, 57*, 457–478.

Skodova, Z., Nagyova, I., van Dijk, J. P., Sudzinova, A., Vargova, H., Studencan, M., & Reijneveld, S. A. (2008). Socioeconomic differences in psychosocial factors contributing to coronary heart disease: a review. *Journal of Clinical Psychology in Medical Settings, 15*, 204–213.

Van Straten, A., Geraedts, A., Verdonck-de Leeuw, I., Andersson, G., & Cuijpers, P. (2010). Psychological treatment of depressive symptoms in patients with medical disorders: a meta-analysis. *Journal of Psychosomatic Research, 69*, 23–32.

White, C. A. (2001). *Cognitive behaviour therapy for chronic medical problems: a guide to assessment and treatment in practice*. Chichester: Wiley.

Williams, E. D., Kooner, I., Steptoe, A., & Kooner, J. S. (2007). Psychosocial factors related to cardiovascular disease risk in UK South Asian men: A preliminary study. *British Journal of Health Psychology, 12*, 559–570.

Zhang, X., Norris, S. L., Gregg, E. W., Cheng, Y. J., Beckles, G., & Kahn, H. S. (2005). Depressive symptoms and mortality among persons with and without diabetes. *American Journal of Epidemiology, 161*, 652–660.

12

CBT with People with Personality Disorders

Kate M. Davidson

Introduction

Training in a specific modality of therapy, such as CBT, does not necessarily prepare us to work with the complexity of clinical problems that our clients present with in mental health settings or in other settings such as prisons. CBT training courses train us in how to work with people who have specific diagnoses such as depression or anxiety and tend to focus on Axis I disorders rather than personality disorders. Research suggests that personality disorders are highly co-morbid with a wide range of Axis I disorders, particularly borderline personality disorder where some researchers have found that over 84 per cent of cases met criteria for one or more Axis I disorders within a 12-month period (Lenzenweger, Lane, Loranger, & Kessler, 2007). Only about 1 in 20 people with this disorder have what could be described as the pure condition (Fyer, Frances, Sullivan, Hurt, & Clarkin, 1988) and multiple co-morbidities with four or more disorders is common in people with a diagnosis of borderline personality disorder. Social impairment and ability to carry out one's life roles is significantly impaired in those with personality disorder (Johnson et al., 2005). Co-morbidity is likely to apply to many people who attend our mental health clinics and in many cases, this will be the co-existence of an Axis I disorder and a personality disorder. We therefore need to be aware that clinical complexity in terms of diagnoses and therefore multiple problems and symptoms is more than just a possibility. We need to be able to recognize personality disorder and we need to know what we can do to help those who come with this additional type of problem.

Formal Assessment of Personality Disorder

Classification of personality disorders

It is worth noting that there is a lively debate about the usefulness of the current classification system and what may be put in place in the revisions of the diagnostic

How to Become a More Effective CBT Therapist: Mastering Metacompetence in Clinical Practice,
First Edition. Edited by Adrian Whittington and Nick Grey.
© 2014 John Wiley & Sons, Ltd. Published 2014 by John Wiley & Sons, Ltd.

manuals (Davidson, 2011; Livesley, 2011; Tyrer et al., 2011). It is likely that any new version of the current classification systems will emphasize chronic interpersonal dysfunction in its criteria. At the time of writing, it seems likely that the American and International Diagnostic systems will diverge in terms of how personality disorders are to be classified in the revisions of these nomenclatures. However, as the psychopathology of personality disorder arises from a complex interaction of genetic vulnerability and environment, interpersonal dysfunction will vary greatly from one individual to another.

Currently there are ten categories of personality disorders in DSM-IV (American Psychiatric Association, 1994) and these are grouped into three clusters: A – odd and eccentric (paranoid, schizoid and schizotypal), B – dramatic and erratic (borderline, narcissistic, histrionic and antisocial), and C – anxious and fearful (avoidant, dependant, and obsessive compulsive). Each personality disorder category is defined by between seven and nine specific criteria, a set number being required for diagnosis of each disorder. Individuals may meet criteria for more than one personality disorder. The category of "not otherwise specified" covers cases who do not fulfil criteria for any single specific category, but who meet the general diagnostic criteria and many people with personality disorder fall into this category.

Personality disorders are categorized differently in ICD 10 (World Health Organization, 1992) and there are eight categories of personality disorder in this system with no clusters. ICD-10 uses different labels to DSM for some categories. For example, the term dissocial is used rather than antisocial and anankastic rather than obsessive-compulsive. Schizotypal is not categorized in the personality disorder section and is instead classified with schizophrenia and related conditions. Narcissistic personality disorder does not appear in ICD-10. Differences exist in the specific criteria used in the two classification systems. Borderline personality disorder is described as a unitary disorder in the DSM-IV but is described by two types in ICD-10, impulsive and emotionally unstable personality disorder, borderline type.

How would I recognize personality disorder?

We can formally diagnose personality disorder by carrying out an assessment using a standardized structured clinical interview such as the International Personality Disorder Examination (Loranger et al., 1994) or the Structured Clinical Interview for DSM (SCID II) (Spitzer, Williams, Gibbon, & First, 1990). Training is required to be able to make the assessment of personality disorder reliably. These assessment interviews also require at least an hour or two and cannot be hurried. There are some briefer ways of assessing the likelihood of the presence of personality disorder. Some of these quicker assessments have been shown to be helpful and reasonably sensitive in picking up the presence of personality disorders (for example, the SAPAS: Moran et al., 2003). However, to be clinically useful there is no substitute for a proper assessment and formal diagnosis being carried out by an appropriately trained clinician.

Consistent difficulties in relationships

There are times when a formal assessment of personality disorder is not possible or available to the clinician or therapist treating a patient. The question is then why do we think an individual may have a personality disorder? Some of this information will come from the clinical and personal histories that we take from individuals presenting for therapy. One of the hallmarks of personality disorder is a longstanding pattern of difficulty getting on with people, or a history suggesting that there is often a breakdown in relationships, or relationships are consistently not maintained. Clearly everyone can fall out with other people or become estranged and this does *not* mean that an individual who falls out with people has a personality disorder. It is the fact that it is a consistent pattern that may suggest that the person has personality difficulties or a disorder.

Does co-morbid personality disorder predict a poorer response to CBT for Axis I disorder?

There is debate surrounding the mixed findings about the impact of personality disorder on Axis I treatment. A review of depression trials (Mulder, 2002) concluded that the results from better designed studies provided little evidence to support the contention that the presence of co-morbid personality disorder has a negative impact on treatment outcome. Others suggest poorer outcomes if there is an Axis II disorder present with major depression and suggest that those with an additional Axis II disorder are about twice as likely to exhibit poor treatment response compared to those patients with major depression and no personality disorder (Newton-Howes, Tyrer, & Johnson, 2006). If studies are more methodologically rigorous, and personality disorder is more fully assessed then the presence of personality disorder may not adversely influence the outcome of CBT for the treatment of depression, whereas the outcome of Interpersonal Therapy for depression is adversely affected (Carter et al., 2011). CBT may be well suited to working with personality disorders with its explicitly structured approach and focus on the here and now problems while not neglecting maladaptive beliefs. These findings suggest we should not stop carrying out cognitive therapy just because someone has a personality disorder. Indeed it may make little difference to the outcome of our therapy for depression though poorer social functioning and some residual symptoms of depression may persist (Shea et al., 1990).

Psychological Therapy for Personality Disorders

Cognitive behavioural therapy for personality disorders (CBTpd)

CBTpd is a structured mutualized therapy for personality disorders, carried out over 12 months in 30 individual sessions (Davidson, 2007). The therapy is based on developmental and cognitive theory. One of the essential features of cognitive therapy for personality disorder is the historical account of the patient's childhood development and background that is essential for deriving a cognitive formulation. Therapists need a sound grasp of child development to gain an understanding of the potential impact of childhood factors on the development of the adult personality disorder. Therapy focuses on beliefs that concern core concepts about the self and others that have developed from childhood onwards and associated behaviours that have developed as potentially maladaptive coping strategies. The content and meaning of the beliefs have had an impact on past and present relationships and are likely to impact on the therapeutic relationship. These beliefs, formed through negative, possibly abusive and neglectful experiences with others, are likely to have resulted in low self-esteem, hypersensitivity to criticism and poor relationships with peers, caregivers and others in adolescence. Cognitive and behavioural strategies to change maladaptive coping styles and belief then come into play in therapy after a clear agreed rationale for change is established.

Evidence for CBTpd

In the past, most clinicians were highly sceptical about the benefit of treatment for those with personality disorders. Indeed, the presence of a personality disorder was often considered a diagnosis of exclusion from treatment. The past two decades have delivered consistent evidence that psychological therapies can benefit people with borderline personality disorder and avoidant personality disorder, though the former disorder has been more extensively subject to randomized controlled trials. No one therapy has been consistently shown to be superior to any other in terms of outcome and good clinical management has been shown to give as good clinical outcomes for those with borderline personality disorder (McMain et al., 2009). Cognitive behavioural therapy for personality disorders – CBTpd – has been shown to be effective in reducing suicidal behaviour and decreasing distress as well as changing the beliefs that those with personality disorder hold, particularly about how they view themselves and others. In a randomized controlled trial of patients with borderline personality disorder who were seriously self-harming or had been psychiatric inpatients, CBTpd was delivered in mental health settings, in 30 sessions over one year, and showed lasting effects with the gains made after one year of therapy maintained in both the short term (at year two) and at a six-year follow-up (Davidson et al., 2006; Davidson et al., 2010). CBTpd is also very cost efficient. There is a long-term financial saving of around one-third after treatment and this saving increases to two-thirds for those who receive CBTpd compared to usual treatment at a six-year follow-up period (Davidson et al., 2010). CBTpd has also been evaluated in a pilot study in men with antisocial personality disorder (Davidson et al., 2009), a group that is often seriously disadvantaged in terms of their access to health services but who have high levels of alcohol misuse and anxiety (Crawford, Sahib, Bratton, Tyrer, & Davidson, 2009).

Other therapies

All treatments for BPD have been found to be effective for most symptoms to some degree and there are very few differences, if any, between therapies. The degree to which the treatment studies are methodologically rigorous varies, and it is possible that the outcomes reported may be overly optimistic since trials of most therapies have not been sufficiently replicated by researchers who are independent of the authors who developed the therapies. In addition, high-quality, structured clinical management has been shown to be equally helpful to psychological therapies such as MBT and DBT for those with BPD (McMain et al., 2009; Bateman & Fonagy, 2009). No one therapy can therefore be regarded as superior to another.

Schema-focused therapy (SFT)
Schema-focused therapy (SFT) was developed by Young, Klosko, and Weishaar (2003). It is highly intensive and consists of twice weekly therapy over three years. A central assumption in SFT is that there are four specific schema modes operating in Borderline personality disorders. These schema modes are sets of schemas expressed in pervasive patterns of thinking, feeling and behaving. In BPD, these modes are detached

protector, punitive parent, abandoned/abused child, and angry/impulsive child. In addition, some presence of the healthy adult is assumed. Change is achieved through a range of behavioural, cognitive and experiential techniques that focus on the therapeutic relationship, life outside therapy and past (traumatic) experiences. The desired outcomes in SFT are when the patient's life is no longer controlled or ruled by these schema modes.

Transference-focused psychotherapy (TFP)
Transference-focused psychotherapy (TFP) (Yeomans, Clarkin, & Kernberg, 2002) is another intensive therapy that lasts at least three years. Central to TFP is a negotiated treatment contract between patient and therapist that then guides all treatment. Patients are thought to change through analysing and interpreting the transference relationship, focusing on the here-and-now context. The main techniques used in TFP are exploration, confrontation and interpretation. Recovery in TFP is reached when good and bad representations of self and others are integrated and when fixed primitive internalized object relations are resolved.

Mentalization-based treatment (MBT)
Mentalization-based treatment (MBT) (Bateman & Fonagy, 2004) is a manualized psychodynamic treatment with its roots in attachment and cognitive theory. The therapy consists of several hours per week over 18 months consisting of combined individual and group psychotherapy and telephone contact. It includes crisis contact and crisis plans, pharmacotherapy, general psychiatric review and written information about treatment. MBT therapists focus on helping patients strengthen their capacity to understand their own and others' mental states in attachment contexts in order to address their difficulties with affect, impulse regulation and interpersonal functioning, which act as triggers for acts of suicide and self-harm (Bateman & Fonagy, 2009).

Dialectical behaviour therapy (DBT)
Dialectical behaviour therapy (DBT) (Linehan, 1993) is probably the most well-known treatment for borderline personality disorder. DBT is a cognitive behavioural treatment programme developed to treat suicidal clients with BPD. DBT directly targets suicidal behaviour and behaviours that interfere with treatment delivery and dangerous, severe or destabilizing behaviours. The therapy promotes the development of adaptive coping behaviour and the generalization of these gains to the natural environment. It attempts to structure the client's treatment environment so that it reinforces functional rather than dysfunctional behaviours. DBT is a highly intensive treatment of a minimum of 3.5 hours per week and includes weekly individual psychotherapy, group skills training, telephone consultation and weekly therapist consultation team meeting.

Systems training for emotional predictability and problem solving (STEPPS)
Systems training for emotional predictability and problem solving (STEPPS) (Blum et al., 2008) is a CBT psychoeducational group programme for working with outpatients with Borderline Personality Disorder. It is carried out over 20 weeks, two hours per week. STEPPS includes a session for family members or significant others and a mental health professional involved in the patient's care treatment approach as well as group work with patients. This latter systems element is innovative and makes a great deal of sense given the interpersonal problems and misunderstandings that arise about the condition in those who are trying to help. It has three phases – psychoeducation, emotion

management skills training and behavioural management skills training. STEPPS is designed to augment usual treatment. Although the systems element is innovative, and intuitively it would appear to be useful clinically, we do not know whether this is an essential element in leading to improvement (Davidson, 2008).

Adaptations to CBT when working with people with personality disorder

A number of differences in the structure and content of therapy are suggested when working with mood disorders in the context of a personality disorder, extrapolating from the major differences between CBT for mood disorders and CBT for personality disorders (Davidson, 2007).

Longer process of engaging the client

Therapy with a patient with a personality disorder is likely to be longer as the process of engagement takes longer and the therapist needs to know much more about the patient than they do if a patient has a mood disorder such as depression on its own.

It is not surprising that people with a personality disorder are thought of as being hard to engage in therapy as they are described as having chronic interpersonal dysfunction. Although they may be aware of their difficulties, they are not necessarily optimistic that they can be helped or that change is possible. People with personality disorders may have been seen many times by other professionals but not have been offered therapy or not been recognized as having a personality disorder. An Axis I disorder may only have been partially treated as a result of their difficulties interpersonally and a failure to engage with the therapist for the reasons stated earlier. Some clinicians continue to believe that those with personality disorder will not be helped by psychological therapies in spite of consistent and growing evidence to the contrary (Leichsenring, Leibing, Kruse, New, & Leweke, 2011). This negative attitude can have a demoralizing effect on the patient.

It helps to give a patient a clear idea about what they are to expect in therapy. This aspect is no different from standard CBT. However, if the individual has a personality disorder, they may not have a clear idea of what might be possible in therapy and may not be sure what problems can be addressed by therapy. This is different from clients who have an Axis I disorder as their problems are characterized by a change in functioning and the client wishes to return to being problem free or at least being less distressed. So for those with personality disorder, it may be best to start therapy by laying out the possibility that we do not know if it would be helpful but we would like to help if possible. However, as therapists we need to know a lot about the person to be able to judge what might be possible in terms of change and to negotiate this with them.

In CBTpd, the initial phase of therapy is therefore designed to engage the patient by taking an in-depth personal, social and psychiatric history. This can take up to five or six sessions with someone with borderline personality disorder. We have found it takes even more sessions with those who have had less contact with clinical mental health services, such as those with antisocial personality disorder. They are not used to "telling their story", describing their problems in a logical order, being questioned systematically and having to think about how relationships and situations in their childhood and adolescence have had an impact on them as adults. Relationships with parents, siblings, other family members and peers are explored in considerable depth to understand how these have affected the patient's view of themselves and other people. Core beliefs such as "I am unlovable", "I am no good", "other people will hurt me", "I cannot trust other people" are understood in the context of the patient's life history. The behavioural strategies that have been over-developed over the patient's lifetime to cope with these beliefs are charted.

From a developmental perspective and from other historical information the therapist can develop a formulation of the patient's problems and their development from childhood into adulthood. The way that this is developed and presented to the patient also differs from standard CBT. In CBTpd, we present the formulation as a narrative and write it as a coherent story of the patient's life. This formulation is our psychological understanding, using CBT and our knowledge of developmental psychology, of how the patient has come to hold the beliefs he has about himself and others and the behaviours that are over-developed and problematic. This narrative formulation is written either as a letter to the patient or more simply as a two or three page account of the patient's life.

Therapy not going as planned

There are likely to be times in therapy when a therapist does not recognize that the person they are treating has a personality disorder. One hint that an individual may have a personality disorder is when therapy is not going as expected. If an individual with a mood disorder also has a personality disorder, he is less likely to respond in a straightforward manner to standard CBT for the mood disorder. However, a lack of improvement does not necessarily signal that the patient has a personality disorder. For example, the patient and therapist may not have developed a level of collaboration required to carry out therapy or the therapy may be being misdirected towards a problem that the client regards as being unimportant.

Patients with personality disorder will often present the therapist with repeated crises that seem to get in the way of conducting systematic therapy for a mental disorder. They may also appear to be changing what they regard as their main problems. This has a stop/start effect in therapy that can be rather bewildering for an unsuspecting therapist. Just when the therapist thinks they are on course, the patient seems to change tack, wants to discuss new problems, they may become upset about something that was not mentioned in the initial sessions, or they seem dissatisfied with the therapist or therapy. The problem list that was drawn up and agreed at the beginning of therapy may keep changing or seem irrelevant to the therapist who suspects that there may be other more significant problems. Within the therapy session, the patient does not seem to want to follow the agenda or the collaborative relationship that the therapist thought they had begun to develop seems to break down. It is not hard to imagine that most therapists would feel rather lost in the clinical session if some of these events occurred and some will admit that they do not know what is going on in the session. These are in fact very useful feelings to have! It is exactly these feelings within the therapist that need to be paid attention to and responded to appropriately. It signals that a therapeutic impasse may have been reached and the therapist needs to change direction and change the strategy to focus on the relationship with the patient and clarify what is happening. Unfortunately, when patients are not on track in therapy, their therapists appear to overcompensate by giving more and more complex explanations and use very different language to their patients (Davidson, Livingstone, McArthur, Dickson, & Gumley, 2007). Instead, it appears helpful for the therapist to communicate clearly, making the problem explicit without appearing to be critical of the patient and whilst remaining empathic and warm in their attitude towards the patient. These are some useful statements and questions for the therapist to use at these times, for example,

> I wonder if you also have the impression that we are not quite managing to work together on your problems. I would really like to help you but I am a bit confused about what is important to you right now. In fact, I am unsure if we are really discussing what is most important to you. Do you feel the same way? (Therapist acknowledges her own feelings, confusion and breakdown in communication. Asks if patient feels the same way)

Or

> Can you help me follow what is happening here in therapy? You seem to want to talk about other things than the ones we agreed might be important at the beginning of therapy – when we first met. Would you like to tell me what is upsetting you? Then maybe I can help you. (Therapist acknowledges that therapy is off track in terms of topic and that the patient is upset. Seeks clarity from patient and offers to try to help)

Or

> You seem to be very upset about something and I am not sure what you are upset about. I will try to help you but I need a clear idea about what is upsetting you. Can you help me to understand what is going on? (Therapist acknowledges patient is upset and asks directly what is upsetting. Makes the point that they cannot help if they do not know what is upsetting the patient)

In each of the suggested ways of approaching a patient, the therapist is distinguishing between what is said overtly in therapy and the process of therapy. In each of these examples, the therapist attempts to explain what is happening in the potential breakdown in relationship with the patient. This is useful to the patient as the therapist may be reflecting what happens to the patient in other relationships when there is a breakdown in communication. It potentially allows the patient to develop an ability to reflect on the process of relationships and how they may become dysfunctional when the mutual understanding between people falters.

Optimizing emotional regulation

Patients with personality disorder have difficulties regulating their emotions and can often be highly emotional in therapy sessions. When emotions are expressed in a highly dysregulated manner, both the therapist and patient will struggle to keep a therapy session on track and this will interfere with progress in therapy. As therapists, we need to be able to help patients understand and manage to gain control of their emotions and be able to express these so that they can deal effectively with personal problems and issues and are able to use appropriate strategies to deal with these.

We need to help patients understand their emotional distress and help them to identify the emotions expressed and the underlying issues, some of which may be long standing with their origins in childhood. We then need to help patients to find an appropriate and controllable level to manage their emotions so that they can be effective in their communication with others. There are often serious consequences for our patients who have difficulty controlling their emotions. Friends and family can feel so overwhelmed and deskilled by frequent emotional outbursts that they are unable to help the person and can retreat from our patients or they can become insensitive to the outbursts and close down communication in an attempt to cope with the patient. Unfortunately, this can make the patient even more emotionally distressed, trying to seek the help they crave and often acting out other negative behaviours. The reaction from others is then often to seek even more physical and emotional distance from the patient, creating a vicious cycle.

If a patient is overly emotional or over stimulated, a therapist can help by taking an opposite stance in expressing emotion. By behaving in an outwardly calm and con-trolled manner, keeping their voice low and slow, they can facilitate the patient in reaching a more optimal level of emotional expression. At these times it is usually unhelpful to use straightforward cognitive strategies as the patient is unlikely to be able to access the ability to think more rationally at these times. Once the patient is calmer, giving some gentle feedback about what has happened is helpful, discussing how the patient managed to gain more control of their emotions and recover a sense of perspec-tive once calmer.

Borderline patients can also avoid emotions and distressing topics and appear to be rather under-aroused or cut off from their emotions. There are, however, often signs that the lack of emotional expression is an attempt to inhibit experiencing distress and patients may act in odd ways, jump from topic to topic, or appear sad while outwardly stating they are relatively okay and coping. At these times, it is important the therapist realizes what is happening, makes a judgement about whether or not to gently point out that the patient seems sad even though they say they are not or appears on edge but not sure why and then move the session forward without labouring the point that the patient may be using avoidance. At these moments in therapy, it is generally more pro-ductive for the therapist to try to work on what might be the issue bothering the patient than on focussing on the avoidance of emotions *per se*. However, the therapist should remember to return to the issue at a later stage in therapy or even within the same session.

Listening and talking: avoiding and confronting
Good collaboration involves the therapist making decisions about when to talk and when to listen. It involves making a judgment about the timing of when to help the patient by confronting an issue that they may be avoiding. Therapists need to be aware of when they may be avoiding an issue that is highly emotive such as abuse or trauma or even a problem in the therapeutic relationship. We need to push therapy forward at times but moving too fast can be highly problematic for a patient who is not at the stage of being able to assimilate new ways of perceiving a problem or coping with a new emotional challenge. We may need to come at the patient's problems using different methods. Getting significant others involved can be help-ful if there is an interpersonal problem. Using historical information to assess how someone has coped in the past with distress before confronting current avoidance can be useful when a patient is too anxious to move forward or does not believe they can cope.

If the problem is in the therapeutic relationship, then this must be confronted gently and promptly. Using a non-defensive open style with the patient will help diffuse the situation and will prevent the patient from feeling criticized. If as therapists we seem to have offended a patient or said something that might be misconstrued, then use com-ments such as, I think I may have done/something to upset you/increased your fear that you cannot trust me/been insensitive. Or if the patient has reacted negatively to something that the therapist believes is important and not negotiable then this must be dealt with openly also. For example, saying: "I am aware that you may not like what I did but I have to be able to ... (communicate with others/make decisions about your safety when you are not able to/express my concern etc.), Can I tell you why I need to do this so that you might be able to see this from my perspective? I will also listen to your views and see if we can come to a better understanding or plan about how to cope with these issues in the future". Having problems discussed openly and frankly will at least allow both therapist and patient to acknowledge that there may be a problem and begin to think of ways to resolve these. It also provides the patient with an alternative model of how to express negative emotions and how to approach difficult and sensitive interpersonal issues.

Irreverent communication: getting the patient back on track
A therapist can use irreverent communication as a way of provoking the patient to "jump the track" (described by Marsha Linehan, 1993, p. 393). Linehan describes irreverent styles of communication as helping therapy get back on track with borderline patients when the therapist and patient are stuck. Irreverent communication can be used in three ways – to get the patient's attention, to shift the patient's emotional response and to get the patient to see a completely different perspective. She says that this style of communication is best delivered in a style opposite to that of the patient's style. If the patient is being highly emotional for example, then a deadpan style and matter of fact tone would be effective in order to contrast with the patient's high emotional tone and more likely to halt the patient in their tracks and change what is happening in the session.

To be effective the therapist has to respond to the patient in a genuine way and must be able to take a compassionate stance towards the patient at the same time. The style is not a ridiculing or undermining one. It can appear paradoxical, even extreme and require a certain degree of boldness on the therapist's part. It also involves rather precise timing to be effective.

Take this example. The therapist and patient are discussing why the patient has not made progress in therapy and both appear to be stuck. The patient has refused to disclose personal details of the circumstances of past incidents of abuse believing that he cannot trust anyone with this sensitive information. This is despite agreeing that her past may be relevant to therapy.

THERAPIST (TH):   So we have finally reached an impasse. We cannot move forward or for that matter backwards. We cannot talk about the now and we cannot talk about the past. I do not know what we can talk about! (Therapist is being blunt about the situation in therapy.)

PATIENT (P):   Well I just don't think I can trust anyone.

TH: I know that and I am experiencing that too! (laughs) This means that I cannot do my job. I need to be able to discuss these matters with you. Effectively, it seems you have sacked me. (Therapist continues to be blunt about the situation and points out that she has no power to change the situation – effectively being sacked. Also note, the therapist is partly calling the patient's bluff as there is no indication that the patient wants to be discharged or would not attend therapy. Only the patient can move therapy forward).

P: (looks shocked) No – I want your help. I just don't know how I can get it without talking about this. Do you think it would help?

TH: Unfortunately I have no idea in your case because you have never discussed the things that upset you with anyone. However, other people seem to find it effective and helpful.

P: Okay, you are telling me to give it a go.

TH: Yes, but only if you want to and feel able to trust me with this information about your past. (Therapist again puts responsibility onto patient).

Without this discussion, therapy would have remained stuck. The blunt fact of the therapeutic impasse, presented in a matter of fact manner, was helpful in pointing out that the patient had responsibility to take advantage of therapy as much as the therapist had in providing therapy. The therapist judged that the patient should be able to trust her at this point in therapy and that the patient now had to make the leap to trusting the therapist with sensitive and highly upsetting information about her past, in order to move forward.

Supervision and the development of a helicopter hovering stance

Supervision is an opportunity for therapists to discuss both the content of therapy sessions and how patients are progressing and how they relate to their patients, including how the therapeutic alliance is developing. Through discussion of the therapeutic alliance, a therapist has the opportunity to reflect on the process of therapy. It allows the therapist to take a "helicopter stance" within sessions, an ability to evaluate the process of therapy while also simultaneously attending to the content of therapy.

There are several ways to judge if the process of therapy is good enough to support the work that needs to be carried out using CBTpd. Is the patient participating in therapy appropriately? Do they seem to be taking responsibility in a shared way with the therapist in the session? Is the therapist sufficiently encouraging the patient to participate? For example are they asking questions to help the patient understand their problems or emotions? Is the style of working suited to the patient's natural learning style? For example, is there too much written work when more practical behavioural work would be more helpful to the patient? Is the therapist talking too much? Is the patient allowed to talk in an unfocused manner either about their problems or off topic? By far the best way to attend to these issues and supervise what goes on in therapy is through recording live sessions.

Summary

Those with personality disorders seek help for their Axis I disorders all the time. We should not be surprised by this and being more aware of this possibility will help us avoid some of the more common interpersonal difficulties that might arise or the experience of the therapy going off track. We can use some of the techniques from CBTpd to help us to get the patients back on track. The therapeutic relationship can be enriched by using these techniques and importantly there is no reason to believe that the Axis I disorder cannot be treated effectively, even with the presence of a personality disorder. The presence of a personality disorder does not necessarily lead to poorer outcome for CBT for mood disorders.

Procedural Rules

- Recognize that co-morbidity is the norm for most personality disorders, both in association with other personality disorders or with mental state or Axis I disorders.
- If you are treating a patient's mood disorder and therapy is not going as planned, with frequent crisis and difficulties following a structured agenda, then consider if the patient has a personality disorder.
- If you think that a patient may have a personality disorder, it may be worth using a screening tool followed by a formal diagnostic assessment.
- If you are treating a patient for a mood disorder with CBT, and that patient also has a personality disorder, the outcome may *not* differ from a patient without a personality disorder.
- If you are treating a patient with a personality disorder, pay more attention to the therapeutic relationship. Make sure that your communication style is open and warm and validate the patient's distressing experiences. Be helpful and active in the sessions and clarify that patients have understood what you have said. Use supervision to discuss both the content of sessions and how you can build a positive therapeutic alliance.
- If you encounter difficulties in the collaborative relationship with a client with borderline personality disorder, consider using "irreverent communication" to get the therapy back on track.
- If you are treating a patient's personality disorder, CBTpd will take up to 30 sessions over one year.

References

American Psychiatric Association (1994). *Diagnostic and statistical manual of mental disorders* (4th rev.). Washington, DC: American Psychiatric Association.

Bateman, A., & Fonagy, P. (2004). *Psychotherapy for borderline personality disorder: mentalisation based treatment*. Oxford: Oxford University Press.

Bateman, A., & Fonagy, P. (2009). Randomized controlled trial of outpatient mentalization-based treatment versus structured clinical management for borderline personality disorder. *American Journal of Psychiatry, 166,* 1355–1364.

Blum, N., St John, D., Pfohl, B., Stuart, S., McCormick, B., Allen, J., … Black, D. W. (2008). Systems training for emotional predictability and problem solving (STEPPS) for outpatients with borderline personality disorder: a randomized controlled trial and 1-year follow-up. *American Journal of Psychiatry, 165,* 468–478.

Carter, J. D., Luty, S. E., McKenzie, J. M., Mulder, R. T., Frampton, C. M., & Joyce, P. R. (2011). *Journal of Affective Disorders, 128*(3), 252–261.

Crawford, M. J., Sahib, L., Bratton, H., Tyrer, P., & Davidson, K. (2009). Service provision for men with antisocial personality disorder who make contact with mental health services. *Personality and Mental Health, 3,* 165–171.

Davidson, K. M. (2007). *Cognitive therapy for personality disorders: a guide for clinicians* (2nd ed.). Routledge: Hove.

Davidson, K. M. (2008). Commentary on Blum et al. (2008). The STEPPS program. *Evidence-Based Mental Health, 11,* 120.

Davidson, K. M. (2011). Editorial. Changing the classification of personality disorders – An ICD11 proposal that goes too far? *Personality and Mental Health, 5,* 243–245.

Davidson, K. M., Livingstone, S., McArthur, K., Dickson, L., & Gumley, A. (2007). Integrative complexity and outcome in cognitive behaviour therapy for borderline personality disorder. *Psychology and Psychotherapy: Theory, Research and Practice, 80*, 513–523.

Davidson, K. M., Norrie, J., Tyrer, P., Gumley, A., Tata, P., Murray, H., & Palmer, S. (2006). The effectiveness of cognitive behaviour therapy for borderline personality disorder: results from the BOSCOT trial. *Journal of Personality Disorders, 20*, 450–465.

Davidson, K., Tyrer, P., Norrie, J., Palmer, S., & Tyrer, H. (2010). Cognitive therapy v. usual treatment for borderline personality disorder: prospective 6-year follow-up. *British Journal of Psychiatry, 197*, 456–462.

Davidson, K. M., Tyrer, P., Tata, P., Cooke, D., Gumley, A., Ford, I., Walker, A., ... Crawford, M. J. (2009). Cognitive behaviour therapy for violent men with antisocial personality disorder in the community: An exploratory randomised controlled trial. *Psychological Medicine, 39*, 569–578.

Fyer, M. R., Frances, A. J., Sullivan, T., Hurt, S. W., & Clarkin, J. (1988). Co-morbidity of borderline personality disorder. *Archives of General Psychiatry, 45*, 348–352.

Johnson, J. G., First, M. B., Cohen, P., Skodol, A. E., Kasen, S., & Brook, J. S. (2005). Adverse outcomes associated with personality disorder not otherwise specified in a community sample. *American Journal of Psychiatry, 162*, 1926–1932.

Leichsenring, F., Leibing, E., Kruse, J., New, A. S., & Leweke F. (2011). Borderline personality disorder. *Lancet, 377*, 74–84.

Lenzenweger, M. F., Lane, M. C., Loranger, A. W., & Kessler, R. C. (2007). DSM-IV personality disorders in the national comorbidity survey replication. *Biological Psychiatry, 62*, 553–564.

Linehan, M. M. (1993). *Cognitive-behavioral treatment of borderline personality disorder*. New York: Guilford Press.

Livesley, J. (2011). Tentative steps in the right direction. *Personality and Mental Health, 5*, 263–270.

Loranger, A. W., Sartorius, N., Andreoli, A., Berger, P., Buchheim, P., Channabasavanna, S. M., ... Ferguson, B. (1994). The international personality disorder examination. *Archives of General Psychiatry, 51*, 215–224.

McMain, S. F., Links, P. S., Gnam, W. H., Guimond, T., Cardish, R. J., Korman, L., & Streuner, D. L. (2009). A randomized trial of dialectical behaviour therapy versus general psychiatric management for borderline personality disorder. *American Journal of Psychiatry, 166*, 1365–1374.

Moran, P., Leese, M., Lee, T., Walters, P., Thornicroft, G., & Mann, A. (2003). Standardised Assessment of Personality- Abbreviated Scale (SAPAS): Preliminary validation of a brief screen for personality disorder. *British Journal of Psychiatry, 183*, 228–232.

Mulder, R. T. (2002). Personality pathology and treatment outcome in major depression: a review. *American Journal of Psychiatry, 159*, 359–371.

Newton-Howes, G., Tyrer, P., & Johnson, T. (2006). Personality disorder and the outcome of depression: meta-analysis of published studies. *The British Journal of Psychiatry, 188*, 13–20.

Shea, M. T., Pilkonis, P. A., Beckham, E., Collins, J. F., Elkin, I., Sotksy, S. M., & Docherty, J. P. (1990). Personality disorders and treatment outcome in the NIMH treatment of depression collaborative research program. *American Journal of Psychiatry, 147*, 711–718.

Spitzer, R. L., Williams, J. B. W., Gibbon, M., & First, M. (1990). *User's guide for the structured clinical interview for DSM-III-R*. Washington, DC: American Psychiatric Association.

Tyrer, P., Crawford, M., Mulder, R., Blashfield, R., Farnam, A., Fossati, A., ... Reed, G. M. (2011). The rationale for the reclassification of personality disorder in the 11th revision of the International Classification of Diseases (ICD-11). *Personality and Mental Health, 5*, 246–259.

World Health Organization (1992). *The ICD-10 Classification of mental and behavioural disorders: clinical descriptions and diagnostic guidelines*. Geneva: World Health Organization.

Yeomans, F. E., Clarkin, J. F., & Kernberg, O. F. (2002). *A primer for transference focused psychotherapy for the borderline patient*. Northvale, NJ: Jason Aronson Inc.

Young, J. E., Klosko, J., & Weishaar, M. E. (2003). *Schema therapy: a practitioner's guide*. New York: Guilford Press.

13

CBT with People with Psychosis

Louise Johns, Suzanne Jolley, Nadine Keen and Emmanuelle Peters

Introduction

Psychosis

Psychosis describes a loss of contact with reality. Clinically, "psychosis" encompasses the positive symptoms of psychotic disorders: unusual beliefs (delusions), anomalous experiences (voices and hallucinations in other modalities, other perceptual changes), and disturbances of thought and language. Individuals may describe being controlled, or people plotting to harm them. Voices may insult or command them to do things. Thoughts may be jumbled, or experienced as inserted into, or stolen from, the person's mind. Thought disturbances can manifest as tangential or circumstantial speech.

Although these are hallmarks of schizophrenia, phenomenologically similar psychotic symptoms occur in mood and personality disorders, and in people without a psychiatric diagnosis. Psychosis is therefore considered to be a continuum, rather than a discrete category (Van Os et al., 2000).

Cognitive behaviour therapy for psychosis (CBTp)

CBTp is an adaptation of standard CBT, informed by research into the psychological mechanisms underpinning psychotic symptoms, and tailored to accommodate the difficulties of people with psychosis. Cognitive models highlight that it is not unusual experiences themselves that are problematic, but their appraisal as external, personally significant and threatening (Birchwood and Chadwick 1997; Freeman, Garety, Kuipers, Fowler, & Bebbington, 2002; Garety, Bebbington, Fowler, Freeman, & Kuipers, 2007; Morrison, 2001). Maladaptive coping and safety behaviours also maintain distress and disability (Brett et al., 2007; Gaynor, Ward, Garety, & Peters, 2013). CBTp aims to break these vicious cycles by helping people to understand their psychotic experiences, promote coping and self-regulation, and counter negative appraisals of self and illness. Table 13.1 provides a list of manuals and self-help guides.

How to Become a More Effective CBT Therapist: Mastering Metacompetence in Clinical Practice,
First Edition. Edited by Adrian Whittington and Nick Grey.
© 2014 John Wiley & Sons, Ltd. Published 2014 by John Wiley & Sons, Ltd.

Table 13.1 CBTp books and therapy manuals

Authors (year of publication)	Book Title
CBT for Psychosis/Schizophrenia	
Kingdon & Turkington (1994)	*CBT of Schizophrenia*
Fowler, Garety, & Kuipers (1995)	*CBT for Psychosis: Theory and Practice*
Nelson (1997)	*CBT with Schizophrenia. A Practice Manual*
Kingdon & Turkington (2002)	*The Case-Study Guide to CBT of Psychosis*
Morrison (2002)	*A Casebook of Cognitive Therapy for Psychosis*
Morrison, Renton, Dunn, Williams, & Bentall (2003)	*Cognitive Therapy for Psychosis: A Formulation-Based Approach*
Kingdon & Turkington (2005)	*Cognitive Therapy of Schizophrenia. 2nd Edition.*
Nelson (2005)	*Cognitive-Behavioural Therapy with Delusions and Hallucinations. A Practice Manual.*
Beck, Rush, Shaw, & Emery (1979)	*Schizophrenia: Cognitive Theory, Research and Therapy*
Wright, Kingdon, Turkington, & Ramierz-Basco (2009)	*Cognitive Therapy for Severe Mental Illness*
Hagen, Turkington, Berge, & Grawe (2010)	*CBT for Psychosis: A Symptom-based Approach*
Steel (2013)	*CBT for Schizophrenia: Evidence-based Interventions and Future Directions*
CBT for Particular Psychotic Symptoms or Phases of Psychosis	
Chadwick, Birchwood, & Tower (1996)	*Cognitive Therapy for Delusions, Voices and Paranoia*
French & Morrison (2004)	*Early Detection and Cognitive Therapy for People at High Risk of Developing Psychosis*
Byrne, Birchwood, Trower, & Meaden (2006)	*A Casebook of CBT for Command Hallucinations: A Social Rank Theory Approach*
Larkin & Morrison (2006)	*Trauma and Psychosis: New Directions for Theory and Therapy*
Gumley & Schwannauer (2006)	*Staying Well after Psychosis: A Cognitive Interpersonal Approach to Recovery and Relapse Prevention*
Freeman, Bentall, & Garety (2008)	*Persecutory Delusions: Assessment, Theory, and Treatment*
Meaden, Keen, Aston, Barton, & Bucci (2012)	*Cognitive Therapy for Command Hallucinations. An Advanced Practical Companion*
Third Wave CBT approaches	
Chadwick (2006)	*Person-Based Cognitive Therapy for Distressing Psychosis*
Morris, Johns, & Oliver (2013)	*Acceptance and Commitment Therapy and Mindfulness for Psychosis*
Wright et al. (in press)	*Treating Psychosis: A Clinician's Guide to Integrating Acceptance and Commitment Therapy, Compassion-Focused Therapy, and Mindfulness Approaches within the Cognitive Behavior Therapy Tradition*
Self-Help Guides	
Freeman, Freeman, & Garety (2006)	*Overcoming Paranoid and Suspicious Thoughts*
Morrison, Renton, French, & Bentall (2008)	*Think You're Crazy, Think Again: A Resource Book for Cognitive Therapy for Psychosis*
Turkington et al. (2009)	*Back to Life, Back to Normality: Cognitive Therapy, Recovery and Psychosis*
Hayward, Strauss, & Kingdon (2012)	*Overcoming Distressing Voices*

Efficacy and effectiveness of CBTp

CBTp consistently reduces positive symptoms and distress and improves functioning compared to routine care, whether in formal trials (Wykes, Steel, Everitt, & Tarrier, 2008; Morrison, Turkington, et al., 2014) or routine services (Lincoln et al., 2012; Morrison et al., 2004; Peters et al., 2010). Effects are modest but persist at follow-up, and reduced admissions result in net cost savings (Sarin, Wallin, & Widerlov, 2011; NICE 2009). Satisfaction with therapy is very high (Miles, Peters, and Kuipers 2007). Clinical guidelines recommend that people with schizophrenia are offered CBTp (National Institute for Care and Health Excellence, 2009) There is, however, a need to strengthen the evidence base for CBTp compared to an alternative therapy (Jones, Hacker, Cormac, Meaden, & Irving, 2012; Lynch, Laws, & McKenna, 2010).

Around half to two-thirds of those offered CBTp engage with therapy. Engagement and outcome are related to the person's views of their problems (Freeman et al., 2013), and outcome is influenced by symptom severity and duration, cognitive flexibility, social support, pre-existing coping skills and functioning, but not IQ or cognitive impairment (Garety et al., 2008; Granholm, et al., 2008; Perivoliotis et al., 2010; Premkumar et al., 2011; Tarrier & Wykes, 2004). Therapeutic alliance is important, and high-quality training and delivery of CBTp specific interventions are necessary to achieve positive outcomes (Bentall et al., 2003; Dunn et al., 2012; Steel, Tarrier, Stahl, & Wykes, 2012).

Practical Application

Approach and format of therapy

CBTp approaches have common basic tenets (Morrison and Barratt, 2010) (see Figure 13.1). Therapy focuses explicitly on the client's distress, and what clients wish to change – note that this may not necessarily be the psychotic symptoms. Client and therapist engage actively and collaboratively to reduce distress, enhance coping, and achieve therapy goals, guided by the case formulation.

CBTp sessions occur weekly to fortnightly, typically over 6–9 months, with follow-up appointments. Therapy sessions follow CBT structure, beginning with agenda setting. Session length and pacing is flexible: therapists must tolerate and adapt to the complexity and heterogeneity of clients' presentations, their emotional sensitivity, cognitive difficulties and rapid changes in mental state. Therapeutic style is collaborative and non-didactic, and two-way feedback is emphasized. Interventions follow a line of least resistance. Therapists focus on what clients are ready to work with, explicitly checking this out ("How does that sound?", "What do you think?"). Socratic questioning may be used less, with more "floating" ideas instead. Open mindedness and genuine curiosity towards clients' beliefs, and empathy with their difficulties, are essential. Therapists take more responsibility for the session, aiming to be containing and careful not to over-arouse clients, which might exacerbate psychotic symptoms. Post-session ratings of therapist empathy and understanding are useful (Burns & Nolen-Hoeksema, 1992).

CBTp involves changing appraisals and behaviour, through new learning, in the context of a good therapeutic relationship. The focus on appraisals helps clients to make sense of unusual experiences and events, to take a different perspective and/or react in new ways. Homework maximizes new learning and setting homework is associated

Explicit, collaborative goal focus
Engagement and therapeutic style
Normalization
Individualized formulation based on cognitive model
Appraisal and behaviour targeted for change
Change occurs through new learning (facilitated through monitoring, guided discovery, testing out)
Strategies for change implemented both within and outside sessions
Aim to reduce distress and improve quality of life

Figure 13.1   Core elements of CBTp. Data from Morrison and Barratt (2010). Jolley and Garety, 2011. Reproduced with permission from Wiley.

with improved outcome and greater satisfaction in CBTp, even though clients may not always complete assignments (Dunn, Morrison, & Bentall, 2006; Glaser, Kazantizis, Deane, & Oades, 2000; Miles, Peters, & Kuipers 2007).

Components of CBTp

CBTp progresses through engagement, assessment, formulation and intervention phases, although in practice these overlap. Assessment, formulation and intervention planning may take much longer than in standard CBT in order to ensure a genuinely collaborative and achievable therapy target. These remain key parts of the work throughout therapy.

Case Example (see Box 13.1)

Engagement and assessment

A non-colluding, non-confrontative therapeutic style is required, using the client's own terminology. Aim for words like "experienced" and "knew" early on, to avoid watering down the client's report, moving to "felt" and "thought" only when this matches the client's understanding. For example, "Can I just check I've understood you correctly? You were walking past somebody and he started coughing. You knew immediately that he was an evil spirit disguised as a person, trying to get at you. Have I got that right?"

Clients should feel understood and taken seriously. It is crucial to convey that you view them as reasonable, and their concerns and reactions as understandable, for example: "I can understand why you feel constantly on the alert with all this going on", "I can see why you choose to stay inside most of the day." Client and therapist puzzle together to understand difficult or unusual experiences. It is important to empathize frequently and to use explicit empathic comments, since clients with psychosis may misinterpret or not pick up more subtle non-verbal cues, for example: "I'm sorry to hear that … that sounds really difficult for you … it sounds like you've been through a tough time".

Box 13.1 Case example: Peter

Peter* reports getting "bad vibes" from strangers. They act in "suspicious" ways: staring, coughing, and using other body language, which creates a discernible "atmosphere". Peter believes that, through their actions and mannerisms, people are suggesting that he should kill himself. He hears people commenting, and commanding him to harm himself, saying "Peter is useless … he will die soon", "kill yourself". Initially, Peter thought that he was imagining things, but after talking to his vicar, he came to the conclusion that the people are actually powerful evil spirits, disguised to look like people, attempting to deceive and ruin him, and prevent him going to heaven. He wonders whether it is a test or punishment for previous drug-related misdemeanours. He feels depressed and anxious when he experiences these bad vibes or hears the voices, and angry towards the spirits. He copes by avoiding busy places, and prays and reads the Bible to ward off evil spirits.

*based on two anonymized cases

It is usually unhelpful to contradict clients' unusual experiences and strongly held beliefs. Aim for an open, neutral, tentative, respectful and helpful stance:

PETER (P):   My brother tells me nothing is going on, it's just my imagination. You believe me, don't you?

THERAPIST (TH): I certainly believe that you are noticing people doing these things, acting in strange ways. I'm afraid I don't know whether they are really evil spirits in disguise. Maybe we can look at that together in therapy.

Specific reassurance can be helpful for fears arising from delusional ideas or about being crazy, for example, if a patient asks if you think they are mad, answer with "No, I don't think so at all". This can be followed up with a normalizing comment such as "It seems like you are going through a really difficult time at the moment, trying to understand and cope with a lot of distressing experiences", before exploring further.

It is important to routinely check for, and deal collaboratively with, any counter-therapeutic or delusional beliefs about the therapist, and any misinterpretations of their intentions and meaning. For example, Peter may misinterpret the therapist coughing, and require specific feedback about their intentions when this occurs.

Voices may impede engagement by distracting the client, increasing anxiety and telling the client not to trust you. Additional engagement strategies include using a symbolic panic button to increase the client's control over the session, seeking permission before asking difficult questions, and having "non-voice talk". It is helpful to pre-empt difficulties, for example, discussing coping strategies in case voices worsen temporarily after sessions. Avoid setting yourself in opposition to the voices, as this can place clients in an uncomfortable "mediating" position. Passing messages onto voices can be helpful, for example, "I wonder if it would be helpful for you to pass a message to the voices that our meetings are not to get rid of them but to help with your distress".

It can be difficult to establish a focus at the beginning of therapy. Let the person tell their story in their own way. Then, once you have an overview of their difficulties and their "model of understanding", you can elicit a problem and goal list. Remain open about therapy priorities; a client may be less distressed by their voices than by their lack of socially-valued roles, indicating a focus on depression and social inclusion. Cognitive-behavioural assessment should not start without a collaborative focus.

Key to assessment is clarifying experience-appraisal links. Ask what the person notices that leads to the appraisals. The "intrusion" may be an internal feeling or emotion, a hallucinatory experience, or an external event (that may also have anomalous percep-tual qualities). Anomalous perceptions can directly influence appraisals (Freeman et al., 2008), and be very powerful in maintaining delusional explanations. Example:

TH: Can you say what's difficult for you at the moment?

P: Yes, people get me down. I'm getting bad vibes from them.

TH: Bad vibes ... (*repeating the client's words, but said in a curious way*) ... what are these?

P: People watching me, looking nervously, coughing, acting strange. I told my vicar a few weeks after it started, and he said maybe they could be spirits in disguise.

TH: OK (*just accepting what the client says*), and what did you think about it before you talked to your vicar?

P: I didn't know what was going on, maybe I was imagining things. I was worried.

TH: Yes, I can imagine. And when the vicar told you it was spirits, what did you think, did you immediately agree with that?

P: Not straight away. But on my way home, I said to a person on the bus "you're a spirit aren't you", in my mind, and the person nodded and looked shocked. He didn't want me to find out. Then I knew I wasn't imagining things, and their game was up.

TH: Is it OK to ask you a bit more about what happens when you go out? (*asking about the "intrusions"*)

P: They don't always mention my name. They give an impression that they are keeping an eye on me, from their body language. You can tell when something is strange, when there's an atmosphere. They say things to me, "Peter is going to die soon", "kill yourself". They quickly mince it with other words, it's hard to explain.

TH: No, you're doing a good job, thank you. That sounds really distressing. So, you're thinking ... something is not quite right, something is going on (*appraisal*), because of what you notice – the way people look at you, a gesture, and sometimes you also hear them speaking to you (*summarizing and clarifying, and not yet probing for the details of exactly what he notices*). Have I got that right? And with the body language, what message are they giving you, what are they communicating? (*asking literally at this stage, rather than asking what he thinks or believes to be the case*)

P: To let me know they're still there. They want me to believe that everyone is an evil spirit. It gets me down.

TH: Yes, that does sound hard. And how do you normally cope with all this?

Promoting self-regulation of psychotic symptoms

Early on, it can help to identify strategies for coping with distressing symptoms or their consequences (e.g., amotivation and avoidance), and for the client to try these between sessions. Clients usually initiate some coping, which can be built on in therapy (Tarrier, Harwood, Yusopoff, Beckett, & Baker, 1990). Coping work can include strategies for particular symptoms, for example, reading aloud or humming for voices (Farhall, Greenwood, & Jackson, 2007). Other strategies can be borrowed from affect work, for example, relaxation, reducing rumination and mindfulness.

Although coping strategies might not be new, clients have often not tried them sys-tematically. Troubleshoot before the client tries them, and then tweak them if they do not work. When reviewing the effect of coping strategies, it is important to reflect on the mechanism and to incorporate positive outcomes into the client's appraisals. A change in experiences, for example, noticing fewer instances of people coughing, that is contingent on the client's behaviour, can be used to question their appraisals, particularly beliefs about power and control over their experiences. For example: "You noticed that you heard fewer people talking to you when you started humming to yourself ... what does that say about your ability to have some control over them? ... and what does that say about the power of these spirits?"

Formulation

The formulation emphasizes the understandability of the client's position by drawing on the roles of vulnerability factors, life events, affect, past and current unusual experiences, appraisal, cognitive biases and behaviour. The therapist's task is to build a tailored understanding of the factors that are maintaining distress and preventing the client reaching their goals. You can use, for example, the models of Freeman et al. (2002: delusion specific), Meaden et al. (2012: voices specific), Morrison (2001: general psychosis model) or Garety et al. (2007: general psychosis model), or you can devise your own formulation, as long as it is a CB formulation incorporating experiences, appraisals and thinking biases, behaviour, and affect, and how these interact in a maintenance cycle. You can formulate all the main difficulties together if they interact closely (e.g., when voices maintain beliefs by providing confirmatory evidence), or it may be better to formulate individual experiences separately (e.g., dealing first with command hallucinations, then with paranoia). When sharing the formulation with the client, a very simple formulation might be used initially, which can be developed as therapy progresses (Kinderman & Lobban, 2000). Figure 13.2 shows a cross-sectional formulation of Peter's psychotic symptoms.

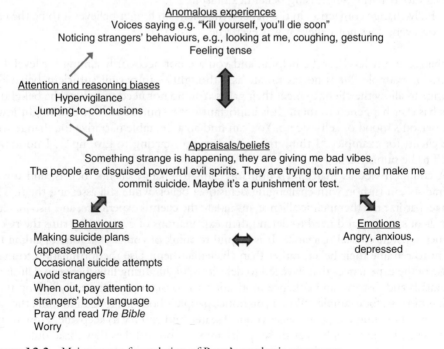

Anomalous experiences
Voices saying e.g. "Kill yourself, you'll die soon"
Noticing strangers' behaviours, e.g., looking at me, coughing, gesturing
Feeling tense

Attention and reasoning biases
Hypervigilance
Jumping-to-conclusions

Appraisals/beliefs
Something strange is happening, they are giving me bad vibes.
The people are disguised powerful evil spirits. They are trying to ruin me and make me commit suicide. Maybe it's a punishment or test.

Behaviours
Making suicide plans
(appeasement)
Occasional suicide attempts
Avoid strangers
When out, pay attention to
strangers' body language
Pray and read *The Bible*
Worry

Emotions
Angry, anxious,
depressed

Figure 13.2   Maintenance formulation of Peter's psychotic symptoms.

Formulation alone, particularly complex, developmental formulation, is useful for therapists but can be perceived as unhelpful by clients (Chadwick, Williams, & Mackenzie, 2003; Morberg Pain, Chadwick, & Abba, 2008). Linking the formulation to the client's goals, and identifying strategies for change, is key. While developmental formulations might be helpful to share with clients whose goal is to gain a better understanding of their experiences (particularly clients with trauma histories), it is often preferable to focus on current maintenance ("vicious") cycles and how to change them (developing "virtuous" cycles). Discuss with clients mechanisms that maintain their unhelpful appraisals and distress, for example, use of safety behaviours, and particular attentional and reasoning biases (e.g., hypervigilance, confirmation bias) (Freeman, 2007). Initial intervention strategies aim to reduce these maintaining factors.

Specific belief change (including beliefs about voices)

Appraisals of experiences in psychosis are usually external, personal and threatening. The emphasis in CBTp is on reducing distress and preoccupation, and increasing the client's sense of control and hope, rather than necessitating major belief change. There are four levels of belief change:

1. No change – just deal with the sequelae. The belief is there, but the person cannot change anything about it. Therapy focuses on improving the client's mood and coping, and different ways of reacting (i.e., working "within the delusion").
2. Change implications of the belief and interference with functioning – beliefs about what the client can do even with the belief present. For example, "There is a risk of giving in to the evil spirits, but I can still go and visit my family".
3. Change one or more aspect of the belief, for example, it is less widespread, or not always true (i.e., increasing belief flexibility).
4. Fully change conviction in the belief – the client no longer believes it to be the case or, even, does not believe it was ever true.

A change at any level can be helpful, and you are not necessarily aiming for level 4. A shift, for example, "it is not as unsafe as I thought" can permit sufficient behaviour change to allow the client to meet their goals. You do not need to reduce the belief that this has ever happened to them. It is important not to pursue change that might lower the person's mood or self-esteem. You can find an acceptable narrative for change with the client, for example, "I think the evil spirits are starting to give up ... I no longer need to be punished".

A common view is that CBTp primarily aims to change clients' beliefs, and novice therapists can rush in with challenging delusional beliefs while still assessing them. This can jeopardize the therapeutic alliance, invalidate the client's experience, and also increase the client's anxiety and need to defend their explanations of events. This runs the risk of inducing psychological reactance. It is helpful to think of your task as one of aiding the client to reframe their beliefs rather than challenge them. Use the formulation to make sense of the experiences that have led to delusions, highlighting links between delusional appraisals and distress, and enhance motivation to consider alternatives by linking these to less distress, for example, "When you notice people's body language and think they are evil spirits targeting you, that makes you feel scared and you try to keep safe. How would you feel ... if you thought that these spirits aren't as powerful as they make out ... or if you thought that people's body language might not always be about you?"

Cognitive change is facilitated by wondering together about possible exceptions for specific situations (Was *everybody* giving you bad vibes when you went out? Was there any other reason why that particular person might have coughed on that occasion?). Alternative explanations for particular instances can be identified, considering with the client whether there is any possibility at all that a single event could be due to something else, such as chance, bad luck or things to do with the other person (i.e., not threatening and not personal to the client). The generation of acceptable alternative beliefs, rather than simply creating doubt, is crucial. Doubt in the absence of plausible alternatives is associated with lower self-esteem (Freeman et al., 2004). You can suggest alternatives as 'possibilities' without taking personal ownership of them, which makes it easier to back down without damaging the therapeutic relationship. Be prepared to suggest or 'float' some ideas, as clients may not be able to generate alternatives themselves (Freeman et al., 2004). The accumulation of alternative explanations for numerous instances can be used as evidence against a delusional belief and to test out beliefs using behavioural experiments. Any new alternative belief needs to be explanatory, acceptable and plausible to the client. A detailed formulation of the client's experiences can often serve as an alternative non-delusional explanation.

Working with emotion

Reducing emotional problems is an important goal of CBTp. There is an increased prevalence of anxiety and depression in those with psychosis, compared with the general population (Achim et al., 2011), and affective processes are a key part of the onset, maintenance and sequelae of psychotic symptoms (Birchwood, 2003; Fowler et al., 2012; Freeman & Garety, 2003). It is often easier to engage clients by assessing and formulating affective disturbance initially, which can be framed as caused by the presenting problem. Affect work with Peter, for example, could include working with: worry about future commands to kill himself; anxiety about dealing with this when he goes out; and depression caused by avoiding activities and by self-blaming appraisals. Strategies for working with affect include standard CB approaches for anxiety and depression, but they are usually adapted to take account of the presence of anomalous experiences and strongly held beliefs.

Use of avoidance and other safety behaviours to reduce anxiety is common in people with voices and paranoia (Morrison, 2001; Freeman et al., 2007), and play a key role in maintaining threatening appraisals and delusional beliefs (Hacker, Birchwood, Tudway, Meaden, & Amphlett, 2008; Nothard, Morrison, & Wells, 2008; Gaynor et al., 2013). These avoidant behaviours can also maintain negative self-beliefs following acute psychosis and fear of adverse outcomes (failure, rejection, relapse), relevant to both social anxiety (Birchwood et al., 2007) and negative symptoms (Rector, Beck, & Stolar, 2005). Graded exposure (GE) can be used to target anxious avoidance of a particular feared situation, and used to test out particular (delusional) thoughts and beliefs. Clients develop a hierarchy of increasingly feared situations, working towards a values-based goal, and approach each situation with the therapist's support. In addition to habituation of the anxiety, and learning that feared outcomes do not occur or are not as bad as imagined, a key cognitive shift following exposure may also be an increased sense of perceived control (Mineka & Thomas, 1999).

In CBTp, you typically approach GE more slowly than in CBT for anxiety, to avoid over-arousing the client and exacerbating psychotic symptoms. Additionally, some clients' fears are so terrifying, for example, believing 100 per cent that they will be killed, that GE seems very risky (or implies that you don't take their fears seriously). In these cases, it is important to do a lot of preparatory work on the client's thoughts and beliefs beforehand. The client will often use coping strategies initially, which may be formulated as safety behaviours. These enable the client to start achieving their goals, and can gradually be dropped. A client may choose to retain some safety behaviours which, although will prevent them fully testing their beliefs, may not matter if the client is able to achieve their goals. CBTp can also target worry processes, which have been found to maintain delusional distress (e.g., Startup, Freeman, & Garety, 2007; Morrison & Wells, 2007). Standard worry strategies can be used to reduce distress associated with delusions (Foster, Startup, Potts, & Freeman, 2010).

Depression is a common reaction to psychosis, and is associated with appraisals of shame, entrapment, loss and self-blame (Birchwood, Iqbal, & Upthegrove, 2005). Clients with negative symptoms also express depressive cognitions around failure and lack of hope for improvement (Grant & Beck, 2009). CBTp incorporates behavioural and cognitive strategies for both depression and negative symptoms. Behavioural activation (BA) focuses on changing behaviours and reduces depression by helping clients to increase levels of rewarding activity (Mazzucchelli, Kane, & Rees, 2009). BA can be used to reduce depression and negative symptoms (Mairs, Lovell, Campbell, & Keeley, 2011; Waller et al., 2013), although the therapist may need to provide more structure and scaffolding. Cognitive techniques for depression, as described by Beck, Rush, Shaw, & Emery (1979), can be used with clients with psychosis, questioning the accuracy of negative thoughts, testing out (negative) predictions and working with cognitive biases (Grant, Huh, Perivoliotis, Stolar, & Beck, 2012).

Working jointly with trauma and psychosis is a relatively new area, despite many studies reporting high rates of trauma and of post-traumatic symptomatology in psychosis clients (Bendall, Alvarez-Jimenez, Nelson, & McGorry, 2013; Mueser et al., 2004; Read, Van Os, Morrison, & Ross, 2005; Varese et al., 2012). Although therapists typically will address trauma by including it in developmental formulations, many are cautious about treating the symptoms of post-traumatic stress disorder (PTSD) in clients who are actively psychotic because of concerns about over-arousing the client, leading to dissociation and/or increased psychotic symptoms. However, there is emerging, tentative evidence that therapists can intervene effectively with PTSD symptoms in clients with psychosis, or other severe mental illness, using either cognitive restructuring (Mueser et al., 2008), reliving (Frueh et al., 2009; van den Berg and van der Gaag, 2012), or an integrated CBT approach using both procedures (Callcott, Standart, & Turkington, 2004; Grubaugh, Zinzow, Paul, & Egede, & Frueh, 2011).

Delivery of CBTp

Therapist competence and adherence can be assessed using rating scales such as the Cognitive Therapy Scale – Revised (CTS-R) (Young & Beck, 1980; Blackburn et al., 2001) and the Revised-Cognitive Therapy for Psychosis Adherence Scale (R-CTPAS) (Startup, Jackson, & Pearce 2002; Rollinson et al., 2008). The National Institute for Care and Health Excellence (NICE) recommendations (NICE, 2009) note that trial therapists were mostly clinical psychologists or other accredited psychological therapists, who received regular clinical supervision. They recommended further research into the training and core competencies required to deliver CBTp. Most recently, as part of Increasing Access to Psychological Therapies for people with severe mental illness (IAPT-SMI), core competences for work with people with psychosis have been developed (see www.ucl.ac.uk/CORE/).

Subjective experiences of CBTp, ascertained from qualitative studies interviewing clients who have received CBTp, group into common themes that overlap with the core elements of CBTp (Figure 13.1). They include CBTp as: a respectful relationship, a process of person-centred engagement, an education process, helping to improve personal understanding, an active process of structured learning, hard work, a healing process, and related to recovery and outcomes (Messari and Hallam, 2003; Kilbride et al., 2013).

Procedural Rules

- A good therapeutic relationship is crucial, and all work in psychosis must be done within the context of this relationship.
- Be curious and collaborative, using the person's terminology and their "model of understanding" to facilitate engagement.
- Focus on what is distressing rather than what is abnormal when setting goals, and focus initially on maintenance cycles and how to change them.
- If put on the spot about whether you believe the client's account, empathize with the distress and reality of the experience for the person, and do not worry about "colluding".
- Don't be tempted to reframe beliefs too early, and don't push for change.
- When working with delusional beliefs, aim to reduce distress, preoccupation, and interference with the client's valued goals before conviction change, and be prepared to work "within the delusion".
- Target affect and/or cognitive biases, which are integral to psychotic symptom change
- Ensure the psychosis work does not jeopardize the person's self-esteem: enhance and protect self-esteem at all times

References

Achim, A. M., Maziade, M., Raymond, E., Olivier, D., Merette. C., & Roy, M. A. (2011). How prevalent are anxiety disorders in schizophrenia? a meta-analysis and critical review on a significant association. *Schizophrenia Bulletin, 37*(4), 811–821. doi: 10.1093/schbul/sbp148

Beck, A. T., Rush, A. J., Shaw. B. F., & Emery, G. (1979). *Cognitive therapy of depression*. New York: Guilford.

Bendall, S., Alvarez-Jimenez, M., Nelson. B., & McGorry, P. (2013). Childhood trauma and psychosis: new perspectives on aetiology and treatment. *Early Intervention in Psychiatry, 7*(1), 1–4. doi: 10.1111/Eip.1

Bentall, R. P., Lewis, S., Tarrier, N., Haddock, G., Drake, R., & Day J. (2003). Relationships matter: the impact of the therapeutic alliance on outcome in schizophrenia. *Schizophrenia Research, 60*(1), 319–319. doi: 10.1016/S0920-9964(03)80274-8

Birchwood, M. (2003). Pathways to emotional dysfunction in first-episode psychosis. *British Journal of Psychiatry, 182*, 373–375. doi: 10.1192/bjp.182.5.373.

Birchwood, M., & Chadwick, P. (1997). The omnipotence of voices: testing the validity of a cognitive model. *Psychological Medicine, 27*(6):1345–1353. doi: 10.1017/S0033291797005552.

Birchwood, M., Iqbal, Z., & Upthegrove, R. (2005). Psychological pathways to depression in schizophrenia – studies in acute psychosis, post psychotic depression and auditory hallucinations. *European Archives of Psychiatry and Clinical Neuroscience, 255*(3), 202–212. doi: 10.1007/s00406-005-0588-4

Birchwood, M., Trower, P., Brunet, K., Gilbert, P., Iqbal, Z., & Jackson, C. (2007). Social anxiety and the shame of psychosis: a study in first episode psychosis. *Behaviour Research and Therapy, 45*(5), 1025–1037. doi: 10.1016/j.brat.(2006).07.011

Blackburn, I. M., James, I. A., Milne, D. L., Baker, C., Standart, S., Garland. A., & Reichelt, F. K. (2001). The revised cognitive therapy scale (Cts-R), psychometric properties. *Behavioural and Cognitive Psychotherapy, 29*(4), 431–446. doi: 10.1017/S1352465801004040

Brett, C. M. C., Peters, E. P., Johns, L. C., Tabraham, P., Valmaggia. L. R., & McGuire, P. (2007). Appraisals of anomalous experiences interview (AANEX), a multidimensional measure of psychological responses to anomalies associated with psychosis. *British Journal of Psychiatry, 191*: S23–S30. doi: 10.1192/bjp.191.51.s23

Burns, D. D., & Nolen-Hoeksema, S. (1992). Therapeutic empathy and recovery from depression in cognitive-behavioral therapy: a structural equation model. *Journal of Consulting and Clinical Psychology, 60*(3), 441–449.

Byrne, S., Birchwood, M., Trower. P. E., & Meaden, A., (2006). *A casebook of cognitive behaviour therapy for command hallucinations: a social rank theory approach.* Hove: Routledge.

Callcott, P., Standart, S., & Turkington, D. (2004). Trauma within psychosis: using a CBT model for PTSD in psychosis. *Behavioural and Cognitive Psychotherapy, 32*(2), 239–244. doi: 10.1017/S1352465804001249

Chadwick, P. D. J. (2006). *Person-based cognitive therapy for distressing psychosis.* Chichester: John Wiley & Sons.

Chadwick, P., Birchwood, M., & Tower, P. (1996). *Cognitive therapy for delusions, voices and paranoia.* Chichester: John Wiley & Sons.

Chadwick, P., Williams, C., & Mackenzie, J. (2003). Impact of case formulation in cognitive behaviour therapy for psychosis. *Behaviour Research and Therapy, 41*(6), 671–680. doi: 10.1016/S0005-7967(02)00033-5

Dunn, G., Fowler, D., Rollinson, R., Freeman, D., Kuipers, E., Smith, B., ... Bebbington, P. (2012). Effective elements of cognitive behaviour therapy for psychosis: results of a novel type of subgroup analysis based on principal stratification. *Psychological Medicine, 42*(5), 1057–1068. doi: 10.1017/S0033291711001954

Dunn, H., Morrison, A. P., & Bentall, R. P. (2006). The relationship between patient suitability, therapeutic alliance, homework compliance and outcome in cognitive therapy for psychosis. *Clinical Psychology & Psychotherapy, 13*(3), 145–152. doi: 10.1002/Cpp.481

Farhall, J., Greenwood, K. M., & Jackson, H. J. (2007). Coping with hallucinated voices in schizophrenia: a review of self-initiated strategies and therapeutic interventions. *Clinical Psychology Review, 27*(4), 476–493. doi: 10.1016/j.cpr.(2006).12.002

Foster, C., Startup, H., Potts, L., & Freeman, D. (2010). A randomised controlled trial of a worry intervention for individuals with persistent persecutory delusions. *Journal of Behavior Therapy and Experimental Psychiatry, 41*(1), 45–51. doi: 10.1016/j.jbtep.2009.09.001

Fowler, D., Garety, P., & Kuipers, E. (1995). *Cognitive behaviour therapy for psychosis: theory and practice.* Chichester: John Wiley & Sons.

Fowler, D., Hodgekins, J., Garety, P., Freeman, D., Kuipers, E., Dunn, G., ... Bebbington, P. E. (2012). Negative cognition, depressed mood, & paranoia: a longitudinal pathway analysis using structural equation modeling. *Schizophrenia Bulletin, 38*(5), 1063–1073. doi: 10.1093/schbul/sbr019

Freeman, D. (2007). Suspicious minds: the psychology of persecutory delusions. *Clinical Psychology Review, 27*(4), 425–457. doi: 10.1016/j.cpr.(2006).10.004

Freeman, D., Bentall, R., & Garety, P. (2008). *Persecutory delusions: assessment, theory, & treatment.* Oxford: Oxford University Press.

Freeman, D., Dunn, G., Garety, P., Weinman, J., Kuipers, E., Fowler, D., Jolley, S., & Bebbington, P. (2013). Patients' beliefs about the causes, persistence and control of psychotic experiences predict take-up of effective cognitive behaviour therapy for psychosis. *Psychological Medicine, 43*(2), 269–277. doi: 10.1017/S0033291712001225

Freeman, D., Freeman, J., & Garety, P. A. (2006). *Overcoming paranoid and suspicious thoughts.* London: Constable and Robinson.

Freeman, D., & Garety, P. A. (2003). Connecting neurosis and psychosis: the direct influence of emotion on delusions and hallucinations. *Behaviour Research and Therapy, 41*(8), 923–947. doi: 10.1016/S0005–7967(02)00104–3

Freeman, D., Garety, P. A., Fowler, D., Kuipers, E., Bebbington, P. E., & Dunn, G. (2004). Why do people with delusions fail to choose more realistic explanations for their experiences? An empirical investigation. *Journal of Consulting and Clinical Psychology, 72*(4), 671–680. doi: 10.1037/0022-006x.72.4.671

Freeman, D., Garety, P. A., Kuipers, E., Fowler, D., & Bebbington, P. E. (2002). A cognitive model of persecutory delusions. *British Journal of Clinical Psychology, 41*, 331–347. doi: 10.1348/014466502760387461

Freeman, D., Garety, P. A., Kuipers, E., Fowler, D., Bebbington, P. E., & Dunn, G. (2007). Acting on persecutory delusions: The importance of safety seeking. *Behaviour Research and Therapy, 45*(1), 89–99. doi: 10.1016/j.brat.(2006).01.014

Freeman, D., Gittins, M., Pugh, K., Antley, A., Slater, M., & Dunn, G. (2008). What makes one person paranoid and another person anxious? The differential prediction of social anxiety and persecutory ideation in an experimental situation. *Psychological Medicine, 38*(8), 1121–1132. doi: 10.1017/S0033291708003589

French, P., & Morrison, A. P. (2004). *Early detection and cognitive therapy for people at high risk of developing psychosis: a treatment approach.* Chichester: John Wiley & Sons.

Frueh, B. C., Grubaugh, A. L., Cusack, K. J., Kimble, M. O., Elhai, J. D., & Knapp, R. G. (2009). Exposure-based cognitive-behavioral treatment of PTSD in adults with schizophrenia or schizoaffective disorder: A pilot study. *Journal of Anxiety Disorders, 23*(5), 665–675. doi: 10.1016/j.janxdis.2009.02.005

Garety, P. A., Bebbington, P. E., Fowler, D., Freeman, D., & Kuipers, E. (2007). Implications for neurobiological research of cognitive models of psychosis: a theoretical paper. *Psychological Medicine, 37*(10), 1377–1391. doi: 10.1017/S003329170700013x

Garety, P. A., Fowler, D., Freeman, D., Bebbington, P. E., Dunn, G., & Kuipers, E. (2008). Cognitive-behavioural therapy and family intervention for relapse prevention and symptom reduction in psychosis: randomised controlled trial. *British Journal of Psychiatry, 192*(6), 412–423. doi: 10.1192/bjp.bp.107.043570

Gaynor, K., Ward, T., Garety, P., & Peters, E. (2013). The role of safety-seeking behaviours in maintaining threat appraisals in psychosis. *Behaviour Research and Therapy, 51*(2), 75–81. doi: 10.1016/j.brat.2012.10.008

Glaser, N., Kazantizis, N., Deane, F., & L Oades, L. (2000). Critical issues in using homework assignments within cognitive-behavioural therapy for schizophrenia. *Journal of Rational-Emotive & Cognitive-Behavior Therapy, 18*, 247–261.

Granholm, E., McQuaid, J. R., Link, P. C., Fish, S., Patterson, T., & Jeste, D. V. (2008). Neuropsychological predictors of functional outcome in Cognitive Behavioral Social Skills Training for older people with schizophrenia. *Schizophrenia Research, 100* (1–3), 133–143. doi: 10.1016/j.schres.2007.11.032

Grant, P. M., & Beck, A. T. (2009). Defeatist beliefs as a mediator of cognitive impairment, negative symptoms, & functioning in schizophrenia. *Schizophrenia Bulletin, 35*(4), 798–806. doi: 10.1093/schbul/sbn008

Grant, P. M., Huh, G. A., Perivoliotis, D., Stolar, N. M., & Beck A. T. (2012). Randomized trial to evaluate the efficacy of cognitive therapy for low-functioning patients with schizophrenia. *Archives of General Psychiatry, 69*(2), 121–127. doi: 10.1001/archgenpsychiatry.2011.129

Grubaugh, A. L., Zinzow, H. M., Paul, L., Egede, L. E., & Frueh, B. C. (2011). Trauma exposure and posttraumatic stress disorder in adults with severe mental illness: a critical review. *Clinical Psychology Review, 31*(6), 883–899. doi: 10.1016/j.cpr.2011.04.003

Gumley, A., & Schwannauer, M. (2006). *Staying well after psychosis: a cognitive interpersonal approach to recovery and relapse prevention.* Chichester: John Wiley & Sons.

Hacker, D., Birchwood, M., Tudway, J., Meaden, A., & Amphlett, C. (2008). Acting on voices: omnipotence, sources of threat, & safety-seeking behaviours. *British Journal of Clinical Psychology, 47*, 201–213. doi: 10.1348/014466507x249093

Hagen, R., Turkington, D., Berge, T., & Grawe, R. W. (2010). *CBT for psychosis: a symptom-based approach.* London: Routledge.

Hayward, M., Strauss, C., & Kingdon, D. (2012). *Overcoming distressing voices.* London: Constable and Robinson.

Jolley, S., & Garety, P. (2011). Cognitive behavioural interventions. In W. Gaebel (Ed.), *Schizophrenia: current science and clinical practice* (pp. 185–215). Chichester: John Wiley & Sons.

Jones, C., Hacker, D., Cormac, I., Meaden, A., and Irving, C. B. (2012). Cognitive behaviour therapy versus other psychosocial treatments for schizophrenia. *Cochrane Database of Systematic Reviews, 4*, CD008712. doi: 10.1002/14651858.CD008712.pub2

Kilbride, M., Byrne, R., Price, J., Wood, L., Barratt, S., Welford, M., & Morrison A. P. (2013). Exploring service users' perceptions of cognitive behavioural therapy for psychosis: a user led study. *Behavioural and Cognitive Psychotherapy, 41*(1), 89–102. doi: 10.1017/S1352465812000495

Kinderman, P., & Lobban, F. (2000). Evolving formulations: sharing complex information with clients. *Behavioural and Cognitive Psychotherapy, 28*, 307–310.

Kingdon, D., & Turkington, D. (1994). *Cognitive behavioural therapy of schizophrenia.* New York: Guilford Press.

Kingdon, D., & Turkington, D. (2002). *The case study guide to cognitive behaviour therapy of psychosis.* Chichester: John Wiley & Sons.

Kingdon, D., & Turkington, D. (2005). *Cognitive therapy of schizophrenia.* New York: Guilford Press.

Larkin, W., & Morrison, A. P. (2006). *Trauma and psychosis: new directions for theory and therapy.* London: Routledge.

Lincoln, T. M., Ziegler, M., Mehl, S., Kesting, M. L., Lullmann, E., Westermann, S., & Rief, W. (2012). Moving from efficacy to effectiveness in cognitive behavioral therapy for psychosis: a randomized clinical practice trial. *Journal of Consulting and Clinical Psychology, 80*(4), 674–686. doi: 10.1037/A0028665

Lynch, D., Laws, K. R., & McKenna, P. J. (2010). Cognitive behavioural therapy for major psychiatric disorder: does it really work? A meta-analytical review of well-controlled trials. *Psychological Medicine, 40*(1), 9–24. doi: 10.1017/S003329170900590x

Mairs, H., Lovell, K., Campbell, M., & Keeley, P. (2011). Development and pilot investigation of behavioral activation for negative symptoms. *Behavior Modification, 35*(5), 486–506. doi: 10.1177/0145445511411706

Mazzucchelli, T., Kane, R., & Rees, C. (2009). Behavioral activation treatments for depression in adults: a meta-analysis and review. *Clinical Psychology-Science and Practice, 16*(4), 383–411.

Meaden, A., Keen, N., Aston, R., Barton, K., & Bucci, S. (2012). *Cognitive therapy for command hallucinations: an advanced practical companion.* Hove: Routledge.

Messari, S., & Hallam, R. (2003). CBT for psychosis: A qualitative analysis of client's experiences. *British Journal of Clinical Psychology, 42*, 171–188.

Miles, H., Peters, E., & Kuipers, E. (2007). Service-user satisfaction with CBT for psychosis. *Behavioural and Cognitive Psychotherapy, 35*(1), 109–116. doi: 10.1017/S1352465806003158

Mineka, S., & Thomas, C. (1999). Mechanisms of change in exposure therapy for anxiety disorders. In T. Dalgliesh & M. Power (Eds.), *Handbook of cognition and emotion* (pp. 747–764). New York: John Wiley & Sons.

Morberg Pain, C., Chadwick, P., & Abba, N. (2008). Clients' experience of case formulation in cognitive behaviour therapy for psychosis. *British Journal of Clinical Psychology, 47*(2), 127–138. doi: 10.1348/014466507X235962

Morris, E., Johns, L., & Oliver, J. (2013). *Acceptance and commitment therapy and mindfulness for psychosis.* Chichester: Wiley-Blackwell.

Morrison, A. P. (2001). The interpretation of intrusions in psychosis: an integrative cognitive approach to hallucinations and delusions. *Behavioural and Cognitive Psychotherapy, 29,* 257–276.

Morrison, A. P. (2002). *A casebook of cognitive therapy for psychosis.* Hove: Brunner-Routledge.

Morrison, A. P., & Barratt, S. (2010). What are the components of CBT for psychosis? a Delphi study. *Schizophrenia Bulletin, 36*(1), 136–142. doi: 10.1093/schbul/sbp118

Morrison, A., J. Renton, J., Dunn, H., Williams, S., & Bentall, R. (2003). *Cognitive therapy for psychosis: a formulation-based approach.* Hove: Brunner-Routledge.

Morrison, A. P., Renton, J. C., Williams, S., Dunn, H., Knight, A., Kreutz, M. S., ... Dunn, G. (2004). Delivering cognitive therapy to people with psychosis in a community mental health setting: an effectiveness study. *Acta Psychiatrica Scandinavica, 110*(1), 36–44. doi: 10.1111/j.1600-0447.(2004).00299.x

Morrison, A. P., Turkington, D., Pyle, M., Spencer, H. Brabban, A., Dunn, G., ... Hutton, P. (2014). Cognitive therapy for people with schizophrenia spectrum disorders not taking antipsychotic drugs: a single-blind randomised controlled trial. *The Lancet,* http://dx.doi.org/10.1016/S0140-6736(13)62246-1

Morrison, A. P., & Wells, A. (2007). Relationships between worry, psychotic experiences and emotional distress in patients with schizophrenia spectrum diagnoses and comparisons with anxious and non-patient groups. *Behaviour Research and Therapy, 45*(7), 1593–1600. doi: 10.1016/j.brat.2006.11.010

Mueser, K. T., Rosenberg, S. D. Xie, H. Jankowski, M. K. Bolton, E. E. Lu, W., ... Wolfe, R. (2008). A randomized controlled trial of cognitive-behavioral treatment for posttraumatic stress disorder in severe mental illness. *Journal of Consulting and Clinical Psychology, 76*(2), 259–271. doi: 10.1037/0022-006x.76.2.259

Mueser, K. T., Salyers, M. P., Rosenberg, S. D., Goodman, L. A., Essock, S. M., Osher, F. C., ... 5 Site Health Risk Study Res Comm. (2004). Interpersonal trauma and posttraumatic stress disorder in patients with severe mental illness: demographic, clinical, & health correlates. *Schizophrenia Bulletin, 30*(1), 45–57.

National Institute for Care and Health Excellence (NICE). (2009). *Schizophrenia: core interventions in the treatment and management of schizophrenia in primary and secondary care* (update). London: Gaskell.

Nelson, H. E. (1997). *Cognitive behavioural therapy with schizophrenia: a practice manual.* Cheltenham: Nelson Thornes Ltd.

Nelson, H. E. (2005). *Cognitive-behavioural therapy with delusions and hallucinations: a practical manual* (2nd ed). Cheltenham: Nelson Thornes Ltd.

Nothard, S., Morrison, A. P., & Wells, A. (2008). Identifying specific interpretations and exploring the nature of safety behaviours for people who hear voices: an exploratory study. *Behavioural and Cognitive Psychotherapy, 36*(3), 353–357. doi: 10.1017/S1352465808004372

Perivoliotis, D., Grant, P. M., Peters, E. R., Ison, R., Kuipers, E., & Beck A. T. (2010). Cognitive insight predicts favorable outcome in cognitive behavioral therapy for psychosis. *Psychosis-Psychological Social and Integrative Approaches, 2*(1), 23–33. doi: 10.1080/17522430903147520

Peters, E. R., Landau, S., McCrone, P., Cooke, M., Fisher, P., Steel, C., ... Kuipers, E. (2010). A randomised controlled trial of cognitive behaviour therapy for psychosis in a routine clinical service. *Acta Psychiatrica Scandinavica, 122*(4), 302–318. doi: 10.1111/j.1600-0447.(2010).01572.x

Premkumar, P., Peters, E. R., Fannon, D., Anilkumar, A. P., Kuipers, E., & Kumari, V. (2011). Coping styles predict responsiveness to cognitive behaviour therapy in psychosis. *Psychiatry Research, 187*(3), 354–362. doi: 10.1016/j.psychres.2010.12.029

Read, J., Van Os, J., Morrison, A. P., & Ross, C. A. (2005). Childhood trauma, psychosis and schizophrenia: a literature review with theoretical and clinical implications. *Acta Psychiatrica Scandinavica, 112* (5), 330–350. doi: 10.1111/j.1600-0447.2005.00634.x

Rector, N. A., Beck, A. T., & Stolar, N. (2005). The negative symptoms of schizophrenia: A cognitive perspective. *Canadian Journal of Psychiatry-Revue Canadienne De Psychiatrie, 50*(5), 247–257.

Rollinson, R., Smith, B., Steel, C., Jolley, S., Onwumere, J., Garety, P. A., ... Fowler, D. (2008). Measuring adherence in CBT for Psychosis: a psychometric analysis of an adherence scale. *Behavioural and Cognitive Psychotherapy, 36*(2), 163–178. doi: 10.1017/S1352465807003980

Sarin, F., Wallin, L., & Widerlov, B. (2011). Cognitive behavior therapy for schizophrenia: A meta-analytical review of randomized controlled trials. *Nordic Journal of Psychiatry, 65*(3), 162–174. doi: 10.3109/08039488.2011.577188

Startup, H., Freeman, D., & Garety, P. A. (2007). Persecutory delusions and catastrophic worry in psychosis: Developing the understanding of delusion distress and persistence. *Behaviour Research and Therapy, 45*(3), 523–537. doi: 10.1016/j.brat.2006.04.006

Startup, M., Jackson, M., & Pearce, E. (2002). Assessing therapist adherence to cognitive-behaviour therapy for psychosis. *Behavioural and Cognitive Psychotherapy, 30*(3), 329–339. doi: 10.1017/S1352465802003077

Steel, C. (2013). *CBT for schizophrenia: evidence-based interventions and future directions.* London: Wiley-Blackwell.

Steel, C., Tarrier, N., Stahl, D., & Wykes, T. (2012). Cognitive behaviour therapy for psychosis: the impact of therapist training and supervision. *Psychotherapy and Psychosomatics, 81*(3), 194–195. doi: 10.1159/000334250

Tarrier, N., Harwood, S., Yusopoff, L., Beckett, R., & Baker, A. (1990). Coping strategy enhancement (CSE) – a method of treating residual schizophrenic symptoms. *Behavioural Psychotherapy, 18*(4), 283–293.

Tarrier, N., & Wykes, T. (2004). Is there evidence that cognitive behaviour therapy is an effective treatment for schizophrenia? A cautious or cautionary tale? *Behaviour Research and Therapy, 42*(12), 1377–1401. doi: 10.1016/j.brat.2004.06.020

Turkington, D., Kingdon, D,. Rathod, S., Wilcock, S. K. J., Brabban, A., Cromarty, P., ... Weiden, P. (2009). *Back to life, back to normality: cognitive therapy, recovery and psychosis.* London: Cambridge University Press.

Van den Berg, D. P. G., & van der Gagg, M. (2012). Treating trauma in psychosis with EMDR: A pilot study. *Journal of Behavior Therapy and Experimental Psychiatry, 43*, 664–671.

Van Os, J., Hanssen, M., Bijl, R. V., & Ravelli, A. (2000). Strauss (1969) revisited: a psychosis continuum in the general population? *Schizophrenia Research, 45*(1–2), 11–20.

Varese, F., Smeets, F., Drukker, M., Lieverse, R., Lataster, T., Viechtbauer, W., ... Bentall, R. P. (2012). Childhood adversities increase the risk of psychosis: a meta-analysis of patient-control, prospective- and cross-sectional cohort studies. *Schizophrenia Bulletin, 38*(4), 661–671. doi: 10.1093/schbul/sbs050

Waller, H., Garety, P. A., Jolley, S., Fornells-Ambrojo, M., Kuipersa, E., Onwumere, J, ... Craig, T. (2013). Low intensity cognitive behavioural therapy for psychosis: a pilot study. *Journal of Behavior Therapy and Experimental Psychiatry, 44*(1), 98–104. doi: 10.1016/j.jbtep.2012.07.013

Wright, N. P., Kelly, O., Turkington, D., Davies, D., Jacobs, A. M., Hopton, J., & Beck, A. T. (In press). *Treating psychosis: a clinician's guide to integrating acceptance and commitment therapy, compassion-focused therapy, & mindfulness approaches within the cognitive behavior therapy tradition.* Oakland, CA: New Harbinger Publications.

Wright, J. H., Kingdon, D., Turkington, D., & Ramierz-Basco, M. (2009). *Cognitive-behavior therapy for severe mental illness.* Washington, DC: American Psychiatric Publishing Inc.

Wykes, T., Steel, C., Everitt, B., & Tarrier, N. (2008). Cognitive behavior therapy for schizophrenia: Effect sizes, clinical models, & methodological rigor. *Schizophrenia Bulletin, 34*(3), 523–537. doi: 10.1093/schbul/sbm114

Young, J., & Beck, A. T. (1980). *Cognitive therapy scale.* Philadelphia: University of Pennsylvania.

14

CBT with Older People

Steve Boddington

Introduction

As life expectancy continues to increase (Office for National Statistics, 2011) older people are now the fastest growing section of the population. People over 65 years of age now account for almost 18 per cent of the total population and over 21 per cent of the adult population in the United Kingdom. Some psychological therapy services have attempted to manage this demographic change by removing the age cut-off in their inclusion criteria. However, Minshull (2007) concluded that these age inclusive services are not adequately addressing the particular needs of older people leading to "indirect discrimination".

This chapter aims to summarize the literature relating to the application of CBT to the needs of older people, so that we do not inadvertently limit the beneficial impact of our interventions when working with older people by adopting a "one-size fits all" approach to our work.

How Common is Depression and Anxiety in Later Life?

The 2007 Adult Psychiatric Morbidity Survey (McManus, Meltzer, Brugha, Bebbington, & Jenkins, 2009) reported lower prevalence rates for common mental disorders in people aged 65–74 (10.6 per cent) and 75+ (9.9 per cent) than for the total adult population (16.2 per cent). However, the Department of Health policy document "No Health Without Mental Health" (Department of Health, 2011) states that 25 per cent of the older people in the community have symptoms of depression that require treatment. Also, higher rates of common mental disorders are found in specific groups of older people including those in residential care, those experiencing chronic physical ill-health and/or social isolation (Craig & Mindell, 2007).

How to Become a More Effective CBT Therapist: Mastering Metacompetence in Clinical Practice,
First Edition. Edited by Adrian Whittington and Nick Grey.
© 2014 John Wiley & Sons, Ltd. Published 2014 by John Wiley & Sons, Ltd.

Less than 20 per cent of older people who experience depression actually report this to their GP (Chew-Graham, Burns, & Baldwin, 2004) and can use language that differs from that of younger people, which may not be picked up by clinicians. We may also view symptoms associated with common mental disorders as normal given the adverse life events often associated with later life, or construe symptoms as the effects of chronic physical health conditions (e.g., preoccupation with pain, fatigue and poor sleep), or medication side effects (e.g., agitation, confusion and sedation) rather than ascribing them to a treatable mental illness. Despite similar profiles being found between older and younger people's reports of somatic and affective symptoms in anxiety, older people's levels of worry tend to be lower (Brenes, 2006) and may have different foci (Gonçalves & Byrne, 2012) with less emphasis on interpersonal relationships, personal health or work and more preoccupation with the needs of loved ones.

How Effective is CBT with Older People?

The evidence for CBT for common mental disorders in later life remains relatively thin when compared to studies for working age adults. A meta-analyses of CBT for late life depression (Gould, Coulson, & Howard, 2012a) identified 14 studies (N = 1178) comparing CBT with non-active control conditions, showing a moderate effect size ($g = -0.57$) in favour of CBT. However, there was no significant difference between the effect of CBT and active talking therapy control conditions using data from five studies (N = 239) ($g = -0.22$). This is comparable to a meta-analysis in which CBT for younger adults was compared to active therapeutic controls ($g = -0.27$) (Lynch, Laws, & McKenna, 2010). CBT is a valuable intervention for older people with depression, but the literature does not strongly support its use over other types of active treatment. Pinquart, Duberstein, and Lyness (2007) identify a number of factors that influence outcome including co-morbidity of depression with physical illness or cognitive impairment. We will consider the challenge of working with these conditions later in the chapter.

Studies of CBT as a treatment for anxiety in later life were reviewed using data from 12 published randomized controlled trials (Gould, Coulson, & Howard, 2012b). This meta-analysis showed a moderate effect size ($g = -0.66$) in favour of CBT over treatment as usual or waiting list control, but no significant difference when compared to active control interventions such as medication (SSRI/SNRIs) ($g = -0.20$). Interestingly, unlike depression, these effect sizes are considerably smaller than those found for younger adults with anxiety ($g = -1.69$) (Covin, Ouimet, Seeds, & Dozois, 2008), suggesting that treatment response is not as marked in older people.

Studies of older people's attitudes to psychological interventions verses medication for common mental illness generally show a preference for psychological treatments or a combination of both (Hanson & Scogin, 2008). In a study investigating the effects of collaborative care for late life depression (Gum et al., 2006) 57 per cent of participants (mean age = 71; S.D. 7.4) expressed a preference for psychological treatment over medication or no treatment if they were to become depressed. A key issue in older people's uptake of CBT may be a lack of understanding of, and familiarity with, psychological therapy. Given the relatively recent development of CBT it is worth remembering that older people's concepts of psychological therapy may be based on historical ideas about the nature and course of such treatments.

How to Adapt Therapy to Address the Needs of Older People

Fundamentally the cognitive behavioural treatment of common mental disorders in older people is rooted in the same model and uses the same techniques as CBT for younger adults. In their review of psychological treatments for older adults Gatz et al. (1998) conclude that the evidence for CBT indicates that *little adjustment of fundamental techniques appears to be required*. However, therapists need to be skilled in conveying the model and techniques so that each client can apply them to their own experience. A number of factors should be considered when applying CBT to older people in a manner that is acceptable and accessible.

Working with diversity

One of the distinctive features of working with older people is the heterogeneity and diversity of this age group. Intuitively it makes sense that, as we age, we are exposed to an increasing variety of life events and life choices that shape our physical, social and psychological make-up. Assimilated life events including our early life experiences, dietary patterns, lifestyle choices, education and career paths, relationships, alcohol and drug use, exercise and hobbies, spiritual/religious observance, financial circumstances and much more. These are compounded by our endowed genetic makeup and conspire to ensure that by the time we reach our later years our unique set of circumstances have shaped our individuality. Thus, when working with older people, all that we have been taught in relation to addressing issues of diversity in therapy will be of relevance. Showing genuine interest in older people's backgrounds, values and life experiences, while being transparent about potential similarities and differences between these and our own, is both fascinating, and rewarding. In turn, such acknowledgement of diversity and difference is likely to improve therapeutic engagement and collaborative working. As a therapist you may need to factor in more time, especially within the early stages of therapy, to understand the specific characteristics that influence your older client's mental health needs and ensure that you have established a common language and framework within which you are both able to communicate. Remember that older people have spent a lifetime assimilating new ideas and knowledge as society evolves around them, and many will therefore be quite at home relating to a younger therapist about matters of a psychological nature!

Assessment tools for anxiety and depression in later life

Most outcome measures have been developed, and validated on younger adult populations and thus vary in their reliability and validity with older cohorts (Dennis, Boddington, & Funnell, 2007; Sperlinger, 2004). It is my impression that assessment tools can underestimate common mental disorders in later life. Our local referrals data indicates that fewer older people reach the cut off point for case consideration than younger referrals. Barkham, Culverwell, Spindler, Twigg, and Connell (2005) found a similar phenomenon for the CORE-OM using data from older people referred to primary care services. Of course this may be a consequence of referrers showing greater sensitivity to the needs of dysphoric older people, but such an explanation contradicts evidence that primary care clinicians under identify common mental disorders in older people (Chew-Graham et al., 2004). An alternative, and in my view more plausible explanation is that older people in general are more circumspect and reticent to disclose mental distress.

Two rating scales that have been developed specifically for use with older people are the Geriatric Depression Scale (GDS) (Yesavage et al., 1983) and its subsequent shorter versions (GDS-15, -12, -10) (Sheikh & Yesavage, 1986; see also Almeida & Almeida, 1999) and the Geriatric Anxiety Inventory (GAI) (Pachana et al., 2007) and it's shorter version (GAI-SF) (Byrne & Pachana, 2010) all of which are available for general use without charge. The Hospital Anxiety and Depression Scale (Zigmond & Snaith, 1983) also has a long history of use with older populations.

Socialization to the model

This early stage in therapy, in which a shared understanding and meaning is created in relation to the older person's mental illness, is by nature a two-way process. While this is true when initiating therapy with someone of any age it may be a particularly important element of engaging older people in CBT (Dick, Gallagher-Thompson, & Thompson, 1996). As a therapist assessing an older person's ability to engage in therapy, you must strive to comprehend the individual factors that contribute to and maintain their condition. You must help them understand their emotional difficulties by using a CBT conceptualization while being vigilant to their use of language, noting terms and phrases and checking to ensure that you have understood the meaning of these correctly. You are more likely to hear phrases such as "down in the dumps", "browned off", "glum" or "melancholic" to describe feeling depressed, and being "vexed", "neurotic", "having trouble with my nerves" or "troubled" to express feeling anxious. Also, it is not uncommon for patients to focus on co-morbid physical conditions rather than disclose emotional weaknesses given the stigma that these can hold. It is also important to check that older patients have understood the psychological language implicit in CBT. Terms such as "attributions", "cognitions", "behavioural experiments", "safety behaviours", and so on, may well be alien to an older person. Likewise, given the co-morbidity of physical and emotional difficulties in later life, some medical jargon and references to basic human biophysiology may also be unfamiliar and require careful explanation.

At its core, the CBT model espouses the principles of *collaborative empiricism* (Burns & Beck, 1978). The current cohort of older people may not immediately expect to relate to a health professional collaboratively. They may not perceive the patient–doctor relationship as necessarily involving mutual understanding and the negotiation of goals, objectives and treatment plans. Rather, they may assume a passive role, believing that their therapist's superior knowledge requires unquestioning acceptance and compliance; freeing them from the responsibility to understand the principles on which decisions are based and thus developing generalizable skills. Therefore, when working with older people check what they infer from the conversation and whether they understand that you expect to work in partnership with them. They may find it difficult when you talk of theories and hypotheses, and suggest that they experiment to see if possible explanations are "helpful". They may not expect to be asked to take an active role in setting up activities (especially as behavioural experiments), keeping accounts of thoughts and wrestling with re-appraising unhelpful cognitions.

Segal et al. (1995) describe a number of factors that underpin effective CBT. Although these were originally developed with younger clients, many of these can be used as a helpful guide to socializing an older person to the expectations and nature of therapy (see Figure 14.1).

- Client's understanding is compatible with cognitive and or behavioural rationale: for instance, patients who insist that their problems are purely the result of a chemical imbalance, physical illness or social adversity are less likely to benefit.

- Ability to differentiate between emotions, forming a common language with the therapist to describe these.

- The ability to identify and describe automatic thoughts or images, relating to their mental illness.

- Acceptance of personal responsibility to change

- The degree of alliance with the therapist that is created in the session.

- The degree to which the patient is willing to acknowledge and discard unhelpful "self-protective strategies/safety behaviours" that serve to avoid feared situations.

- Ability to identify and stick to specific objectives and goals for therapy

Figure 14.1   Factors that may help to assesses suitability for CBT and may be addressed in the early stages of therapy with older people (adapted from Segal et al., 1995).

Charlesworth and Greenfield (2004) identify stereotypical prejudices for both clients and therapists, which act as barriers to effective engagement of older people:

- ageist attitudes, rather than specific disabilities are used to explain barriers to change;
- pessimism towards therapy (therapeutic nihilism) often triggered by overwhelming adversity, leading to a sense of helplessness and hopelessness on the part of either client or therapist;
- the risk of attributing too much importance to intrapsychic factors and explanations (*psychopathologism*) while undervaluing other aetiological factors; or
- conversely having insufficient regard for psychological components, and focussing on purely physical or social explanations.

It may be helpful to suggest strategies to overcome such prejudices as part of the therapeutic process. Address sample bias, which may occur without an understanding of normal/successful ageing, and balance the experience of adversity in later life with examples of people who have coped well with the challenges of their later years. Sir Winston Churchill's courageous leadership through World War II, becoming Prime Minister at 65 years of age, and his well-known struggle with "the black dog" is one such example. Prejudice may be broken down by experiences that counter such beliefs and therefore older patients may be encouraged to embark on therapeutic endeavours to see if their beliefs are correct.

> Elsie became avoidant of using buses following a fall caused by a driver pulling away before she had reached her seat. Following a discussion of her conviction that this would happen again as "*people* (in this case bus drivers) *have no regard for the elderly*" she agreed to sit at the town centre bus stop and observe the behaviour of drivers towards elderly passengers. She returned to the subsequent session having realized that drivers were, on the whole, very considerate towards their passengers. Also, she observed one particularly feisty elderly lady command the driver to remain stationary until she was properly seated. This inspired Elsie to realize that she need not be powerless in such situations.

It is important to set small and achievable goals, which will foster hope and increase confidence as they are successfully achieved. Look for opportunities to instil hope, such as explaining the rationale for therapy or providing examples and wider evidence of constructive change. As part of supervision we may need to address our own tendency towards pessimistic expectations, and to hold in balance the multiple mechanisms that can contribute to emotional disorders in later life, using a CBT framework that embraces a bio-psycho-social understanding.

Developing a CBT conceptualization: "comprehensive" vs. "comprehensible"

In his paper "On Psychotherapy" (1905) Freud stated that:

> Persons near or over the age of fifty lack, on the one hand, the plasticity of the psychic processes upon which the therapy depends – old people are no longer educable – and on the other hand, the material which has to be elaborated, and the duration of the treatment is immensely increased.

The issue of the "plasticity of the psychic processes" (or the concept of "psychological mindedness" in modern psychobabble!) will be considered later. However, Freud's assertion about the excessive amount of material to be considered when working with older people is also encountered within CBT formulations.

A significant development in the use of CBT with older people occurred with Laidlaw et al.'s (2003; 2004) proposed CBT conceptualization for depression, which draws on a broader gerontological framework within which emotional needs can be understood (Figure 14.2). Essentially this places the traditional longitudinal cognitive conceptualization of depression proposed by Beck, Rush, Shaw, & Emery (1979) within the wider context of later life.

Cohort beliefs (about ageing, therapy, psychological difficulties, etc.) may be important to explore; any issue for which there is a distinctive belief held by the age cohort that is pertinent to the patient's specific emotional distress. Examples include: when working with elderly couples where one partner requires residential or nursing care and the other experiences powerful feelings of guilt and betrayal of their spouse based on a strong social disapproval of "putting your loved-one away' rather than caring for them to the bitter end, no matter what the cost; or the social stigma associated with mental illness, senility, or reliance on state benefits, which can arise from early formative experiences of the traumas associated with mental institutions and the workhouse prior to the health and social care reforms of the second half of the twentieth century.

Role transitions such as retirement, widowhood, or increasing dependence on others, are often significant triggers and influences on emotional ill-health in later life. It is important to consider how such transitions are being negotiated to enable reinvestment in other roles, as the following example illustrates:

> Harry became depressed when he had to move to sheltered housing near his son following the death of his wife who had been his primary source of friendship and support for over sixty years. He was able to identify and grieve for the multiple losses associated with this transition, and began to make new friends and became an active member of the unit's social committee.

Physical health and well-being is likely to be an increasingly significant factor in older people's circumstances. It will be important to explore the personal meaning associated with illness for each patient and to assess their understanding of the relationship between their physical and emotional difficulties. This will be considered in more detail.

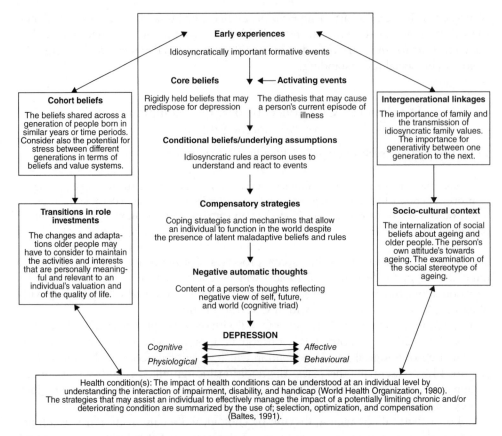

Figure 14.2 CBT conceptual framework for older people (adapted from Laidlaw et al. 2003; Laidlaw et al., 2004).

Inter-generational linkages may also play a part in understanding the context of an older patient's mental illness. Both historical and current family relationships may act as important mediators to emotional well-being. Family history, traditions and values may be important to explore as influences on patient's behavioural and cognitive patterns and habits, for example:

> Bill was an independent-minded man with depression and mild cognitive impairment who became increasingly socially isolated as his self-confidence waned. He was angry towards his carers for "stealing his money". On further exploration he disclosed that he had been a heavy drinker through much of his adult life and was ashamed that his family had needed to hide his weekly pay to prevent him from squandering it on alcohol. While he hated being "controlled" by others he could see that such steps had been necessary in his younger days and that receiving more help now, as he aged, did not equate with his previous problems. Grudgingly, he began to accept care from others without making allegations against them. Understanding the associations that relinquishing control to others evoked also helped his carers to respond more sensitivity so that they could mitigate his hostility.

The broader socio-cultural context and the degree to which an older patient is able to engage constructively with this, will affect emotional well-being. The extent to which wider society and older people's immediate communities value and respect their

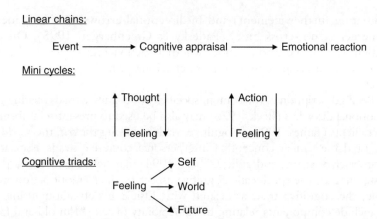

Figure 14.3   Using mini formulations to enhance older people's psychological understanding of their emotional disorder (adapted from Charlesworth & Reichelt, 2004).

roles will make a difference to their sense of self. The extent to which older people assimilate new technology also affects their well-being: The increasing importance of computer literacy to maintain active and productive lives (e-mail, social networking, Internet banking, on line shopping, interaction with many public and voluntary organizations and obtaining information via organizations' websites) provides a distinct advantage to those who keep abreast of such technology.

While all these factors are clearly relevant to a therapists' work with older clients, one can't help but agree with Freud, that the amount of potential material that could be brought to bear could become overwhelming. This may be compounded by reduced "plasticity in their psychic processes". Loss of cognitive flexibility, speed of information processing, working memory, and so on, may limit some older people's ability to process novel, elusive and abstract concepts, especially at a time of heightened emotional distress. Therefore, while therapists seek to develop a broad and holistic conceptualization of their older client's mental disorder, such "kitchen sink" formulations (James, 2008) are unlikely to be helpful to the clients themselves. Therapists need to develop skill in identifying and focussing on key psychological concepts that provoke the most salient insight and subsequent change in thoughts and behaviours and enable the intended shift in mood (Grant & Casey, 1995).

Charlesworth and Reichelt (2004) proposed a number of types of "mini-formulations" for use as a means of focussing CBT interventions with elderly family caregivers experiencing emotional distress (Figure 14.3). These may be of relevance to older people more generally:

- The introduction of simple "*linear chains*" in which the patient is helped to link one aspect of their circumstances with a related thought or behaviour and the resultant change in mood. Once this has been achieved, therapy may progress towards considering whether alternative cognitive or behavioural responses may have resulted in different emotional states and thus to the development of behavioural or cognitive strategies that can be tested.
- *Mini cycles* can introduce the concept of maintaining patterns and explore the interplay of mood and thoughts or mood and behaviours. This may be extended into more complex models to explain the maintenance of emotional disorders,

incorporating further elements and bi-directional arrows, akin to Padesky and Greenberger's "hot-cross bun" (Padesky & Greenberger, 1995). Once again, the patient can be asked to consider whether such vicious cycles can be reversed by introducing alternative thoughts or behaviours, which might prompt a change in affect.

- Aaron Beck's description of the content specificity of cognitive triads relating to different emotional disorders (Beck, 1976) may also be used to present mini-formulations to older clients (James, 1999). Cognitive triads involving the *self*, the *world* and the *future*, (and the similar concept of interpersonal cognitive dyads associated with emotions such as shame and guilt; Gilbert, 1994) may help clients develop a better understanding of the specifically cognitive aspect of their emotional disorder. For example, the cognitive triad associated with Elsie's anxiety about using the bus might include components relating to vulnerability of self ("I'm old and frail, with poor balance and brittle bones"), the hostility and danger of the world around ("Nobody shows any thought or concern for the elderly") and the unpredictability of future events ("the driver may pull away before I've sat down").

Secker, Kazantzis, and Pachana (2004) emphasize the importance of the structured nature of CBT in helping older clients negotiate the experience of psychological therapy to a constructive conclusion. Structuring sessions in a clear, collaborative way helps to provide order and understanding to the wealth of material that older people may bring. While allowing for a modified pace of therapy (the amount of material dealt with in each session) they highlight techniques such as setting session by session goals and agendas to help maintain a focus, starting each session by "bridging" to earlier work to aid recall and continuity, and eliciting feedback to gauge the extent to which older clients have understood issues and concepts discussed. Particularly careful consideration should be given to the setting of between session tasks to ensure that they are understood, relevant and realistic.

How to Adapt Therapy for Older People with Specific Impairments

James (2008) suggests a helpful framework (Figure 14.4) for considering whether to modify CBT techniques for older people. This involves assessing the patient's needs along two axes: one for *cognitive ability* and one for *physical health*.

CBT for older people who fit in the top left quadrant will require little structural adaptation beyond the principles already outlined in this chapter. Such referrals' cognitive and physical difficulties will be mild, resulting in only small degrees of handicap/ loss of ability. Most of the evidence for the efficacy of CBT with older people is based on this population.

Adapting therapy for older people with mild cognitive impairment (MCI)

Older people may develop MCI for a number of reasons including age-related cognitive decline and cognitive symptoms of depression and/or anxiety or in the very early stages of a dementia. These clients will require adaptations to therapy to help them compensate for their impairment as summarized in Table 14.1. They may require

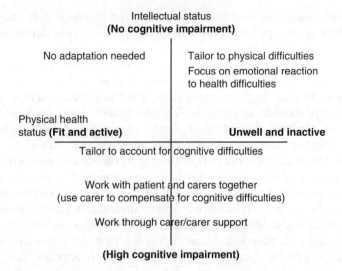

Figure 14.4 James' four quadrant framework for applying CBT to the needs of older people (adapted from James, 2008).

Table 14.1 Strategies for adapting CBT in older people with mild cognitive impairments

Cognitive deficits	*Compensatory strategies*
Memory problems	<ul><li>Use diaries, checklists and notebooks</li><li>Record the sessions on audio or video tape</li><li>Repetition of main points/themes</li><li>Use much *feedback* within/between sessions</li><li>Highly structured formats</li><li>Involve relatives/carers to prompt patient between sessions</li><li>Therapist fills gaps</li></ul>
Language difficulties	<ul><li>Receptive problems can be helped by using handouts, pictures, diagrams and audio aids.</li><li>Use alternative communication strategies and appropriate writing, drawing or visual material.</li><li>Use relatives/carers</li></ul>
Mental inflexibility (concreteness)	<ul><li>Use simple structured material with which the person can be easily socialized to the CBT model.</li><li>Use regular feedback; frequently asking the person to describe the main themes of the therapy.</li><li>Consolidate through role-play and behavioural work.</li></ul>
Attention problems	<ul><li>Set short-term, specific and highly relevant goals.</li><li>Slower pace and simple objectives (resist urge to rush to fit more in)</li><li>Use sensitively paced therapy with appropriate breaks within the session.</li><li>Increase frequency and decrease duration on appointments</li></ul>
Interpersonal difficulties arising from cognitive impairment	<ul><li>Work with families/carers</li><li>Work with patient and carer together</li></ul>

involvement of carers and care staff if their level of impairment is more advanced. However, adapting therapy for people with moderate to severe cognitive impairment is beyond the scope of this chapter.

The focus of therapy may need to consider aetiological factors associated with cognitive decline. Such clients may become anxious or depressed as a result of their attributions relating to their cognitive difficulties, and the consequences of this on their current and future activities and lifestyle. They are likely to make predictions about the implications of cognitive decline based on the experience of others who they have witnessed developing a dementia such as Alzheimer's disease. Where this is the case it may be helpful to encourage the person to seek further assessment. Often people in the early stages of cognitive decline attribute the consequences of their forgetfulness (such as losing personal belongings) to theft or even intentional repeated harassment by particular individuals. Such beliefs can lead to altercations with family members and friends, increasing social isolation, paranoia and depression. As with the example of Bill misattributing well intentioned care to people trying to control him, skilled application of CBT in a timely manner may help such clients re-appraise their understanding of the situation and take more appropriate steps to compensate for their difficulties. Addressing issues of cognitive decline in a respectful, empathic manner may facilitate valuable discussions regarding the provision of care and support both in the current circumstances and potential further decline, ensuring that the client's wishes are taken into account.

In the early sessions of therapy it is important to gauge the extent to which a client with MCI is able to retain information from the session. It is expedient to set clear and simple assignments between sessions (such as a simple activity/mood diary) and then begin each session by checking what can be remembered from the previous session and how they have progressed with their assignments. If the client is unable to recall the contents of sessions and forgets to complete homework tasks, you will need to consider introducing supportive strategies to aid recall and adherence, or whether to refer to more specialist services or alternative treatment strategies.

Applying CBT for anxiety/depression in older people with co-morbid physical illness

The top right quadrant in Figure 14.4 describes referrals with diseases and disorders such as cancer, arthritis and stroke. Such patients are discussed in greater detail in Chapter 11 with CBT interventions designed to address common mental disorders associated with chronic physical conditions not defined by age. However, in my experience of working with older people with a complex presentation of emotional and physical disorders typically the intervention will focus on one or both of the following areas:

- Fears and anxieties associated with specific aspects of the physical illness and its impact on the person's lifestyle.
- Depression associated with a sense of loss and hopelessness caused by the illness.

Depression is a common co-morbid condition with long-term physical ill health (Craig & Mindell, 2007) and interventions will often need to draw on a "coping" rather than "curing" model of CBT in which the reality of disability is directly acknowledged (Grant & Casey, 1995). It is important to elicit any disempowering assumptions that physical illness somehow directly causes depression.

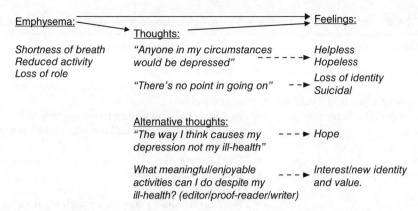

Figure 14.5   Mini formulation of depression in patient with chronic emphysema.

Figure 14.5 shows a mini-formulation for Mary:

> Mary was a retired drama teacher who became increasingly depressed with the progression of her emphysema. Having been an active, outgoing person she became housebound due to her shortness of breath on physical exertion. Initially, she was scathing of therapy, claiming that depression was inevitable and was cynical of anyone who disagreed with her "rational" wish to end her life. Therapy was slow until a friend persuaded her to join the editorial team for a book of short plays to be performed by a local theatre company. The emotional benefits from this involvement challenged her formulation and spurred her to take up writing herself.

Once your client understands the significance of their thought processes, activities and behaviours in mediating emotions it becomes possible to consider more constructive patterns of thinking and behaving to improve their quality of life and emotional state while acknowledging the reality of the underlying medical/physical condition.

A summary of practical adaptations when working with patients with physical disabilities is provided in Table 14.2. A number of the ideas outlined in this table are derived from the work of Baltes and Baltes (1990) who proposed a behavioural model of successful ageing based on the principles of "selection" (of activities that derive highest personal meaning), optimization (maintaining performance of these activities, e.g., through practice) and compensation (problem solving to find ways of overcoming the barriers to achieving these activities).

Ending Therapy

As with patients of any age it is important to manage the process of ending therapy, applying techniques such as relapse prevention plans and written summaries of the main learning points developed during the course of treatment. Such documents are pertinent to ending therapy with older people where clear, structured information may help as an aid-memoir both to the client, but also, with their consent, to inform relatives and carers who can remind the older person if their mental health begins to deteriorate.

As loneliness and social isolation are common challenges in later life, some patients may find the loss of the supportive and trusting therapeutic relationship difficult. Several

Table 14.2 Strategies for adapting CBT in older people with co-morbid physical illness

Ill-health & disability	*Compensatory strategies*
Managing risk of exacerbation of illness. Judging what is physical handicap vs. excessive illness behaviour	• Consult with medics/GPs • Negotiate very gradual increases/exposure and monitor effects. • Be collaborative in setting treatment objectives • Include wider family who know the client's previous functioning
Fatigue	• Shorter sessions • Home-based treatment • Small goals/aspirations • Build up stamina/tolerance through regular exercise/ activity
Impact of illness on lifestyle (handicap)	• Problem solve (compensatory strategies) • Identify new/modify old interests/meaningful activities (selection) • Optimize skills that help to reduce handicap
Avoidance due to fear of health crisis	• Provide information and correct misconceptions about biological/psychological aspects of the illness. • Negotiate very graded exposure and review impact on health • Look for dis-confirmatory evidence (self & others)
Pain	• Differentiate between acute pain (indicating new damage) and chronic pain (indicating no new damage) • Monitor impact of lifestyle on (a) pain and (b) emotional wellbeing

strategies have been recommended to help with this adjustment (Laidlaw et al., 2003; Secker, et al., 2004). It is helpful to regularly orientate your client to the point that you have reached in therapy and the remaining number of sessions/length of time over which you will be meeting. By clearly articulating the process and structure of therapy you help to ensure that the client is not caught out by ending, and has time to adjust as therapy progresses. Provide opportunities to reflect on the implications of ending and the potential challenges anticipated when this occurs. Spacing the final few sessions can also provide older patients who are anxious about ending with experience of coping with longer intervals during which they manage more independently. Offering "booster sessions", which may be used to reinforce newly acquired skills and techniques, can also provide reassurance of further contact. Check that the client understands how to access further psychological therapy in the future, should the need arise, and ensure that this is recorded as part of the written summary and relapse prevention plan.

Issues of dependency are core anxieties that may re-emerge during later life. Fears of isolation and abandonment on the one hand, and loss of independence or "becoming a burden" on the other, are often challenging aspects of older peoples' adjustment to adverse life events. These issues may be played out in the therapeutic relationship, particularly in relation to ending therapy. As therapists, we should also reflect on our own preconceptions regarding dependency in later life, which we bring to our work with older patients.

Personal note

As an undergraduate I worked night shifts in a local residential care home for elderly people. Early each morning the residents would be woken, washed, dressed and given breakfast, ready for the morning shift to arrive. During this routine I would regularly prepare a blind, very elderly, retired admiral for his day. Each morning, at 6.30 a.m., I would shave and dress him and as we talked my prejudices about this washed up, abandoned old relic, dependent on others for the most basic of personal functions, were exposed and challenged. Here was a man facing the vicissitudes of very old age, ignored by the "real world" apart from very occasional flying visits from a child, grandchild or other relative while on their way to their "business". As the mornings passed I developed a fascination for the man within the withered shell; the amazing life concealed and the vibrant personality being ignored. At the age of 20 I was hooked! I challenge you to look beyond the façade of the older person sitting in your waiting room. It won't necessarily be comfortable but it will usually be worthwhile and will always be fascinating!

Procedural Rules

Assessment

- When you assess an older person don't make assumptions about the causes of symptoms and be careful how you interpret formal measures of depression and anxiety.
- Avoid pre-judging older patients and enjoy the privilege of learning about and working with people and the diversity of their life experiences
- Check your older patient's understanding of their mental health needs and the language they use.

Socializing older people to CBT

- Be explicit about your expectations of their role in therapy and the focus on collaborative experimentation.
- Check their understanding of the concepts/ideas and language you refer to.
- Watch for stereotypes and prejudice in yourself and your patient that may militate against constructive engagement in therapy.
- Endeavour to assess and understand the broader gerontological framework that contextualizes your patients' immediate mental illness.
- Identify and focus therapy on the key "psychological concept" to enable the most salient insight; subsequent changes in thoughts and behaviours and their associated shift in mood.
- Seek to convey a simple "mini-formulation" so as to optimize the likelihood of comprehension and retention by your patient. This can be expanded if necessary.

Adapting therapy for people with mild cognitive impairment

- Assess the extent to which this affects the process of therapy and whether there are ways of compensating for the impairment.
- Investigate the extent to which the person's emotional needs are generated by their reaction to the cognitive impairment and work with this.
- Make use of wider systems of support that can provide assistance to the therapeutic process.

Adapting therapy for people with co-morbid physical illness

- Don't be afraid to be explicit about the reality of the physical condition.
- Determine whether the emotional need is driven by unrealistic attributions relating to the illness or the relationship between the illness and their mental state.
- Adopt a "coping with" model of recovery rather than "cure".
- Successful adaptation to chronic illness involves "selection", "optimization" and "compensation".

Ending

- Be explicit about the time-limited nature of therapy from the beginning, and the planned number of sessions, so that ending doesn't come as a surprise
- Look for ways of empowering older people to demonstrate their ability to cope after therapy has ended
- Be aware of your own attributions regarding dependence/independence and how these influence your work.

Acknowledgements

I would like to acknowledge the valuable contributions of my colleagues, Adrienne Little, Debbie Walker, Grace Wong and Becky Gould who collated much of the material covered in this chapter and provided valuable feedback on the manuscript.

References

Almeida, O. P., & Almeida, S. A. (1999). Short versions of the geriatric depression scale: a study of their validity for the diagnosis of a major depressive episode according to ICD-10 and DSM-IV. *International Journal of Geriatric Psychiatry, 14*(10), 858–865.

Baltes, P. B. (1991). The many faces of human aging: toward a psychological culture of old age. *Psychological Medicine, 21*, 837–854.

Baltes, P. B., & Baltes, M. M. (1990). Psychological perspectives on successful aging: The model of selective optimization with compensation. In P. B. Baltes & M. M. Baltes (Eds.), *Successful aging: perspectives from the behavioral sciences* (pp. 1–34). New York: Cambridge University Press.

Barkham, M., Culverwell, A., Spindler, K., Twigg, E., & Connell, J. (2005). The CORE-OM in an older adult population: psychometric status, acceptability, and feasibility. *Aging and Mental Health, 9*, 235–245.

Beck, A. T. (1976). *Cognitive therapy and the emotional disorders*. New York: International Universities Press.

Beck, A. T., Rush, A. J., Shaw, B. F., & Emery, G. (1979). *Cognitive therapy of depression*. New York: Guildford Press.

Brenes, G. A. (2006). Age differences in the presentation of anxiety. *Aging & Mental Health, 10*(3), 298–302.

Burns, D. A., & Beck, A. T. (1978). Cognitive behaviour modification of mood disorders. In J. P. Foreyt & D. P. Rathjen (Eds.), *Cognitive behavior therapy: Research and application* (pp. 109–134). New York: Plenum.

Byrne, G. J., & Pachana, N. A. (2010). Development and validation of a short form of the Geriatric Anxiety Inventory – the GAI-SF. *International Psychogeriatrics, 18*, 1–7.

Charlesworth, G., & Greenfield, S. (2004). Overcoming barriers to collaborative conceptualisation in cognitive therapy with older adults. *Behavioural and Cognitive Psychotherapy, 32*,411–422.

Charlesworth, G. M., & Reichelt, F. K. (2004). Keeping conceptualisations simple: examples with family carers of people with dementia. *Behavioural and Cognitive Psychotherapy, 32*, 401–409.

Chew-Graham, C., Burns, A., & Baldwin, R. (2004). Treating depression in later life: we need to implement the evidence that exists. *British Medical Journal, 329*: 181–182.

Covin, R., Ouimet, A. J., Seeds, P. M., & Dozois, D. J. (2008). A meta-analysis of CBT for pathological worry among clients with GAD. *Journal of Anxiety Disorders, 22*(1), 108–116.

Craig, R., & Mindell, J. (Eds.). (2007). *Health survey for England 2005: health of older people*. Leeds: NHS Information Centre.

Dennis. R. E., Boddington, S. J. A., & Funnell, N. J. (2007). Self-report measures of anxiety: are they suitable for older adults? *Ageing & Mental Health, 11*, (6), 668–677.

Department of Health (2011). No health without mental health: a cross-government mental health outcomes strategy for people of all ages. Retrieved from: http://www.dh.gov.uk/prod_consum_dh/groups/dh_digitalassets/documents/digitalasset/dh_124058.pdf

Dick, L. P., Gallagher-Thompson, D., & Thompson, L. W. (1996). Cognitive -behavioural therapy. In R. T. Woods (Ed.), *Handbook of the clinical psychology of aging* (pp. 509–544). Chichester: John Wiley & Sons.

Freud, S. (1905). *On psychotherapy* (Standard ed., Vol. 7). London: Hogarth Press.

Gatz, M., Fiske, A., Fox, L. S., Kaskie, B., Kasl-Godley, J. E., McCallum, T. J., & Wetherell, J. L. (1998). Empirically validated psychological treatments for older adults. *Journal of Mental Health and Aging, 4*(1), 9–46.

Gilbert, P. (1994). *Counselling for depression*. London: Sage

Gonçalves, D. C., & Byrne, G. J. (2012). Who worries most? Worry prevalence and patterns across the lifespan. *International Journal of Geriatric Psychiatry, 28*(1): 41–49.

Gould, R. L. Coulson, M. C., & Howard, R. J. (2012a). Cognitive behavioral therapy for depression in older people: a meta-analysis and meta-regression of randomized controlled trials. *Journal of the American Geriatrics Society, 60*(10), 1817–1830.

Gould, R. L. Coulson, M. C., & Howard, R. J. (2012b). Efficacy of cognitive behavioral therapy for anxiety disorders in older people: a meta-analysis and meta-regression of randomized controlled trials. *Journal of American Geriatrics Society, 60*(2), 218–229.

Grant, R. W., & Casey, D. A. (1995). Adapting cognitive behavioral therapy for the frail elderly. *International Psychogeriatrics, 7*, 561–571.

Gum, A. M., Arean, P. A., Hunkeler, E., Tang, L., Katon, W., Hitchcock, P., … Unutzer, J. (2006). Depression treatment preferences in older primary care patients. *The Gerontologist, 46*(1), 14–22.

Hanson, A. E., & Scogin, F. (2008). Older adults' acceptance of psychological, pharmacological, and combination treatments for geriatric depression. *The Journals of Gerontology, 63*(4), P245–P248.

James, I. A. (1999). Using a cognitive rationale to conceptualize anxiety in people with dementia. *Behavioural and Cognitive Psychotherapy, 27*, 345–351.

James, I. A. (2008). Stuff and nonsense in treatment of older people: essential reading for the over-45s. *Behavioural and Cognitive Psychotherapy, 38*, 735–747.

Laidlaw, K., Thompson, L. W., & Gallagher-Thompson, D. (2004). Comprehensive conceptualisation of cognitive behaviour therapy for late life depression. *Behavioural and cognitive psychotherapy, 32*, 389–399.

Laidlaw, K., Thompson, L. W., Gallagher-Thompson, D., & Dick-Siskin, L. (2003). *Cognitive behaviour therapy with older people*. Chichester: John Wiley & Sons.

Lynch, D., Laws, K. R., & McKenna, P. J. (2010). Cognitive behavioural therapy for major psychiatric disorder: does it really work? A meta-analytical review of well controlled trials. *Psychological Medicine, 40*, 9–24.

McManus, S., Meltzer, H., Brugha, T., Bebbington, P., & Jenkins, R. (2009). *Adult psychiatric morbidity in England. 2007: results of a household survey*. NHS Information Centre for Health and Social Care. Retrieved from http://www.ic.nhs.uk/pubs/psychiatricmorbidity07

Minshull, P. (2007). *Age equality: what does it mean for older peoples' mental health services?* Sutton, UK: Care Services Improvement Partnership.

Office for National Statistics (2011). Life expectancy at birth and at age 65 by local areas in the United Kingdom, 2004–06 to 2008–10. Retrieved from http://www.ons.gov.uk/ons/dcp171778_238743.pdf

Pachana, N. A., Byrne, G. J. A., Siddle, H., Koloski, N., Harley, E., & Arnold, E. (2007). Development and validation of the Geriatric Anxiety Inventory. *International Psychogeriatrics, 19*(1), 103–114.

Padesky, C. A., & Greenberger, D. (1995). *Mind over mood: change how you feel by changing the way you think*. New York: Guilford Press.

Pinquart, M., Duberstein, P. R., & Lyness, J. M. (2007). Effects of psychotherapy and other behavioral interventions on clinically depressed older adults: A meta-analysis. *Aging and Mental Health, 11*(6), 645–657.

Secker, D. L., Kazantzis, N., & Pachana, N. A. (2004). Cognitive behaviour therapy for older adults: practical guidelines for adapting therapy structure. *Journal of Rational-Emotive & Cognitive-Behavior Therapy, 22*, 93–109.

Segal, Z. D., Swallow, S. R., Bizzini, L. and Rouget, B. W. (1995). How we assess for short-term cognitive behaviour therapy. In C. Mace (Ed.), *The art and science of assessment in psychotherapy* (pp. 102–116). London: Routledge.

Sheikh, J. I., & Yesavage, J. A. (1986). Geriatric depression scale (GDS): Recent evidence and development of a shorter version. In T. L. Brink (Ed.), *Clinical gerontology: a guide to assessment and intervention* (pp. 165–173). New York: Haworth Press.

Sperlinger, C. D. (2004). *Measuring psychosocial treatment outcomes with older people*. Leicester: British Psychological Society, CORE.

World Health Organization (1980). *International classification of impairments, disabilities and handicaps: a manual of classification relating to the consequences of disease*. Geneva: World Health Organization. Retrieved from http://whqlibdoc.who.int/publications/1980/9241541261_eng.pdf

Yesavage, J. A., Brink, T. L., Rose, T. L., Lum, O., Huang, V., Adey, M. B., & Leirer, V. O. (1983). Development and validation of a geriatric depression screening scale: a preliminary report. *Journal of Psychiatric Research, 17*, 37–49.

Zigmond, A. S., & Snaith, R. P. (1983). The hospital anxiety and depression scale. *Acta Psychiatrica Scandinavica, 67*(6), 361–370.

15

CBT with People with Intellectual Disabilities

Biza Stenfert Kroese

Introduction

The term "intellectual disability" (also known in the United Kingdom as "learning disability", and formerly as "mental handicap" or "mental retardation") is used to describe a condition of significant impairment of both intellectual ability (usually defined as a Full-Scale IQ below 70) and functional ability, acquired before adulthood (British Psychological Society, 2000).

As a result of methodological problems, especially problems with self-report, the proportion of people with intellectual disabilities (ID) that also have mental health problems is not known. However, there is strong evidence of higher rates of psychological and emotional difficulties. A recent study found that if challenging behaviour and autistic spectrum disorders are included, over 40 per cent of the adult population with ID can be said to have additional mental health needs (Cooper, Smiley, Morrison, Williamson, & Allan, 2007). A number of reasons have been proposed for higher prevalence, which are discussed.

Causes of mental health problems have been linked to the difficulties that people have encountered as a result of their disabilities. For example, being highly dependent on others and having limited opportunities to make choices can prevent people from developing self-esteem, a sense that life is worth living, and an expectation that the future holds interesting and achievable challenges. Meaningful relationships are often lacking and few adults with ID develop the roles of paid worker, consumer, sexual partner or parent in their lifetime (see Figure 15.1) that is, roles that provide most adults with positive experiences, albeit at times stressful. This, together with frequently encountering failure, stigma, prejudice and a lack of competence-enhancing social support, are likely to result in psychological distress and enduring mental health problems (Jahoda, Dagnan, Jarvie, & Kerr, 2006).

As is the case for the rest of the population, trauma and abuse (including physical, sexual, financial and emotional abuse) are also reasons why people with ID may suffer psychological problems, particularly psychotic symptoms such as hearing voices or having

How to Become a More Effective CBT Therapist: Mastering Metacompetence in Clinical Practice,
First Edition. Edited by Adrian Whittington and Nick Grey.
© 2014 John Wiley & Sons, Ltd. Published 2014 by John Wiley & Sons, Ltd.

The Department of Health with Central England People First and Lancaster University (Emerson et al., 2005) carried out a survey of nearly 3,000 adults with a range of ID in England. The results showed that:

- 40 percent said they were bullied at school

- One-third said they did not feel safe in their homes

- 64 percent in supported accommodation had no choice over who they lived with or where

- Half were still living with their parents

- Only 17 percent were in paid work and many of these worked less than 16 hours a week

- Two-thirds who were unemployed said they wanted a job

- 31 percent said they did not have any contact with friends

- One in 15 had children and of these only 52 percent looked after them

- More than half said someone else controlled their money and less than 20 percent received direct payments

Figure 15.1   Risk factors.

chronic delusions (Morrison, Frame, & Larkin, 2003). Rates of abuse are higher in the ID population (because of high dependency on others and difficulties in recognizing and reporting abuse), which may account for the finding that the prevalence rates for the diagnosis of, for example, schizophrenia have been reported to be three times higher than expected (Morgan, Leonard, Bourke, & Jablensky, 2008).

Moreover, people with ID are more likely to be exposed to a number of further social factors that are considered determinants of (general but also mental) health: poverty, poor housing, unemployment, social exclusion and overt discrimination (Emerson & Hatton, 2007).

Many people with *severe* ID are said to show challenging behaviour with an age-specific prevalence peak of between 20 and 49 years (Emerson et al., 2001). Causes associated with challenging behaviour include environmental, psychological, specific genetic factors and in some cases physical pain due to untreated medical disorders (e.g., Kwok & Cheung, 2007). When people have limited ability to express themselves (and therefore struggle to report feelings and thoughts) it is difficult to distinguish between mental illness and challenging behaviour, as clinicians may not be able to establish what the underlying psychological experiences are that are causing the observed challenging behaviours.

Efforts to reduce the psychological distress experienced by people with ID must consider the quality of current services and how they can best provide prevention, early intervention and good crisis management. Also, as most adults with ID are likely to spend large amounts of time in service settings and in contact with paid support workers and other service providers whose input and interventions can help or hinder recovery, the quality of services and staff expertise is vital in determining the impact of service users' mental health problems on them and those around them.

The traditional model of service provision was a medical one where people with ID (whether they had mental health problems or not) were considered to be lifelong patients, best placed in long-stay hospitals, cared for by medical and nursing staff (e.g., Stenfert Kroese & Holmes, 2001). More recently, community care is considered to be a more acceptable and effective model of support and many adults with ID, including those with mental health problems who now live in integrated settings. Social role valorization as a service objective (Wolfensberger, 1998) has had a major influence and has made commissioners and providers consider ways in which to help people who are at risk of being labelled, devalued and excluded, achieve "valued roles" in their families and communities, so as to improve their living conditions and thus their psychological well-being.

However, services for adults with ID are still said to be lacking in both quantity and quality. Despite a more holistic and social approach being adopted by most services, to this day psychotropic medication is a common first choice response to psychological distress and challenging behaviour. A high proportion of adults are prescribed such drugs (which may have considerable harmful side-effects), often without a specific diagnosis and no evidence for their effectiveness (e.g., Stenfert Kroese, Dewhurst, & Holmes, 2001). Recently produced UK guidelines (Unwin & Deb, 2010) for prescribing and reviewing psychotropic medication for people with ID and challenging behaviour may help to improve this situation.

Talking therapies, especially CBT, which are now the treatment of choice for many mental health problems in the general population, are rarely accessible to adults with ID although there has been a recent trend for (the few) mental health clinicians working with people with ID to incorporate adapted versions of CBT and other psychotherapies and counselling approaches into their clinical practice. There is growing evidence that these treatments are both effective (Willner & Hatton, 2006) and highly valued by service users and their carers (Pert et al., 2013; Stenfert Kroese et al., 2014). One user's view of CBT was: "I talk about it more now and I feel a lot better, relaxed. I feel this great big weight come off my shoulders and I feel thingy, and that weight can stay away altogether and I feel a lot better" (Pert et al., 2013).

That few people with ID are in receipt of talking therapies may also be due to a lack of training received by staff working in ID services on mental health and likewise the lack of knowledge and experience mental health workers have of ID (Stenfert Kroese & Rose, 2011). Although the majority of professional and support staff working in ID services come in regular contact with service users who have mental health problems, a minority receive training in this complex area (Rose, Rose, & Kent, 2012) yet evidence indicates that even brief training can increase confidence, attitudes and working practices in staff (Costello, Bouras, & Davies, 2007). It is important that "front line" workers are able to recognize the symptoms of mental illness and have the confidence to refer to specialist services such as CBT when needed, as often service users themselves do not have the ability or opportunity to self-refer.

Evidence of CBT Efficacy for Adults with ID

The necessary research on effectiveness of psychological therapies for this population is still in its infancy. It is only recently that CBT has been adapted for people with intellectual disabilities and outcome studies have been conducted. Nevertheless, there is a relatively large case-study literature describing successful outcomes for CBT in a variety of mental disorders (Taylor, Lindsay, & Willner, 2008). Case studies have shown that depression (McCabe, McGillivray, & Newton, 2006), anxiety (Lindsay, Neilson, & Lawrenson, 1997) and PTSD (Stenfert Kroese and Thomas, 2006) can be successfully treated, and evidence from controlled trials has recently started emerging. The most recent of these (Willner et al., 2013) employed a cluster-randomized controlled trial (RCT) of a 12-week group-based CBT anger management intervention, delivered by staff ("lay therapists") working in the service settings where the intervention was delivered. Participants were 179 service users with mild to moderate ID, identified as having problems with anger control. They attended 30 services, which were randomly assigned either to anger management groups or to support-as-usual. Before randomization, four months and ten months post-intervention, service users, their key-workers, and their home carers completed a battery of anger, anger coping, challenging behaviour, and mental health assessments.

Although the intervention had only a small and non-significant effect on participants' reports on a provocation inventory (the primary outcome measure), staff ratings of service users' anger decreased significantly, as did service-users' ratings on a more personally meaningful anger measure. Both service users and staff reported significant increases in clients' anger coping skills, and both staff and home carers reported significant decreases in challenging behaviour. The intervention did not have a significant impact on mental health measures. This study provides the first evidence from a robust RCT for the effectiveness of a CBT intervention for people with intellectual disabilities.

In addition to CBT outcomes studies, recent research has addressed CBT process issues (Jahoda et al., 2009). Verbatim transcripts of therapy sessions of 15 clients with borderline to mild ID were coded using an initiative-response method of analysing power distribution in dialogue, to investigate collaboration at the level of therapeutic interaction. The results indicate that power was relatively equally distributed between clients and therapists. Analyses of the pattern of interaction showed that while the therapists asked most questions, the clients contributed to the flow of the analysis and played an active part in dialogues, suggesting that clients with ID adopted a collaborative rather than a passive role in the therapeutic process.

There remains, however, scepticism that the cognitive components (as opposed to solely the behavioural ones) are the active ingredients of CBT as applied to adults with ID (e.g., Sturmey, 2004). A deficit model of psychological distress is most commonly employed as opposed to a distortion model. Deficit models involve consideration of problems with language, memory, attention and other meta-cognitive processes. Harchick, Sherman, and Sheldon (1992) reviewed 59 studies that used self-management techniques for people with ID. Nine of these studies aimed to reduce challenging behaviour and 50 aimed to increase social skills or performance in academic or work settings. Few of these studies considered or treated cognitive distortions or mentioned collaborative relationships between clients and therapists or the psychological well-being of the client, focusing instead on self- monitoring, self-control and contingency management of adaptive and maladaptive behaviours, with aims largely determined by the therapists.

Distortion models as proposed by Beck (1974) and Ellis (2004) suggest a form of CBT that assumes that a person's reaction to an event is influenced by the *meaning they attach to the event*. Emotional and behavioural responses are assumed to be a function of how an event is perceived and recalled, the attributions that are made about its causes, and the way in which the event affects self-perception.

Although CBT distortion models of psychological distress are now more widely applied by ID specialists, we have as yet no evidence that the techniques designed to identify and address dysfunctional beliefs are the effective ingredient in the intervention.

Recent qualitative studies of clients' with ID experiences and recall of group (McMahon et al., in preparation) and individual therapy (Pert et al., 2013) sessions indicate that what was most positively considered by the majority of participants, focussed on social and process issues rather than specific CBT intervention models or techniques applied. Participants especially appreciated opportunities to develop their relationships with the therapists and (in the case of group therapy) other group members. They also reported their appreciation of opportunities to talk and be listened to and to be treated as an equal and an adult, indicating that the therapeutic alliance (Bordin, 1994) and the relationships established are important potential vehicles for therapeutic change in CBT interventions for adults with ID.

These qualitative studies also found that participants reported on newly acquired knowledge and described use of newly acquired skills, suggesting that in addition to process issues, the content of the therapy also influenced psychological change. Interestingly, in both studies none of the participants reported using cognitive strategies, focusing instead on behavioural strategies, such as "walking away" and "asking for help". It remains to be determined whether this reflects the participants' limited abilities to comprehend and utilize these more complex cognitive strategies, their ability to recall and report them during the research interview, the ability of the therapists in delivering these more abstract components of the therapy, or some interaction between these factors. How much the component parts of a CBT intervention contribute to outcome must be further investigated.

Adapting CBT for Adults with ID

One of the main considerations when adapting CBT for people with ID is this client group's limited ability to generalize and maintain the techniques learned in the therapy sessions. This constitutes a challenge partly due to a well-recognized cognitive deficit associated with ID, namely self-regulation (Whitman, 1990) but also due to a lack of autonomy and opportunities to make one's own decisions and take control of one's lifestyle and routines (e.g., Stenfert Kroese & Holmes, 2001). Moreover, sole focus on individual cognitions fails to acknowledge the importance of social factors that influence and provide context for people's perceptions of themselves and their world (Dagnan, Jahoda, & Stenfert Kroese, 2007). The following sections consider how CBT can be adapted to become accessible and meaningful for people with ID, taking account of their cognitive limitations as well as their particular social position and status, typified by a lack of power and autonomy.

Assessment

When first meeting a person with an ID it takes time to gauge the level of their cognitive functioning as well as their communication and functional skills. These can only be established after the therapist has engaged the client in conversation. Even then, it is easy to under- or over-estimate ability levels. It is not unusual for people with even severe ID to have unexpected "pockets of excellence". Examples from my own clinical practice are:

- A young woman with Down's syndrome with limited functional skills and unclear speech had a clear insight into her problems and being surprisingly psychologically minded to the extent that she spontaneously presented an almost complete formulation of her PTSD symptoms including activating events and negative automatic thoughts.

- A middle-aged man who had spent most of his life in large institutions had an excellent long-term memory. He was able to remember names, numbers, addresses, telephone numbers and other factual details of many years ago.
- A young mother whose child had recently been taken into care was a competent dancer with an extensive knowledge of the ballet world.

Other examples include musical or mathematical talents, good social skills and/or an ability to pick up on other people's moods and (unexpressed) inter-personal conflict, knowledge of birds or other specialist subjects and advanced levels of performance on computer games. It is important to recognize that IQ tests such as the WAIS IV (Wechsler, 2008) do not measure many such skills and talents and during informal conversations other cognitive deficits may "overshadow" a person's strengths. In the context of the therapeutic environment it is particularly relevant to acknowledge that cognitive intelligence (IQ) is not correlated with emotional intelligence (Goleman, 1998).

On the other hand, it is also possible to over-estimate a person's ability and this can occur when clients have reasonable communication and social skills. They may have learned to "cover up" their lack of comprehension and understanding by using stock phrases such as "Yes, you're right" or "I'm not bothered" when asked a closed question (i.e., a question that demands a "yes" or "no" answer). A lack of understanding will most likely lead to high levels of acquiescence, making the assessment process invalid and therefore useless.

It is not practical to assess every aspect of a person's cognitive, functional and emotional repertoire before CBT is embarked on but it may be helpful for the therapist to have a mental checklist that includes some of the most relevant aspects of a person's functioning, such as:

- limits of attention span;
- limits of verbal expression and comprehension;
- limits of memory;
- ability to project self into past or future;
- ability to conceptualize abstract concepts such as death, dreams, illness etc.;
- emotional awareness/expression;
- experience and confidence in expressing self: self-reporting, giving opinions, making decisions;
- ability to self-regulate (applying new skills in daily life);
- an understanding of the therapeutic relationship;
- motivation to engage in therapy (may be low if referred by others);
- ability to trust the therapist (previous experiences may have been disappointing and/or abusive); and
- unidentified sensory deficits (hearing and sight problems often unrecognized having been "overshadowed" by ID).

There are a number of formal assessments that can be applied to assess some of these items listed above. For example, a standardized assessment by Reid and Clements (1989) uses simple illustrated scenarios to test emotional awareness ("You take your dog for a walk, it runs away. Do you feel happy or sad?"). To assess the ability to identify mediating cognitions, Dagnan, Chadwick, and Proudlove, (2000) developed an assessment based on simple scenarios and an associated emotion. For example, "Chloe walks into a room where there are a group of her friends. As she walks in they start to laugh. She feels sad." The person is asked to suggest what they would be "thinking or saying to themselves". The same scenario can then be presented at a later stage with a different emotion. The degree to which clients are able to alter their response in order to accommodate the different emotion is an indication of how well they are able to use a cognitive model.

This type of assessment allows the therapist to adjust the therapy to match their clients' cognitive and emotional skills and identify areas where pre-therapy didactic input may be required, for example, helping people to recognize certain emotions by teaching them to label a number of emotional states either verbally or with a sign or a picture.

Session content and structure

Adults with ID are frequently referred and taken to therapy without sufficient explanation of the therapeutic process to give informed consent. In order to develop a collaborative relationship, it is important that from the start the therapist involves the client in decision making and whether or not they attend is surely one of the most important decisions that is to be made. In order to help people decide whether they want to engage in psychological therapy we have developed and implemented a video information pack that presents a brief description of what is involved in therapy in order to provide potential clients with accessible information to allow them to make an informed choice.

Such a video has been found to significantly improve knowledge and understanding (Dunn, Stenfert Kroese, Thomas, McGarry, and Drew, 2006) and, although leaflets may serve the same function, we found that a video provides more detailed and more memorable information.

One of the most challenging aspects of CBT for people with ID is helping them understand the cognitive mediation model. The way to assess a person's understanding of this model is already described above (Dagnan et al., 2000). These authors stress that a substantial proportion of clients with ID without a grasp of this model may be referred for CBT. This does not mean that they cannot be taught and there are many opportunities during sessions to illustrate the importance of cognitive mediation. Different emotions can be identified that are experienced on different occasions and examining why emotional responses are not always the same constitutes a useful way of reinforcing the cognitive model. Basing these explanations on real and recently experienced events is particularly important for clients with ID who may struggle with hypothetical and /or abstract examples. Discussing thoughts and emotions that occur in everyday life will also allow the therapist to understand the personal meaning that their clients attach to particular events. It is important that this process is active and engaging and role-plays, drawings of matchstick people with speech bubbles, and film clips of "soaps" can all be employed to make it so.

Not all people with ID will be able to understand the concepts of cognition and thought and may struggle to differentiate thoughts from feelings (e.g., *T*: "What were you feeling?", *C*: "Very, very angry", *T*: "What were you thinking?", *C*: "I was thinking I'm very, very angry!"). However, people use specific (albeit limited) vocabularies to describe past events and the world they live in. Their use of language will give the therapist many clues as to personal meaning, evaluations, thoughts and beliefs held. Similar to the techniques employed in qualitative research methodology (e.g., McLeod, 2011), the therapist can scrutinize the language employed to deduct underlying meaning, automatic thoughts and assumptions that can then be fed back to the client in order to check whether the hypotheses made can be verified. In order to do this, closed questions must be avoided, as acquiescence can be a problem. Instead, techniques such as sentence completion or multiple-choice tasks can be used. With the latter, one or two of the options should be unlikely and/or humorous in order to assess whether the client has understood the options and the task, and is not making a random choice. For example: I get very upset when my parents go out without me because:

- I want them to spend more time with me.
- They always get into trouble when I'm not there to look after them.
- I worry they may not come back.
- They may get lost.

There is a substantial body of evidence that people with ID have particular problems with the identification of emotions (e.g., Wood and Stenfert Kroese, 2007) and for CBT to be effective it is important that clients are able to distinguish between at least the most basic emotions such as sadness, happiness, anger, anxiety and fear. There are standardized materials available to assess types of errors made and levels of ability. However, the use of non-standardized materials can also be useful, particularly when working to engage and motivate clients; using materials that include their role models and/or people they are familiar with (such as members of staff) is likely to have a greater impact and be better understood and recalled.

Most mainstream therapists depend exclusively on verbal communication and it is important with this client group to have a wider focus and consider other media to explain and prompt. For example, after many group sessions on assertiveness during which we failed to explain the component parts of assertiveness, or at least failed to explain it in such a way that people were able to remember and put them into practice, we used "hand signals" for staying calm, feeling good about yourself, listening to other people and speaking up for yourself. This had an immediate impact not only on recall but also on the ability to implement the techniques in real life (Winchurst, Stenfert Kroese, & Adams, 1992).

Use of role-play can make it easier to access cognitions and feelings especially when the therapist takes the client's part and asks the client to "direct the scene" and explain the incident in as much detail as possible. In group work various group members and co-therapists can take on acting roles and become "co-directors", "producers" or "stage hands" in order to involve everyone in the role-play. Seeing a therapist act angry or out of control is not only amusing for clients (e.g., "See, when (therapist) was getting angry, I thought he was getting angry at us but he wasnae, it's just 'cause he was acting (…) you felt a wee bit scared, you were like that, Oh no … he's gonna hit me … aahhh!"; McMahon et al., in preparation) but can also make a lasting impression which can "normalize" difficult feelings and make clients aware that everyone has to cope with frustration and disappointment in their daily life. Subsequently re-playing the scene but with an agreed adaptive way of responding and with the main actor "thinking aloud", can give insight into the cognitive model (i.e., illustrating that how we think can determine how we behave and feel) and the value of more functional ways of thinking and responding.

Planning sessions, setting agendas, eliciting feedback and reviewing previous sessions are all essential parts of standard CBT protocols. They become even more important for clients with ID as they will reduce fear of the unknown (and of failure), increase confidence, understanding and memory, and facilitate an equal, collaborative partnership between client and therapist. In addition, using resultant notes and records during clinical supervision will facilitate insight into why sessions may have failed to engage the client and/or move the therapeutic process forward or, on the other hand, have been helpful and productive.

Providing clients with accessible summaries of sessions allows them to review and recall essential components. Summaries can be in the form of drawings, diagrams, cartoons or digital photos. I have also found that a recording of "an ending interview" serves this purpose, as well as constituting a clear and enjoyable final task that can be planned and executed by the client and the therapist as equal collaborators. If the client agrees, sharing the recording can also be a useful way of explaining a formulation to other significant people who thus can be encouraged to support the client in generalizing and maintaining their progress in everyday life.

Some people with ID may be sensitive to what they consider childish, patronizing approaches and it is therefore important not to use language or illustrations taken from resources designed for children. Some clients may consider even a term such as "homework" age-inappropriate and frequent checking that they are comfortable with terms and expressions and negotiating a shared vocabulary of terms used in session is advisable.

A number of extra measures are required to ensure that people will engage with tasks between sessions as many people with ID have memory, attention and self-regulatory deficits to cope with, as well as a lack of control and autonomy. These potential barriers must be dealt with in addition to those typically encountered by most mainstream clients, such as having to find motivation to prioritize new repertoires and change long-standing habits. For example, it is important to adapt diaries and charts to people's literacy and numeracy skill levels and to personalize them in a way that they not only understand the measure, but also are motivated to complete it regularly. In many cases, it will be helpful to recruit a friend or supporter who is willing and able to prompt the client to complete the task or the diary. However, issues of confidentiality and boundaries that are raised by this will need to be considered carefully with the client.

The therapist will need to be prepared to be flexible in planning the frequency, number, length and venue of the sessions as some clients will not be able to cope with the "standard package" and may require, for example, more but shorter sessions, planned closely together in time to cater for attention span, rate of learning and other cognitive deficits. Transport to the venue can be a problem if people are not able to travel alone and they depend on others. It is therefore essential that the latter are convinced of the importance of the therapy and for this the therapist needs to spend time and effort to get carers and support workers "on board".

Home visits to conduct therapy sessions are not recommended as the home environment is too distracting for both client and therapist and confidentiality cannot always be assured when family members, friends or staff are present.

Case Study: Jim

Jim, a man in his 40s with moderate ID living with his brother Martin, was referred five months after an unprovoked attack as he walked home from the bus stop. He suffered multiple injuries and spent some time in hospital. At the time of referral he suffered sleep loss, loss of appetite and did not want to leave the house on his own.

Prior to the attack Jim worked four days a week at a local sports club. He spent his free time at the local pub, where he had many acquaintances. Although after the attack he still worked and socialized, Jim often had to be cajoled into going out and frequently complained he did not feel well enough. He would only go out if another person agreed to take and fetch him.

Jim reported symptoms of post-traumatic stress disorder (PTSD) including intrusive images, increased arousal symptoms and avoidance behaviours. He suffered nightmares and would often wake up finding it difficult to breathe. He also mentioned that thoughts and questions about the attack would enter his head frequently. He was particularly puzzled why one of his attackers had called him "mate" before hitting him ("Why did he call me mate if he was going to hurt me? Mates don't do that"). He was also confused about having gaps in his memory due to losing and regaining consciousness during and after the attack.

Jim was aware that Martin found it difficult to talk about the attack as he also reported to have been severely traumatized by the events that took place near their home; Martin had been called to the scene while Jim was still on the ground and bleeding profusely. Jim therefore had stopped talking to Martin about his own upsetting thoughts and feelings and felt that he had to protect his brother from further distress.

In Ehlers and Clark's (2000) model PTSD develops when people process trauma in a way that leads to a sense of serious, current threat. Sense of threat is influenced by excessively negative appraisals of the trauma itself and the consequences of the trauma. The nature of the trauma memory is also implicated in that if a person has a poorly elaborated and contextualized memory they are more likely to experience PTSD. McNally and Shin (1995) found that people with low intellectual ability process memories in terms of sensory impressions rather than processing the meaning and context of the event. They propose this as an explanation for the higher incidence of PTSD in this group. Jim's account of his trauma memory indicates that he indeed lacked the ability and opportunity for conceptual processing due to his ID, his intermittent loss of consciousness after the attack (and the resultant confusion caused by these gaps in his memory), and his reluctance to ask a vital informant, his brother Martin, to explain the meaning and context of the event and to make sense of some of the physical sensations he experienced during the assault.

The intervention consisted of simple relaxation training, education and normalization of the physical sensations and injuries (based on the reported intrusive questions that he reported), Imagery Rehearsal Therapy (Krakow & Zadra, 2006) for the nightmares and flashbacks and "Keeping Safe" training and facilitating agreements with family and carers about safe travel arrangements. The latter part of the intervention was most challenging as Jim had been a deliberately selected victim by his assailants, who (on bail) remained at large in the local area. Jim's perception of threat was, therefore, based on a functional assumption and it would have been potentially dangerous to attempt to modify his avoidance behaviours.

Jim received a total of 16 weekly sessions and throughout completed illustrated recording forms (that did not require writing but only ticks to complete) on a daily basis to assess the extent of his intrusive thoughts and nightmares. Although he had limited reading ability, he demonstrated that he was able to use the forms by determining the days of the week by sequential order, and severity of symptoms and day/night by the symbols provided.

In addition to a daily diary, adapted versions of the Hospital Anxiety and Depression Scale (HADS; Zigmond & Snaith, 1983) and the Impact of Event Scale–Revised (IES-R; Weiss & Marmar, 1997) were completed using an illustrated four-point scale after establishing that Jim was able to use such a scale (asking him to rate favourite and least favourite foods and repeating this to gauge test–retest reliability). All items were read out and expanded upon if the meaning was not immediately clear to him. He completed these measures with the therapist's support at baseline, after 16 sessions and during a four-week follow-up session.

The repeat measures indicate that Jim's self-reported HADS anxiety score reduced from a score of 15 (severe) to 6 (normal) and that his "Intrusion" score on the IES-R reduced from 27 to 14. His "Avoidance" score on the same measure, however, remained stable (11 before and after intervention), which is in accordance with the observation that the threat of further attack remained real and that avoidance was an adaptive response in this context.

His diary recordings which were kept by Jim for 20 weeks in total (four weeks baseline, 12 weeks intervention and four weeks follow-up) indicate a decrease in frequency of PTSD symptoms: during baseline intrusive images occurred on average more than three times per week, post-intervention this dropped to less than once a week. Nightmares occurred on average more than five times a week and this also dropped to less than once a week.

At the end of the intervention a review letter summarizing the formulation and techniques covered in therapy (as well as an audio-taped copy of this letter) were presented to Jim and (with Jim's consent) to his brother.

Jim reported feeling "a lot better" but still pre-occupied with the danger of a repeat attack. Considering the circumstances this was not a dysfunctional pre-occupation and part of the intervention was to liaise with other people involved in Jim's life to put practical measures in place to ensure his safety and reduce his anxiety levels, rather than cognitive restructuring which was not considered to be ethically or clinically justified.

Summary and Conclusions

This case study illustrates a typical clinical intervention that utilizes adapted CBT approaches in order to cater for specific cognitive deficits. It provides evidence that adults with ID can achieve real cognitive and behavioural changes and that self-report and diary recordings can provide insight into the problems and can function as outcome measures.

There is now a sufficient evidence base to justify clinicians devoting clinical time to adapting and applying CBT for people with learning disabilities with a wide range of psychological problems. Although time and enthusiasm are needed to adapt or design appropriate measures and approaches, and the formulation of the problems may rely on third party as well as self-report, productive therapeutic relationships can be established and positive outcomes can be achieved and maintained, provided the clients can depend on long-term support from informed and committed others.

Procedural Rules

- Consider the specific psychological impact of having an ID, including vulnerability to abuse, reduced opportunities for developing positive self-esteem and meaningful relationships, and lack of power and autonomy.
- Invest time and effort in assessing cognitive, psychological and social strengths and deficits before therapy is planned and commenced.
- Language and materials used must be accessible but also age appropriate for the client.
- Establish motivation to engage in therapy by making sure the client is provided with sufficient information to give informed consent.
- Not all clients with ID will understand the cognitive model. This can be assessed and if necessary taught during therapy sessions.
- Emotion recognition and expression may also need to be assessed and taught in order for the client to be able to engage in therapy.
- The therapist can use the language used by clients to gain insight into the personal meaning, evaluations, thoughts and beliefs held.
- Non-verbal media can be employed when the client's verbal comprehension, memory and expression are limited.
- Session planning must consider the particular cognitive limitations of the client such as short sessions for someone with a short attention span.
- To achieve maintenance and generalization the therapist needs to consider involving other people who may be able to support and encourage the client in between sessions and after therapy has ended.
- When others are involved in the therapeutic process, their motivation and understanding needs to be assessed and issues of confidentiality and boundaries must be negotiated with the client.

References

Beck, A. T. (1974). The development of depression: a cognitive model. In R. F. Friedman & M. M. Katz (Eds.), *The psychology of depression* (pp. 3–27). New York: John Wiley & Sons.

Bordin, E. S. (1994). Theory and research on the therapeutic working alliance: new directions. In A. O. Horvarth & L. S. Greenberg (Eds.), *The working alliance: theory, research and practice* (pp. 13–37). New York: John Wiley & Sons.

British Psychological Society (2000). *Learning disability: definitions and contexts*. Leicester: British Psychological Society.

Cooper, S. A., Smiley, E., Morrison, J., Williamson, A., & Allan, L. (2007). Mental ill-health in adults with intellectual disabilities: prevalence and associated factors. *British Journal of Psychiatry, 190*, 27–35.

Costello, H., Bouras, N., & Davies, H. (2007). The role of training in improving community care staff awareness of mental health problems in people with intellectual disabilities. *Journal of Applied Research in Intellectual Disabilities, 20*(3), 228–235.

Dagnan, D., Chadwick, P., & Proudlove, J. (2000). Towards an assessment of suitability of people with mental retardation for cognitive therapy. *Cognitive Therapy and Research, 24*, 627–636.

Dagnan, D., Jahoda, A., & Stenfert Kroese, B. (2007). Cognitive behaviour therapy. In A. Carr, G. O'Reilly, P. Noonan Walsh, & J. McEvoy (Eds.), *The Handbook of Intellectual Disability and Clinical Psychology Practice* (pp. 281–299). London: Routledge.

Dunn, A., Stenfert Kroese, B., Thomas, G., McGarry, A., & Drew, P. (2006). "Are you allowed to say that?" Using video materials to provide accessible information about psychology services. *British Journal of Learning Disabilities, 34*, 215–219.

Ehlers, A., & Clark, D. M. (2000). A cognitive model of posttraumatic stress disorder. *Behaviour Research and Therapy, 38*, 319–345.

Ellis, A. (2004). *Rational emotive behavior therapy: it works for me it can work for you*. New York: Prometheus.

Emerson, E., Malam, S., Davies, I., & Spencer, K. (2005). *Adults with Learning Difficulties in England 2003/4 Survey*. Retrieved from http://webarchive.nationalarchives.gov.uk/+/www.dh.gov.uk/en/publicationsandstatistics/publications/publicationsstatistics/dh_4120033

Emerson, E., & Hatton, C. (2007). The mental health of children and adolescents with intellectual disabilities in Britain. *British Journal of Psychiatry, 191*, 493–499.

Emerson, E., Kiernan, C., Alborz, A., Reeves, D., Mason, H., Swarbrick, R., ... Hatton, C. (2001). The prevalence of challenging behaviors: a total population study. *Research in Developmental Disabilities, 22*(1), 77–93.

Goleman, D. (1998). *Working with emotional intelligence*. New York: Bantam Books.

Harchik, A. E., Sherman, J. A., & Sheldon, J. B. (1992). The use of self-management procedures by people with developmental disabilities: A brief review. *Research in Developmental Disabilities, 13*, 211–227.

Jahoda, A., Dagnan, D., Jarvie, P., & Kerr, W. (2006). Depression, social context and cognitive behavioural therapy for people who have intellectual disabilities. *Journal of Applied Research in Intellectual Disabilities, 19*, 81–89.

Jahoda, A., Selkirk, M., Trower, P., Pert, C., Stenfert Kroese, B., Dagnan, D., & Burford, B. (2009). The balance of power in therapeutic interactions with individuals who have intellectual disabilities. *British Journal of Clinical Psychology, 48*, 63–77.

Krakow, B., & Zadra, A. (2006). Clinical management of chronic nightmares: imagery rehearsal therapy. *Behavioral Sleep Medicine, 4*(1), 45–70.

Kwok, H., & Cheung, P. W. H. (2007). Comorbidity of psychiatric disorder and medical illness in people with intellectual disabilities. *Current Opinion in Psychiatry, 20*, 443–449.

Lindsay, W. R., Neilson, C., & Lawrenson, H. (1997). Cognitive behaviour therapy for anxiety in people with learning disabilities. In B. Stenfert Kroese, D. Dagnan and K. Loumidid (Eds.), *Cognitive behaviour therapy for people with learning disabilities* (pp. 128–144). London: Routledge.

McCabe, M. P., McGillivray, J. A., & Newton, D. C. (2006). Effectiveness of treatment programmes for depression among adults with mild/moderate intellectual disability. *Journal of Intellectual Disability Research, 50*(4), 239–247.

McLeod, J. (2011). *Qualitative research in counselling and psychotherapy*. London: Sage.

McMahon, P., Stenfert Kroese, B., Stimpson, A., Rose, N., Jahoda, A., Rose, J. L., & Willner, P. (in preparation). "I'm in control" – The experiences of service users in a group-based cognitive behavioural therapy anger management intervention for adults with intellectual disabilities.

McNally, R., & Shin, L. (1995). Association of intelligence with severity of posttraumatic stress disorder symptoms in Vietnam combat veterans. *American Journal of Psychiatry, 152*, 936–938.

Morgan, V. A., Leonard, H., Bourke, J., & Jablensky, A. (2008). Intellectual disability co-occurring with schizophrenia and other psychiatric illness: a population-based study. *British Journal of Psychiatry, 193*, 364–372.

Morrison, A. P., Frame, L., & Larkin, W. (2003). Relationships between trauma and psychosis: a review and integration. *British Journal of Clinical Psychology, 42*, 331–353.

Pert, C., Jahoda, A., Stenfert Kroese, B., Trower, P., Dagnan, D., & Selkirk, M. (2013). Cognitive behavioural therapy from the perspective of clients with mild intellectual disabilities: a qualitative investigation of process issues. *Journal of Intellectual Disability Research, 57*(4), 359–369.

Reid, J., & Clements, J. (1989). Assessing the understanding of emotional states in a population of adolescents and young adults with mental handicaps. *Journal of Mental Deficiency Research, 33,* 229–233.

Rose, N., Rose, J., & Kent, S. (2012). Staff training in intellectual disability services: a review of the literature and implications for mental health services provided to individuals with intellectual disability. *International Journal of Developmental Disabilities, 58*(1), 24–39.

Stenfert Kroese, B., & Holmes, G. (2001). "I've never said 'No' to anything in my life": Helping people with learning disabilities who experience psychological problems. In C. Newnes, G. Holmes & C. Dunn (Eds.), *This is madness too* (pp. 71–80). Ross-on-Wye: PCCS Books.

Stenfert Kroese, B., Dewhurst, D., & Holmes, G. (2001). Diagnosis and drugs: help or hindrance when people with learning disabilities have psychological problems? *British Journal of Learning Disabilities, 29*(1), 26–33.

Stenfert Kroese, B., Jahoda, A., Pert, C., Trower, P., Dagnan, D., and Selkirk, M. (2014). Staff expectations and views of cognitive behaviour therapy (CBT) for adults with intellectual disabilities. *Journal of Applied Research in Intellectual Disabilities, 27*(2), 145–153.

Stenfert Kroese, B., & Rose, J. L. (2011). *Mental health services for adults with learning disabilities.* London: The Judith Trust.

Stenfert Kroese, B., & Thomas, G. (2006). Treating chronic nightmares of sexual assault survivors with an intellectual disability. *Journal of Applied Research in Intellectual Disabilities, 19*(1), 75–80.

Sturmey, P. (2004). Cognitive therapy with people with intellectual disabilities: a selective review and critique. *Clinical Psychology and Psychotherapy, 11,* 222–232.

Taylor, J. L., Lindsay, W. R., & Willner, P. (2008). CBT for people with intellectual disabilities: Emerging evidence, cognitive ability and IQ effects. *Behavioural and Cognitive Psychotherapy, 36,* 723–734.

Unwin, G. L., & Deb, S. (2010). The use of medication to manage behaviour problems among adults with an intellectual disability: a national guideline. *Advances in Mental Health and Intellectual Disability, 4*(3), 4–11.

Wechsler, D. (2008). *Wechsler adult intelligence scale-UK* (4th ed.). Pearson: London.

Weiss, D. S., and Marmar, C. R. (1997). The impact of event scale-revised. In J. P. Wilson & T. M. Keane (eds.) *Assessing psychological trauma and PTSD* (pp. 399–411). New York: Guilford Press.

Whitman, T. L. (1990). Self-regulation and mental retardation. *American Journal on Mental Retardation, 94*(4), 347–362.

Willner, P., Rose, J. L., Jahoda, A., Stenfert Kroese, B., Felce, D., Cohen, D., … Gillespie, D. (2013). Group-based cognitive-behavioural anger management for people with mild to moderate intellectual disabilities: cluster randomised controlled trial. *The British Journal of Psychiatry, 203*(4), 288–296.

Willner, P., & Hatton, C. (2006). CBT for people with intellectual disabilities. *Journal of Applied Research in Intellectual Disabilities, 19,* 1–3.

Winchurst, C., Stenfert Kroese, B., & Adams, J. (1992). Assertiveness training for people with a mental handicap: a group approach. *British Journal of Mental Handicap, 20*(3), 97–101.

Wood, P. M., & Stenfert Kroese, B. (2007). Enhancing the emotion recognition skills of individuals with learning disabilities: a review of the literature. *Journal of Applied Research in Intellectual Disabilities, 20,* 576–579.

Wolfensberger, W. (1998). *A brief introduction to social role valorization* (3rd ed.). Syracuse, NY: Training Institute for Human Service Planning, Syracuse University.

Zigmond, A. S., & Snaith, R. P. (1983). The hospital anxiety and depression scale. *Acta Psychiatrica Scandinavica, 67*(6), 361–370.

IV
Mastering Metacompetence

16

Using Self-Practice and Self-Reflection (SP/SR) to Enhance CBT Competence and Metacompetence

Richard Thwaites, James Bennett-Levy, Melanie Davis and Anna Chaddock

Introduction

As therapists we have all experienced "stuckness" with certain types of clients. Maybe it is those clients that are so depressed that we find ourselves getting sucked into their sadness and hopelessness. Maybe it is people who attend regularly yet are not benefitting and do not quite seem to be engaging ("I'm sorry I just didn't get time to do my homework again ..."). Perhaps basic CBT competences don't seem to work; we might have an idea that we could be doing something differently but just don't know how to flexibly adapt a standard approach. We may notice that we respond in characteristic, yet unhelpful ways that we struggle to change. For some therapists (especially when training) such experiences can lead them to have doubts about what they are providing. We may think "Well I know what the evidence base says, and the theories make sense, but can this really make a difference to people's lives?"

In our personal lives, away from the therapy room, we may also notice ourselves getting stuck in characteristic ways of thinking or behaving. Maybe we fall into the same traps that our clients do? Or do we assume that, as therapists, we should never get lost in ruminative self-doubt, avoid anxiety-provoking situations or become depressed? Unfortunately, being a competent CBT therapist does not automatically lead to the instant transfer of evidence-based approaches to ourselves!

Research over the past decade has shown that practising CBT methods on oneself and reflecting on the experience can help therapists to address the kinds of professional and personal issues identified above (Bennett-Levy et al., 2001; Davis, Thwaites, Freeston, & Bennett-Levy, in press; Haarhoff, Gibson, & Flett, 2011), which standard training methods may fail to address (Bennett-Levy McManus, Westling, & Fennell, 2009a). In this chapter, we suggest that self-practice/self-reflection (SP/SR) is an integrative training

How to Become a More Effective CBT Therapist: Mastering Metacompetence in Clinical Practice,
First Edition. Edited by Adrian Whittington and Nick Grey.
© 2014 John Wiley & Sons, Ltd. Published 2014 by John Wiley & Sons, Ltd.

strategy, ideally suited to enhancing the skills of therapists who have learned the basic techniques of CBT, and now wish to move towards developing therapeutic artistry by learning CBT "from the inside" (Bennett-Levy, Lee, Travers, Pohlman, & Hamernik, 2003).

Accordingly, this chapter is aimed at therapists who, having achieved competence in CBT, are now keen to develop and "fine-tune" their delivery of CBT. This does not mean abandoning evidence-based protocols. Rather, SP/SR may enable therapists to apply them more sensitively and with a higher degree of finesse and flexibility (especially for the most difficult or personally challenging clients) while remaining true to the key principles of CBT.

The aims of this chapter are to: (1) to provide a basic description of SP/SR; (2) to discuss the evidence-base supporting different methods of delivering SP/SR; (3) to provide illustrative examples of tasks from SP/SR programmes; and (4) to discuss the important issue of ensuring safety and maximizing benefit from the approach.

What is SP/SR?

SP/SR is a focused training strategy that gives therapists a structured experience of using CBT on themselves (SP) and reflecting on that experience (SR). The primary purpose of SP/SR is to enhance therapist skills. The SP component is typically delivered in one of three main formats:

- A group-based intervention in which participants use a manualized workbook method to complete a programme of therapeutic tasks typical of CBT (e.g., activity schedules, thought diaries, behavioural experiments) over a period of 6 to 12 weeks (Bennett-Levy et al., 2001; Bennett-Levy, Thwaites, Haarhoff, & Perry, 2014; Chaddock, 2007; Davis et al., in press; Farrand, Perry, & Linsley, 2010).
- A co-therapist method with pairs of participants alternating between the role of therapist and client. They usually receive four to six sessions in each role (Bennett-Levy et al., 2003).
- Self-guided SP/SR from workbooks, for therapists wishing to "go it alone" (at this stage, unevaluated as a delivery method) (Bennett-Levy et al., 2014).
- Workbook and co-therapy SP/SR are formalized, structured approaches for bringing SP/SR into therapist training (Haarhoff & Farrand, 2012). However, it should be noted that CBT training programmes and clinical supervision sometimes include self-experiential tasks or role-plays in less intensive ways. For instance, trainers or supervisors may ask students to use mild to moderate personal issues in order to experience the impact of a particular technique (e.g., a behavioural experiment).

There are different ways in which an SP/SR experience can be focused to address specific CBT competencies. In the co-therapy condition, goals are negotiated in much the same way as they would be within standard therapy. Orientation to our group-based SP/SR programmes includes personalized goal setting, so while the self-practice exercises that follow are standard, the learning process can be specific and idiosyncratic, depending on what the person is aiming to achieve and the way they choose to focus their reflections. We would encourage anyone undertaking self-guided SP/SR to create meaningful personal and professional goals for themselves.

All three formal SP/SR procedures include a process of structured reflection, which approximately follow the progressively deepening structure below:

1. Observe the experience (e.g., how did I feel, what did I notice?).
2. Clarify the experience (e.g., was it helpful, what did not change?).
3. Implications of the experience for clinical practice (e.g., for one-to-one therapy, for supervision and training).
4. Implications of the experience for how I see myself as "a person" and/or as a "therapist".
5. Implications of this experience for my understanding of CBT theory and practice.

There are slight variations in how the self-reflection (SR) component is delivered. In the group-based workbook method, participants usually complete weekly written reflections, which are then collated, anonymized and shared with the full cohort in order to maximize learning and provoke further reflection. In the co-therapy condition, participants reflect in pairs on their learning, then complete written reflections and circulate to the other participants. One study utilized a web-based blog/discussion board to enable participants to post their reflections, which led to reflections and comments from other participants and then onto further reflections (Farrand, Perry, & Linsley, 2010). Experiencing the reflective styles of fellow students apparently enabled students to challenge and adapt their own reflective style (Haarhoff & Farrand, 2012).

It should be noted that the SR component differs from much of the reflection that typically takes place in CBT practice (e.g., in supervision), where the reflective process is usually focused on the client. Previously, we have made a distinction between this kind of "general reflection" (e.g., reflecting on a client formulation) and self-reflection "in which the content for reflection is self-referenced to one's thoughts, feelings, behaviours or personal history" (Bennett-Levy, Thwaites, Chaddock, & Davis, 2009b, p. 121; Bennett-Levy and Thwaites, 2007). SP/SR involves both kinds of reflection: self-reflection on our experience, and how we see ourselves as a person or therapist; and general reflection on the implications of our experience for clinical practice and for our understanding of CBT theory.

In the following sections we summarize the past 15 year's SP/SR research findings with both inexperienced and experienced therapists, provide examples of the kind of activities in which participants might engage, and demonstrate the benefits and difficulties experienced. A summary of the findings to date is shown in Table 16.1. It is important to note that in addition to consolidating competence, SP/SR has been found to develop metacompetencies such as reflective skills, which are essential to both identifying when and how to flexibly adapt standard competencies, but also crucially, to be able to learn effectively from future clinical experiences.

Using SP/SR to Enhance the Competencies and Meta-competencies of Inexperienced Therapists

SP/SR enhances CBT competencies

An early qualitative study of trainee therapists' experiences of SP/SR found evidence to suggest that SP/SR can cement competencies gained through other methods such as reading and workshops (Bennett-Levy et al., 2001). Participants perceived an increase

Table 16.1   Summary of main SP/SR research findings

Domain	Research findings
Declarative knowledge (knowledge that we might write about, talk about or read about)	• A clearer (Haarhoff et al., 2011) and deeper (Bennett-Levy et al., 2001) understanding of the CBT model (declarative knowledge) • An increased understanding of processes of change in therapy and potential difficulties in making changes (Bennett-Levy et al., 2001; Bennett-Levy et al., 2003)
Procedural skills (when and how we implement declarative knowledge in practice)	• Increased level of specific CBT skills (e.g., explaining model, process and tasks) (Bennett-Levy et al., 2001; Davis et al., 2014) • A specific primary impact on interpersonal aspects of therapist performance such as empathic attunement and interpersonal communication skills (Bennett-Levy et al., 2003) • Increased self-awareness and knowledge of self (Bennett-Levy et al., 2001) affecting procedural skills • Changes in beliefs relating to both therapist self and personal self (Chaddock, 2007; Davis, Freeston, Thwaites, & Bennett-Levy, in preparation; Fraser & Wilson, 2010) • Increased therapist flexibility and creativity (Bennett-Levy et al., 2003) • Better understanding of CBT processes, specific therapeutic methods and the development of a therapeutic style (Laireiter & Willutski, 2003)
Reflective skills (using our experiences to learn which skill to apply to which client under which set of circumstances at which point in time in therapy)	• Increased self-reflection skills (both during and after sessions) (Bennett-Levy et al., 2003; Farrand, Perry, & Linsley, 2010).

in their conceptual understanding of CBT including their understanding of the therapist's role in therapy, the cognitive model and their understanding of the process of change in therapy. In a more recent study, Haarhoff et al. (2011) reported that "developing a theoretical understanding of the CBT conceptual model" was the most frequent theme emerging from thematic analysis of trainee's reflections on their SP/SR experience. All participants reported understanding CBT more clearly, and suggested that it was the act of doing and experiencing the impact of CBT interventions that enabled them to gain a deeper understanding of the model. To provide a flavour of the way in which goals, activities and reflections are linked we have included some examples from "Laura", one of our group-based SP/SR participants (see Table 16.2).

Table 16.2 SP/SR Case example: Laura

Example learning goal: I would like to develop more skills and confidence in knowing when and how to apply different change techniques.

Self-Practice	Self-Reflection
Thought diary	I've become more aware of how my thoughts affect my everyday life. I realize that I doubt my abilities in a number of different areas, but this is helping me to become more aware of this and to challenge these thoughts. I'm noticing a difference in how I feel and this is helping me not only to see what thought diaries do and how they work, but also for me to be able to engage more in my training and give things a go.
Behavioural experiment	I really struggled with this to begin with … I had a few goes before I settled on an experiment that was relevant enough to have some impact. It made me think about how much of a collaborative effort the setting up of experiments needs to be and I am adjusting my practice as a result. I'm starting to understand the difference between applying a technique and doing it skillfully or effectively and the implications for collaboration.
Historical test	In thinking about the schema I was aware of a knot in my stomach and noticed that as I did the historical test and I identified quite a lot of evidence to the contrary, it began to unwind. It wasn't until actually reviewing the historical evidence that I realized just how little evidence there is to support my schema. I have noticed changes over the past 11 weeks and am aware that this exercise has probably added to the change in my thinking and attitude towards myself and my abilities. I understand the role of historical tests more now that I have completed one myself and I think it has helped me to be less harsh on myself. Through reading and trying the test myself, I think it would be good to break the person's life up into small age ranges to gather the full extent of data.

SP/SR starts to build metacompetencies

Beyond the benefits of typical learning methods during training, SP/SR starts the process of developing metacompetencies, providing a springboard for later developments towards clinical artistry, potentially at an earlier stage than might usually occur. Since reflection is a key element of SP/SR, reflective skills are often enhanced, with benefits both for reflecting "in-action" (in the moment with the client) and "on-action" (e.g., post-session or in supervision) (Bennett-Levy et al., 2003). Reflective skill can facilitate the learning of the inexperienced therapist and increase the sophistication of their delivery of therapy. For instance, they may use their "lived" knowledge and experience of CBT to explain the model to clients in a flexible and attuned manner, or use their reflective skills to predict potential barriers, which can be addressed in advance.

Participants report that SP/SR has a specific impact on their interpersonal skills, because they experience first-hand the challenges of using CBT techniques on themselves, and feel increased empathy for their clients. They report paying increased attention to the therapeutic relationship and finer attunement to the client's experience (e.g., subtly judging the cognitive and emotional state of the client in the moment) (Bennett-Levy et al., 2001, 2003; Bennett-Levy et al., 2009a). This is a particularly valuable impact of SP/SR, since interpersonal aspects of therapy are often given the least focus in CBT training (Niemi & Tiuraniemi, 2010; Thwaites, 2011). These data lead us to suggest that SP/SR may enhance the ability to flexibly apply CBT-approaches to engage ambivalent clients or address therapeutic ruptures in an effective way, but this hypothesis awaits empirical verification.

SP/SR can help manage the emotional impact of training and development

Bennett-Levy and Beedie (2007) describe how through exposure to training, we gain a greater understanding of the standards required for professional competence and become more aware of the gap between our own skills and where we would like them to be. Our confidence can be dented as we adjust to new understandings of what "competence" actually means and to what extent our skills match up to that standard. Bennett-Levy et al. (2001) found that SP/SR resulted in "enhanced confidence and self-perception of competence" and a greater belief in CBT as an effective tool for personal change. Haarhoff et al. (2011) found that some of their participants experienced increased self-awareness and that this led to increased acceptance of current skill level.

Research also suggests that SP/SR can effect personal change in therapists (Sanders & Bennett-Levy, 2010). We can see an example of this in Laura's reflection on completing a Historical Test (see Table 16.2). As well as learning about the felt impact of the historical test and the implications for her use of the technique with her clients, Laura has reflected on the emotional impact of the task, has realized things about herself that she was not previously aware of, and has noticed a change in attitude to herself and her skills over the course of her SP/SR experience.

Using SP/SR To Enhance the Artistry of Experienced Therapists

Having completed training and gained experience working as a therapist, different challenges emerge for the therapist both personally and professionally. Confidence can grow, and with that, the potential for complacency or therapeutic drift. Consequently, continued engagement with SP/SR offers an opportunity for ongoing reflective practice, not just to aid personal and professional development as a therapist, but also to help develop competence and metacompetence in potential newer roles such as supervisor and trainer.

Current requirements for continual professional development and ongoing accreditation once qualified (e.g., British Association for Behavioural and Cognitive Psychotherapies, 2010) further support the need for evidence-based methods to continue enhancing CBT knowledge and skill. SP/SR's self-experiential approach can provide an avenue for professional growth and skill development in ways that other CBT training methods are less equipped to do. Even those therapists with advanced skills following many years of experience have shown benefit from the programme. Research has demonstrated that SP/SR can result in a measurable change in self-rated CBT skills and empathy skills in CBT therapists with an average of 18 years professional experience (average of nine years post-CBT training) (Davis et al., in press). Furthermore, impact was demonstrated not only at the level of the "therapist self", but also the "personal self", with participants rating their own self-identified dysfunctional beliefs (about themselves personally, and as a therapist) as significantly lower following SP/SR. (Davis et al., in preparation).

While the primary functions of SP/SR as a training and development tool remain across different levels of experience, SP/SR with more experienced practitioners brings the need for a different focus within SP/SR. A more experienced therapist is likely to see a higher degree of complexity in their caseload, and so there may be an increased need for sensitive handling of interpersonal processes. Ongoing self-awareness and reflective skills will aid a therapist's ability to manage such processes through helping fine tune key interpersonal skills. While it could be assumed that more experienced therapists may have honed their therapeutic skills over a number of years, there will still be client presentations that pose significant challenges. For example, some therapists may find that they over- or under-match with certain groups of clients (Leahy, Tirch, & Napolitano, 2011), leading to the possibility that the same mistakes are being repeated year on year. If engaged with fully, SP/SR can foster this self-awareness and enhance the development of therapeutic skills and confidence in areas of clinical practice, and with client groups that have started to elicit a "heart sinking" feeling in us. Indeed, a consistent finding in Davis et al.'s (in press) study was that the greatest self-reported skill change came from the ratings that participants gave in relation to their "most difficult" client of the week, which could be seen as a big motivating factor to engage with SP/SR.

Given the above, we have utilized an adapted SP/SR manual for experienced therapists, which includes not only "core" CBT activities such as goal-setting and behavioural experiments but also tasks aimed at encouraging self-examination at ever more deepening emotional levels coupled with matching reflective questions. As a more specific example: in Week 3 of an SP/SR Programme for experienced therapists, participants were asked to complete the first three columns of a standard thought record over the course of one week (SP), and then respond to the questions, shown in Table 16.3, designed to progressively deepen reflection (SR). (In this adapted version, these reflective questions are also designed to capture the additional roles of the therapist at more experienced levels of practice; self-as-trainer and self-as-supervisor).

Table 16.3   Example of reflective questions for a specific thought diary task

Q1:	What did I notice about my experience of completing the first three columns of the thought record? What feelings would have come up for me if someone else had read what I had written?
Q2:	Was I able to carry the record around with me during the week and complete it as I went along? What difficulties did I face with this?
Q3:	How difficult was it to only complete the first three columns of the thought record and not go on to consider how to challenge the thoughts? How did it feel just to sit and notice the negative thoughts or images?
Q4:	With what type of client, or under what circumstances am I most likely to run into problems using thought records? How do I overcome these difficulties? How could I use this knowledge to help an inexperienced trainee to use thought records with client? What would I need to take into account if I was training someone to use this skill?
Q5:	Has noticing and recording my thoughts throughout the week changed my understanding of myself or 'selves' (e.g. self-as-CBT therapist, self-as-supervisor, self-as-partner, self-as-parent)?

Although many of the benefits previously described for inexperienced therapists can apply equally for experienced therapists, there are also some more specific benefits for therapists experiencing SP/SR at a later point in their career. A number of the main themes are illustrated below through participants' reflections.

SP/SR can help to remind us of the emotional impact of therapy

First, given that the experienced therapist is likely to have seen hundreds of clients, and performed the basic tasks of CBT thousands of times (e.g., agenda setting), the self-practice element can really bring back into focus what it *feels* like to be on the receiving end of a therapeutic technique. For the therapist with many years post-qualification experience, this experience can be eye-opening, providing an experiential reminder of just how emotionally challenging therapy can be:

> When I looked back however I was taken aback at the thoughts and strength of feeling. Therefore I wouldn't want people to read my diary. I would feel a bit embarrassed and probably ashamed.

SP/SR can enhance empathy with the client's experience

As well as the sheer challenge of *feeling* the emotion, SP/SR can help the therapist understand better just how difficult making sense of our own emotional and cognitive experiences can be. For instance, even core CBT tasks undertaken early in the therapeutic process, such as observing changes to mood and thoughts, are not always straightforward; "It was very difficult for me to notice changes in mood … On some occasions I was completely unable to identify any thoughts."

So, although more experienced therapists are likely to have well-honed procedural skills, and high awareness of the difficulties that clients commonly encounter in completing CBT, SP/SR can help draw the therapist's attention more acutely to the reality and pull of avoidant behaviours and what it feels like *not* to complete the task: "What I have experienced as a result of not doing it is a sense of shame and not wanting to fill out the reflections as I would have to admit to not doing the 'homework' and a sense of failure."

SP/SR can aid reflection on clinical practice

SP/SR is key to further fine tuning metacompetencies such as reflective skills. For experienced therapists, the process of completing the SP/SR tasks through the weeks seems to lead to new learning, which then prompts reflective questions within everyday clinical practice. For example, even the most routine of clinical tasks completed regularly in therapy, such as recording information through diaries and completing questionnaires are seen in a new light, through the client's eyes.

SP/SR can highlight the need for CBT skill readjustment

For some participants, SP/SR encourages a re-examination of their core CBT skills, and how they communicate and work with these tasks with clients (re-adjusted procedural skill):

> I was struck by how strong the automatic thoughts could be and how powerful the emotional reactions were. I was struck by the realization this was something I do so often with patients yet not with myself despite being clearly affected by negative thoughts and feelings

and finding it useful to identify them. I would have been very uncomfortable about any-one else reading this ... yet I expect patients to do this freely for me as their therapist. I talk about how difficult they may be to spot and differentiate –the technical stuff – but not about the process of possibly feeling embarrassed or even ashamed about sharing them.

Through the research evidence gained to date, the potential benefits of SP/SR appear to be extensive; however, these benefits appear to be dependent on the level and quality of trainees' engagement with the SP/SR process (Bennett-Levy & Lee, 2014; Chaddock, 2007; Davis et al., in press). For therapists and trainers wondering how to utilize SP/SR for maximum benefit, the next section lists our recommendations.

Core Conditions Recommended for SP/SR

As discussed above, an initial decision to make will be how to engage in SP/SR; self-guided, with a partner or colleague, or in a group. Table 16.4 highlights the pros and cons of each approach.

Whichever the chosen method of delivery, and whether considering utilizing SP/SR for your own professional development needs or planning to implement as a trainer, we would suggest a consideration of the following questions:

1. *Can I do SP/SR now?* SP/SR can, and should, have some level of emotional impact and therefore it is important for potential participants to consider the availability of time and energy to commit to a programme. Higher engagement appears to reap more rewards, therefore being realistic about the time requirement, especially for the self-reflection component, is essential from the start. The benefits of the struc-tured versions of SP/SR in groups or pairs is that part of the commitment is to allocate and protect sufficient time for SP/SR. However, if time commitment is a difficulty, or an entire SP/SR programme is simply not a possibility, then there is the alternative to engage in self-guided SP/SR activity.

2. *Should I do SP/SR now?* Given the potential impact on personal beliefs, as well as the further honing and fine tuning of therapy skills, it may be that with new insight and self-awareness comes a "shaking up" of confidence and a questioning of compe-tence level, not just for the trainee (Chaddock, 2007) but also for the more experi-enced therapist. Therefore, it will be important for SP/SR participants to be aware of the possibility of feeling deskilled. As SP/SR is designed to be a "therapy-like" experience, it may be the case that the self-practice element draws out emotional responses that are unexpected for the participant. Therefore, another important condition to consider is the self-care and safety aspect of the programme (Bennett-Levy & Lee, 2014). It will be necessary from the start to be clear about what steps should be taken if the process feels unsafe for any reason. For example, there may be times when SP/SR may not be advisable due to other competing life demands, which may require significant emotional resources. Previous SP/SR studies have addressed the safety aspect by having an agreed personal safeguard strategy in place prior to the commencement of the programme (e.g., identify personal warning signs, withdrawal from programme) (Bennett-Levy et al., 2001, 2014).

3. *What is the best way to engage with SP/SR?* In order to gain the most from the pro-gramme, goal-setting is an important starting point, as in therapy. For example, it may be a very specific skill enhancement that a participant is seeking, such as

Table 16.4   Advantages and disadvantages of different methods of SP/SR delivery

Method	Advantages	Disadvantages
Group-based SP/SR using a workbook	• Support and motivation from doing SP/SR in groups • Value of group feedback – can contextualize own experience against others (similarities and differences) • Recognize importance of therapist through their absence (e.g., difficulty of doing self-guided behavioural experiments) • Can be done online, using online blogging • In principle group can be formed from anywhere in the world • Strongest evidence-base of different SP/SR methods	• Not get "real therapy" experience • Potential for "exposure" even if anonymous – may be guarded • Availability limited by the need for a group facilitator • No flexibility in timeline if personal issues prevent completion of weekly SP/SR exercise
SP/SR in Pairs (limited "co-therapy", 4–6 sessions)	• The most "therapy-like" process • Can work through single issue in detail • Can derive significant personal benefits (possibly more so through other forms of SP/SR?) • Have direct experience of the therapeutic relationship, and directly experience which elements are important • Some evidence-base	• The value of the experience is heavily dependent on the quality of the partner • May get exposure only to a limited range of CBT techniques • Probably needs to be face-to-face (though video communication may be a possibility) • Pairs need careful monitoring by facilitator
Self-guided SP/SR	• Can be self-paced • Can self-select techniques to practice • No "exposure" issues • Recognize importance of therapist through their absence (e.g., difficulty of doing self-piloted behavioural experiments) • No facilitator required, can be made widely available	• Not get "real therapy" experience • No group reflections to compare own experience with, so cannot determine singularity or generality of personal experience of SP/SR • Needs self-motivation and self-discipline • No current evidence base • Reliance on self-questioning to deepen self-reflections, may be limitations due to therapist "blind spot"

agenda-setting or it might be a more general increase in self-awareness such as wishing to know what it feels like to complete a positive data log over an extended period of time. Specifying the focus and desired outcomes have proved an essential component in previous programmes (Chaddock, 2007; Davis et al., in press). Self-monitoring can help to identify any measurable change.

4. *What do I need to engage with SP/SR?* If a group programme is undertaken then confidentiality of the shared reflections on process will be important. To aid this, a facilitator is necessary to co-ordinate this process and preserve anonymity; and also to encourage engagement and keep participants motivated, especially when other life and work pressures can compete for attention. The facilitator, and the SP/SR workbook itself, can also act as a way of structuring the process by providing a clear framework and ensuring the reflection process is progressive and deepening.

5. *How do I gain the most from SP/SR?* To gain the most, research suggests that participants should fully engage with the process, and be realistic in goal setting, the time it will take, and the level of commitment it will require. The evidence-base is stronger for SP/SR, which involves participating simultaneously with others in a group-based setting, or having some level of dialogue with an "other" (be that a co-therapist, supervisor or colleague) to aid experiential learning and foster reflection. Finally, a willingness to be honest with ourselves and keep an open mind will allow for new levels of insights to be gained at a personal as well as a professional level.

Concluding Remarks

Throughout the world the community of CBT therapists continues to grow, especially rapidly in the United Kingdom as part of the Improving Access to Psychological Therapies Program (Department of Health, 2008). One of the challenges of such large scale training expansions is to help staff develop metacompetence as therapists, and, for some, competence and metacompetence as supervisors.

SP/SR may be regarded as an integrative training technique: it seems to put the icing on the cake of therapeutic skill development. It links the experiential with the conceptual, the interpersonal and the technical, the "therapist self" and "personal self", and the declarative and procedural with the reflective. It enables therapists to take responsibility for their own learning and development, and appears to add flexibility, creativity and empathic sensitivity to the delivery of evidence-based protocols. The consistency of participants' responses across different formats and countries gives us some confidence that there are identifiable benefits, particularly in the interpersonal and reflective domains (Bennett-Levy et al., 2009a).

However, we should be clear that there is much work to be done to develop the SP/SR evidence base. At this stage, the evidence base remains largely (though not completely) qualitative, and there has been no evaluation of the longevity of the benefits.

In this chapter we have articulated some of the theoretical underpinnings of SP/SR, and given examples of the kind of benefits that can be expected from making a commitment to such an approach. Some benefits will apply across the full span of therapist development, from the trainee to the highly experienced therapist, supervisor and trainer. Other benefits may be more specific to the level of knowledge and learning needs of the practitioner. We have also detailed the initial tantalizing findings that SP/SR programmes can provide benefits on a personal level in addition to the self-as-therapist level.

Taking part in a group or self-guided SP/SR programme requires a significant degree of personal motivation and honesty with oneself. Our experience has been that typically the benefits justify the commitment, as illustrated in this final quote from an SP/SR participant:

> SP/SR ... greatly increased my understanding of how the techniques used are experienced by clients ... and perhaps how these techniques work, not just a rational explanation of "why" they work. In a strange way, I feel "closer" to the cognitive model ... As "scientific" health professionals, a majority of our knowledge comes from listening to people's research findings/following tried and true methods yet somehow it is still vicarious. Not that I am knocking our channels of learning and research, but I believe things are more powerful when we also experience ... this has allowed me to feel more genuine with my understanding and I feel this is fed back implicitly to my patients.

Procedural Rules

- Consider the pros and cons of doing SP/SR on your own, with a partner, or with a group. Decide which will best suit your needs.
- Choose an appropriate "issue" to address in your SP/SR programme: consider whether this should be a professional or personal issue.
- Set yourself goals for the SP/SR programme.
- For maximum benefit, engage fully with both the self-practice and self-reflection components of SP/SR.
- Plan when to do SP/SR, setting aside sufficient time to engage fully with the programme.
- If working with a partner or in a group establish clear confidentiality agreements.
- Keep yourself safe: avoid doing SP/SR at times of high personal stress. In case you do become distressed during the process, establish a personal safeguard strategy prior to starting SP/SR.
- Develop your reflective capacity by remaining open to experience; by developing your Socratic self-questioning skills; and through writing.

References

Bennett-Levy, J., & Beedie, A. (2007). The ups and downs of cognitive therapy training: what happens to trainees' perception of their competence during a cognitive therapy training course? *Behavioural and Cognitive Psychotherapy, 35,* 61–75. doi: 10.1017/S1352465806003110

Bennett-Levy, J., & Lee, N. K. (2014). Self-practice and self-reflection in cognitive behaviour therapy training: what factors influence trainees' engagement and experience of benefit? *Behavioural and Cognitive Psychotherapy, 42,* 48–64. doi: 10.1017/S1352465812000781

Bennett-Levy, J., Lee, N., Travers, K., Pohlman, S., & Hamernik, H. (2003). Cognitive therapy from the inside: enhancing therapist skills through practicing what we preach. *Behavioural and Cognitive Psychotherapy, 31,* 143–158. doi: 10.1017/S1352465803002029

Bennett-Levy, J., McManus, F., Westling, B., & Fennell, M. (2009a). Acquiring and refining CBT skills and competencies: which training methods are perceived to be most effective? *Behavioural and Cognitive Psychotherapy, 37,* 571–583. doi: 10.1017/S1352465809990270

Bennett-Levy, J., & Thwaites, R. (2007). Self and self-reflection in the therapeutic relationship: A conceptual map and practical strategies for the training, supervision and self-supervision of interpersonal skills. In P. Gilbert and R. L. Leahy (Eds.), *The therapeutic relationship in the cognitive-behavioural psychotherapies* (pp. 255–281). London: Routledge.

Bennett-Levy, J., Thwaites, R., Chaddock, A., & Davis, M. (2009b). Reflective practice in cognitive behavioural therapy: the engine of lifelong learning. In J. Stedmon and R. Dallos (Eds.), *Reflective practice in psychotherapy and counselling* (pp. 115–135). Maidenhead: McGraw-Hill.

Bennett-Levy, J., Thwaites, R., Haarhoff, B. & Perry, H. (2014). *Experiencing CBT from the inside out: A self-practice/self-reflection workbook for therapists.* New York: Guilford.

Bennett-Levy, J., Turner, F., Beaty, T., Smith, M., Paterson, B., & Farmer, S. (2001). The value of self-practice of cognitive therapy techniques and self-reflection in the training of cognitive therapists. *Behavioural and Cognitive Psychotherapy, 29,* 203–220. doi:10.1017/S1352465801002077.

British Association for Behavioural and Cognitive Psychotherapies. (2010). *Standards of conduct, performance and ethics.* Retrieved from http://www.babcp.com/Files/About/BABCP-Standards-of-Conduct-Performance-and-Ethics.pdf

Chaddock, A. V. (2007). *Can the use of a self-practice/self-reflection approach enhance the therapeutic skills and attitudes of trainee cognitive-behavioural therapists?* (Unpublished DClinPsy Thesis). University of Newcastle-upon-Tyne, Newcastle-upon Tyne.

Davis, M. L., Freeston, M. H., Thwaites, R. & Bennett-Levy, J. (in preparation). Engaging the self in SP/SR: evidence with experienced practitioners.

Davis, M. L., Thwaites, R., Freeston, M. H. & Bennett-Levy, J. (in press). Measurable impact of a self-practice/self-reflection programme on the therapeutic skills of experienced cognitive-behavioural therapists. *Clinical Psychology and Psychotherapy.* doi: 10.1002/cpp.1884

Department of Health. (2008). *Improving access to psychological therapies implementation plan: national guidelines for regional delivery.* London: Department of Health.

Farrand, P., Perry, J., & Linsley, S. (2010). Enhancing self-practice/self-reflection (SP/SR) approach to cognitive behaviour training through the use of reflective blogs. *Behavioural and Cognitive Psychotherapy. 38,* 473–477. doi: 10.1017/S1352465810000238

Fraser, N., & Wilson, J. (2010). Self-case study as a catalyst for personal development in cognitive therapy training. *The Cognitive Behaviour Therapist, 3,* 107–116. doi: 10.1017/S1754470X10000097

Haarhoff, B., & Farrand, P. (2012). Reflective and self-evaluative practice in CBT. In W. Dryden and R. Branch (Eds.), *The CBT handbook* (pp. 475–492). London: Sage.

Haarhoff, B., Gibson, K., & Flett, R. (2011). Improving the quality of cognitive behaviour therapy case conceptualization: The role of self-practice/self-reflection. *Behavioural and Cognitive Psychotherapy, 39,* 323–339. doi: 10.1017/S1352465810000871

Laireiter, A.-R., & Willutzki, U. (2003). Self-reflection and self-practice in training of cognitive behaviour therapy: an overview. *Clinical Psychology and Psychotherapy, 10,* 19–30.

Leahy, R. L., Tirch, D., & Napolitano, L. (2011). *Emotional regulation in psychotherapy: a practitioner's guide.* New York: Guilford.

Niemi, P., & Tiuraniemi, J. (2010). Cognitive therapy trainees' self-reflections on their professional learning. *Behavioural and Cognitive Psychotherapy, 38,* 255–274. doi: 10.1017/S1352465809990609

Roth, A. D., & Pilling, S. (2008). Using an evidence-based methodology to identify the competencies required to deliver effective cognitive and behavioural treatment for depression and anxiety disorders. *Behavioural and Cognitive Psychotherapy, 36,* 127–147. doi: 10.1017/ S1352465808004141

Sanders, D., & Bennett-Levy, J. (2010). When therapists have problems: what can CBT do for us? In M. Mueller, H. Kennerley, F. McManus, & D. Westbrook (Eds.), *The Oxford guide to surviving as a CBT therapist* (pp. 457–480). Oxford: Oxford University Press.

Thwaites, R. (2011). *Does the IAPT program ignore the therapeutic relationship?* Paper presented at the BABCP Conference, Guildford, July.

17

Using Outcome Measures and Feedback to Enhance Therapy and Empower Patients

Sheena Liness

Introduction

The use of outcome measures, in the form of self-report questionnaires, in therapy can polarize opinion. There is debate around when to use them, which are the most useful and valid measures, how best to use them, and even whether to use them at all. They may be seen as an unwelcome and mechanical imposition, or an obstacle that will create rupture in the therapy alliance. Therapists may believe that patients dislike measures, or feel that they take too long to administer and waste precious therapy time. When working across different locations with large caseloads and a variety of clinical presentations, outcome measures can quickly become an expendable part of therapy.

Outcome measures have long been accepted as essential in clinical trials, but have been used less systematically within routine therapy. This is changing: Patient Reported Outcome Measures (PROMs) have been introduced across the healthcare system in the United Kingdom (Black, 2013; Department of Health, 2010, 2011b).

Many studies have found that the best outcomes were achieved when therapists collected and shared information about progress with their patients (e.g., Harmon et al., 2007; Lambert, Hansen, & Finch, 2001; Lambert, Harmon, Slade, Whipple, & Hawkins, 2005; Lambert et al., 2003). Providing feedback to clinicians regarding progress significantly improved outcomes for patients who were not improving in therapy (Sapyta, Riemer, & Bickman, 2005) and therapists who fail to seek feedback can have significantly poorer outcomes and more drop-outs (Miller, Duncan, Brown, Sorrell, & Chalk, 2006). Whatever our confidence in our clinical decisions and self-assessment of therapy competence, evidence suggests therapists' clinical judgement alone is a poor judge of patient progress and outcome (Lambert et al., 2005; Sapyta et al., 2005). Lambert et al. (2005) suggest clinicians should routinely and formally monitor their clinical outcomes and effectiveness, not least because we have an ethical responsibility to do so (Newnham & Page, 2010).

How to Become a More Effective CBT Therapist: Mastering Metacompetence in Clinical Practice,
First Edition. Edited by Adrian Whittington and Nick Grey.
© 2014 John Wiley & Sons, Ltd. Published 2014 by John Wiley & Sons, Ltd.

Types of Outcome Measures/Self-Report Questionnaires

Numerous outcome and process measures, both general and specific have been developed across a range of difficulties. It is beyond the scope of this chapter to cover all clinical outcome measures. Some of the most regularly used and clinically helpful measures for adults with depression and anxiety disorders will be presented, with examples of how best to use them to inform therapy and engage your patient into the process.

The UK's Improving Access to Psychological Therapies (IAPT) programme has introduced and established a Minimum Data Set for session-by-session reporting (Department of Health, 2011a). This includes symptom measures of low mood, the PHQ-9 (Kroenke, Spitzer, & Williams, 2001), and general anxiety, the GAD-7 (Spitzer, Kroenke, Williams, & Löwe, 2006). These measures were chosen due to their good psychometric properties, for being brief, and for being available without charge. Importantly a measure of functioning is also included, the Work & Social Adjustment Scale (WSA) (Mundt, Marks, Shear, & Greist, 2002). The WSA reports on the impact of current psychological difficulties on functioning across work, social life, leisure time and relationships. It can helpfully track more global improvement and is also useful for goal setting. Another commonly used measure is the Clinical Outcomes in Routine Evaluation-Outcome Measure (CORE-OM) (Barkham et al., 2001). It targets overall well-being, functioning and risk to self and others, as well as symptoms of depression, anxiety, physical conditions and trauma.

IAPT have also introduced disorder specific outcome measures for each anxiety disorder. The GAD-7 is not a good measure of avoidance and clearly avoidance is a key feature of anxiety disorders. A person can present with a low score on a generic measure such the GAD-7 but very high on the anxiety disorder specific measure, especially if the presentation is characterized by avoidance. Without the use of disorder specific measures it is possible that some people who need treatment would not be offered it, or that it appears progress is being made in treatment when this is not the case.

In addition to measures of symptoms and functioning, more specific measures can provide ongoing assessment and monitoring of cognitions, behaviours and other processes. Table 17.2 (at the end of the chapter) shows some examples of outcome and process measures for adults with depression and anxiety disorders. For other disorders (e.g., eating disorders, psychosis) and for other populations (e.g., children) more appropriate and specific measures have been developed and should be used. The principles of their use remain the same as laid out in this chapter.

Using outcome measures effectively requires specific skills. These are set out in Roth and Pilling's (2008) competence framework for delivering CBT for depression and anxiety disorders. They include:

- the knowledge to select the most appropriate measures;
- the ability to interpret the scores (i.e., norms/cut offs);
- the ability to help patients use self-monitoring procedures;
- the ability to share information gleaned from the measures with the patient with the aim of giving them feedback about progress; and
- the ability to integrate the measures into a therapy intervention and adapt interventions in response to feedback.

The Art of Using Outcome Measures and Patient Feedback Throughout Treatment

Assessment

Conducting a thorough assessment of patients' difficulties, sometimes in the face of complexity and limited time, can be a difficult task. A good assessment is crucial if we are to understand presenting problems, help the patient make sense of their difficulties, and deliver a sound rationale for therapy, which also indicates where we might start in therapy. Self-report measures at assessment aid us in our detective work. They can give us an overall picture, signpost difficulties, help clarify themes and highlight priorities for therapy. Measures can be sent out with the appointment letter with the patient asked to complete them prior to, and bring them along to the assessment appointment. It is helpful to add some lines of explanation for patients from the outset:

> Please complete the enclosed questionnaires in the day or two before your appointment and bring them with you to the assessment interview. The answers that you provide will be of great assistance in ensuring that your problems are fully assessed and that the right type of treatment is organized.

This process of acknowledgement, explanation and engagement should be continued at the start of the first meeting:

> Thank you very much for completing the questionnaires. I would like to have a look at them before we start. Can I just ask if they made sense to you? Did they seem relevant to your difficulties? Was there anything that you did not understand or did not find helpful?

Often patients are surprised that measures have been created that so clearly mirror their own problems. Other times they might say they did not make sense. Either answer is helpful clinically. In the first we know we are hopefully on the right track, the second indicates more exploration is necessary. More importantly, this process starts a therapist–patient dialogue and engenders a collaborative approach to therapy with therapist and patient feedback at the core. Clearly, outcome measures do not replace a thorough and comprehensive assessment, but they are valuable tools in the decision-making process of differential diagnosis. Generic and disorder specific outcome measures can also be used to inform goal setting, making them more specific, achievable and measurable, while therapy goals also create an idiosyncratic measurement for therapy overall.

Using measures at assessment

- Send out measures with the appointment letter asking patients to complete and bring them along to the assessment appointment. If you ask the patient to arrive 15 minutes early you can pick them up before the session and review them quickly, highlighting areas you may wish to clarify.
- Familiarize yourself with the measures that you use. If you are short of time or the patient is late, be aware of key measures or one or two items that you want to check on.

- If your assessment leaves you and the patient unclear about the way ahead, do ask them to complete further measures to help clarify.
- Tailor measures to your patients' needs and available time.
- Encourage dialogue through Socratic questioning and exploration of their responses.
- The more complex a presentation, the more helpful outcome measures can be.

Therapy

It is helpful to touch base about outcome measures in the first therapy session. You may not have assessed this patient, there may be a gap between assessment and therapy commencing, or it may be you want to check the patient's understanding of the rationale for filling them in. At this point we would recommend revisiting the rationale with them:

> We will ask you to complete these measures on a weekly basis. The reason for this is so that we can keep track of your progress and get an idea of areas that might be improving, and in particular areas that it may be helpful to focus on. I will also use them as an opportunity to ask for feedback on therapy overall. What we have found most helpful is if I give them to you at the end of each session and you take them away and complete them the night before our next session and bring them along with you. We will always allocate some time at the beginning of each session to review them. Does this sound acceptable to you? Do you have any questions or doubts? Equally is there anything you can think of that might get in the way of this?

Using measures early in treatment

- Have sets of measures readily available to give out.
- Revisit the rationale for use of outcome measures at the beginning of a course of therapy.
- Always acknowledge the measures, thank them for filling them in and review them together.
- Elicit any doubts or obstacles that may interfere and brainstorm solutions.
- If the patient has not completed them choose 1 or 2 key questions for them to complete in the initial minutes of the session.
- Do not spend whole chunks of a therapy session reviewing the measures. They are a tool to enhance and finesse your focus; they should not become the focus.
- Avoid as much as possible patients completing a lot of measures in session time. Have some awareness of the previous scores, and a quickly tot up the new ones (this can be done quickly).

Developing a shared formulation

Initial sessions of CBT usually involve deriving a collaborative idiosyncratic formulation or model of the patient's current difficulties. We often ask the patient to take us through a recent problematic situation step by step: this can provide invaluable insights into their view of the world and how different factors inter-relate. Outcome measures and patient feedback can enrich this process. Disorder specific measures will have already highlighted problematic emotions, physical sensations, maintenance factors, safety behaviours and the related thoughts and misinterpretations driving the cycle.

Sometimes recent situations explored in therapy nicely cover all key areas, but more often than not they are tightly tied to that one situation. Information from measures enables us to both check we are on the right track, but also helps broaden out the detail within the formulation to encapsulate other areas of concern. Outcome measures may also highlight themes, persistent avoidances or specific concerns that may not have been raised by the patient, but which would, without attention, increase their likelihood of future relapse.

THERAPIST (TH): Ok if we look at the model we have drawn out together so far, we can see we have lots of helpful information about what was happening for you at that time. You were on a tube, noticed feeling hot, sweaty, and lightheaded and then worried you were going to faint. To make sure you didn't faint, you started to breathe deeply, sip water, and then asked someone to give up their seat so that you could sit down. Does that look accurate?

CLIENT (C): Yes

TH: Is there anything missing? When you felt hot and sweaty was there anything else you worried might happen?

C: Not that I can remember

TH: Ok, so looking at the measures you have completed, what is interesting is that you are rating some other fears as also quite problematic in a panic attack (look at measures together). So you rate "I will suffocate" and also "I will lose control" at 90 per cent. You have also highlighted "holding on" and "monitoring yourself" as safety behaviours. Did any of these come into this situation? Can we add to what we have or can we draw out a new situation?

Here we can see how the therapist uses the measures to explore and expand the active misinterpretations and safety behaviours. The formulation becomes more open, broad and inclusive, which in turn gives us more to work on and with in therapy.

Clients often feedback at this point that it is the first time their problem has been broken down into clear areas, and that it now feels more manageable. They can also begin to see a way forward.

Enhancing the Course of Therapy

Using measures session-by-session helps us to check in with the patient at the beginning of every session. From the outset, we have set up the premise that a two-way dialogue regarding progress is useful. This includes picking up on events occurring between sessions and agreeing how to best use the session. This encourages an ethos of continual reflection and adaptation of therapy to address the current problems. Keeping a log or measure for each patient can help track progress and highlight areas for concern. The following case example illustrates how outcome measures can aid decision making.

Case study

Deborah was a 55-year old housewife whose children had recently left home. She was unemployed as a result of low mood and persistent social anxiety, which had affected her since her teens. She worried she had nothing to say, would babble and freeze, others would notice and think her boring and inadequate. She completed generic and disorder specific outcome measures, which were charted from the outset.

	PHQ9	GAD7	SCQ Freq	SCQ Beliefs	Leibowitz (LSAS)	SPIN
1	15	17	69	1650	103	46

Her scores on these questionnaires provide an overview of her current difficulties. Her PHQ9 indicates a moderate level of low mood, her GAD7 is in the severe range of general anxiety. Of the specific social anxiety questionnaires the Leibowitz Social Anxiety Scale (LSAS: Baker, Heinrichs, Kim, & Hofmann, 2002) and Social Phobia Inventory (SPIN: Connor et al., 2000) are in the severe range so we can see she is both anxious and avoiding across a broad range of situations. The Social Cognitions Questionnaire (Clark, 2005) is also high indicating a broad range of problematic socially anxious beliefs. As we track progress in therapy we can see below her measures are improving nicely across all areas.

	PHQ9	GAD7	SCQ Fre	SCQ Bel	Leibowitz (LSAS)	SPIN
1	15	17	69	1650	103	46
2	6	18	62	1110		
3	6	19	58	1120		
4	4	13	40	900	78	37
5	1	13	33	630		
6	1	7	25	260	78	35

At session 6 she announced she could only attend one more session. Looking at her measures it was clear that specific social situations remained problematic, as measured on the LSAS. Looking at the set of questionnaires she brought to this session, situations that jumped off the page related to themes of high anxiety and avoidance when she was the centre of attention and in group settings. This is a transcript of setting the agenda for this session (session 6):

TH: Ok, let's think about what might be helpful to focus on today. I guess I'd be keen to find out how you got on with the experiments you set off to do from last week's session. For today's session, I think last time we spoke about possibly doing some work on imagery today, (*bridging from the previous week*) however, having just looked again at your questionnaires along with the fact that we have fewer sessions, it may be helpful to use today to focus on something else.

CLIENT (C):   OK

TH: Given this is now our last but one session, is there anything that you would really like to look at today, or anything pressing from the week that you'd like to put on the agenda?

C: I don't think so. I haven't done everything on the list, well I kind of have, but I haven't managed to speak up at a meeting at work (voluntary).

TH: Sure, now that's interesting because I noticed on the form you filled in which highlights the situations you are still finding difficult, groups are still really causing you quite severe difficulties.

C: Yeah, well doing anything in front of people is still difficult.

TH: Ok, now given it looks like this is to be our last session, what do you see as most problematic at the moment? Certainly from these questionnaires there are a few things standing out, (therapist and patient look at the questionnaires together) which are: working in front of other people, interviews, if you look here, what is also coming out on here is speaking up at meetings, entering a room when others are already seated, being the centre of attention.

C: The problem is I think that it's all stuff I haven't done for such a long time although I can remember even before it was a big problem.

TH: OK, so given we have fewer sessions and we want to make you as robust as we can when you finish here, I wonder if it would be helpful for us to do something on this today. And also where you have just started your voluntary work is group dominated, this is clearly causing you high levels of anxiety.

So, by looking at the questionnaires together during the agenda setting, the therapist and patient are able to identify a cluster of remaining difficulties that would benefit exploration. A small group is organized for the patient to join and participate in a brief discussion. Her anxious predictions are identified (again the therapist checks that these fit with her formulation, her outcome measures and self–report).

She is able to speak up in the group. The meeting is recorded and the therapist and patient observe it afterwards together. Written feedback is received from the other group members. The patient wrote down her learning from this experiment to take away:

I didn't look as anxious as I felt.
Even though I felt 100 per cent anxious it wasn't noticeable.
Even though I had done nothing at the weekend no one thought I was boring.
People don't analyse everything like I do.

This intervention took 30 minutes in total. In reviewing the outcome measures, therapist and client were able to identify key problematic areas. A change method was then tailored to target her specific concerns in these situations in the form of a behavioural experiment. By continuing to track outcome we can see that at session 7 there is a significant reduction in her outcome measures and in particular the Leibowitz, which was standing out as less improved, is now in the normal population range. The patient was also able to attend a follow-up session one month later and had maintained the gains made in therapy. The patient related this functional improvement to the key experiment described above in session 6, which was guided by the measures.

Session	PHQ9	GAD7	SCQ Fre	SCQ Bel	Leibowitz (LSAS)	SPIN
1	15	37	69	1650	103	46
6	1	7	25	260	78	35
7	0	4	24	60	35	12
FU1	0	4	25	30	23	8

Outcome measures can also be invaluable with lack of progress (Hawkins, Lambert, Vermeersch, Slade, & Tuttle, 2004; Lambert et al., 2001; Lambert et al., 2005). A person with PTSD midway through therapy arrived at his session in a state of distress and frustration: he felt he had got much worse after a specific trigger had caused his main intrusions to recur. By sharing his weekly measures with him he was able to see that in fact despite his setback, his PTSD was still much improved from his assessment. This is also particularly important when working with fluctuations in mood in depression. Setbacks are a common part of recovery. Outcome measures highlighting fluctuations encourages discussion and exploration.

Using measures throughout therapy

- Always look at completed measures and reflect with the patient on progress/areas that are not responding to therapy.
- Chart progress in a table or graph format for use in therapy (and supervision).
- Monitor completion and adapt use to the individual presentation (e.g., poor literacy/lack of time/engages well with them).
- Make them quick and make them matter.
- Have outcome measurement aid therapy interventions and treatment decisions as a shared open process.
- Don't be didactic or over-zealous (e.g., totting up scores before asking a client a question or telling a client what the score means "you are severely depressed" before some exploration of this.

Blueprint/relapse prevention

At the end of therapy, time is allocated to focus on relapse prevention. A therapy blueprint can be created, highlighting key learning points, change methods, specific behavioural experiments that were helpful in creating belief change. Strategies to remember at difficult times in the future can also be emphasized. The rationale for the Blueprint is to have as much learning as possible within one document that can be easily accessed in the future. Outcome measures can inform the blueprint in identifying any remaining problematic situations, residual beliefs or behaviours that the therapist's or patient's attention is drawn to. This is also an opportunity to zoom in on any residual scores and explore ways the patient might be able to work on these in the future to maintain and improve progress.

Using measures at the end of therapy

- Do use outcome measures as part of discharge planning, highlighting areas for further work (e.g., remaining problematic beliefs or safety behaviours).
- Offer patients blank measures to take away. Part of their relapse prevention plan is then to complete them as a way of monitoring their mood after therapy ends. An increase in scores can act as a prompt to take skilful action such as looking at worksheets and reminding them to get more active.

When using measures in therapy there are a number of problems that may be encountered. Some of these, and possible solutions, or approaches to adopt are shown in Table 17.1.

Table 17.1 Troubleshooting problems with measures

Problem	Solutions
Complexity	Therapists are often suspicious of the use of measures when faced with complexity and will claim they are not suitable for use with their particular client group. We would argue that complexity lends itself all the more readily to the use of outcome measures to engage the client in the process of therapy and aid the teasing out of the focus of therapy that will lead to most substantial change. Remember there is evidence that patients who are not improving in therapy benefit the most from on-going feedback regarding progress (Lambert et al., 2005; Sapyta et al., 2005).
Patient distress	Take time to explore the distress Use supervision to reflect Role play use of measures Revisit the rationale Tailor measures to one or two key features of benefit
Literacy problems	Adapt measures – use of pictures, symbols, images Ask patient to attend a few minutes early and help them complete them or find an assistant to help Tailor/fine tune measures to their difficulties: e.g., before and after photographs (for example, clutter in a hoarders home) Use of friend or family member (as appropriate)
Persistent non-completion	Share the dilemma Revisit the rationale for their use and benefit Problem solve/time management

Using Outcomes Measures in Supervision

Bringing outcomes measures to supervision can greatly enhance the process for both supervisee and supervisor. Bringing a copy of initial and current scores on key measures gives immediate feedback on progress and stuck points. Using measures in supervision can also help in assessing clinical effectiveness and areas of difficulty for the therapist: for instance, a trend for less improvement with a particular presentation. This can help focus the content of supervision, or suggest follow-up CPD. It is helpful for supervisors to lead by example, and actively use outcome measures in their own work. Reviewing charts and graphs together with a non-threatening approach can also encourage openness and sharing of information to aid reflection and improvement. See Chapter 18 (this volume), for a supervision record to help with this process.

Using measures in supervision

- Use outcome measures to aid clinical supervision.
- Elicit and work on any therapist interfering beliefs.
- If there is resistance, set up as an experiment to use outcome measures for a set period and review.
- Lead by example and facilitate a culture of reflection on outcome within and across therapy (e.g., by sharing your own outcome grids/templates).
- Review progress in a non-threatening objective style.
- Highlight both content and process issues.

Table 17.2 Examples of outcome and process measures for adults with depression and anxiety disorders

	Symptomatology	Specific Cognitions	Safety Behaviours & Avoidance
Depression	**Patient Health Questionnaire (PHQ-9)** (Kroenke et al., 2001) Severity of symptoms of depression	**Automatic Thought Questionnaire** (Hollon & Kendall, 1980) Frequency of automatic negative thoughts	**Work & Social Adjustment Scale** (Mundt et al., 2002) Level of general impairment in work, social, home, leisure and relationships
	Beck Depression Inventory (Beck et al., 1988) Assesses depressive symptoms and attitudes	**Dysfunctional Attitudes Scale** (Weissman & Beck, 1978) Negative attitudes re self, world and future	
OCD	**Obsessive Compulsive Inventory (OCI)** (Foa et al., 1998) Frequency and distress of obsessive thoughts and compulsions	**Responsibility Attitudes Scale (RAS)** (Salkovskis et al., 2000) Assesses beliefs about responsibility	**Compulsive Activities Checklist** (Steketee & Freund, 1993) Level of impairment due to compulsive behaviours on a range of activities.
	Yale-Brown Obsessive-Compulsive Symptoms Checklist (Y-BOCS) (Goodman et al., 1989) Distress of obsessive thoughts and compulsions common in OCD.	**Responsibility Interpretations Questionnaire (RIQ)** (Salkovskis et al., 2000) Frequency and belief interpretations of intrusive thoughts about possible harm.	
Panic Disorder with/ without Agoraphobia	**Panic Disorder Severity Scale** (Shear et al., 2001) Frequency, avoidance, impact of panic symptoms	**Agoraphobic Cognitions Questionnaire (ACQ)** (Chambless, Caputo, Bright, & Gallagher, 1984) Frequency and strength of belief for specific panic cognitions (e.g., heart attack, faint, lose control)	**Safety Behaviours Questionnaire (SBQ)** (Clark & Salkovskis, 2009 unpublished) Frequency of specific safety behaviours
	Panic Disorder Weekly Summary Scale (Clark, 1994 unpublished) Frequency, severity and avoidance of panic symptoms on three individual items	**Body sensations questionnaire** (Chambless, Caputo, Bright, & Gallagher, 1984) Frequency and distress of bodily sensations which can be tied in to anxious misinterpretations.	**Mobility Inventory (MI)** (Chambless, Caputo, Jasin, Gracely, & Williams, 1985) Agoraphobic avoidance, when alone and accompanied

	Symptomatology	Specific Cognitions	Safety Behaviours & Avoidance
GAD	**Penn State Worry Questionnaire** (Molina & Borkovec, 1994) Measures symptoms of pathological worry	**Meta Cognitions Questionnaire** (Cartwright-Hatton & Wells, 1997) Assesses beliefs about worry & intrusive thoughts.	
Social Anxiety Disorder	**Social Phobia Inventory (SPIN)** (Connor et al., 2000) Fear, avoidance and physiological symptoms re social anxiety **Social Summary Rating Scale** (Clark et al., 2003). Avoidance, symptom severity and level of internal focus of attention, anticipatory processing and rumination.	**Social Cognitions Questionnaire (SCQ)** (Clark, 2005 unpublished) Frequency & strength of belief of specific social cognitions (e.g., I'll blush, sweat, look anxious, I'm boring) **The Social Attitudes Questionnaire (SAQ)** (Clark, 2005 unpublished) Strength of conviction for attitudes often held by people with social anxiety.	**Social Behaviour Questionnaire (SBQ)** (Clark, 2005 unpublished) Frequency of specific in-situ social safety behaviours **Leibowitz Social Anxiety Scale** (Baker et al., 2002) Fear and avoidance of social situations
PTSD	**Impact of Events Scale (Revised)** (Creamer, Bell, & Failla, 2003) Measures symptoms of re-experiencing, avoidance and hyper-arousal	**Response to Instrusions Questionnaire (RIQ)** (Clohessy & Ehlers, 1999; Murray, Ehlers, & Mayou, 2002) Explores responses to intrusive memories and associated safety behaviours **Post-trauma Cognitions Inventory (PTCI)** (Foa et al., 1999) Trauma related thoughts and beliefs re self, world, self-blame	
Health Anxiety	**Health Anxiety Inventory** (Salkovskis, Rimes, Warwick, & Clark, 2002) Severity of symptoms of health anxiety	**Illness Cognitions Questionnaire** (Clark et al., 1998) Frequency and belief of specific health cognitions **Illness Attitudes Scale** (Kellner, 1987) Strength of conviction for fears attitudes and beliefs often associated with health anxiety.	

Patients Like Them (Yes They Do!)

There are many accounts of patients giving positive feedback about outcome measures in therapy even if presenting as very distressed (Black, 2013; Hawkins et al., 2004). Patients value access to the information, appreciate when the measures reflect their difficulties and many also talk about the measures normalizing their problems. Patients like engaging with the process and generally find it helpful to review changes over time or notice when things haven't moved forwards. Measures can also help patients understand their condition more and clarify on what to focus. This is what some patients had to say:

> So one of the things I've found helpful was the questionnaires. I've had to fill in loads. It really focused me on my problems because I think I was a bit vague as to what I was anxious about. I just had a general feeling I was an anxious person all the time.

> It is as if this was written for me, if there's a questionnaire about it, it means other people must have the same difficulties.

> They gave me a clearer picture of my problems.

> They helped me to see the things I'm confident about.

Another patient informed us that she liked to see her progress mapped out and asked for a print out of her weekly measures mid-way through therapy. She said that seeing them in print really helped her to see progress, and areas that still needed work, which gave her the confidence to do further out of session experiments.

Procedural Rules

- Do not assume patients dislike outcome measures.
- Actively engage patients in the process and encourage reflection and ongoing feedback on their use in and out of session.
- Use them to inform clinical choice points at a number of therapy stages: assessment, through treatment and ending treatment.
- Use them to enhance the therapy relationship with collaborative treatment planning.
- Use measures to inform supervision.
- Always get feedback from patients on their use.

Acknowledgements

Many thanks especially to Hannah M. Parker, and also Alicia Deale, Suzanne Byrne and Nick Grey for comments on this chapter. The guidance and input from David M. Clark on the use of measures in my clinical practice has been invaluable, and a final thank you to all the patients who have helped to inform this chapter.

Useful resources

General information re IAPT measurement, the IAPT data handbook (which includes the key measures) and to access to measures in different languages: www.iapt.nhs.uk

Access to other freely available measures including some of the currently unpublished, although validated, Clark and Salkovskis ones: www.kcl.ac.uk/cadat

References

Baker, S. L., Heinrichs, N., Kim, H. -J., & Hofmann, S. G. (2002). The Liebowitz social anxiety scale as a self-report instrument: a preliminary psychometric analysis. *Behaviour Research and Therapy, 40*(6), 701–715.

Barkham, M., Margison, F., Leach, C., Lucock, M., Mellor-Clark, J., Evans, C., … McGrath, G. (2001). Service profiling and outcomes benchmarking using the CORE-OM: Toward practice-based evidence in the psychological therapies. *Journal of Consulting and Clinical Psychology, 69*(2), 184–196.

Beck, A. T., Steer, R. A., & Carbin, M. G. (1988). Psychometric properties of the Beck Depression Inventory: twenty-five years of evaluation. *Clinical Psychology Review, 8*(1), 77–100.

Black, N. (2013). Patient reported outcome measures could help transform healthcare. *British Medical Journal, 346.*

Cartwright-Hatton, S., & Wells, A. (1997). Beliefs about worry and intrusions: the Meta-Cognitions Questionnaire and its correlates. *Journal of Anxiety Disorders, 11*(3), 279–296.

Chambless, D. L., Caputo, G. C., Bright, P., & Gallagher, R. (1984). Assessment of fear of fear in agoraphobics: the body sensations questionnaire and the agoraphobic cognitions questionnaire. *Journal of Consulting & Clinical Psychology, 52*(6), 1090–1097.

Chambless, D. L., Caputo, G. C., Jasin, S. E., Gracely, E. J., & Williams, C. (1985). The mobility inventory for agoraphobia. *Behaviour Research and Therapy, 23*(1), 35–44.

Clark, D. M. (1994). *Panic disorder weekly summary scale.* Unpublished manuscript. King's College London, UK.

Clark, D. M. (2005). *Three questionnaires for measuring central constructs in the cognitive model of social phobia.* Unpublished manuscript. King's College London, UK.

Clark, D. M., Ehlers, A., McManus, F., Hackmann, A., Fennell, M., Campbell, H., … Louis, B. (2003). Cognitive therapy versus fluoxetine in generalized social phobia: a randomized placebo-controlled trial. *Journal of Consulting and Clinical Psychology, 71*(6), 1058–1067.

Clark, D. M., & Salkovskis, P. (2009). *Safety behaviours questionnaire.* Unpublished manuscript. UK.

Clark, D. M., Salkovskis, P. M., Hackmann, A., Wells, A., Fennell, M., Ludgate, J., … Gelder, M. (1998). Two psychological treatments for hypochondriasis. A randomised controlled trial. *The British Journal of Psychiatry, 173*(3), 218–225.

Clohessy, S., & Ehlers, A. (1999). PTSD symptoms, response to intrusive memories and coping in ambulance service workers. *British Journal of Clinical Psychology, 38*(3), 251–265.

Connor, K. M., Davidson, J. R. T., Churchill, L. E., Sherwood, A., Weisler, R. H., & Foa, E. (2000). Psychometric properties of the Social Phobia Inventory (SPIN): New self-rating scale. *The British Journal of Psychiatry, 176*(4), 379–386.

Creamer, M., Bell, R., & Failla, S. (2003). Psychometric properties of the impact of event scale – revised. *Behaviour Research and Therapy, 41*(12), 1489–1496.

Department of Health. (2010). *Equity and excellence: liberating the NHS* (White Paper). UK: The Stationary Office Limited. Retrieved from www.gov.uk/government/publications/liberating-the-nhs-white-paper

Department of Health. (2011a). *IAPT data handbook* (Version 2). Retrieved from http://www.iapt.nhs.uk/silo/files/the-iapt-data-handbook.pdf

Department of Health. (2011b). *The NHS outcomes framework 2012/13.* Retrieved from www.gov.uk/government/publications/nhs-outcomes-framework-2012-to-2013

Foa, E. B., Ehlers, A., Clark, D. M., Tolin, D. F., & Orsillo, S. M. (1999). The posttraumatic cognitions inventory (PTCI): development and validation. *Psychological Assessment, 11*(3), 303–314.

Foa, E. B., Kozak, M. J., Salkovskis, P. M., Coles, M. E., & Amir, N. (1998). The validation of a new obsessive-compulsive disorder scale: the obsessive-compulsive inventory. *Psychological Assessment, 10*(3), 206–214.

Goodman, W. K., Price, L. H., Rasmussen, S. A., Mazure, C., Fleischmann, R. L., Hill, C. L., … Charney, D. S. (1989). The Yale-Brown obsessive compulsive scale: I. development, use, and reliability. *Archives of General Psychiatry, 46*(11), 1006.

Harmon, S. C., Lambert, M. J., Smart, D. M., Hawkins, E., Nielsen, S. L., Slade, K., & Lutz, W. (2007). Enhancing outcome for potential treatment failures: Therapist–client feedback and clinical support tools. *Psychotherapy Research, 17*(4), 379–392.

Hawkins, E. J., Lambert, M. J., Vermeersch, D. A., Slade, K. L., & Tuttle, K. C. (2004). The therapeutic effects of providing patient progress information to therapists and patients. *Psychotherapy Research, 14*(3), 308–327.

Hollon, S. D., & Kendall, P. C. (1980). Cognitive self-statements in depression: development of an automatic thoughts questionnaire. *Cognitive Therapy and Research, 4*(4), 383–395.

Kellner, R. (1987). *Abridged manual of the illness attitudes scale.* Albuquerque: Department of Psychiatry, School of Medicine, University of New Mexico.

Kroenke, K., Spitzer, R. L., & Williams, J. B. W. (2001). The PHQ-9: Validity of a brief depression severity measure. *Journal of General Internal Medicine, 16*(9), 606–613.

Lambert, M. J., Hansen, N. B., & Finch, A. E. (2001). Patient-focused research: using patient outcome data to enhance treatment effects. *Journal of Consulting and Clinical Psychology, 69*(2), 159–172.

Lambert, M. J., Harmon, C., Slade, K., Whipple, J. L., & Hawkins, E. J. (2005). Providing feedback to psychotherapists on their patients' progress: clinical results and practice suggestions. *Journal of Clinical Psychology, 61*(2), 165–174.

Lambert, M. J., Whipple, J. L., Hawkins, E. J., Vermeersch, D. A., Nielsen, S. L., & Smart, D. W. (2003). Is it time for clinicians to routinely track patient outcome? a meta-analysis. *Clinical Psychology: Science and Practice, 10*(3), 288–301.

Miller, S. D., Duncan, B. L., Brown, J., Sorrell, R., & Chalk, M. B. (2006). Using formal client feedback to improve retention and outcome: Making ongoing, real-time assessment feasible. *Journal of Brief Therapy, 5*(1), 5–22.

Molina, S., & Borkovec, T. D. (1994). The Penn state worry questionnaire: psychometric properties and associated characteristics. In G. C. L. Davey & F. Tallis (Eds.), *Worrying: perspectives on theory, assessment and treatment* (pp. 265–283). Oxford, England: John Wiley & Sons.

Mundt, J. C., Marks, I. M., Shear, M. K., & Greist, J. M. (2002). The work and social adjustment scale: a simple measure of impairment in functioning. *The British Journal of Psychiatry, 180*(5), 461–464.

Murray, J., Ehlers, A., & Mayou, R. A. (2002). Dissociation and post-traumatic stress disorder: two prospective studies of road traffic accident survivors. *The British Journal of Psychiatry, 180*(4), 363–368.

Newnham, E. A., & Page, A. C. (2010). Bridging the gap between best evidence and best practice in mental health. *Clinical Psychology Review, 30*(1), 127–142.

Roth, A. D., & Pilling, S. (2008). Using an evidence-based methodology to identify the competences required to deliver effective cognitive and behavioural therapy for depression and anxiety disorders. *Behavioural and Cognitive Psychotherapy, 36*(2), 129–147.

Salkovskis, P. M., Rimes, K. A., Warwick, H. C., & Clark, D. M. (2002). The health anxiety inventory: development and validation of scales for the measurement of health anxiety and hypochondriasis. *Psychological Medicine, 32*(5), 843–853.

Salkovskis, P. M., Wroe, A. L., Gledhill, A., Morrison, N., Forrester, E., Richards, C., ... Thorpe, S. (2000). Responsibility attitudes and interpretations are characteristic of obsessive compulsive disorder. *Behaviour Research and Therapy, 38*(4), 347–372.

Sapyta, J., Riemer, M., & Bickman, L. (2005). Feedback to clinicians: theory, research, and practice. *Journal of Clinical Psychology, 61*(2), 145–153.

Shear, M. K., Rucci, P., Williams, J., Frank, E., Grochocinski, V., Vander Bilt, J., ... Wang, T. (2001). Reliability and validity of the Panic Disorder Severity Scale: replication and extension. *Journal of Psychiatric Research, 35*(5), 293–296.

Spitzer, R. L., Kroenke, K., Williams, J. W., & Löwe, B. (2006). A brief measure for assessing generalized anxiety disorder: The gad-7. *Archives of Internal Medicine, 166*(10), 1092–1097.

Steketee, G., & Freund, B. (1993). Compulsive activity checklist (CAC): further psychometric analyses and revision. *Behavioural and Cognitive Psychotherapy, 21*(1), 13–25.

Weissman, A. N., & Beck, A. T. (1978). *Development and validation of the dysfunctional attitude scale: a preliminary investigation.* Proceedings of the meeting of the American Educational Research Association. Toronto, ON.

18

Making CBT Supervision More Effective

Nick Grey, Alicia Deale, Suzanne Byrne and Sheena Liness

Background to CBT Supervision

What is supervision?

A key function of CBT supervision is to facilitate the development and maintenance of therapist competence. More broadly supervision also may include case management and the governance of safe practice. However the emphasis in this chapter is on clinical skill development and being a more effective therapist, with supervision provided by a more experienced CBT therapist. Differing definitions of supervision exist but Roth and Pilling suggest supervision is "a formal but collaborative relationship which takes place in an organizational context, which is part of the overall training of practitioners, and which is guided by some form of contract between a supervisor and supervisee … with the primary aim of facilitating development of supervisee's therapeutic competences" (Roth & Pilling, 2008, p. 4). Supervision aimed at increasing therapist competence is not simply to help the supervisee with a specific client but to help them learn the relational, conceptual and technical skills of CBT (Newman, 2010).

Models of learning and CBT supervision

Liese and Beck (1997) and Padesky (1996) have written seminal chapters outlining the way CBT supervision explicitly links to the way in which CBT treatment is provided. They suggest that supervision includes the same structure, such as agenda setting, focusing on key problems and setting homework, and a similar process, including collaboration, giving and receiving feedback and using experiential methods. In supervision these experiential methods should ideally include role-play and live observation of the supervisee's therapy. The key methods used within a CBT supervision session are well documented and comprise of:

- case discussion,
- use of audio/video recordings of therapy sessions,

How to Become a More Effective CBT Therapist: Mastering Metacompetence in Clinical Practice,
First Edition. Edited by Adrian Whittington and Nick Grey.
© 2014 John Wiley & Sons, Ltd. Published 2014 by John Wiley & Sons, Ltd.

- role-play,
- discussion of therapeutic techniques, and
- focusing on therapists' beliefs.

In attempting to advance supervision practice others have built on this initial supervision model and integrated more formal theories of learning and teaching (Armstrong & Freeston, 2006; Milne, 2009; Townend, 2008). These have all, to some degree, been theoretically founded on Kolb's (1984) experiential learning model. Kolb's (1984) learning cycle is an integral component of learning for healthcare professionals and has four stages that suggest learning is an ongoing sequential process: reflection, conceptualization, planning, and doing.

These stages fit well within the context of developing therapeutic competences. The premise is that the learner must go through each stage in order for deeper learning to occur. However, individuals learn differently and this poses a challenge for supervision. Honey and Mumford (2006) based their learning styles questionnaire around Kolb's learning cycle and suggest four learning styles that can be mapped onto the learning cycle: activist (prefers doing), reflector (prefers reflection), theorist (prefers conceptualization) and pragmatist (prefers planning). A therapist's preferred learning style may interfere with processes at a particular stage of the learning cycle, for example, within a supervision session a theorist may be reluctant to participate in role-play while an activist may find it difficult to reflect on their work with a client. Supervisors need to create a learning environment within supervision that not only suits the particular learning styles of a supervisee but which will also help to develop the other non-dominant learning styles. Furthermore a supervisor should be mindful of their preferred learning styles and ensure that this does not impede the learning process (see also Chapter 19).

A criticism of Kolb's model is that it does not account for the developmental aspects of learning within supervision (Milne, 2009). Therefore a supervisor might find it useful to consider Inskipp and Proctor's (1993) use of four stages of learning readiness for counsellors: (1) "unconscious incompetence" when one is not aware of deficits, for example a novice therapist at the start of a training programme can be unaware that he/she is not proficient or skilled; (2) "conscious incompetence" when a therapist becomes aware of their skills deficits, for example, after bringing a recording to supervision; (3) "conscious competence" when a therapist is competent but still very conscious of what it is they are doing, for example, shortly after completing therapy training; and (4) "unconscious competence" when a therapist is proficient and doing things implicitly by "second nature", for example, after treating a number of clients with the same type of difficulty such as depression. Considering how best to support a therapist to progress through the stages is important for a supervisor to consider. In particular the second stage of learning is understandably a difficult process and therapists' respond in a number of ways when they learn that they are not yet competent. This may explain some of the more "unhelpful" behaviours often observed in supervision, for example, a trainee could become anxious and avoid bringing recordings to supervision.

Furthermore, learning may not always follow the sequence proposed and a degree of flexibility is required (supervision metacompetence). A key question in a supervision session might be "what is going to help my supervisee learn most at this point?" In response to this question a supervisor may decide when in the planning stage that it is best to guide the supervisee back to the reflective stage to help the therapist reflect further on their practise (Armstrong & Freeston, 2006). Throughout this chapter it has been left open as to whether the supervision is provided individually or in groups. Most issues will apply in each situation but supervising in groups has a number of differing demands (see also Kennerley & Clohessy, 2010). These include the type of group such whether it is a peer group, a led group or a facilitated group. Agreeing group rules to keep the sessions constructive, supportive and safe will be important. An advantage of group supervision is that there are more people's ideas and experience to draw on. A possible difficulty may be trying to meet very varying learning needs within a single setting.

Competency model of supervision

Roth and Pilling's Supervision Competences Framework (2008) gives a comprehensive outline of generic supervision and metacompetences applicable to all therapy modalities and then outlines specific modality supervision competences.
Generic supervision competences include:

- the ability to employ educational principles that enhance learning,
- the ability to enable ethical practice,
- the ability to form and maintain a supervisory alliance, and
- the ability to gauge a supervisee's level of competence.

CBT specific supervision competences include:

- an ability to combine sound knowledge of general and specific, theoretical and applied CBT and to use this to recognize and remedy limitations in supervisee practice;
- an ability to structure supervision sessions in a way that reflects CBT practice using an agenda, so that topics are prioritized, homework and previous practice is reviewed, key issues are discussed and feedback is exchanged; and
- specific supervisory techniques such as an ability to use observational and participative methods to develop CBT skills and to help the supervisee identify thoughts that interfere with therapy or with supervision.

In addition the use of supervision competences is guided by metacompetences that include:

- adapting the process and content of supervision,
- giving feedback,
- managing concerns about the supervisees ability to use supervision, and
- managing serious concerns about practice.

The Roth and Pilling (2008) therapy and supervision competencies interact to provide an overall heuristic model as shown in Figure 18.1. In this the basic CBT competences of the supervisee and the supervision competences of the supervisor are guided by their respective metacompetences. The key one of these for both therapist and supervisor is the development of "flexibility within fidelity", of adjusting and adapting the basic tools to the specific individual and circumstances. Furthermore the CBT competences of the supervisee can only be demonstrated and addressed by what and how they present in supervision sessions. The supervisee may provide good therapy to clients but if, for example, the supervisor never sees or hears this it will be more difficult to provide suitable feedback and guidance. The competences of the supervisee to use supervision

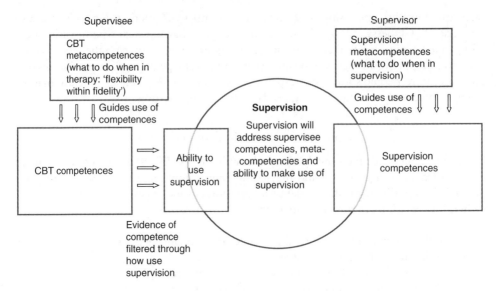

Figure 18.1   Competency model of supervision. © Nick Grey, Alicia Deale, Suzanne Byrne and Sheena Liness.

may need to be a focus of supervision itself. These abilities are discussed in the next section of the chapter. Supervision of course will also focus on the basic CBT competences, such as how to introduce activity monitoring and recording, or metacompetences, such as how to adapt this for people with poor literacy skills.

Effectiveness of supervision

A key factor in the design and delivery of clinical trials for CBT is the provision of supervision and monitoring of therapists' work via review of recorded therapy sessions and client outcomes. Supervision in clinical trials is usually rigorous but an inherent difficulty is that this has not been made explicit within research publications (Roth, Pilling, & Turner, 2010). There have been a number of studies that have shown that brief CBT training programmes for specific disorders, which have included the provision of CBT supervision led to the development of competence (e.g., Addis et al., 2004; Gillespie, Duffy, Hackman, & Clark, 2002). However, these studies did not look at the direct effect of supervision on both skill development and the maintenance of competence. A few studies have investigated this and found both that provision of supervision leads to increased skills and competence, and also that discontinuation of supervision leads to a deterioration of skills. Sholomskas and colleagues (2005) found that the effects of a manualized training programme were enhanced with the provision of supervision, being associated with increased skills. Beck (1986) found that the absence of supervision following training in CBT led to a deterioration of therapist competence and skills to pre-training levels. A UK study by Mannix and colleagues (2006) found that providing ongoing supervision following CBT training for palliative care practitioners led to a significant improvement in competence and a maintenance of confidence while the discontinuation of supervision post training lead to a reduction in both confidence and competence.

However, these studies have not measured the competence of the supervision provided. Assessing competence in CBT supervision is still a somewhat new concept. Some competency rating scales have been developed (James, Blackburn, Milne, & Freeston, 2005; Kennerley & Clohessy, 2010; Milne, 2009) although these are not yet widely used and there is currently a lack of empirical data.

Using CBT Supervision

The ability to make good use of supervision is fundamental to being an effective therapist, whatever one's level of experience. It is also part of being a good supervisor – all supervisors are also supervisees, so being proactive in and reflecting on this process is likely to improve the quality of supervision you can offer. At the end of this section there is a summary of how you can get the most out of your supervision, focused on development of clinical competence.

The ability to make use of supervision is a generic skill in the CBT competences framework (Roth & Pilling, 2008). The factors that contribute to the ability to make use of supervision are:

- An ability to work collaboratively with the supervisor (e.g., goals for supervision, presenting one's work in a focused manner).
- Capacity for self-appraisal and reflection (e.g., reflect on feedback and apply these reflections in future work).
- Capacity for active learning (e.g., taking the initiative on relevant reading).
- Capacity to use supervision to reflect on developing personal and professional role (e.g., reflect on personal impact of work).
- Capacity to reflect on supervision quality.

Being open, working collaboratively

Supervision works best when it is a shared responsibility, with supervisor and supervisee working collaboratively. This can fall at the first hurdle if we as supervisees become too caught up in concerns about exposing our own shortcomings, being evaluated negatively or in being seen to fail in some way. Unacknowledged, such fears can lead to avoidance, anxiety and defensiveness – all processes that interfere with learning. These concerns are common and however uncomfortable it may feel, we will be much more effective supervisees if we can be open, honest and non-defensive, disclosing difficulty and being open about not knowing. Supervisor and supervisee should have a shared and explicit agreement to work together to understand difficulties, build success experiences and develop skills.

It is easier to use supervision effectively if there is a clear understanding of mutual expectations and responsibilities in the supervisory relationship. This includes negotiating what is and isn't discussed in supervision, confidentiality and arrangements for giving feedback on and reviewing supervision. You should also plan with your supervisor what to do if predicted difficulties arise – for example, if you have difficulty in following up on suggestions made in supervision, you may agree that this will be a regular agenda item, or that when it arises the supervisor will look at and explore what got in the way rather than just accepting or overlooking it.

Supervisors will often use a questioning style to help us think through things – and the job of being a supervisee is both to engage with this (just as we want our patients to engage with it), but also to have the confidence to not know, and to say that you don't know. This may of course lead to a discussion of how you could find out, which is part of being an active learner.

Self-assessment, learning style and learning goals

Like therapy, effective supervision is tailored to an individual's specific needs and learning style. As supervisees, we can help this process when starting with a new supervisor by reflecting on past experiences of supervision (what has worked well, what has worked less well and what has been actively unhelpful); our personal learning style – how we learn best (e.g., through experiential methods, through direct observation, through reading, or discussion). It is helpful to make a self-assessment of strengths, areas to improve, gaps in knowledge and skills. This can help in formulating a joint plan for the structure, style and focus of supervision sessions. It can also take us into thinking about what we want to take away from supervision, and to develop specific learning objectives. Clear learning goals (like therapy goals) are SMART: specific, measureable, achievable, realistic and time-limited. For example: a learning goal of "get better at using formulations" might be SMARTENED up into "develop a shared formulation with all new clients, choose a disorder specific model that explains the main problem and deliver therapy that links interventions to the formulation". It is also worth thinking about how we will know when this has been achieved, and how it can be measured (for instance, by bringing copies of formulations to supervision, by getting feedback from patients, by having the supervisor review recordings of drawing out a formulation in a therapy session). It can help in the selection of cases to bring to supervision and with specific skills to focus on. Reviewing progress towards goals is also a way of evaluating supervision itself – so an effective supervisee will share the responsibility for reviewing and fine tuning goals – agreeing a date or regular intervals with the supervisor in advance will help with this.

We can understand our current competences and learning needs better if we can make a reasonably objective self-appraisal (avoiding being overly self-critical or over estimating our abilities). Tracking and auditing our own treatment outcomes can be useful, or rating our own therapy sessions (either a whole session or part of a session) using a structured instrument such as the CTS-R (Blackburn et al., 2001). Newman (2013) suggests that self-appraisal is best achieved through cultivating a supervisory relationship with oneself – rating ones' own therapy session in the manner of a supervisor; thinking and acting as we would with a real supervisee focussing on strengths, providing constructive feedback to ourselves with commitment to wellbeing of both patient and our own development.

Thinking ahead and active learning

The supervision session itself is not the time to *start* thinking about a case: some thinking should have been done beforehand. In particular, this means reflecting on what we want to address in supervision, and developing a specific supervision question. A good supervision question is much more likely to get a good answer than a poorly thought out or vague supervision question. In fact, the very process of preparing for supervision can often help us to answer our own question, at least in part. This is the process of active learning. To aid this process, Padesky's (1996) supervision "road map" contains a list of questions designed to help supervisees think about the specific supervision focus, and prepare their material in order to best answer the question. The questions, in an adapted form, are:

- Is there a cognitive model for understanding and treating this client's problem? If not, is it necessary to devise one?
- Am I following the treatment plan suggested by the model? If not, why not? Are there alternatives that may help?
- Do I have the knowledge and skills to carry out treatment? What have I learnt so far that may help? How can I find out the knowledge and skills? How can I acquire them?
- What is there in the conceptualization or in my own beliefs, experiences or reactions, or in the therapeutic relationship that might interfere?

Supervision questions we have found to be less useful are "what do I do next?' or "how do I do this?", although for supervisees with less training and experience these might still be relevant questions to ask. More useful supervision questions have included "how can we understand/formulate the lack of emotion in the session?", "in this section of the recording have I identified the key belief underlying the low mood?", "I would like to have feedback on my use of guided discovery in this section of recording".

A structured supervision plan and record is important, especially when dealing with many cases (see Figure 18.2). It should include a summary of client outcome measures and work done so far, as well as prompting thinking about a specific supervision question, and how best to answer it, together with a section for reflecting on what has been learnt. Typically all columns are complete except for the last "learning and action point column" that is completed during supervision. This record should be used collaboratively by supervisee(s) and supervisor, and both (all) should have copies in supervision.

Being an active supervisee involves considering everything that may help our learning – not only bringing recordings of therapy tapes, and copies of therapy materials, but also looking out for and pursing avenues that help increase learning. This can include reading, relevant CPD activities, requesting live supervision and looking for opportunities to carry out joint work or to observe the supervisor's clinical practice. Keeping written reflections can also help – in therapy, we sometimes ask patients to keep a therapy notebook in order to keep track of key learning points, and this can be just as useful in for us as supervisees – keeping a supervision diary with key learning points and reflections can embed learning.

Reflection and ability to work with our own beliefs and experiences

We all have personal blind-spots, experiences and beliefs that can interfere with therapy (or supervision). We need to be willing to bring this to supervision, or to work with supervisors in becoming aware of and addressing factors that may affect therapy. Our own beliefs may be interfering with therapy if we repeatedly fail to enact specific suggestions made in supervision, if we repeatedly find reasons not to provide the indicated treatment (e.g., to carry out behavioural experiments in panic disorder); if there is a recurring difficulty across several patients; or difficulty sustaining a therapeutic relationship with a particular patient; and if we experience a strong emotional reaction to a patient. We may have beliefs about introducing recording sessions to our clients "they'll just say no", about playing tapes in supervision "everyone will see what a bad therapist I am", about suggesting ideas of our own "my ideas will be useless", and about the process of supervision "I'm here to be told what to do".

Name: _____ Date: _____

My Supervision goals: (1)
(2)
(3)

Client ID	Main problem / diagnosis	Sessions completed	Session 1 scores	Current scores	Action following last supervision Brief update and plan for next session	Supervision Question Use role-play or tape? Which supervision or training goal addressed?	What learned? Action points

Other items for agenda:

Figure 18.2 A structured supervision plan. © Centre for Anxiety Disorders and Trauma and Institute of Psychiatry PgDip in CBT.

Supervision is not personal therapy, but the process of working together to ensure the well-being of patients and our own development as an effective therapist. With this in mind, it is important that we tell our supervisor if we feel their questions are crossing a boundary or if supervision is becoming too much like therapy.

Giving feedback

Giving feedback is an important skill: we need to be able to let the supervisor know if there is anything they are doing that is impacting negatively on supervision or on learning. This might include asking the supervisor to slow down; to say explicitly when you feel your question has been answered sufficiently. We might also ask them to change from being Socratic to didactic, or to move from discussion into demonstration. It is also helpful to let the supervisor know what is working well (not least because this shapes behaviour). This can include feeding back on successes as well as difficulties, and letting your supervisor know the outcome of things that go well, and what you are learning. Giving feedback about supervision is easiest if it is regular – so giving short feedback at the end of every session as well as having regular more detailed reviews and feedback is helpful. It is also important to have (from the outset) a specific understanding of steps to take if the supervisory relationship breaks down.

Preparing for supervision

It is important to plan the time around supervision. It is hard to make best use of a supervision session that is squeezed in between back-to-back appointments with no time to think about it in advance or reflect afterwards. As far as possible, an effective supervisee will make some space for preparation and reflection outside the supervision session itself (just as we expect patients to make time for therapy outside of the therapy session).

Working collaboratively in supervision also involves sharing responsibility for making best use of the time. This includes thinking ahead about what can realistically be covered, prioritizing and choosing a realistic number of areas to address. Presenting material succinctly is important – this includes being selective with the information that is needed in order to illustrate the supervision question (and trusting the supervisor to ask relevant questions if more information is needed). Usually an extract of a therapy recording will be more illuminating than a deluge of verbal background. An effective supervisee will bring a therapy recording, a copy of the formulation, questionnaire scores (baseline assessment and most recent), and any other therapy materials relevant to the question (e.g., a behavioural experiment sheet). Furthermore the recording of the session illustrating the supervision question should be cued to the correct place and ready to play.

Preparing for supervision also involves preparing for disclosing things that go wrong, or showing ourselves doing badly. This is easier to do if we also bring examples of things that we do well – this might be feedback about successful interventions or outcomes, examples of formulations that work well, and audio/video clips of a therapy session that show work we are proud of.

Getting the most from our supervision

The following (non-exhaustive) list may help you get the most out of your supervision:

- Make time outside supervision to prepare and reflect.
- Use a written supervision record.

- Come to supervision on time, regularly and well prepared.
- Think about what you want to address and define a clear supervision question.
- Bring recordings of therapy sessions to illustrate the supervision questions.
- Bring copies of the formulation and relevant therapy materials.
- Follow up on supervision suggestions and tell your supervisor what happened.
- Give your supervisor honest feedback.
- You can learn from what has worked well – share your successes as well as your difficulties.
- Periodically rate an entire therapy session, and ask your supervisor to do the same, then compare notes.

Avoid drift and keep supervision active by bringing recordings, varying the methods, suggesting role-plays, and keeping the content and learning lively. Finally, don't expect your supervisor to do all the work – be an active learner. As in therapy, the more we put into supervision, the more we are likely to get from it.

Providing CBT Supervision

The competency framework of supervision suggests that supervision will include three areas of supervisee competence on which to focus supervision: the ability to use supervision; CBT competences; and CBT metacompetences. The sometimes quite general questions that supervisees commonly bring to supervision such as "what do I do next with this patient?" or "how do I do the usual treatment as this patient has these additional problems that get in the way?", may be linked to metacompetences, that is, "flexibility within fidelity". However, in order to be able to develop metacompetence therapists first need to ensure that foundational skills are in place.

It may be that early in the development of therapist competences the lack of attention to basic competences such as agenda setting, assessment questions, socializing to the CBT model, means that the questions supervisees bring about "what to do when" may not be able to be answered. This may lead to frustration in the supervisee and trying to cover too much on the part of the supervisor. As in therapy, ensuring you have the goals right at the start usually saves difficulties later. The goals set will need to be appropriate to the level of skill of the supervisee. Learning models suggest that skills are learnt incrementally and that people move from novice to competent to expert (Dreyfus, 1986). At different levels of expertise the style of supervisor will need to adapt accordingly. For novices the supervision sessions will have a greater proportion of time that is didactic and supervisees relatively more passive. As expertise increases the sessions will become more Socratic. As discussed earlier there is evidence that people learn through doing and hence the use of role-play is very important.

Supervision goals related to the "ability to use supervision" may include specific targets such as always bringing the formulation, having a specific supervision question, and having recordings to highlight the questions. Supervision goals related to CBT competences may include becoming confident in helping to socialize clients to the CBT model, setting an agenda each session and homework at the end. Supervision goals related to metacompetences may include how to use trauma-focused therapy techniques with people who dissociate, and when to use and when not to use "out of the office" behavioural experiments.

How to make a supervision session more effective

As a supervisor you should be trying to model good practice through demonstrating the competences you are trying to instil. This will help supervisees make more effective use of supervision. Ensure that as a supervisor you:

- Structure the supervision like a therapy session with an agenda, regular summaries, active learning, homework and feedback.
- Be punctual and committed (i.e., not attending to emails, texts or calls in the supervision).
- Keep up to date with the evidence base and link theory to practice.
- Give constructive feedback that builds on supervisee strengths, without overplaying them or avoiding areas of weakness.
- Share dilemmas and ignorance – you're not meant to know everything, but can help model how to be an active learner.
- Use active learning methods such as role-play and listening to recordings.
- Switch modes of supervision regularly – recordings, role-play, use whiteboard, etc.

It is helpful for the supervisor and the supervisee together to have an overview of the medium and longer term learning needs of the supervisee not just those for the next week. One aim of CBT supervision is to help supervisees develop CBT skills that can be used across patients, rather than say helping an individual patient by trying to do "therapy-by-proxy". Of course there will be occasions when supervisors may need to be more directive around risk or other case management issues. Supervision should help supervisees draw on their own resources, and to learn how to facilitate their own learning. This is comparable to clients learning skills in therapy that they can continue to use in future when sessions have finished. Finally, an overall aim of developing CBT competences is to lead to the therapist being able to use an internal supervisor to provide self-supervision. Using this internal supervisor during a session to adapt treatment for the particular circumstances before you is a true metacompetence.

The supervision record in Figure 18.2 should help issues including guiding a supervisee's preparation, using outcome monitoring as a part of supervision (see Chapter 17), structuring the session and addressing key questions. If supervisees are not specifying supervision questions, and ideally these should tie in with their overarching supervision goals, then this needs addressing first (i.e., improve competences in "ability to use supervision"). In order to address the agreed question Gordon (2012) helpfully suggests 10 steps.

1. Clarify the supervision question.
2. Elicit relevant background information.
3. Request an example of the problem (best by listening or viewing a recording).
4. Check supervisee's current understanding.
5. Decide the level or focus of the supervision work.
6. Use of active supervision methods.
7. Check if supervision question has been answered.
8. Format a client-related action plan.
9. Homework setting.
10. Elicit feedback on supervision.

Within the literature there have been concerns raised about the actual practice of supervision in the "real world" with insufficient attention being given to agenda setting, giving feedback, using experiential methods such as role-play and live observation of supervisee therapy (e.g., Milne, 2009; Roth et al., 2010; Townend, Ianetta, & Freeston, 2002). As a supervisor therefore it can be helpful to keep a record of methods used within each supervision session. This can include case discussion, watching/listening to recordings, and role-play/demonstration. In addition the focus of the supervision can also be noted, such as conceptualization, mastery of CBT methods, therapeutic relationship, therapist reactions and supervision process. Padesky (1996) and Kennerley and Clohessy (2010) provide useful tables for recording this information that can be adapted dependent on the needs of the supervisee, supervisor, service and/or training course.

Preventing supervisor drift

Gordon (2012) also suggests that there is a parallel between supervision becoming purely case discussion focused and Waller's (2009) "therapist drift" from "doing therapies" to purely "talking therapies". To prevent such "supervisor drift" both supervisor and supervisee need to agree that active supervision methods are a shared goal and in the supervision contract. While lengthy role-plays in supervision might be an ideal, it

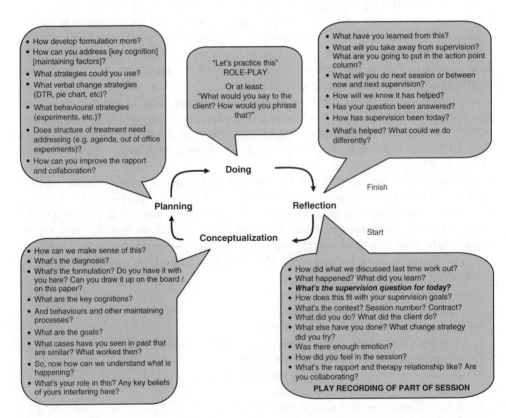

Figure 18.3 Examples of questions that may be used in a supervision session, which centre on the Kolb cycle.

may be difficult to allocate sufficient time to them. A way of always trying to be thinking practically is to make simple "role-plays" routine: ask the supervisee, "how would you say that to the client?" Supervisors can also use other active methods in supervision such as doing a hyperventilation experiment together rather than simply talking about it. We wonder how many supervisors have been "out of the office" in their supervision? For example, if the supervisee has a question about how you might set up and conduct out of office behavioural experiments or exposures, it might be better to practically demonstrate this rather than simply describing and discussing them in the office. A rule might be "don't just tell your supervisees what to do with clients, *show* them what to do" (Newman, 2013). In order to help facilitate learning in this way you will often need to try to guide the supervisee around the Kolb cycle. Some examples of questions that can be asked and how this might look in a supervision session are shown in Figure 18.3.

How to Become a More Effective Supervisor

There is some preliminary evidence that training supervisors can improve self-rated supervision competences (Newman Taylor et al., 2013). Both this chapter and Newman (2013) outline possible course content and process for CBT supervision courses. If you haven't had specific supervisor training this should be your first step and courses in CBT supervision are now more widely available.

Within a supervision session you will meet many if not most of the Roth and Pilling's (2008) supervision competencies by (1) using a supervision record to help elicit feedback and structure the session, and (2) guiding a supervisee round the Kolb (1984) cycle, including some experiential learning. As with providing CBT treatment this still leaves the key question of developing metacompetences – to be flexible about what you do and when you do it. We think that the most effective way to address this is through "supervision of supervision". This has also been referred to as "meta-supervision" (Newman, 2013). For this you will need to record supervision sessions themselves, have supervisor goals and questions for supervision of supervision. As yet there is no evidence base for the value of meta-supervision.

As in usual clinical skill supervision it is helpful to play segments of recordings of supervision relevant to your questions and learning goals. While it would be ideal to listen to and rate whole supervision session recordings, even reviewing segments is very helpful. You could formally use any of the available CBT supervision competency scales or simply use these as a guide. As in clinical practice, you as a supervisor may also have unhelpful beliefs such as "I'm here to tell my supervisees what to do with every client", and "I don't know enough about this sort of problem to offer useful supervision". Addressing such beliefs may form a useful part of supervision of supervision.

In addition, Bennett-Levy's (2006) Declarative-Procedural-Reflective model of therapist skills development has similar components to Kolb's learning cycle and could also be applied to supervisor skill development. It would be possible to adapt the self-practice/self-reflection (SP/SR) (Bennett-Levy & Thwaites, 2007) exercises for use within a supervision context (see Chapter 16, this volume, for a description of SP/SR), although we have not yet done this ourselves.

Procedural rules

- Identify supervision and learning goals – agree a contract to address these.
- Keep on track using a written record of each supervision session.

As a supervisee

- Be prepared for supervision. You don't go to supervision to start thinking about a case; you think about a case beforehand so you can get the most out of supervision.
- Bring supervision questions, formulations and recordings.
- Keep a supervision log/diary with key learning points and reflections.

As a supervisor

- Try to help the supervision session move round the Kolb learning cycle.
- Ensure you are not falling into "supervisor drift", with it becoming "talking supervision" rather than "doing supervision".
- Ask regularly "How would you say that to your client?"
- Keep in mind helping the supervisee with overall learning not just the specific client they bring.
- Get supervisor training and arrange supervision of supervision.

Acknowledgements

Many thanks to supervisors and supervisees on the Institute of Psychiatry PgDip in CBT, King's College London, and at the Centre for Anxiety Disorders and Trauma, South London and Maudsley NHS Foundation Trust. The supervisors include Linda Atkinson, Kathy Burn, Marion Cuddy, Deborah Cullen, Simon Darnley, Linda Fisher, Alice Kerr, John Manley, Stirling Moorey, Jane Muston, Rachel Mycroft, Victoria Oldfield, Maggie Rosairo, Blake Stobie and Tracey Taylor.

Early versions of the supervision record were developed by Beth Skillicorn and Janet Hogg together with their supervisors. Group consultation sessions with Christine Padesky have been very helpful developing our ideas about supervision.

References

Addis, M. E., Hatgis, C., Krasnow, A. D., Jacob, K., Bourne, L., & Mansfield, A. (2004). Effectiveness of cognitive-behavioural treatment for panic disorder versus treatment as usual in managed care setting. *Journal of Consulting and Clinical Psychology, 72,* 625–635.

Armstrong, P., & Freeston, M. (2006). Conceptualising and formulating cognitive therapy supervision. In N. Tarrier (Ed.), *Case formulation in cognitive behaviour therapy* (pp. 349–371). New York: Routledge.

Beck, A. T. (1986). Cognitive therapy: A sign of retrogression or progress. *Behavior Therapist, 9,* 2–3.

Bennett-Levy, J. (2006). Therapist skills: a cognitive model of their acquisition and refinement. *Behavioural and Cognitive Psychotherapy, 34,* 57–78.

Bennett-Levy, J., & Thwaites, R. (2007). Self-practice and self-reflection in the therapeutic relationship: a conceptual map and practical strategies for the training, supervision and self-supervision of interpersonal skills. In R. Leahy & P. Gilbert (Eds.), *The therapeutic relationship in the cognitive behavioural therapies* (pp. 255–281). London: Routledge.

Blackburn, I. -M., James, I. A., Milne, D. L., Baker, C., Standart, S. H., Garland, A., & Reichelt, F. K. (2001). The revised cognitive therapy scale (CTS-R): psychometric properties. *Behavioural and Cognitive Psychotherapy, 29*, 431–446.

Dreyfus, H. L., & Dreyfus, S. E. (1986). *Mind over machine: The power of human intuition and expertise in the era of the computer.* New York: Free Press.

Gillespie, K., Duffy, M., Hackmann, A., & Clark, D. M. (2002). Community based cognitive therapy in the treatment of post-traumatic stress disorder following the Omagh bomb. *Behaviour Research and Therapy, 40*, 345–357.

Gordon, K. (2012). Ten steps to cognitive behavioural supervision. *The Cognitive Behaviour Therapist, 5*(4), 71–82. doi: 10.1017/S1754470X12000050

Honey, P., & Mumford, A. (2006). *The learning styles helpers guide.* Maidenhead: Peter Honey Publications.

Inskipp, F., & Proctor, B. (1993). *Making the most of supervision; professional development for counsellors, psychotherapists, supervisors and trainees.* London: Cascade.

James, I., Blackburn, I. M., Milne, D., & Freeston, M. (2005). *Supervision training and assessment scale (STARS-CT).* Unpublished consultation paper.

Kennerley, H., & Clohessy, S. (2010). Becoming a supervisor. In M. Mueller, H. Kennerley, F. McManus, & D. Westbrook (Eds.), *Oxford guide to surviving as a CBT therapist* (pp. 323–370). Oxford: Oxford University Press.

Kolb, D. A. (1984). *Experiential learning: experience as the source of learning and development.* Englewood Cliffs, NJ: Prentice Hall.

Liese, B. S., & Beck, J. S. (1997). Cognitive therapy supervision. In C. Watkins (Ed.), *Handbook of psychotherapy supervision* (pp. 114–131). New York: John Wiley & Sons.

Mannix, K. A., Blackburn, I. V., Garland, A., Gracie, J., Moorey, S., Reid, B., ... Scott, J. (2006). Effectiveness of brief training in cognitive behaviour therapy techniques for palliative care practitioners. *Palliative Medicine, 20*, 579–584.

Milne, D. (2009). *Evidence-based clinical supervision.* Chichester: BPS/Blackwell.

Newman, C. (2010). Competency in conducting cognitive behavioral therapy: foundational, functional and supervisory aspects. *Psychotherapy: Theory, Research, Practice, and Training, 47*, 12–19.

Newman, C. (2013). Training cognitive behavioral therapy supervisors: didactics, simulated practice and "meta-supervision". *Journal of Cognitive Psychotherapy: An International Quarterly, 27*, 5–18.

Newman Taylor, K., Gordon, K., Grist, S., & Olding, C. (2013). Developing supervisory competence: preliminary data on the impact of CBT supervision training. *The Cognitive Behaviour Therapist, 5*(4), 83–92. doi: 10.1017/S1754470X13000056

Padeksy, C. (1996). Developing cognitive therapist competency: teaching and supervision model. In P. M. Salkovskis (Ed.), *Frontiers of cognitive therapy* (pp. 266–292). New York: Guilford Press.

Roth, A. T., & Pilling, S. (2008). *A competence framework for the supervision of psychological therapies.* Retrieved from http://www.ucl.ac.uk/clinical-psychology/CORE/supervision_framework.htm

Roth, A.T., Pilling, S., & Turner, S. (2010). Therapist training and supervision in clinical trials: implications for clinical practice. *Behavioural and Cognitive Psychotherapy, 38*, 291–302.

Sholomskas, D. E., Syracuse-Siewert, G., Rounsaville, B. J., Samuel, A. B., Nuro, K. F., & Caroll, K. M. (2005). We don't train in vain: A dissemination trail of three strategies of training clinicians in Cognitive-behavioural therapy. *Journal of Consulting and Clinical Psychology, 73*, 1,106–115.

Townend, M. (2008). Clinical supervision in cognitive behavioural psychotherapy: development of a model through grounded theory. *Journal of Psychiatric and Mental Health Nursing, 15*(4), 328–339.

Townend, M., Ianetta, L., & Freeston, M. (2002). Clinical supervision in practice: A survey of UK cognitive behavioural psychotherapists accredited by BABCP. *Behavioural and Cognitive Psychotherapy, 30*, 485–500.

Waller, G. (2009). Evidence-based treatment and therapist drift. *Behaviour Research and Therapy, 47*, 119–127.

19

Take Control of your Training for Competence and Metacompetence

Adrian Whittington

Basketball is an intricate, high-speed game filled with split-second, spontaneous decisions. But that spontaneity is possible only when everyone first engages in hours of highly repetitive and structured practice – perfecting their shooting, dribbling, and passing and running plays over and over again … spontaneity isn't random.

Malcolm Gladwell, *BLINK: The Power of Thinking without Thinking*[1]

Introduction

Traditional education has been criticized for emphasizing the delivery of facts from an educator to a passive learner. This "banking" model of training has severe limitations, especially when applied to the development of competence in complex situations such as therapy (Freire, 1970). Facts and abstract knowledge can never guarantee therapist skill. "Experiential" and skills-acquisition models of learning propose a radically different approach, with practical procedural learning from real-life experience integral to the process of competence development (Kolb, 1984; Bennett-Levy, 2006). To develop metacompetences (the application of multiple procedural rules to tailor CBT to different circumstances), "how-to" procedural learning through practice is likely to require an even greater emphasis.

This chapter draws on theories of learning and the evidence base for CBT training and applies these to the development of competences and metacompetences, arriving at a series of proposed "procedural rules" for making learning most effective, for both therapists and for CBT trainers.

As a therapist wanting to develop your skills, you are encouraged to take active control of your learning opportunities, matching these to the next steps in your learning path and taking account of your own preferred learning style. The wide diversity of training available in CBT will not automatically guarantee that you develop competence and metacompetence. Therapists need substantial specific CBT training to achieve

---

How to Become a More Effective CBT Therapist: Mastering Metacompetence in Clinical Practice, First Edition. Edited by Adrian Whittington and Nick Grey.
© 2014 John Wiley & Sons, Ltd. Published 2014 by John Wiley & Sons, Ltd.

levels of competence likely to produce good clinical results, so it is important to evaluate whether you have reached this standard of foundation competence and to undertake further core training as needed. Many underestimate the need for significant, extended programmes of study and supervision to be able to deliver the therapy as it was intended. Some top-up training and development may need to focus specifically on maintaining adherence and preventing drift from evidence-based approaches (Waller, 2009). It is then possible to build on foundation competence with new competences through briefer training, for example to apply CBT with new client groups, but the integration of this training with supervision is essential for maximum benefit. The development of metacompetences in CBT requires particular attention to practice, informed by feedback and reflection, yet metacompetence has often been left to chance or has been assumed to "come with experience". A worksheet tool is provided to help you build your own programme of training and development activity to support your ongoing competence and metacompetence development after you have reached foundation level competence in CBT.

If you are a CBT trainer, a number of strategies are proposed to enhance your delivery of training to ensure it has an impact on metacompetence, as well as competence. These strategies include attending to both adherence and flexibility in the approaches you are teaching, incorporating sufficient procedural learning opportunities in training, identifying explicit metacompetence procedural rules where possible, and always linking your training to underpinning theory and principles.

Theories of Learning

Active learning approaches based on students' real-life experience and questions have been found to be more effective for developing professional competence than the passive receipt of information (e.g., Neville, 2009). Two active learning models with implications for CBT training and development are presented here. Kolb's experiential learning model proposes an active role for the learner in piecing together experience with more abstract knowledge in order to gain competence (Kolb, 1984). Learning methods for achieving this in CBT are identified by James Bennett-Levy's three systems model of CBT skills development (Bennett-Levy, 2006).

Kolb's experiential learning cycle

David Kolb's model of experiential learning suggests that learning takes place when a series of steps are followed to reflect on experience, draw generic conclusions from it, and on this basis plan how to act and adapt. This model has been influential in the design of practitioner training in the field of mental health. Figure 19.1 provides an example of how it may apply to learning CBT.

Bennett-Levy's declarative procedural reflective (DPR) model

Specific learning activities to support experiential learning of CBT are proposed by James Bennett-Levy's DPR model of CBT skills acquisition (Bennett-Levy, 2006). This model distinguishes between three cognitive systems within which learning takes

Concrete experience
A real life experience
e.g., Doing therapy with a
particular client

Active experimentation

Doing something based on the new
understanding
e.g., Planning how to deliver the therapy
based on the conceptualization, choosing
the most fitting intervention methods
and agreeing these in your next
supervision

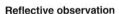

Reflective observation

Reflecting on what happened
e.g., A review of the therapy in
group work during a training
workshop

Abstract conceptualization

Making sense of what happened and
linking this to more general theory or
knowledge
e.g., Within the same workshop,
learning about a disorder-specific
model used in research trials, then
creating an idiosyncratic CBT
conceptualization for your client
based on this model.

Figure 19.1   Kolb's Experiential Learning Cycle, applied to learning CBT.
Note: Kolb's model highlights different types of activities that need to be linked in order to
enable learning, and shows that learners need to take up an active role in making the links and
ensuring that they are progressing around the cycle.

place. It proposes that, supported by different learning activities, these cognitive systems interact and result in skill acquisition by therapists:

1. The *declarative* system concerns "facts" or pure theory, such as the evidence that
    relapse is common in depression, or knowledge of a specific cognitive behavioural
    model of a disorder. Declarative knowledge is typically gained through reading,
    lectures or observation.
2. The *procedural* system concerns rules about what to do when, for example, about how
    to introduce a dysfunctional thought record to a moderately depressed client in the best
    way. Procedural knowledge is gained through practice, observation and role-play.
3. The *reflective* system concerns the process of therapist reflection, which links
    declarative and procedural knowledge, allowing one to impact on the other. For
    example, reflection on a case in supervision (reflective system) may lead to further
    reading on evidence-based treatment for health anxiety (declarative system), which
    through further reflection (reflective system) allows the development of a helpful
    plan for working with this specific case (procedural system).

To develop *competence*, this model suggests that the training methods that work tap
into a mixture of the three systems: declarative knowledge acquisition through lectures

and reading; procedural skill acquisition through observation, role-play and self-practice using CBT methods; and reflective practice through supervision and structured reflection on self-practice. The focus of these activities, especially in the early stages of therapist training, is to enhance adherence to a "usual" way of doing things, if possible with relatively simple presentations of mental health difficulties. Declarative knowledge acquisition may be especially important in driving procedural learning at an early stage of training (Bennett-Levy, 2006).

To develop *metacompetence*, the model suggests that therapists need to focus particularly in the procedural domain, identifying and practicing a set of complex procedural rules for adapting and flexing CBT in a myriad of individual circumstances. The procedural and reflective systems are likely to be more important in driving the development of procedural expertise at this later stage of therapist development (Bennett-Levy, 2006).

How to Learn Competence and Metacompetence

This section proposes theory and evidence-based ways of using training and other learning activities to develop and maintain competence and metacompetence. These proposed "procedural rules" invite you to take control of your learning, starting with self-awareness: knowing where you are up to with competence and metacompetence development and working with your own learning style. From here, you will need to make an honest assessment of whether you need to undertake further foundation training to achieve CBT competence. To expand competent practice to new client groups brief training can work, if accompanied by supervision. To develop metacompetences as defined by Roth and Pilling (2007), a specific individual training plan for procedural learning through practice and reflection will be the most beneficial.

Know your next stage of learning

An important first step in working out how to focus your learning and what training to take up is to work out your next stage of learning. The concept from educational theory of the "zone of proximal development" or ZPD is helpful here. Psychologist Lev Vygotsky developed this concept in the 1930s to refer to the area of learning between what someone can already do independently and what he or she can only do with significant guidance and assistance. Deliberately focusing learning efforts within this zone stretches the learner and leads to new skill development, whereas working beyond this zone is unlikely to lead to the development of independent skill (Berk & Winsler, 1995).

As a CBT therapist, some learning will be within your reach as a sensible next step, in your ZPD, and other learning will be a step too far for now. In trying to identify your own ZPD, it is worth returning to the model in Chapter 1, which differentiates *competent adherence* from *metacompetent adherence*. Competent adherence refers to the ability to apply CBT interventions in the "usual" way where there is a good fit between evidence-based protocol and a specific problem or case, whereas metacompetent adherence involves appropriate adaptation of usual tactics and techniques while remaining true to the underlying principles and theoretical frame of CBT.

With some problem types, your ZPD may include the development of skill in how to adhere to the empirically supported interventions. For example, if you have never used CBT for psychosis you will first want to focus on mastering competent adherence – to apply typical therapy with this group. In other areas it may be that your ZPD includes the development of metacompetent practice. For example, if you are already skilled in the use of CBT for depression and individual anxiety disorders you may want to learn how to adapt the usual approaches when multiple disorders present together. It will be important to use supervision to help identify ZPD areas, drawing on a range of sources of information including observation of your practice and evaluation using a rating tool such as the Cognitive Therapy Scale – Revised (Blackburn et al., 2001).

Know your own learning style and avoid its pitfalls

It will be useful to understand your own preferred learning style and use this knowledge to maximize learning. Honey and Mumford (1992) identified four specific learning styles that were based on the work of Kolb (1984). The proposed learning styles are:

1. Activist – someone who learns best by doing (through concrete experience in Kolb's model). They tend to get stuck into action straight away, without the need for lots of preparation. An activist prefers learning methods such as role-play, live supervision and self-practice of CBT methods.
2. Reflector – someone who learns best by reflecting on experiences (through reflective observation in Kolb's model). They tend to stand back, think about what to do and be rather cautious. A reflector prefers learning methods such as reflection on process in supervision, and reflecting on self-practice.
3. Theorist – someone who learns best through theory and evidence (through abstract conceptualization in Kolb's model). They tend to be attached to models, theories and facts and like to analyse the broader meaning of experience. A theorist prefers learning methods such as reading, lectures and research.
4. Pragmatist – someone who learns best by trying out methods to see how they can work in practice (through active experimentation in Kolb's model). They tend to be practical problem-solvers, who like identifying what works by trying it out. A pragmatist prefers learning methods such as the consideration of case studies, directed role-play and using client feedback and measures.

This framework has been criticized for lacking an evidence-base but it has good face validity as a tool for allowing people to start thinking about their approach to learning (Coffield, Moseley, Hall, & Ecclestone, 2004). Most people identify with all of these learning styles to different degrees, rather than just one. It can be helpful to consider which styles you prefer or identify with most, then to tailor your training plan to take these styles into account.

   Honey and Mumford (1992) proposed that to make learning most effective it is important to engage with a mix of styles of learning: playing to your learning style strengths but not avoiding your weaker styles of learning. If you identify very strongly with the Theorist learning style, for example, models and data will be important to you as a framework for learning. However, you will need to make sure you also engage in active learning and reflection even though this may come less naturally to you.

Achieve competence first, by undertaking sufficient core training

Before setting out to enhance metacompetence, take a good honest look at the extent to which you are able to practice with competence, adhering to the treatment methods and processes that are known to be effective. There may be a tendency for practitioners to overestimate or overstate their competence in CBT after more generic mental health training. Many therapists describe themselves as offering CBT when in fact the therapy offered does not match the most basic CBT characteristics. The treatment histories of people with Obsessive Compulsive Disorder, for example, reveal that 60 per cent of those who had received therapy described as CBT had received incompetent treatment, for example, lacking any exposure element, or spending most of the sessions talking about childhood (Stobie, Taylor, Quigley, Ewing, & Salkovskis, 2007).

A substantial amount (approximately 200 hours) of core CBT training appears to be required to become good enough at the therapy to stand a reasonable chance of replicating the outcomes of research trials. Trials that have demonstrated the efficacy of CBT have tended to use highly trained and experienced therapists with at least a Masters or Doctorate level training and mean experience of over nine years practice (Roth, Pilling, & Turner, 2010). Typically, trial therapists have been monitored for competence using the Cognitive Therapy Scale (CTS) or its revised version (CTS-R). The same scales and score levels have been used to determine the competence of CBT trainees, and despite some known inter-rater reliability problems, higher ratings have been shown to predict better therapy outcomes for clients (McManus, Westbrook, Vazquez-Montes, Fennell, & Kennerley, 2010).

A review of studies of the relationship between training, competence and outcome suggested that a recognized level of therapist competence or client outcome akin to that expected in efficacy trials was only achieved by a mean of 199 formal training hours (Rakovshik & McManus, 2010). Conversely, after a mean 93 hours training inexperienced or novice therapists showed improvements in competence but did not reach a recognized standard, and after a mean of 33 hours training novice therapists typically did not improve in competence or produce improved client outcomes.

There is good reason to believe that the best way to maximize competence is to undertake a specific postgraduate training in CBT. One year Postgraduate Diploma (36–40 training day) programmes with integral supervision have demonstrated student progression through significant improvements in CTS-R or CTS scores from the start to the end of training when recordings were rated blind (McManus, et al., 2010; Milne, Baker, Blackburn, James, & Reichelt, 1999). A small study of 24 UK mental health practitioners claiming to deliver CBT found that those with a substantial training in CBT beyond their core mental health professional training showed a significantly higher level of competence than those without (Brosan, Reynolds, & Moore, 2006). Worryingly, however, a significant proportion of accredited CBT therapists in this sample did not meet minimum standards of competence on the Cognitive Therapy Scale.

If you are in doubt about whether your foundation level of CBT competence matches the level expected to deliver the desired outcomes, seek out a formal evaluation of your practice using a measure such as the CTS-R, rated by colleagues with suitable expertise.

Seek out training that will help to prevent therapeutic drift

Therapists can drift away from core methods of CBT such as collaboratively working towards behavioural change, and changes of direction such as this can have negative effects on outcome (Waller, 2009; Schulte & Eifert, 2002). For this reason, once you have reached a foundation level of CBT competence, it will be important for you not only to seek out training that has the objective of building new competences or meta-competences, but also to identify and undertake training activities that maintain CBT fidelity and reduce drift. Feedback from supervision, in particular live, video or audio supervision or CTS-R ratings from a supervisor may help you to identify areas of drift and identify training to correct this. Training events that offer extended opportunities for "behavioural rehearsal" through being observed doing role-play have been proposed as an effective method of maintaining fidelity (Beidas, Cross, & Dorsey, 2013).

Approach any "maintenance" training events with openness to the possibility that you have drifted away from the evidence-based approach, and deliberately look for ways to correct this. The risk of drift away from core CBT methods may be exacerbated by the expansion of alternate evidence-based models of therapy. It is not known what effect there may be on CBT fidelity when CBT therapists also train in alternate approaches. Integrative practice does not have a strong evidence base compared to single model approaches, so if you are training in alternate approaches the safest course will be to focus on maintaining fidelity within each specific evidence-based intervention.

To gain competences in specific new areas or client groups look for training linked to supervision

Despite the limitations of briefer training programmes these can clearly contribute to building competence and can help disseminate specific, targeted interventions to those who already have essential therapy skills. Effective brief trainings that have improved patient outcomes have had supervision of practice as an integral element. Three dissemination trials illustrate the point:

1. A two-day training in CBT for depression for experienced therapists led to increased CTS scores (maintained during one year of ongoing supervision) and improved outcomes for clients (Simons et al., 2010).
2. A three-day training for counsellors in cognitive therapy for panic disorder (followed by fortnightly group supervision) led to 54 per cent of their clients becoming panic free by the end of treatment, compared to 17 per cent of their clients in the period before the training (Grey, Salkovskis, Quigley, Clark, & Ehlers., 2008).
3. A two-day training workshop followed by monthly supervision allowed comparable outcomes for PTSD to be achieved by experienced therapists with modest previous CBT training to those demonstrated in efficacy trials of trauma focused CBT, despite no major exclusion criteria for clients (Gillespie, Duffy, Hackmann, & Clark, 2002).

Supervision appears to have been an important element of ensuring competence is embedded and translated into practice in each of these trials. Without ongoing supervision, any gains in competence may be lost after brief training. For example, a 12-day training in CBT for palliative care nurses, occupational therapists and social workers led to significant gain in CBT skills. However, if supervision was discontinued at this point the gains were not maintained six months later. Those who did receive ongoing supervision made further advances in competence over the next six months (Mannix et al., 2006).

In choosing how to expand your repertoire of areas of competence, try to find training opportunities with attached supervision from experts in the field. In reality, this integrated training and supervision is rarely available beyond foundation CBT training. In this case, consider whether your regular supervisor is competent in the new approaches that you will be learning, so that these can be consolidated during and after the training. If not, perhaps you could look into seeking specialist supervision elsewhere, or whether you and your regular supervisor could both complete the training, to enable the new approach or area of work to be built into future supervision of your practice. Your organization may wish to set up whole-team training. Whatever the new approaches being adopted, enlisting organizational support from service leaders will be essential if team practice is to change and develop.

Build metacompetences by linking your further training to deliberate practice

Metacompetence, defined as the acquisition of multiple procedural rules, necessarily needs you to do a lot of procedural learning – learning about what to do when (Bennett-Levy, 2006). This will require a large amount of practice. Anders Eriksson's studies of the psychology of expert performance across a number of disciplines such as elite sport, music and chess came to the startling conclusion that to be the very best (i.e., international level) requires a minimum of 10,000 hours practice (Ericsson, Prietula, & Cokely, 2007). If you were providing 20 hours of therapy per week, this would take over 10 years to achieve. Arguably, you are aiming for "good enough" performance of CBT rather than elite performance, but it may be no coincidence that therapists chosen to deliver CBT in RCTs have tended to have, on average, about 10 years' experience (Roth, Pilling, & Turner, 2010).

Practice on its own is a hit and miss way to gain metacompetences, however. Rather, Ericsson and colleagues have proposed "deliberate practice" as the key to enhancing performance (Ericsson et al., 2007, p. 2). Deliberate practice refers to the deliberate targeting of practice towards things that you can't already do well, drawing on reflection and coaching. Deliberate practice of CBT in order to gain metacompetences would mean choosing types of practice slightly beyond what you can comfortably do already, setting up opportunities for case work that stretch you into your learning zone (ZPD). It would also mean setting aside time for reflection and seeking out specific feedback on your practice, where possible based on direct observation.

Experienced CBT therapists appear to recognize the value of a "deliberate practice" approach to developing metacompetence. The methods of learning perceived as most helpful for developing procedural skill in a survey of 120 such therapists were: reflection on therapists' own clinical practice, observation of experienced colleagues working with real clients, active practice in the form of role-play and self-practice using CBT methods (Bennett-Levy, McManus, Westling, & Fennell, 2009).

Postgraduate CBT training programmes incorporate supervision of practice and extensive practical training. However, the list of preferred learning methods for procedural learning matches poorly onto the types of activity typically available as continuing professional development (CPD) training for qualified CBT therapists. This tends to occur in the form of workshops, lectures and research seminars, which may not include significant practical components or opportunities for feedback and reflection, and are only rarely linked to supervision. For these reasons, once you have completed your core training in CBT you will need to work actively to build a fruitful learning programme for yourself to support metacompetence development. This programme of "training" could usefully include:

1. supervision of targeted case work,
2. observation of your practice,
3. observation of expert practice,
4. self-practice/self-reflection,

5. attending lectures and workshops, and
6. reading.

This is not an exhaustive list. Other activities such as peer learning sets, journal clubs and e-learning can all play a part. The suggested activities span the procedural, reflective and declarative cognitive systems. The emphasis for metacompetence development will need to be on activities linked to the procedural and reflective systems, in other words a programme of deliberate practice. Learning theory (Bennett-Levy, 2006; Kolb, 1984) also highlights the potential value in making explicit the procedural rules that are being learnt during this practice, as declarative, generalizable knowledge.

Make a training plan for competence and metacompetence

It is useful to identify a programme of learning activity to target particular areas of competence and metacompetence development. This may involve a wide range of activities, beyond just those usually thought of as "training". The "Training target tool" (see Figure 19.2) can be used to plan and make the most of learning activity to bind it together into a programme to target specific areas of learning.

First, you will need to identify the particular questions that you want to answer in order to develop your competences and metacompetences. To identify specific questions to focus on you may find it helpful to consider and discuss in supervision and your appraisal:

1. your learning zone or ZPD;
2. Roth and Pilling's (2007) competency framework and any gaps in your competence that this highlights (see Chapter 1); and
3. whether you may be "drifting" from competent practice in any areas.

Once you have identified a question, use the tool to guide you in planning specific learning activities that can help you to answer it (Column 1). Next, list the specific questions you hope to address with each activity (Column 2) and identify any procedural rules that you learn (Column 3) (see Figure 19.3). You can photocopy and use the "Training target tool" for each competence or metacompetence question that you decide to target.

The development of both competences and metacompetences can include the explicit identification of procedural rules to guide therapy. The focus of rules for competence will be on typical adherence to the therapy (e.g., with severe depression start with behavioural activation rather than cognitive work), whereas procedural rules for metacompetence will focus on adaptation and individualization of therapy across an array of different circumstances (e.g., if there has been a previous successful course of CBT, cognitive work may come earlier in therapy for severe depression at re-referral).

Addressing questions to develop competences may involve using traditional training activities and linking these to supervision and practice. Questions related to developing metacompetences are likely to be addressed by a programme of activities that particularly emphasizes deliberate practice, so your plan will have a different emphasis, including:

1. Setting up additional opportunities to practice, reflect and receive feedback, such as seeking out particular types of clients to work with under expert supervision.
2. Being creative about developing new systems and structures if the ideal opportunities for reflection on practice are not available, for example, by establishing reflective

Competence or metacompetence question: _____

Method	Specific activity In this column specify the activity you will undertake to support your learning	Specific questions for this activity In this column try to identify specific questions or targets for your learning from each activity	Procedural rules identified In this column note relevant procedural rules identified from any of the activities you undertake
Specific supervised case work What specific types of case work can you seek out/take on to support your learning?			
Observed practice How can you be formally observed and receive feedback, e.g., live, audio, video, CTS-R			
Observation of practice How can you observe an expert at work in this area live, or by audio or video, e.g., your supervisor, or an expert on commercially available video?			
Self-practice/self-reflection What specific SPSR activities might support your learning in this area, e.g., applying particular methods to your own life?			
Training events What training events are available that you could attend that can add to your learning in this area?			
Reading What books or journal articles are particularly relevant?			
Other Any other learning activities that are relevant			

Figure 19.2 Training target tool. © Adrian Whittington (2013).

Competence or metacompetence question: *How to adapt trauma-focused CBT that I have used with single-event trauma in the context of multiple childhood trauma*

Method	Specific activity In this column specify the activity you will undertake to support your learning	Specific questions for this activity In this column try to identify specific questions or targets for your learning from each activity	Procedural rules identified In this column note relevant procedural rules identified from any of the activities you undertake
Specific supervised case work What specific types of case work can you seek out/take on to support your learning?	*Take on 4–5 cases under supervision from Sam, an expert in this field*	*(1) How to balance establishing safety and trust with the need to move on with trauma processing* *(2) What to do about dissociation*	*(1) Set out a clear plan and check regularly that the client is happy to proceed* *(2) Set up grounding methods in advance of reliving work and use these to manage dissociation*
Observed practice How can you be formally observed and receive feedback, e.g., live, audio, video, CTS-R	*Ensure Sam listens to an audio recording of at least one whole session of this work*	*Am I appropriately managing the level of affect in the session to allow work/processing to take place?*	*(3) Be open with the client and manage level of affect together*
Observation of practice How can you observe an expert at work in this area live, or by audio or video, e.g., your supervisor, or an expert on commercially available video?	*Watch a video of one of Sam's sessions of TFCBT with a relevant client*	*How does Sam deal with interpersonal issues in the therapy?*	*(4) When the client expresses anger or mistrust, allow time and space to review this together and respond*
Self-practice/self-reflection What specific SPSR activities might support your learning in this area, e.g., applying particular methods to your own life?	*Explore own anxieties and other emotions about this field of work in supervision*	*How do I stay engaged with the experience of clients who have experienced childhood trauma, without feeling overwhelmed by the emotions I feel about what they have experienced?*	*(5) Use supervision to discuss my reactions to client histories* *(6) Avoid vicarious trauma to others through unnecessary recounting of details of traumatic histories*
Training events What training events are available that you could attend that can add to your learning in this area?	*Attend a masterclass on trauma focused CBT by an expert in the field*	*What is the best way to identify target memories when there appear to be hundreds that carry equal affect*	*(7) Ask your client which memories to target first*
Reading What books or journal articles are particularly relevant?	*Read Nick Grey's casebook of cognitive therapy for traumatic stress reactions (Grey, 2009)*	*What are the main adaptations needed to carry out single-event trauma work?*	*(8) Actively manage dissociation when there are traumatic childhood events*
Other Any other learning activities that are relevant	*N/A*		

Figure 19.3 Training target tool: completed example. © Adrian Whittington (2013).

practice groups with peers, or making some reflection time in your week to listen to recordings of your own practice with a specific learning intention. It is best to programme this sort of activity for times when you are fresh and will not be disturbed.

3. Making sure you make best use of the procedural learning opportunities available, for example, including regular use of audio or video recordings and role-play in your supervision.

4. Making the most of training events or reading to identify explicit declarative knowledge of procedural rules – what to do when. This may involve being prepared to ask specific questions at training events to expand your knowledge of procedural rules or going into reading with a specific question in mind.

Training Others for Metacompetence

If you are a CBT trainer, there are a number of things you can do to build the capacity for both core and CPD training in order to contribute to metacompetence development. The procedural rules for CBT trainers proposed here are additions to more generic frameworks for planning and delivering training described in an excellent chapter by Melanie Fennell (2010).

Train for both adherence and how to flex the usual approach

Some training will be focused on developing competent adherence, especially for more novice therapists in any particular field of CBT practice. Other, more advanced training may have a greater emphasis on flexing the usual approach in the light of individual differences or client characteristics. In planning your training, consider where the balance needs to lie for the event you will be delivering.

It will be helpful to be explicit with learners about when you are training for competent adherence and when you are suggesting evidence-based ways of adapting or flexing the usual approach. For example, you might present a more "standard" case followed by one that contains explicit variations on the standard approach. Seeking feedback from learners on the differences between the approaches can help them to develop an explicit understanding of metacompetences.

If the focus of the training you are delivering is competent adherence, as it will be at the start of core CBT training, it is worth highlighting the fact that there may be potential evidence-based ways to adapt the approach in future as the learner gains more knowledge and experience. Without this explicit acknowledgement, learners can have the experience of being taught competent adherence in core training and all of the necessary adaptations or flexibilities they start to introduce later becoming a guilty secret. Bringing appropriate adaptation and flexibility into the open as an explicit if deferred goal means it is possible to highlight the difference between therapist drift and metacompetent adherence.

Make sure your training includes plenty of procedural learning opportunities

Training that aims to enhance metacompetence should be balanced to include more procedural and reflective type learning activities than declarative. It may be tempting to organize your training by opening your presentation software (PowerPoint is one example) and starting to fill it in. This usually leads to too much didactic teaching, addressing mainly the declarative system, and not enough time for procedural and reflective learning using other methods such as role-play, watching video and case discussions. Procedural learning is likely to be more effective if training is organized from the starting point of specific learning objectives. Trainers can assist learners to travel around the Kolb learning cycle to achieve these objectives by identifying a sequence of activities based on practice and reflection on practice, linked to theory and evidence (see Fennell, 2010 for a fuller description of how to do this).

Be explicit about what to do when

Most training could lead to the explicit identification of procedural rules for practice. Consider whether you can highlight explicit what-to-do-when rules in training that you offer. If your training includes opportunities for practice, for example, through role-play, or other forms of procedural learning such as watching video examples, active engagement can be enhanced by asking participants to reflect and identify explicit procedural rules from these activities themselves.

Link training to conceptual underpinnings and principles

Metacompetent practice may be thought of as staying tight to the principles and conceptual underpinnings of CBT while appropriately flexing the tactics and techniques used in any individual session with any particular client (see Chapter 1). With this in mind, it will be important always to attach training in CBT to an understanding of the core principles and conceptual basis, such as the principle that cognition, emotion and behaviour interact to maintain difficulty or distress, or the principle that interventions should be formulation driven. This will avoid the trap of learners taking only specific tactics or techniques from training, and then ending up adrift or pushing too hard on technique if these specific methods don't work well in a particular case.

Contribute to a new paradigm for advanced training – linked to supervision, observation and coaching

Advanced CBT training needs to move beyond the brief workshop or lecture series as the main method of delivery. Instead, a new paradigm of advanced training could work within a framework for deliberate practice – with more opportunities for experienced practitioners to receive expert supervision, to have their work observed, and to be coached in order to improve or return from therapeutic drift. Technology may contribute helpfully – making video examples of expert practice more widely available and increasing the possibilities for remote coaching by the most able supervisors. We would not expect to improve our basketball, tennis or chess by going to a one- or two-day seminar event with a series of lectures on the topic, and it would be equally foolish to expect this to work for CBT. All involved in training for CBT therapists can contribute to developing this new culture of advanced training for metacompetence.

Conclusion

Learning to deliver effective CBT requires extensive foundation training, based on the balanced combination of information, practice and reflection. Additional competences, for example, for working with new client groups, can be gained through briefer training linked to supervision and some top-up training should focus on maintaining competence and preventing drift. Metacompetence development, consisting of the learning of multiple procedural rules, is likely to require an emphasis on extensive "deliberate practice", that is, practice informed by reflection and feedback. Learning in all of these forms may not automatically be available through advertised training "events". To gain competence and metacompetence it will therefore be important to take control of your learning opportunities to ensure that you are matching the right learning activities to your learning needs. If you are a CBT trainer, you can enhance your training by incorporating metacompetence development and help to build a new paradigm for advanced CBT training.

Procedural Rules

For therapists

- Identify your next stage of learning: use supervision to identify development goals that stretch you and which might include both competences and metacompetences.
- Know your own learning style and avoid its pitfalls. In order to maximize your learning, include learning methods that fit your preferred learning style. However, make sure you cover all types of learning activity, as competence and metacompetence acquisition require a range of learning methods.
- Achieve competence first, by undertaking sufficient core training. You need a minimum of approximately 200 hours of CBT instruction to become competent, preferably including specific postgraduate CBT training. Take stock of your competence honestly and if in doubt have your practice reviewed by a suitably qualified colleague using the CTS-R.
- To gain competences in specific new areas or client groups look for training linked to supervision. Alternatively link training to supervision yourself by seeking specialist supervision, attending training with your supervisor, or undertaking whole-team training.
- Seek out training that could help to prevent or reverse "drift" from proven ways of working. Ask your supervisor to help identify ways in which you may be "drifting" based on observation of your practice.
- Build metacompetences by linking your further training to deliberate practice. Make a specific plan to practice aspects of CBT required in your work setting that stretch you or require adaptations to your usual ways of working and seek out as many opportunities for feedback as possible.
- Make a plan to learn more in specific competence or metacompetence areas. Use the Training target tool to identify the most relevant learning opportunities and derive explicit procedural rules from them.

For CBT trainers

- Train for both competent adherence and how to flex the usual approach. Train novices to focus on competent adherence but to know that some adaptation and flexibility will be appropriate later in their learning. Present case examples for both usual practice and adaptations to usual practice, being explicit about which is which.
- Make sure your training includes plenty of procedural learning opportunities: do away with an overdose of slides and organize your training to include a good dose of modelling, role play, video presentation and case discussion.
- Be explicit about what to do when. Ensure where possible that learners take away explicit procedural rules from your training.
- Link training to conceptual underpinnings and principles of CBT. Ensure that learners take away more than a toolkit of techniques. They need a deep understanding of principles in order to apply these in unique situations.
- Contribute to a new paradigm for advanced training – linked to supervision, observation and coaching: design engaging and effective ways for advanced learners to develop by making your training sessions into deliberate practice opportunities.

Acknowledgements

With thanks to Nick Grey, Lydia Turner and Helen Curr for their ideas and feedback.

Note

1 Reproduced with kind permission of Penguin UK/Hachette.

References

Beidas, R. S., Cross, W., & Dorsey, S. (2013). Show me, don't tell me: behavioural rehearsal as a training and analogue fidelity tool. *Cognitive and Behavioural Practice, 17*: 142–153. doi: 10.1016/j.cbpra.2013.04.002

Bennett-Levy, J. (2006). Therapist skills: a cognitive model of their acquisition and refinement. *Behavioural and Cognitive Psychotherapy, 34*: 57–78. doi: 10.1017/S1352465805002420

Bennett-Levy, J., McManus, F., Westling, B. E., & Fennell, M. (2009). Acquiring and refining CBT skills and competencies: which training methods are perceived to be most effective? *Behavioural and Cognitive Psychotherapy, 37*: 571–583. doi: 10.1017/S1352465809990270

Berk, L. E., and Winsler, A. (1995). *Scaffolding children's learning: Vygotsky and early childhood education*. Washington DC: National Association for the Education of Young Children.

Blackburn, I.-M., James, I. A., Milne, D. L., Baker, C., Standart, S., Garland, A., & Reichelt, F. K. (2001). The revised cognitive therapy scale (CTS-R): psychometric properties. *Behavioural and Cognitive Psychotherapy, 29*: 431–446. doi: 2001-09643-004

Brosan, L., Reynolds, S., & Moore, R. G. (2007). Factors associated with competence in cognitive therapists. *Behavioural and Cognitive Psychotherapy, 35*: 179–190. doi: 10.1017/S1352465806003304

Coffield, F., Moseley, D., Hall, E., & Ecclestone, K. (2004). *Learning styles and pedagogy in post-16 learning. a systematic and critical review.* London: Learning and Skills Research Centre.

Eriksson, A., Prietula, M. J., & Cokely, E. (2007). The making of an expert. *Harvard Business Review,* July/August, 1–8.

Fennell, M. (2010). Training skills. In M. Mueller, H. Kennerley, F. McManus, & D. Westbrook (Eds.), *Oxford guide to surviving as a CBT therapist* (pp. 371–406). Oxford: Oxford University Press.

Freire, P. (1970). *Pedagogy of the oppressed.* New York, Continuum.

Gillespie, K., Duffy, M., Hackmann, A., & Clark, D. M. (2002). Community based cognitive therapy in the treatment of post-traumatic stress disorder following the Omagh bomb. *Behaviour Research and Therapy, 40*: 345–357. doi: 10.1016/S0005-7967(02)00004-9

Gladwell, M. 2006. *BLINK: the power of thinking without thinking.* London: Penguin

Grey, N. (Ed.). (2009). *A casebook of cognitive therapy for traumatic stress reactions.* Hove: Routledge.

Grey, N., Salkovskis, P., Quigley, A., Clark, D. M., & Ehlers, A. (2008). Dissemination of cognitive therapy for panic disorder in primary care. *Behavioural and Cognitive Psychotherapy, 36*: 509–520. doi: 10.1017/S1352465808004694

Honey, P., & Mumford, A. (1992). *The manual of learning styles* (3rd ed.). Maidenhead: Peter Honey.

Kolb, D. A. (1984). *Experiential learning: experience as a source of learning and development.* New Jersey: Prentice Hall.

Mannix, K. A., Blackburn, I. -M., Garland, A., Gracie, J., Moorey, S., Reid, B., ... Scott, J. (2006). Effectiveness of brief training in cognitive behaviour therapy techniques for palliative care practitioners. *Palliative Medicine, 20*: 579–584. doi: 10.1177/ 0269216306071058

McManus, F., Westbrook, D., Vazquez-Montes, M., Fennell, M., & Kennerley, H. (2010). An evaluation of the effectiveness of diploma-level training in cognitive behaviour therapy. *Behaviour Research and Therapy, 48*, 1123–1132. doi: 10.1016/j.brat.2010.08.002

Milne, D. L., Baker, C., Blackburn, I. -M., James, I., & Reichelt, K. (1999). Effectiveness of cognitive therapy training. *Journal of Behavior Therapy and Experimental Psychiatry, 30*: 81–92.

Neville, A. J. (2009). Problem-based learning and medical education forty years on. a review of its effects on knowledge and clinical performance. *Medical Principles and Practice, 18*, 1–9.

Rakovshik, S. G., & McManus, F. (2010). Establishing evidence-based training in cognitive behavioural therapy: a review of current empirical findings and theoretical guidance. *Clinical Psychology Review, 30*: 496–516. doi: 10.1016/j.cpr.2010.03.004

Roth, A, D., & Pilling, S. (2007). The competences required to deliver effective cognitive and behavioural therapy for people with depression and with anxiety disorders. London: Department of Health. Retrieved from http://www.ucl.ac.uk/clinical-psychology/CORE/CBT_Competences/CBT_Competence_List.pdf

Roth, A, D., Pilling, S., & Turner, J. (2010). Therapist training and supervision in clinical trials: implications for clinical practice. *Behavioural and Cognitive Psychotherapy, 38*: 291–302. doi: 10.1017/S1352465810000068

Schulte, D., & Eifert, G. H. (2002). What to do when the manuals fail? the dual model of psychotherapy. *Clinical Psychology Science and Practice, 9*: 312–328.

Simons, A. D., Padesky, C. A., Montemarano, J., Lewis, C. C., Murakami, J., Lamb, K., ... Beck, A. T. (2010). Training and dissemination of cognitive behavior therapy for depression in adults: a preliminary examination of therapist competence and client outcomes. *Journal of Consulting and Clinical Psychology, 78*: 751–756. doi: 10.1037/a0020569

Stobie, B., Taylor, T., Quigley, A., Ewing, S., & Salkovskis, P. M. (2007). "Contents May Vary": A pilot study of treatment histories of OCD patients. *Behavioural and Cognitive Psychotherapy, 35*: 273–282. doi: 10.1017/S135246580700358X

Waller, G. (2009). Evidence-based treatment and therapist drift. *Behaviour Research and Therapy, 47*, 119–127. doi: 10.1016/j.brat.2008.10.018

An Afterword about Therapist Style

Simon Darnley and Nick Grey

Be yourself. Everyone else is already taken.

Oscar Wilde

At its most fundamental CBT is about communication. Much has been written about the content of that communication, the concepts and the techniques but in the CBT literature little has focused on an individual therapist's style. We believe that your style can play an important role in that communication. Our style influences how we express ourselves and the therapy we are trying to convey. This includes the way in which something is said, done, expressed or performed. Every one of us has our own style, including you.

What is *Your* Style?

Think of five therapists you admire (or better still write down their names). They can be real or fictional. Think what their style is like. How would you describe that style in one or two words? Think about how much you would like to be like each of them. Which of these therapists would you *most* want to be like? What are the aspects about her or him and his or her style that you most admire? Now consider your own therapy style. How would you describe it? How would your supervisor? If you get stuck, we suggest you ask some of your honest friends or family to (1) describe your style in general life, (2) describe how they imagine you would be as a therapist, (3) list your strengths, and (4) list what irritates them about you. Ask yourself how these qualities apply to your style in therapy. Now contrast your personal style with your therapy style. How different are you in therapy to how you are as a "real" person (therapists are people too!)? You should have two lists of qualities, one from the admired therapist and one for yourself. We hope some aspects coincide. The good news is that we believe we can all improve in delivering therapy and develop some of the skills and competences that other therapists already have. However, even though you may want to be like other therapists you can only ever be yourself.

How to Become a More Effective CBT Therapist: Mastering Metacompetence in Clinical Practice,
First Edition. Edited by Adrian Whittington and Nick Grey.

There could be various ways in which your therapy style could become unhelpfully divorced from your own personal style. First, you may have a specific view (belief!) on how a therapy session should proceed. You may think that you have to be ultra professional at all times and formal in your therapist style. There is a big difference in being informal and unprofessional. Some therapists think that by being very formalized and ridding themselves of their usual personality and style they are somehow being a better therapist. We can use our personal style to help people understand concepts, challenge their own beliefs and encourage people to act in different ways. Second, you may have been heavily influenced in your training by others who were particularly charismatic. This might be a supervisor or another "expert". Ask yourself, if you try to model your style on them, how they provide a rationale or explain aspects of treatment. This is understandable and role modelling is an important aspect of supervision and training. Much like a band can have many musical influences, it is still important they have their own sound (unless you are Oasis...). We suggest that you don't simply want to be a therapist playing "covers" of others' greatest hits. Third, you may overplay strengths. Once we find that something works with one client its very tempting to then use it repeatedly. This does not just refer to style or performance issues but also specific CBT techniques. This can become problematic with the therapist trying to shoe horn a once successful approach into every session. Fourth, you may be anxious in sessions, perhaps especially early in training regarding one's own competence. Such anxiety and associated processes such as self-focused attention will impair performance. There is a difficult balance between having a helpful "internal supervisor" and unhelpful self-monitoring, probably associated with comparing against some internal ideal standard (like the admired therapists you thought of earlier).

First Impressions: An Example of How Styles Differ

The first impressions the client will take in will include the way you are dressed, your opening line and the way your office is laid out and decorated. Your style will have started to make an impact on the client even before you set the agenda. I (SD) remember my father telling me "Never trust a doctor with dead plants in his office, if he can't even look after plants then he can't look after humans." We've known eminent therapists with very different office styles, one with high end furniture, books neatly, well ordered and professionally shelved, and another whose office is much more shambolic, packed full of piles of papers, open journals and half empty, week-old coffee cups.

The first time you meet a new client what is your opening line? Do you always use the same line/style irrespective of who you are meeting? Have you used the same opening line for 10 years (some of us nearly 30 years)? If you have a range of opening lines what are the factors that you would take into account when deciding how formal or informal to be? Is it informal "Hi, Jack? I'm Simon, shall we go in here and have a chat?" or a more formal, "Hello Mr Roche, I'm Mr Darnley the Cognitive Behavioral Therapist you were expecting to meet at 4.00 p.m. Would you like to follow me Sir?"

What about the way you are dressed? Many (most?) therapists have "work clothes" and "home clothes". We've known therapists who deliberately prefer very casual clothes and even clogs (you know who you are!). Others would never be seen at work in nothing less than a full suit and tie. In my clinical psychology training I (NG) always wore a tie, thinking it made me look more professional to make up for being, and looking, young for a psychologist.

Style and Competence

Will adopting a particular style make you a more effective and competent therapist? Certainly there is no substantial evidence to show this. Some therapists fear that providing specific treatment protocols from manuals mean that we will all become interchangeable therapy-bots. We'd argue that this wouldn't be possible even if it were desirable (which it isn't). Style is mentioned in three places within the CBT competences map (Roth & Pilling, 2007). These are: the generic competence of engaging a client, the CBT competence of the Socratic questioning approach, and as a CBT disorder specific competence within CBT for social anxiety disorder. We suggest "style" is unavoidable in providing CBT across the competences.

When first learning a new skill like CBT it is right to first focus on the technical and theoretical aspects. When learning any new skill there is always the prospect of first feeling deskilled. This is very common when learning CBT for the first time. It's similar to learning a musical instrument or learning to drive, everything can feel clumsy. Inexperienced therapists react in different ways. Some new therapists can become reliant on procedures and prefer manualized approaches, wanting every aspect of therapy to be minutely detailed. Other therapists will try to overcompensate for their lack of knowledge and technical skill by overplaying their strengths at developing rapport and a warm therapeutic relationship. They may point out rightly, that the patient really likes them and they have a great therapeutic relationship. Sometimes they will find a patient makes significant progress, but they may not be providing CBT (see also Chapter 1). We suggest that a greater awareness of your own style, once familiar with the concepts and techniques of CBT, may be helpful in achieving competence and metacompetence.

In musical performance, in many cases it is the most eminent performers whose performance styles are most exaggeratedly different, both from each other and from the statistical mean. However, a feature of expert musical performance is the astonishing level of technical consistency on successive performances of the same piece. By analogy we suggest that even though we may observe very different styles in experienced therapists the fundamental competences will be present. It's just that the expressive and performance skills may mask the technical skills that are being used at that time. Christine Padesky tells a story about watching a recording of a session by A. T. Beck. When she first saw it early in her career she thought it just looked like two people chatting rather than a specific therapy. Some years later she saw the same recording again, but now with greater experience. She could now more clearly see that this recording demonstrated great conceptual understanding and technical skill, but that Beck's individual charm and style simply made it look like a conversation. We need to emulate the technical mastery first, rather than attempting to copy others' personal styles.

There is some evidence that the most effective therapists across different modalities achieve significantly quicker and more lasting effects than the least effective ("supershrinks"; Okiishi, Lambert, Nielsen, & Ogles, 2003). However, this has not examined to what degree the therapists across the levels of effectiveness were achieving basic competency in their therapies. It may be that the most effective therapists were those most competent in a technical sense. Furthermore, even among "supershrinks" we propose there will be differing therapeutic styles. Certainly within CBT we argue that achieving competence is our first goal.

Developing Styles

There are no typologies of therapeutic style of which we are aware. The most common arena to find such frameworks is the management and leadership literature. For example, Goleman (2000) outlined six leadership styles found in managers, based on emotional intelligence competences. These leadership styles are: coercive ("do what I tell you"); authoritative ("come with me"); affiliative ("people come first"); democratic ("what do you think?"); pace-setting ("do as I do, now."); and coaching ("try this"). Coercive and pace-setting styles have an overall negative impact on organizational climate while author-itative, affiliative, democratic and coaching styles have a positive effect on such climate.

While care needs to be taken not to overextend the comparison between corporate leadership styles and therapeutic styles, we believe Goleman's typology offers some useful ideas when considering therapeutic style. An affiliative style may reflect most emphasis on developing the therapeutic relationship. A democratic style may reflect the ideal of collaboration. We suggest that therapists should be able to adapt their style as the situation and particular person demands. As such, different client groups may require different styles – see Part III of this book for some examples. It is this style-switching that may be difficult and require attention. For example, we have seen therapists working with people with anxiety disorders who are excellent at developing working alliances with people and shared formulations, but who then struggle to make the shift to the behavioural experiments or exposure needed to help the person make active changes. This could be conceptualized as a shift from using a more affilia-tive and democratic style to a more coaching and even authoritative style.

Your personality and personal style, linked with beliefs about therapy and therapeutic relationship will lead to developing certain types of working alliance and use of CBT competences. The personal characteristics associated with a positive working alliance are being flexible, honest, respectful, trustworthy, confident, warm, interested and open (Ackerman & Hilsenroth, 2003). The development of a repertoire of one's own styles and ability to switch between aspects of these flexibly will be aided by reflective practice, and an understanding of one's own therapy beliefs. The chapters by Stirling Moorey and Richard Thwaites and colleagues in this volume will help this process.

One specific aspect of therapist style that has been examined is the role of self-disclosure. The evidence suggests that self-disclosure has a generally positive effect on clients (Henretty & Levett, 2009). Therapists who self-disclose are liked more and perceived as warmer, and clients self-disclosed more to those therapists who self-disclosed. Importantly clients had a more positive response to therapist self-disclosures regarding thoughts and feelings about the client than to therapist self-disclosures about out of therapy experiences.

Humour and its use is currently a metacompetency within the CBT competence framework (Roth & Pilling, 2007). However there are no guidelines or framework for its use. Could there be? A sense of humour is one of those things we think we all have. Few people say they don't have one. While it's true we all have a sense of it, we all know that not everyone is able to use it appropriately all the time. What makes a good comedian? Is it his or her jokes? Not really, when we try and tell the same jokes to our friends afterwards they often don't have the same impact. So humour is not only about telling jokes but in the *style* of their telling. In therapy it is also about hav-ing what Paul Gilbert calls "a lightness of touch" or "playfulness". We have heard him impersonate a whole range of voices when describing compassionate mind concepts.

It immediately brings laughter and lightness to the proceedings even though he is conveying some quite complex concepts. Not only are these explanations engaging, the playfulness and humour can activate the affiliative affect system.

Similarly it is a common part of CBT to use metaphors as a way of tapping into concepts and new ideas (Blenkiron, 2010; Stott, Mansell, Salkovskis, Lavender, & Cartwright-Hatton, 2010). The performance and style in which those metaphors are delivered and shared are key to their effectiveness. We have heard Paul Salkovskis have an audience (and patients) laugh out loud and think deeply with a variety of his metaphors.

Be Yourself

We suggest that as a therapist you need to "be yourself". This doesn't mean acting exactly the same with your clients as you do with your friends, but rather that you need to be authentic while taking up your role. We encourage you to become more aware of your own style or styles and how they may impact therapy. We should all try to broaden our repertoire and have some flexibility in aspects of the styles we adopt. Metacompetence is this flexibility, while ensuring that we remain true to the fundamental conceptual underpinnings of CBT.

The most effective therapists don't explicitly think about flexing style but do so naturally. Equally we don't think that you can simply learn which style to apply in which situation mechanistically – it will always depend on the patient, formulation and fuller context of treatment. As supervisors we need to allow supervisees to have their own style. It may take time to fully dovetail CBT approaches with your own style, and may not always be a smooth transition. Be gentle on yourself. Overall, we think these ideas have some clinical utility but ultimately it is an empirical question as to whether style (in all its guises) makes a real difference.

Acknowledgements

Many thanks to Adrian Whittington, Alison Roberts and other colleagues at the Centre for Anxiety Disorders and Trauma and the Anxiety Disorders Residential Unit. Credit is also due to the other fantastic therapists we have learned from over the years (and finally learned not to try to copy).

References

Ackerman, S.J., & Hilsenroth, M.J. (2003). A review of therapist characteristics and techniques positively impacting the therapeutic alliance. *Clinical Psychology Review, 23,* 1–33.

Blenkiron, P. (2010). *Stories and analogies in cognitive behaviour therapy.* London: John Wiley and Sons.

Goleman, D. (2000). Leadership that gets results. *Harvard Business Review, 78*(2), 78.

Henretty, J.R., & Levitt, H.M. (2009). The role of therapist self-disclosure in psychotherapy: a qualitative review. *Clinical Psychology Review, 93*(1), 63. doi: 10.1016/j.cpr.2009.09.004

Okiishi, J., Lambert, M.J., Nielsen, S.L., & Ogles, B.M. (2003). Waiting for supershrink: an empirical analysis of therapist effects. *Clinical Psychology and Psychotherapy, 10,* 361–373.

Roth, T., & Pilling, S. (2007). *The competences required to deliver effective cognitive and behavioural therapy for people with depression and with anxiety disorders. Improving access to psychological therapies (IAPT) programme.* Retrieved from http://www.ucl.ac.uk/clinical-psychology/CORE/CBT_Competences/CBT_Competence_List.pdf

Stott, R., Mansell, W., Salkovskis, P., Lavender, A., & Cartwright-Hatton, S. (2010). *Oxford guide to metaphors in CBT: building cognitive bridges.* Oxford: OUP.

Index

How to Become a More Effective CBT Therapist: Mastering Metacompetence in Clinical Practice,
First Edition. Edited by Adrian Whittington and Nick Grey.
© 2014 John Wiley & Sons, Ltd. Published 2014 by John Wiley & Sons, Ltd.